The MAILBOX®

The Education Center®

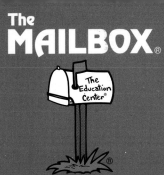

SUPERBOOK® Grade 2

D1479542

Everything You Need For a Successful Year!

- Language Arts
- Math
- Science and Health
- Social Studies
- Graphic Organizers
- Centers
- Games
- Differentiation Tips
- Bulletin Boards
- Management Tips

And Much More!

Revised and Updated!

Managing Editor: Debra Liverman

Editorial Team: Becky S. Andrews, Kimberley Bruck, Diane Badden, Thad H. McLaurin, Jennifer Bragg, Amy Erickson, Gerri Primak, Kelly Robertson, Hope Taylor Spencer, Karen A. Brudnak, Juli Docimo Blair, Hope Rodgers, Dorothy C. McKinney

Production Team: Lori Z. Henry, Pam Crane, Rebecca Saunders, Chris Curry, Sarah Foreman, Theresa Lewis Goode, Greg D. Rieves, Eliseo De Jesus Santos II, Barry Slate, Donna K. Teal, Zane Williard, Tazmen Carlisle, Marsha Heim, Lynette Dickerson, Mark Rainey, Karen Brewer Grossman, Amy Kirtley-Hill

www.themailbox.com

ISBN10 #1-56234-735-7 • ISBN13 #978-156234-735-2

Manufactured in the United States
10 9 8 7 6 5 4 3 2 1

Table of Contents

Language Arts

Math

Science and Health

Social Studies

Classroom Helpers

Table of Con

4

Holidays and Seasonal Activities

Fact
Opinion
A stegosaurus had bony plates on its back.
The stegosaurus was the scariest type of dinosaur.
likes to camp
draws curtains
funny
mixes things up
makes people mad
she's silly
plays ball
Amelia Bedelia
dresses the chicken
goofy
Egg
Caterpillar
Butterfly
Chrysalis
The Sun
It gives Earth heat and light.
The light helps feed the plants.
People eat the plants. They also eat animals that eat plants.

BACK-TO-SCHOOL

Andy
Becky
Kim
Zoe

ABC Lineup

Besides helping you learn your students' names, nametags can be used to play this fun alphabetizing game early in the year. Give each child a nametag to wear; then place your students in groups of four or five children. Ask each group to arrange itself in alphabetical order. After checking each arrangement for accuracy, regroup students for another round. Your students will enjoy learning their classmates' names while they practice a valuable skill. For a fun finale, have the whole class form a large group and arrange themselves alphabetically.

Paper-Bag People

Use this clever activity to help students get to know one another. During the first week of school, give each student a paper lunch bag and a variety of scrap materials. Ask the student to transform his paper bag into a puppet that looks like himself. Then have him fill out a copy of page 7, cut it out, and glue it to the back of the puppet. Have students use the finished puppets to introduce themselves to their classmates; then place the puppets in a center for students to explore on their own. These puppet people will help your students get acquainted without the usual inhibitions.

Name: Sam
Favorite Color: green
Favorite Book: Jumanji
Things I Like to Do:
ride bike
in-line skate
A Place I Like to Go:
beach

Summer Similarities

Create a large graph with columns titled as shown. Read each listed question aloud. If a child answers the question affirmatively, have him write his name in the matching column. The completed graph will give each student the opportunity to get to know his classmates and to find friends with similar summer experiences. For another getting-to-know-you activity, have students complete page 9.

- Did you go on a vacation?
- Did you go swimming?
- Did you climb a tree?
- Did you play an instrument?
- Did you go to the movies?

Vacation	Swimming	Climb Tree	Play Instrument	Movies
Maggie	Justin	Eli	Holly	Matt
Jacob	Joseph	Bobby	Maggie	Enriqué
Alyssa	Bobby		Jacob	Alyssa
Michael	Shammar			Michael
	Eli			
	Enriqué			
	Alyssa			
	Michael			
	Beau			
	Holly			

Robin
Connecticut

Mount Rushmore

Personalized Postcards

Ease students' first-day jitters by giving them an early glimpse at some of your interests. During the summer, collect a class supply of postcards that reflect something about you. For example, gather cards with a scene from your home state, from a vacation spot you visited, or of an animal or flower you like. Prior to the first day of school, mail a postcard to each of your students. Include a personal message about the upcoming school year, and ask each child to bring her postcard on the first day of school. During the first-day introductions, ask each student to share her postcard and to tell the class something about you. Sharing bits of information about you will make your students feel special and in-the-know on the first day of school.

Cool Coupons

Place coupons on your students' desks to greet them as they take their seats on the first day of school. Program a copy of the coupon on page 8 (see programming suggestions on this page); then make a class supply to distribute. Your students will enjoy redeeming the coupons, and you will have an opportunity to meet each student one-on-one. Continue using the coupons throughout the year when students earn special rewards.

Incentive Ideas

- a sticker of choice
- one pencil
- 15 minutes of free time
- sit by a student of choice during lunch
- skip a homework assignment
- read a story to the class

Cool Work Coupon!
Dana
Cool Work Coupon!
Stan
student's name
is entitled to
skip a homework assignment
reward

Get-Acquainted Interviews

Use this fun and informative process to help students get better acquainted. Pair students; then give students ten minutes to question their partners—finding out as much as possible about each other. At the end of the interview time, ask a general question, such as "What is your partner's middle name?" Give each student a chance to answer the question, and let his partner confirm or deny the answer. After asking several questions, your students will feel well acquainted with their partners and other classmates, and you will know more about your students too!

Sample Questions

What is your partner's favorite color?

What is your partner's favorite food?

What pets does your partner have?

How many brothers and sisters does your partner have?

How old is your partner?

When is your partner's birthday?

What is your partner's favorite school subject?

What is a sport your partner likes to play?

What is your partner's favorite book?

What is your partner's favorite movie?

How does your partner get to school?

Get-to-Know-Me Patterns

Use with "Paper-Bag People" on page 4.

Name: ____________

Favorite Color: ____________

Favorite Book: ____________

____

Things I Like to Do:

____

____

____

A Place I Like to Go:

____

Name: ____________

Favorite Color: ____________

Favorite Book: ____________

____

Things I Like to Do:

____

____

____

A Place I Like to Go:

____

©The Mailbox® • *Superbook®* • TEC61049

Coupon Patterns

Use with “Cool Coupons” on page 6.

Cool Work Coupon!

____

student’s name

is entitled to

____

reward

Cool Work Coupon!

____

student’s name

is entitled to

____

reward

Cool Work Coupon!

____

student’s name

is entitled to

____

reward

Name ____________________

We're the Same, Yet Different

Write answers to tell about yourself.
Find someone with the same answer.
Then find someone with a different answer.

	Me	Someone Who's the Same	Someone Who's Different
Eye color			
Hair color			
Number of brothers and sisters			
Freckles?			
Age			
Favorite season			
Favorite holiday			
Favorite sport			

And Then What Happened?

Provide an opportunity for writing as you encourage students to use prediction skills. Begin reading a chosen short story to the class and stop just before the ending. Ask students to imagine what might happen in the conclusion. Then give a sheet of writing paper to each student and instruct her to write a logical ending for the story. Have volunteers share their endings with the class before you read aloud the original ending. Ask students to evaluate the different endings. Their favorite may be one written by a classmate instead of the story's original author! **Making predictions**

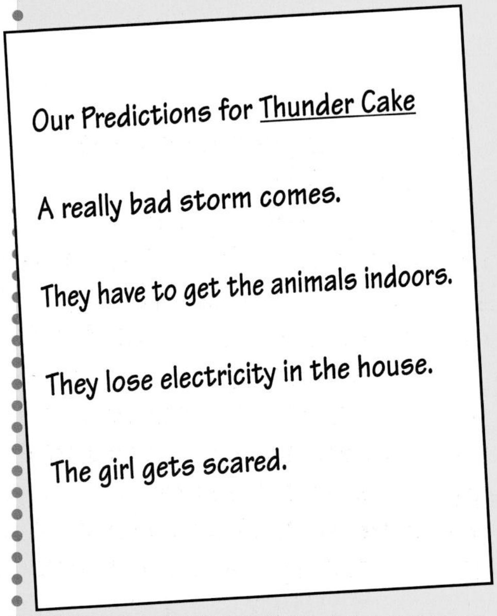
Our Predictions for Thunder Cake
A really bad storm comes.
They have to get the animals indoors.
They lose electricity in the house.
The girl gets scared.

Story Sleuths

With this picture book idea, students use illustrations and prior knowledge to gather clues to a story. Before you read aloud a chosen picture book, title a sheet of chart paper, as shown, with the name of the book. Then post the paper. Next, tell students that they will be story detectives and will search illustrations to find clues to the story. Show students the book cover and read the title aloud. Then, as you show students several illustrations in the book, invite them to make predictions about the story. Write the predictions on the poster and build on students' responses as appropriate to introduce new vocabulary and concepts. After you recap the predictions, have students confirm or modify them as you read the book aloud. **Making predictions**

Glimpse the Future!

A look at this crystal ball reveals what students think will happen in a story. Choose a story to read aloud or for students to read independently. Stop the reading just before the conclusion. Next, instruct each student to write the title of the story on a copy of the crystal ball pattern on page 25. Have him illustrate the crystal ball to show what he predicts will happen at the end of the story. Then ask him to complete the sentence and lightly color the base of the crystal ball. After each student cuts out his crystal ball, finish reading the story to students or have them read the conclusion on their own. Then ask each youngster to write about the actual story ending on the back of his crystal ball. **Making predictions**

Title: The Chalk Box Kid
In my story crystal ball, I see Ivy taking the teacher to Gregory's garden.

Nate the Great
detective,
lost,
picture,
orange,

In So Many Words

With this prereading activity, a few well-chosen words give valuable clues to a story. To prepare for a small group, label the top of an 8½″ x 11″ sheet of paper with the title of a storybook suitable for the students' reading abilities. Below the title, list several words or phrases that are significant to the story. Give each student a copy of the list.

Next, have the youngsters discuss the words and make story-related predictions. Ask each student to write his predictions on his paper. Then have the youngsters read the book. When students finish reading, instruct each youngster to draw a check beside each of his predictions that was confirmed. To check students' understanding, invite them to tell you how their predictions compare with the story events. **Making predictions**

Prediction Wisdom

Here's an easy way to encourage students to support and check their predictions. At a chosen point in a reading selection, give each youngster a copy of the graphic organizer on page 26. Have him write the title where indicated. Then invite him to jot down his predictions and explain his reasoning in the appropriate boxes. Next, encourage each youngster to check his predictions as you (or he) continue reading. At the end of the reading selection, instruct each student to draw an X in the appropriate box to show whether his predictions were confirmed. Then have him write about the actual story events. Making predictions

Paired to Share

Make a read-aloud interactive with this prediction activity. Pair students and have each youngster sit near his partner. Begin reading the story aloud. Then stop at a chosen point in the book and announce, "Pair and predict!" Have one student in each twosome tell her partner what she predicts will happen next in the story and explain her reasoning. After a few minutes, invite volunteers to tell the group about the predictions they discussed. Then resume reading. Periodically pause in the reading as described to have students make more predictions, asking partners to switch roles each time. It's a great strategy for increasing students' comprehension as well as their engagement in the story! **Making predictions**

Lights! Camera! Action!

Set the stage for purposeful reading with this kid-pleasing strategy. In advance, obtain a megaphone or make one from construction paper. To begin, give each child a sticky note and a book suitable for her reading ability. Call out, "Lights!" with the megaphone and then have each youngster focus her attention on her book title and cover. Next, announce, "Camera!" and encourage each child to look briefly at her book's illustrations. Finally, announce, "Action!" and have each child write on her sticky note what she wants to find out by reading the book. Then instruct her to adhere her sticky note to her book. No doubt it will focus her attention as she reads! **Setting a purpose for reading**

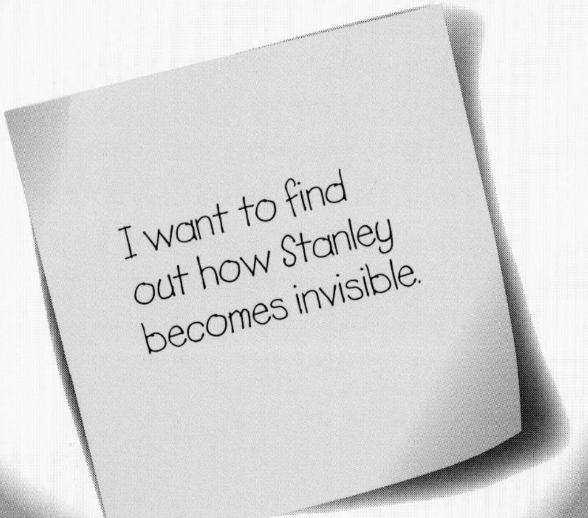
I want to find out how Stanley becomes invisible.

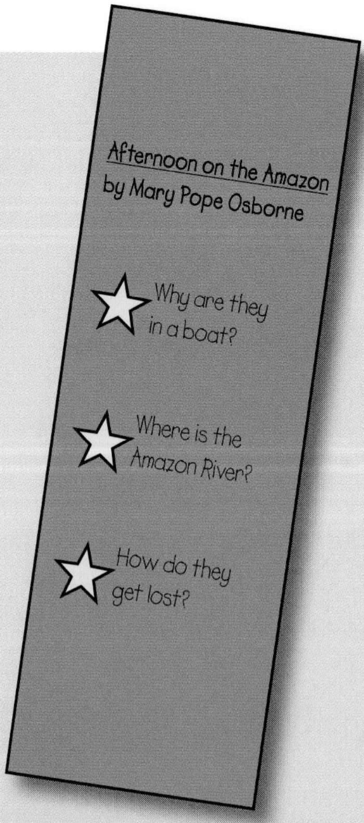
Afternoon on the Amazon
by Mary Pope Osborne
Why are they in a boat?
Where is the Amazon River?
How do they get lost?

Just Curious!

This bookmark idea encourages thoughtful reading. Give each youngster three self-adhesive stars and a 3" x 9" strip of construction paper (bookmark). Instruct him to vertically position the book-mark and write near the top the title and author of a book he will read. Ask him to adhere the stars near the left edge of the bookmark, as shown, leaving writing space between them. Next, instruct each student to study the front cover of his book, and if appropriate, have him read the back cover. Then ask him to write a book-related question beside each star. As he reads the book, encourage him to write on the back of the bookmark any answers he finds. **Setting a purpose for reading**

Read and Learn!

Use this idea to help your students zero in on specific information in nonfiction books. To begin, remind youngsters of several features of nonfiction books that make finding information easier, such as a table of contents, an index, captions, and headings. Next, set out a supply of sticky notes and give each youngster an index card. Instruct her to write on the index card two or more things that she would like to learn by reading the book. Then, each time she finds desired information during her reading, have her jot it down on a sticky note and flag the corresponding page with it.
Reading for specific information

Inquiring Minds

Monitor comprehension and keep students' interest high with this chapter book idea. At the end of each chapter of a chosen book, invite students to tell the class questions they have about the story. Since youngsters will be eager to find the answers to their questions, they'll focus their attention and look forward to continuing the book! **Questioning**

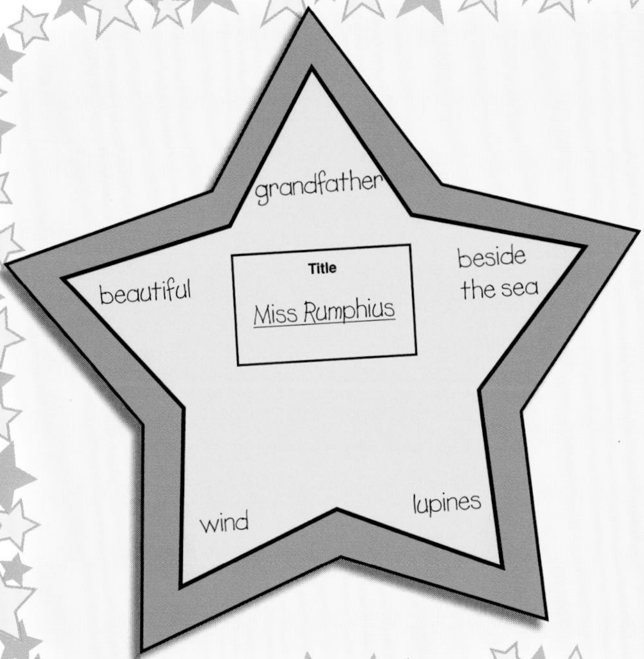
grandfather
beside the sea
beautiful
Title
Miss Rumphius
wind
lupines

Stellar Stories

Students' comprehension is sure to shine when they focus on important story details! To prepare this display idea, title a bulletin board "These Details Shine Bright!"

To decorate the board, give each youngster a colorful copy of the star pattern on page 27. Have him write in the center of the star the title of a book that you recently read to the class. Then, on each arm of the star, instruct him to write a different word or phrase related to an important story detail. Next, invite him to mount the star on a slightly larger piece of colorful paper and then trim the paper to leave a narrow border. After each student completes his star, have each student tell the class one word that he wrote and why he thinks it is important to the story. Then arrange the stars on the board as desired. **Story details**

Group Effort

To promote story recall, divide students into small groups before reading aloud a chosen book. Assign the groups a few different parts of the story, such as selected characters, the setting, or the conclusion. (Give each group the same assignments.) As you read the book, encourage students to pay particular attention to story details relevant to the assigned parts. At the book's conclusion, have each group list significant details they recall for each assigned part of the story. After the students finish writing their lists, invite the groups to compare them. If desired, help students compile the information to create one list for each assigned part of the story. **Story details**

The Donkey
not strong
can't work as hard
scares the robbers when it brays
kicks a robber

One day a fish with many beautiful scales was swimming in the ocean.
2
3

First, Second, Third

Use this simple booklet project to help students recall story events in order. To make a booklet, a student stacks two 8½" x 11" sheets of white paper and positions them vertically. She slides the top paper upward about one inch and then folds the top of the stack forward, creating four graduated layers. She staples the stack along the fold.

To complete her booklet, each youngster writes the title of a chosen book on her booklet cover and illustrates the cover as desired. She numbers the pages as shown. Then she writes about the beginning of the story on the first page, the middle of the story on the second page, and the end of the story on the third page. Finally, she illustrates each page. **Beginning, middle, and end**

Story Chains

Encourage students to think about how story events link together! After you read aloud a chosen book, divide students into small groups. Give each group clear tape, a supply of 2" x 12" light-colored paper strips, and a sheet of paper. In each group, the students list several important story events on their paper. Then they write each event in the center of a separate strip of paper. One student also writes the title and author on a blank strip. Next, the students sequence the event strips and place the titled strip at the beginning of the sequence. They tape the ends of the strips together, linking them, as shown, with blank strips between them. The resulting chain is a great tool for recapping the story! **Sequencing events**

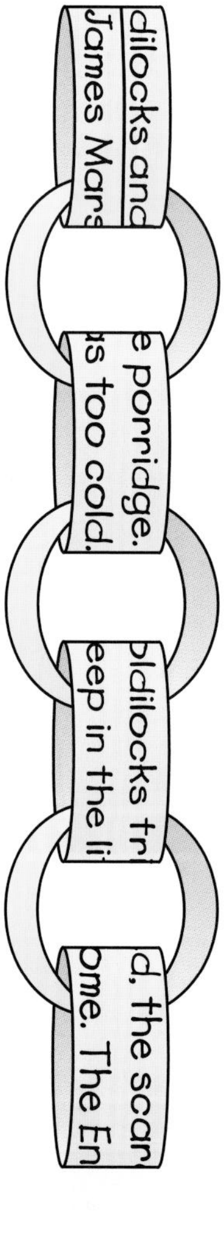
dilocks and
James Mars
e porridge.
s too cold.
oldilocks tr
eep in the li
d, the scar
ome. The En

Comic Relief Sequencing

Here's a grin-inducing approach to sequencing events. Gather several comic strips from the Sunday paper. Glue the strips to a sheet of tagboard, laminate them, and cut the frames apart. For each strip, number the backs of the frames for self-checking. Store each set in a separate envelope and lace the envelopes at a center. A student chooses an envelope and takes out the frames. He sequences the frames and then flips them to check his work.
Sequencing events

TV Time!

Invite youngsters to use televisions to present story events in order. Duplicate the patterns on page 28 onto construction paper to make a class supply. Slit the dotted lines on each television pattern with an X-acto knife. Then read aloud a story to the class. After the reading, a student colors her television pattern and then cuts out the television and the strips. She glues the strips together where indicated. Next, she writes the title and the author's name in the first section; then she illustrates the main story events in order in the remaining sections. To use her television, the student inserts the strip in the slits, as shown, and slides the strip as she tells the story. **Sequencing events**

Charlotte's Web
by
E. B. White
SOME PIG
HUMBLE

Sequencing Seat

Have your youngsters recall the events of a story by playing this sequencing game. To begin, read aloud (or have students independently read) a short passage or story. Invite one youngster to take a seat in a designated chair. Have the student start the game by telling the beginning event of the story and then asking a different student to come sit in the chair. The second child tells the next event in the story; then he asks another student to take his place. Continue to have youngsters tell the events of the story in the same manner until they reach the ending. **Sequencing events**

Daily Events

Spark your students' interest in sequencing with pantomimes! To begin, ask each student to think of an everyday activity that he participates in, such as brushing his teeth or combing his hair. Instruct each child to list the steps of the activity on a sheet of paper without revealing his activity to his classmates.

Next, ask a volunteer to pantomime each step of his activity while his classmates try to identify it. Once they guess it correctly, have one or more different volunteers pantomime their activities for students to guess. Then have each youngster cut apart the steps he wrote. After each student writes his initials on the back of his strips, have each youngster trade strips with a classmate. Then instruct him to arrange the steps he received in sequential order. To check his work, encourage him to read each step, in turn, and visualize his classmate acting it out. **Sequencing steps**

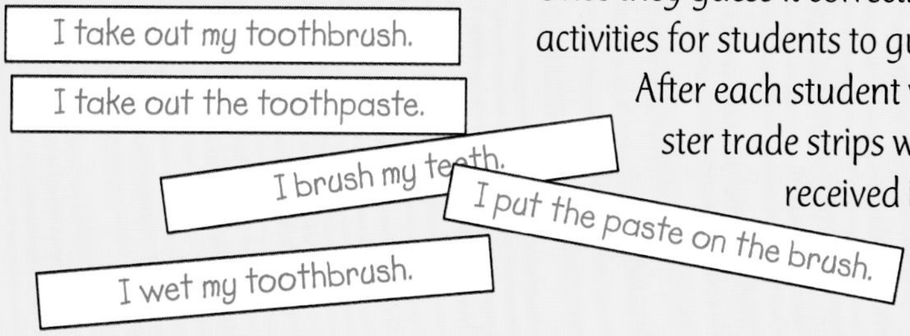
I take out my toothbrush.
I take out the toothpaste.
I brush my teeth.
I put the paste on the brush.
I wet my toothbrush.

The Art of Visualizing

Creating these masterpieces is a picture-perfect way to enhance students' comprehension! Select a book or a chapter from a book that has vivid setting details and hide the illustrations from students' view. To begin, encourage students to visualize the setting as you read the selection aloud. Then have each youngster draw her mental image of the setting on provided paper. When she is satisfied with her artwork, ask her to write words or phrases from the story that influenced her mental image. After each student completes her work, pair students. Have partners compare the details in their drawings. Then display students' artwork on a bulletin board titled "Picture the Story!"
Visualizing story details

Pop-Up Comparison

Follow up a nonfiction selection with this minibooklet project. Give each youngster a copy of the booklet pattern on page 29. Have him write a fact from the reading in the first blank section and a topic-related opinion in the second blank section. Invite him to add any desired crayon details and then have him cut out his pattern. To complete his project, have him follow the steps below. **Fact and opinion**

Steps:

1. Fold the pattern in half along the center line.
2. Fold the curved section downward as shown.
3. Unfold the paper. Reverse the fold on the curved section and push that section inward.
4. Close the booklet with the pop-up section inside. Crease the folds.
5. Title and illustrate the cover.

Step 2

DINOSAURS
by
Jamal

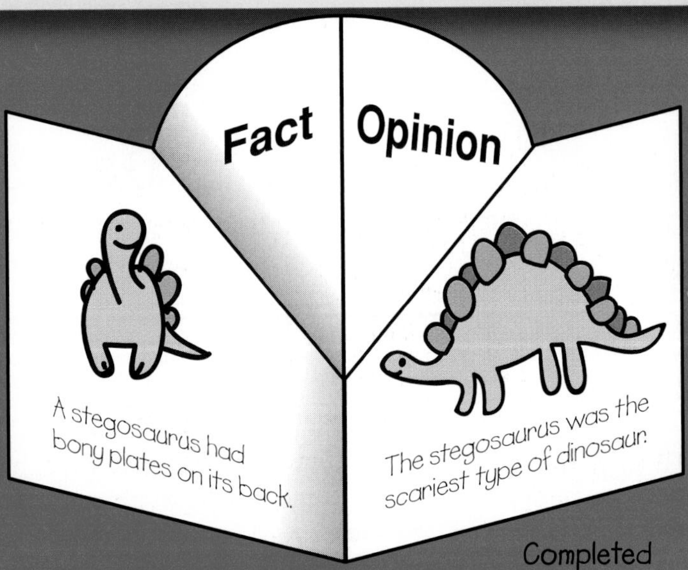
Fact
Opinion
A stegosaurus had bony plates on its back.
The stegosaurus was the scariest type of dinosaur.

Completed Project

Sensational Statements!

This interactive bulletin board is a surefire way to review facts and opinions! To prepare, title a bulletin board as shown. Post either a fact or an opinion in the middle of the board. Also, label one side of the board "Fact" and the other side "Opinion." Ask youngsters to read the statement on the board and silently decide whether it is a fact or an opinion. Have each student write his name on a sticky note and post it below the appropriate heading on the board. Reveal the answer and encourage students to discuss their responses. Change the statement weekly or monthly to keep youngsters' skills sharp. **Fact and opinion**

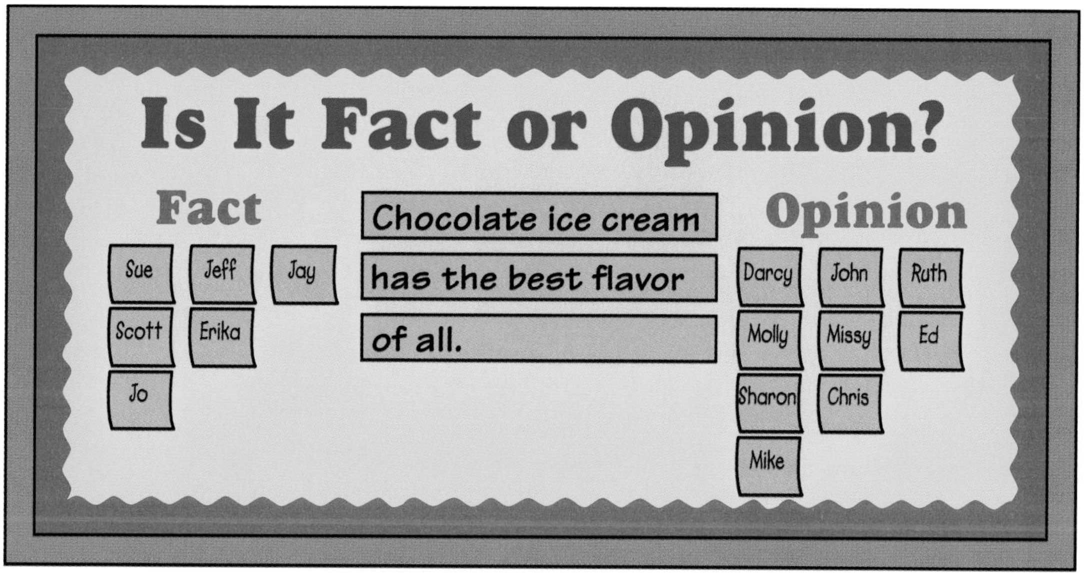
Is It Fact or Opinion?
Fact
Sue
Jeff
Jay
Scott
Erika
Jo
Chocolate ice cream
has the best flavor
of all.
Opinion
Darcy
John
Ruth
Molly
Missy
Ed
Sharon
Chris
Mike

Take a Sentence!

After reviewing with students the difference between a fact and an opinion, announce a topic such as pets or toys. Then have each student write her name on two index cards. On one card, ask her to write an opinion about the topic. On the other card, ask her to write a topic-related fact. Place all of the students' cards in a large bowl or a similar container and scramble them. Next, invite a student to take a card at random and read the sentence to his classmates. Ask youngsters whether the sentence is a fact or an opinion. Confirm the answer. Then have another student take a card. Continue as described until all of the facts and opinions have been identified. **Fact and opinion**

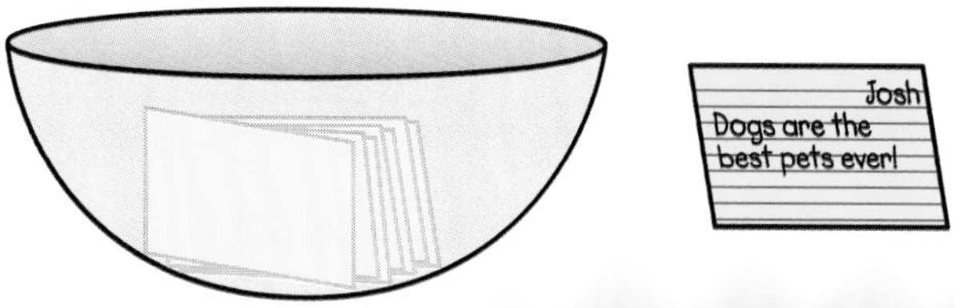
Josh
Dogs are the
best pets ever!

In a Flash

No doubt your students will enjoy Fact-or-Opinion Flash! To prepare this group activity, give each student two blank cards and a craft stick. Have him write "Fact" on one card and "Opinion" on the other card. Then instruct him to glue one card to each side of the craft stick, as shown, to make a two-sided sign.

To begin, ask each student to set his sign down. Then announce a statement. Have each youngster silently determine whether the statement is a fact or an opinion and then hold up his sign to show you the appropriate side. After you scan students' responses, announce the correct answer and provide any needed explanation. Then ask each child to set his sign down. Present a desired number of different sentences for students to identify in the same manner. To extend the activity, have students write facts and opinions to use during a later round of play. **Fact and opinion**

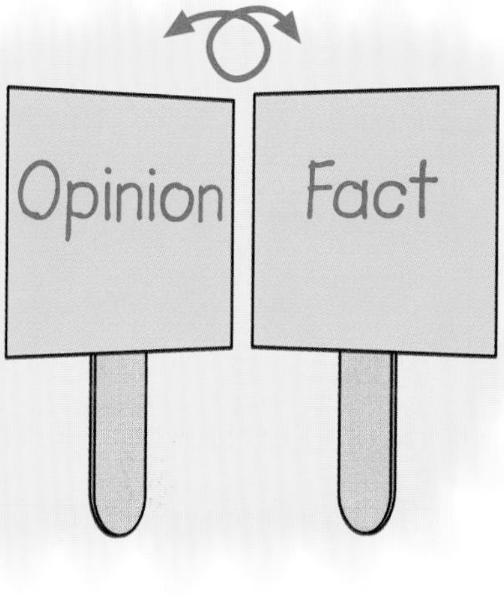
Opinion
Fact

A Perfect Fit

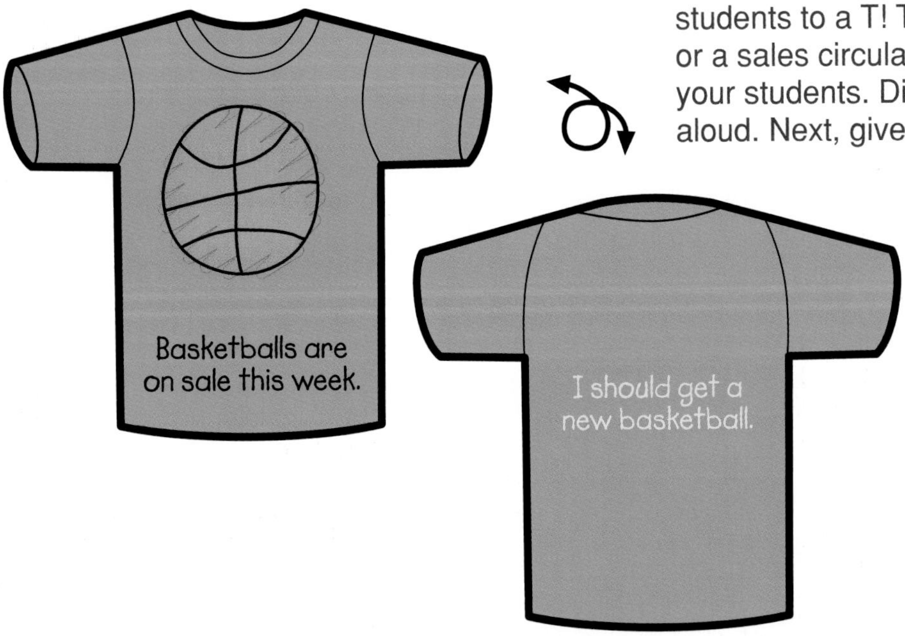
Basketballs are on sale this week.
I should get a new basketball.

Count on this fact-and-opinion idea to suit your students to a T! To prepare, cut from a newspaper or a sales circular two or three ads likely to interest your students. Display the ads and read them aloud. Next, give each student a construction paper T-shirt. Have her write near the bottom of the shirt a fact from a chosen ad on display. Ask her to draw a corresponding illustration above the fact. Then instruct her to write a relevant opinion on the back of her shirt. If desired, clip students' completed shirts to a clothesline to create an eye-catching display. **Fact and opinion**

Fries, Facts, and More

When it comes to checking students' understanding of fact and opinion, this idea is sure to hit the spot! To prepare, make a randomly ordered list of five facts and five opinions. Cut a supply of yellow construction paper strips (french fries). Also, copy the french fry container on page 30 on red paper to make a class supply.

To begin, give each student eight fries and a copy of the list. Have him identify four facts and four opinions on the list and write each one on a separate fry. Next, instruct him to cut out a copy of the french fry container. After he folds it on the thin lines, ask him to secure the sides with tape and glue the container to the middle of a paper plate. Ask him to arrange the opinions on the plate so that they can be read easily. Then have him glue the opinions in place. Once he tucks the facts in the container, his mouthwatering work will be complete! **Fact and opinion**

You should eat french fries every day.
The large size has too many fries
Some fries are cooked in
French fries are made with
The fries are sold in two sizes.
Some people put ketchup o
French fries taste better with salt on them.
Supersize Facts
Fries taste good with ketchup.

Matchmakers

Shhhh!
Where is it?
Cause
Henry lost his library book.
Effect
He had to pay a fine.

For this large-group activity, copy the cause-and-effect cards on page 31. If you have more than 20 students, program copies of the blank cards with additional cause-and-effect situations to make a class set. Cut out the cards. Begin the activity with a demonstration, such as walking across the room wearing an untied shoe and tripping. Ask students to describe the cause and effect of your situation. Next, hand out the cards. Ask a child with a cause card to read his sentence aloud. Then ask the student with the matching effect to read her card aloud. Continue until all the cause-and-effect situations are found. Provide time for each duo to create a two-part illustration of its cause-and-effect situation. Post the completed artwork around the room. **Cause and effect**

Story Slice

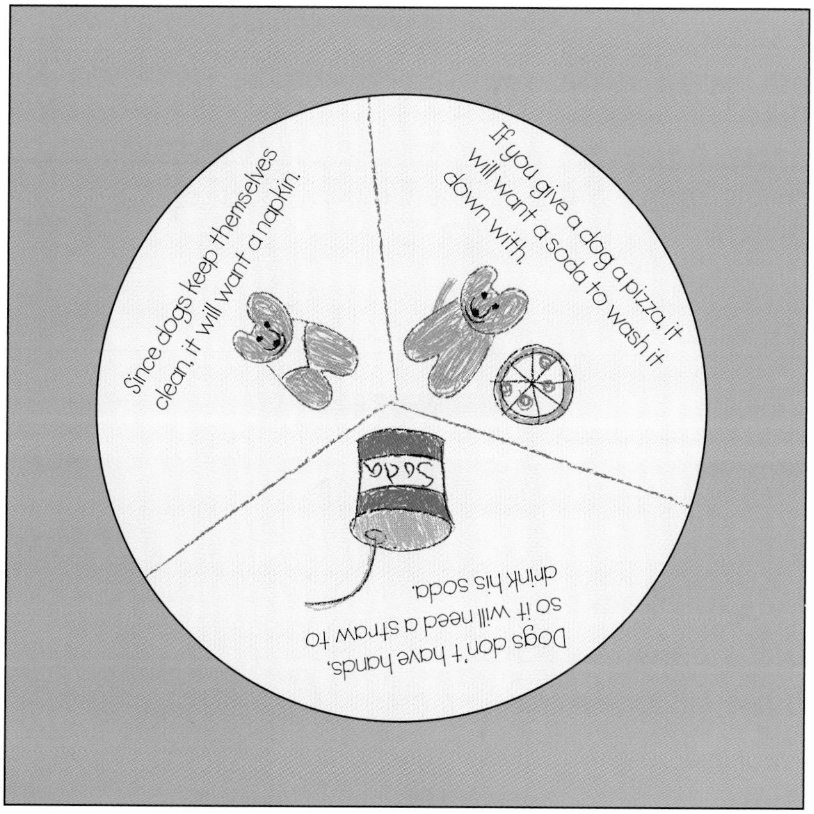
If you give a dog a pizza, it will want a soda to wash it down with.
Since dogs keep themselves clean, it will want a napkin.
Soda
Dogs don't have hands, so it will need a straw to drink his soda.

To prepare, cut a supply of large paper circles into thirds. Then read aloud *If You Give a Mouse a Cookie* by Laura Joffe Numeroff. Have students recall several cause-and-effect situations from the story. Next, divide students into groups of three and give each student a third of a circle. Announce a title such as "If You Give a Dog a Pizza." Ask each group to brainstorm cause-and-effect events for the story and then describe and illustrate its favorite events on the circle slices. Then have each group put its thirds together to re-form a circle and glue it on construction paper. Invite each group to share its completed story aloud. If desired, bind the completed pages into a class book. **Cause and effect**

Tabletop Tents

Teach youngsters about cause and effect as they make these tabletop tents. Ask students to stand beside their seats if they have a favorite story; then ask them why they are standing. Tell them that your request caused them to respond. The effect was that the students stood up at their seats. Ask students to brainstorm additional examples of cause and effect. Write the students' responses on the board; then ask each child to select one from the list. Each student then folds a sheet of construction paper lengthwise into fourths. Next, he writes "cause" at the bottom of the second section and "effect" on the third section; then he illustrates a picture for each one. Finally, he glues the first section atop the last section to create a tent like the one shown. Invite youngsters to share their tents with their classmates. Then display the tents on a table to create a cause-and-effect village.
Cause and effect

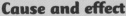

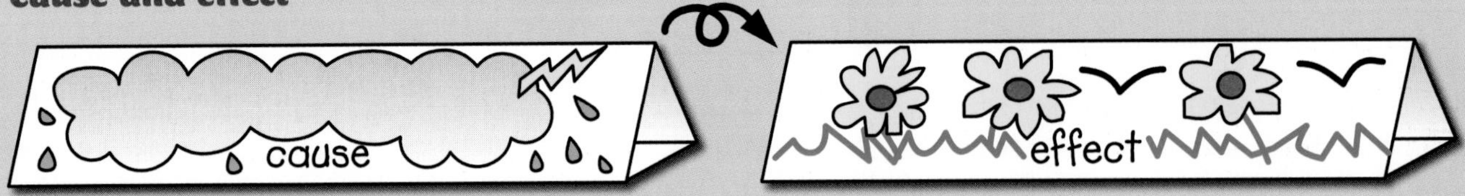
cause
effect

Kid-Friendly Words

Introduce cause and effect with words that are easier to understand: *when* and *then.* Review the actions of a character in a well-known story. Tell students that *when* and *then* can be used to link the actions to the consequences or results. Make a chart on the board, like the one shown, and write a story event in the "when" column. Then have a student tell its effect as you write it in the "then" column. Reread the statements as a single idea by inserting the words *when* and *then.* Once students understand this format, begin using the formal terms. **Cause and effect**

When	Then
Goldilocks sat in Baby Bear's chair.	The chair broke.

When Goldilocks sat
in Baby Bear's chair...
then the chair broke.

C
I have a brother who makes me mad sometimes too.

Take Note

During a read-aloud, stop periodically and share personal connections with the story. Encourage students to share other connections at those times as well. After finishing the story and sharing connections as a whole class, have students practice on their own. Give each child a small supply of sticky notes before he reads an assigned story or chapter. Have him label the top of each note with the letter *C* as shown. Then, as he reads, have him write on a sticky note a brief description of any connection he makes. He marks the page with the sticky note and continues reading, writing, and placing more notes as needed. When the assigned reading time is over, he meets with a partner to share connections. **Making connections**

Me
I like to sing songs.
I have a mom.
I have to be careful.
My friend hurt my feelings.
I don't get tricked.
Kelsey
Frances from A Bargain for Frances
She makes up songs.
She has a mom.
She has to be careful.
Her friend hurt her feelings.
She got tricked.

Side by Side

Copy the character pattern on page 32 onto tagboard and cut it out. Place the cutout at a center with a supply of large paper. After reading a narrative story, a child visits the center and folds a sheet of paper to make two halves. She traces the character cutout onto each half and then labels one side with her name and the other side with the name of a character. She writes characteristics related to each around the appropriate outline; then she circles the similarities. If desired, she completes the activity by drawing details on each outline as shown. **Making connections**

I am embarrassed, and I hope Mr. Slinger isn't mad at me. I really want him to like me as much as I like him.
Lilly told Mr. Slinger that she was sorry.

What's on Your Mind?

Bring inferring skills to mind with this easy art activity. Give each child a sheet of paper and have him draw an important event from a story, focusing on the main character. He includes text from the story to help explain or describe the scene. Then the student uses prior knowledge, such as personal experiences and information from the story, to record what the character might be thinking in a thought bubble as shown. If desired, have the student draw attention to the thought bubble by outlining it with puff paint. **Making inferences**

Take a Trip

Have youngsters take imaginary trips to learn about drawing conclusions. Give each student a copy of page 33; then ask each student to think of a special place where she would like to take a trip, keeping it a secret. Have her list on her sheet words and ideas that describe her place. Then have student volunteers read aloud their clues to their classmates. Students will enjoy trying to guess their classmates' destinations! **Drawing conclusions**

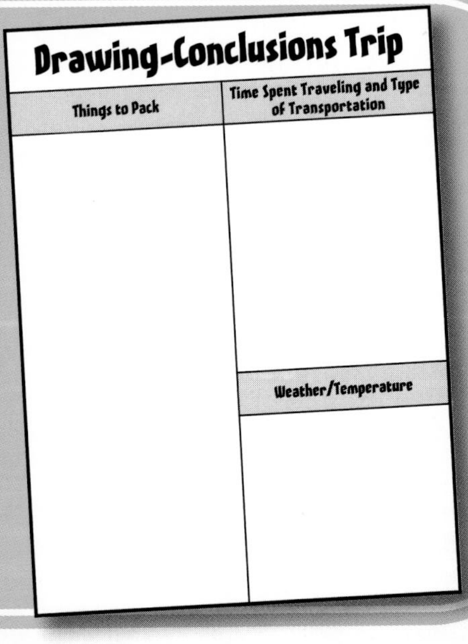
Drawing-Conclusions Trip
Things to Pack
Time Spent Traveling and Type of Transportation
Weather/Temperature

Mystery Items

Challenge your youngsters to guess mystery items as they practice drawing conclusions. Select an item and place it in a shoebox. Write a number of clues about the item on separate cards. Each day have a student read a new clue aloud to the class. After all the clues have been read, have each student write his guess and his name on a slip of paper. Collect the papers and reveal the mystery item. Provide time for students to discuss their answers. Spotlight a different mystery item each week to aid in your students' understanding of drawing conclusions! Drawing conclusions

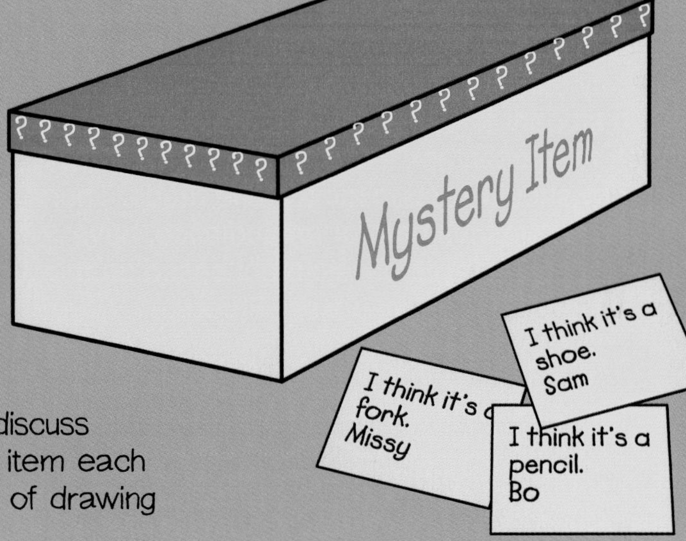
Mystery Item
I think it's a shoe. Sam
I think it's a fork. Missy
I think it's a pencil. Bo

Missing From the Menu

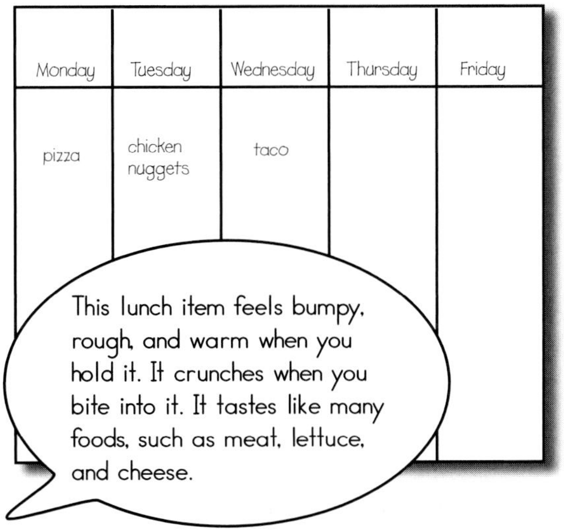
Monday
Tuesday
Wednesday
Thursday
Friday
pizza
chicken nuggets
taco
This lunch item feels bumpy, rough, and warm when you hold it. It crunches when you bite into it. It tastes like many foods, such as meat, lettuce, and cheese.

Build on students' prior knowledge with this partner activity. In advance, write clues about five cafeteria foods, focusing on how each food smells, feels, sounds, and tastes. Tell students to pretend that the lunch menu for the following week has been changed and that it is their job to use your clues to rewrite the menu. Next, have each student pair divide a piece of paper into five columns, writing the name of each school day at the top of a column. Read the clues aloud and have students work together to name the food described and write it on their paper. After reading all five sets of clues, review the answers and discuss with students how they used the clues to name the foods. Relate their strategies to drawing conclusions when reading. **Drawing conclusions**

Look a Little Closer

Put your student detectives to work using story clues to draw conclusions. After assigning a story or chapter for students to read, give each child a copy of page 34. A student writes evidence from the story that tells what the main character was like at the beginning and at the end of the story. Then she uses the story references to generate her own ideas about the character. **Drawing conclusions**

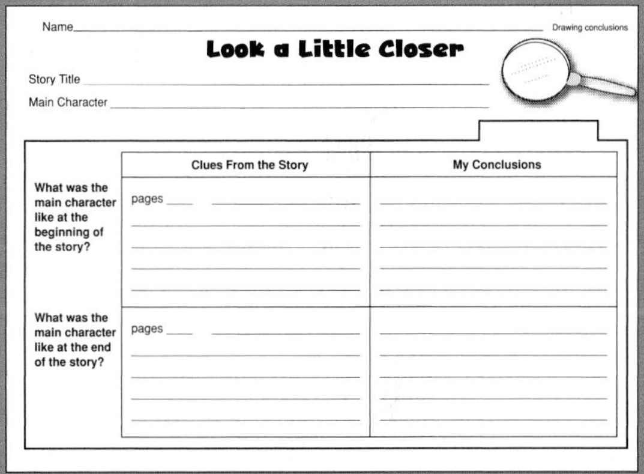

Name ______ Drawing conclusions

Look a Little Closer

Story Title ______

Main Character ______

	Clues From the Story	My Conclusions
What was the main character like at the beginning of the story?	pages ___	
What was the main character like at the end of the story?	pages ___	

Reading Lines

Use readers' theater to pinpoint and improve fluency skills. Provide several opportunities for a student to practice his assigned part. For each rehearsal, ask a different guiding question that he should keep in mind as he reads. Then, after he reads his part for an audience, have him complete a self-assessment based on the guiding questions you posed. **Fluency**

Name ________________________

Did you pause when you saw punctuation? Yes No

Did your voice change when you read questions or exclamatory sentences? Yes No

Did you read your words so that the audience understood how your character feels? Yes No

Did you do all you could to make the story sound interesting? Yes No

A Frog's Tale

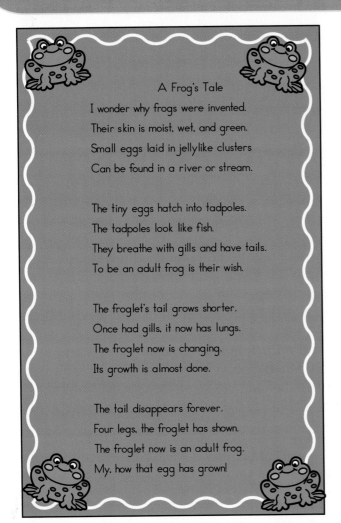

I wonder why frogs were invented.
Their skin is moist, wet, and green.
Small eggs laid in jellylike clusters
Can be found in a river or stream.

The tiny eggs hatch into tadpoles.
The tadpoles look like fish.
They breathe with gills and have tails.
To be an adult frog is their wish.

The froglet's tail grows shorter.
Once had gills, it now has lungs.
The froglet now is changing.
Its growth is almost done.

The tail disappears forever.
Four legs, the froglet has shown.
The froglet now is an adult frog.
My, how that egg has grown!

Poetry With a Punch

Post a copy of a poem, like the one shown, on chart paper. Model reading it expressively and fluently. Next, have students read the poem along with you. Then assign small groups to read each stanza. Each time the poem is read, remind students to use an expressive tone and follow the rhythm of the poem. Repeat the activity with other poems your students enjoy. **Fluency**

Follow Along

Provide access to models of fluent reading by setting up a listening center in your classroom. Gather a supply of books with tapes and store each set in a gallon-size plastic bag. Or make your own books on tape by recording yourself reading some of your classroom books. Place the bags in a large tub or basket along with a cassette player and headphones. Encourage students to visit the center and follow along in the books as the stories are read. For further practice, have them listen to a story a few times and then read it aloud with the tape. **Fluency**

Check out the skill-building reproducibles on pages 35–37.

Crystal Ball Pattern

Use with “Glimpse the Future!” on page 10.

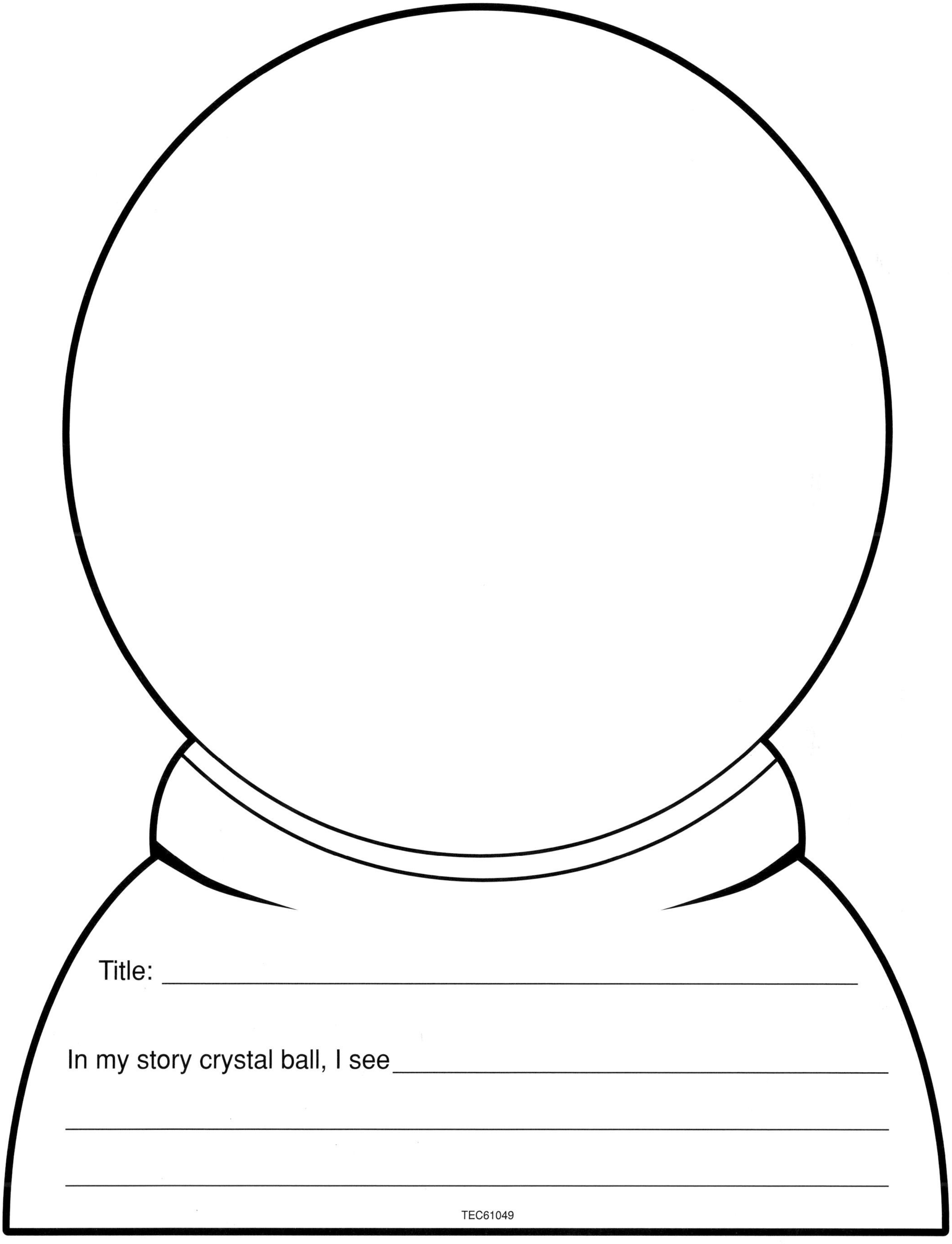
Title: ____________________
In my story crystal ball, I see ____________________
____
____
TEC61049

 Name ______________________________

Prediction Wisdom

Title: ______________________________

My Predictions

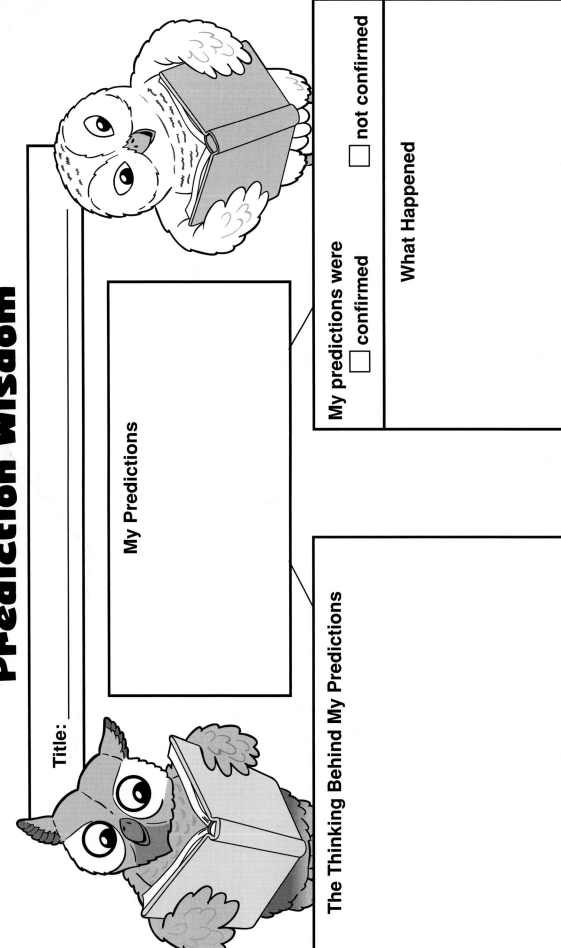

The Thinking Behind My Predictions

My predictions were

☐ **confirmed** ☐ **not confirmed**

What Happened

Note to the teacher: Use with "Prediction Wisdom" on page 11.

Star Pattern

Use with "Stellar Stories" on page 13.

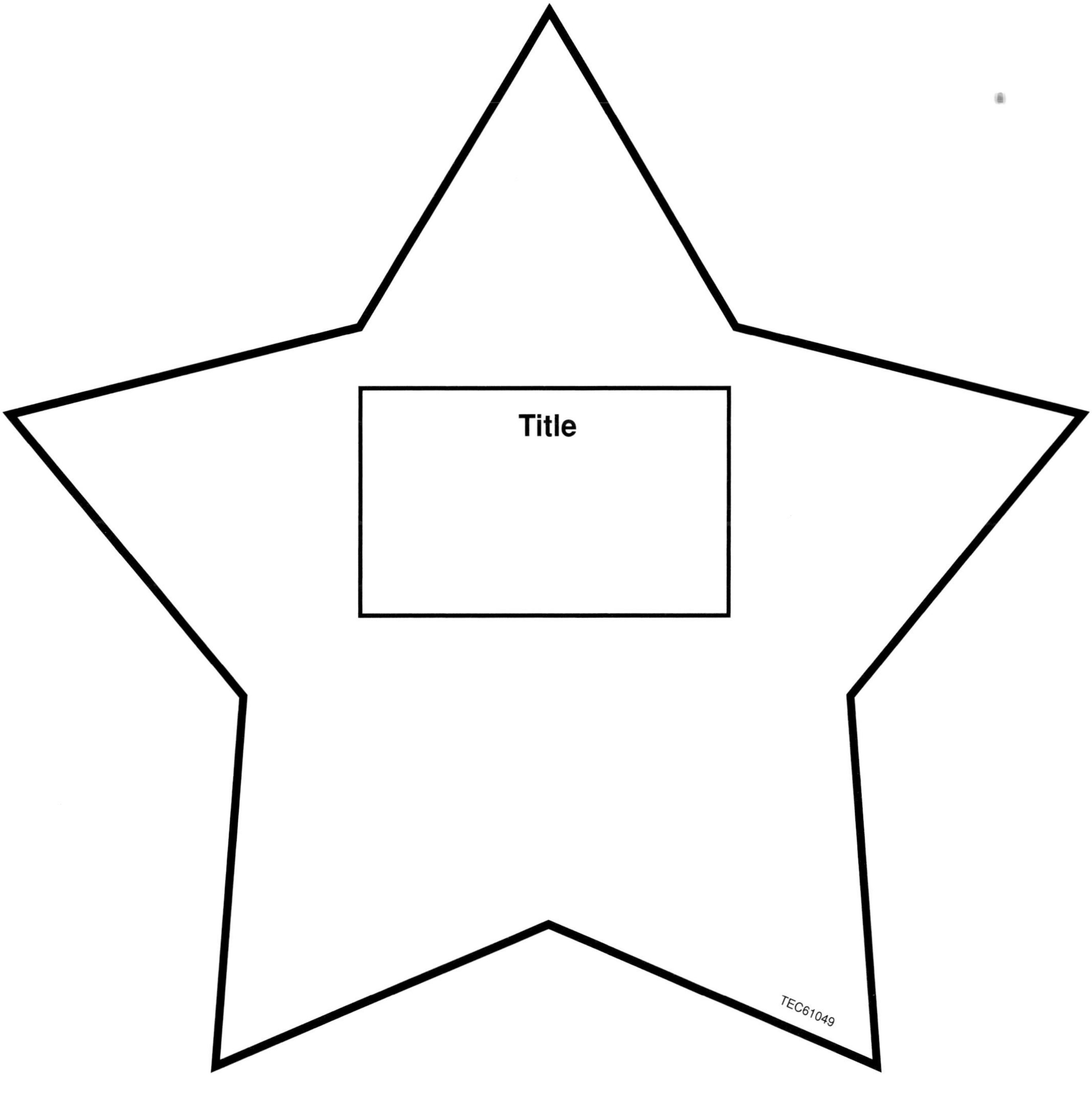
Title
TEC61049

Television and Strip Patterns

Use with "TV Time!" on page 15.

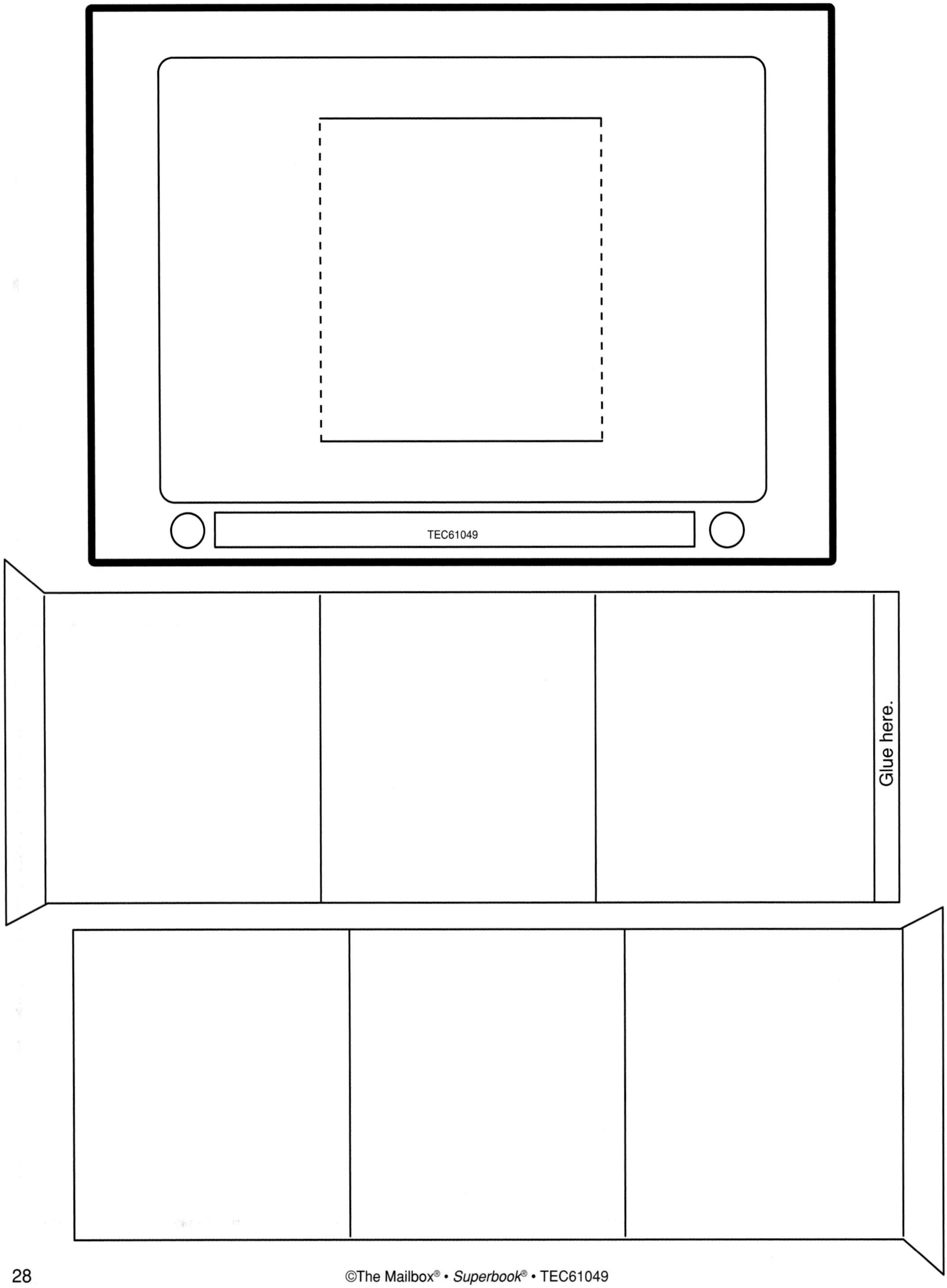
TEC61049
Glue here.

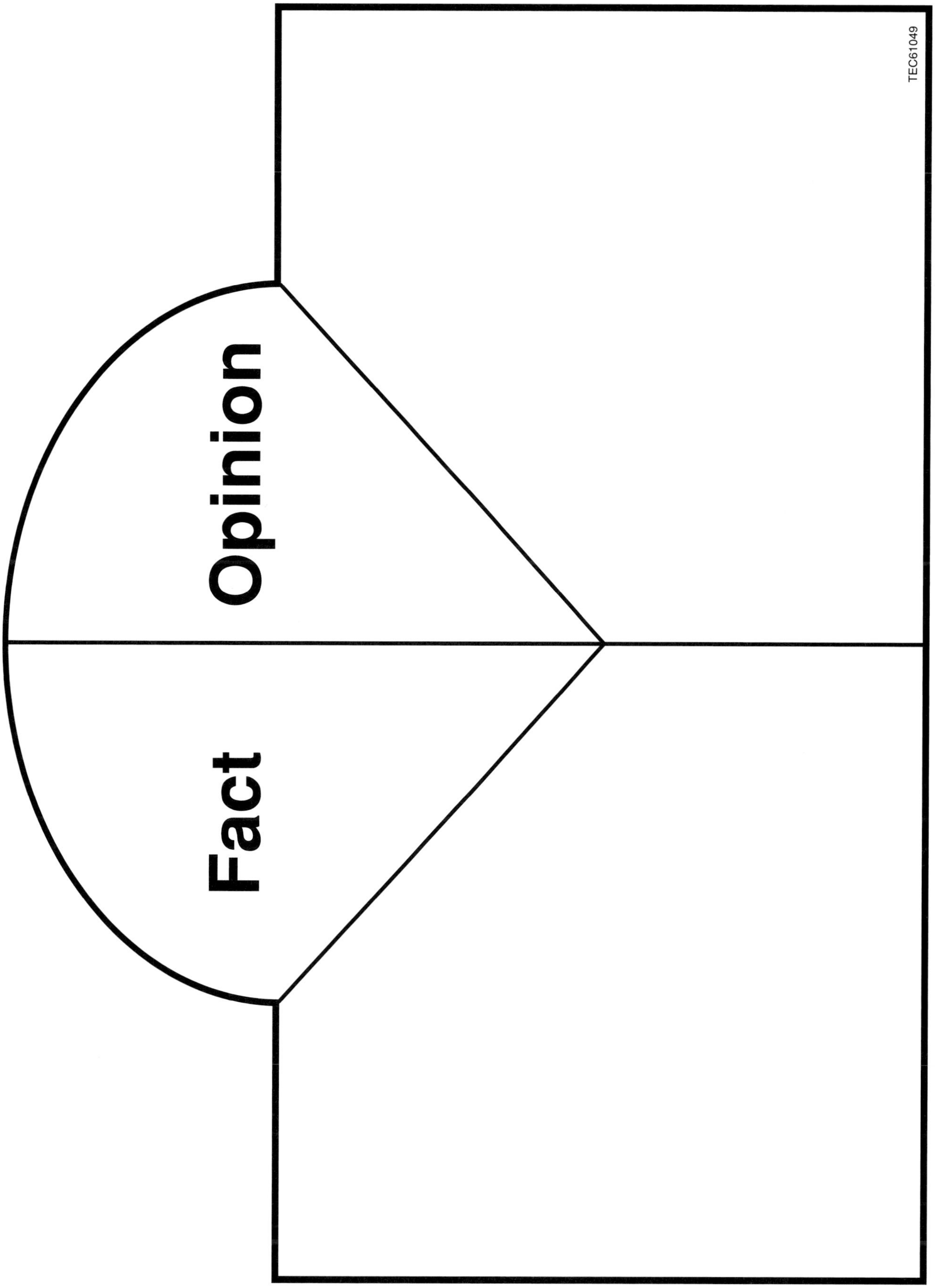
TEC61049
Opinion
Fact

French Fry Container Pattern

Use with "Fries, Facts, and More" on page 18.

Supersize Facts
TEC61049

Use with "Matchmakers" on page 19.

Cause	Effect
Cause Dan got the flu. TEC61049	**Effect** He couldn't play in his baseball game. TEC61049
Cause Jill dropped a bottle of juice. TEC61049	**Effect** The floor was sticky. TEC61049
Cause Tim swung hard at the ball. TEC61049	**Effect** He got a base hit. TEC61049
Cause Hannah slept through her alarm. TEC61049	**Effect** She was late for school. TEC61049
Cause Todd did all of his chores. TEC61049	**Effect** He got his weekly allowance. TEC61049
Cause Kara did not eat all of her dinner. TEC61049	**Effect** She did not get dessert. TEC61049
Cause Henry lost his library book. TEC61049	**Effect** He had to pay a fine. TEC61049
Cause Kendra watered the plant. TEC61049	**Effect** It grew big and tall. TEC61049
Cause Don ran all the way home. TEC61049	**Effect** He was tired when he got there. TEC61049
Cause Tess carefully followed the recipe. TEC61049	**Effect** Her cookies were yummy! TEC61049
Cause TEC61049	**Effect** TEC61049
Cause TEC61049	**Effect** TEC61049

Character Pattern

Use with "Side by Side" on page 21.

TEC61049

Drawing-Conclusions Trip

Things to Pack	Time Spent Traveling and Type of Transportation
	Weather/Temperature

Note to the teacher: Use with "Take a Trip" on page 22.

Name ____________________

Look a Little Closer

Story Title ____________________

Main Character ____________________

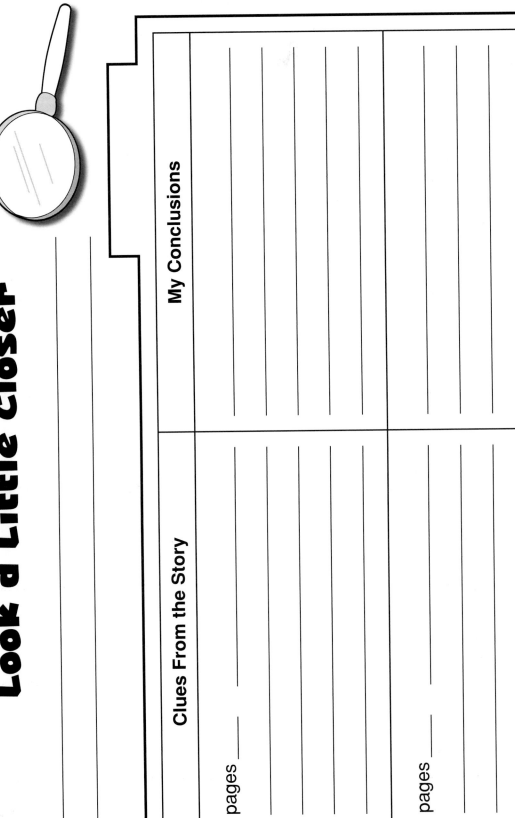

	Clues From the Story	My Conclusions
What was the main character like at the beginning of the story?	pages ____	
What was the main character like at the end of the story?	pages ____	

Note to the teacher: Use with "Look a Little Closer" on page 23.

Name____ Sequencing events

Beach Bound

Welcome
to the
Beach!

Cut out each strip.
Place the sentences in the correct order.
Glue them to a sheet of paper.

The Stone family started getting ready for a trip to the beach.

TEC61049

Then the family climbed into the car.

Next, they put some food and drinks into a cooler.

After that, they loaded up the car with their things.

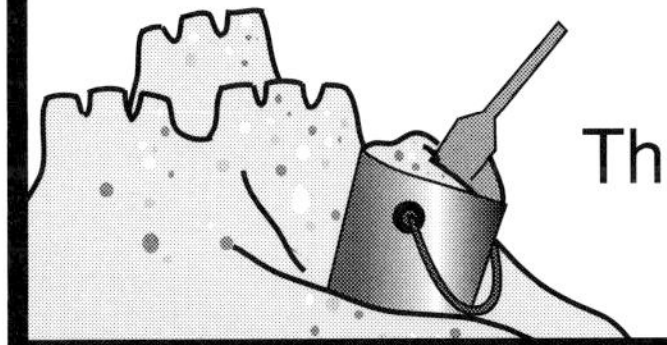
The Stone family took off for the beach.

First, they packed their suitcases.

After they went home for the map, the Stone family was on the road again.

Oops! They forgot to bring the map.

Name ____________________

Thinking Ahead

Fold the paper on the dotted line.
Read the story below.

Kate needed a gift for her sister's birthday. But Kate did not have any money. So she thought about what she could do. Time was running out when she finally came up with a plan. Kate got some paper and markers and went to work.

Prediction: What do you think will happen next? ____________________

____

____

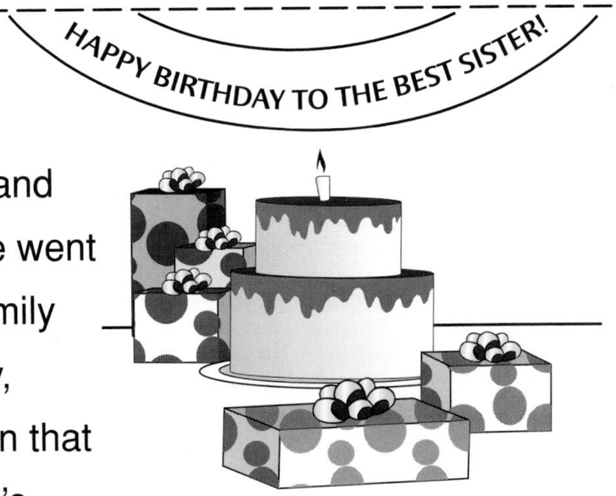
HAPPY BIRTHDAY TO THE BEST SISTER!

Now finish reading the story.

Kate worked hard to make the letters neat and big. She also used her best spelling. Then she went downstairs to finish her surprise. When the family gathered for cake and ice cream later that day, Kate's gift hung in the room. It was a huge sign that read "Happy Birthday to the Best Sister!" Kate's sister loved the gift!

Was your prediction right? Tell why or why not. ____________________

____

____

____

Note to the teacher: Have the student fold the bottom half of the paper behind the top half before reading the story. After the prediction is made, the child may unfold the paper to continue the activity.

Name ____________________

The Bad Day

Read.

Ben's day went badly from the minute he awoke. When he got out of bed, he tripped on his toys. That hurt! At breakfast, he spilled orange juice down the front of his shirt. That meant he needed to change. Wouldn't you know it, that made Ben late and he missed the bus. He got a ride from his dad and Ben finally got to school. Things seemed to be going well until lunchtime. He had forgotten his lunch. As a result, Ben had to buy his lunch at school. He had to eat spinach soup. Yuck! That was not Ben's favorite food. He could not wait to get home, crawl into bed, and start a new day. It would have to be better than this one!

Complete the chart.
Use the passage to help you.

Cause	Effect
Ben tripped on his toys.	
	He had to change his shirt.
	He missed the bus.
Ben forgot his lunch.	

Details, Details, Details!

This idea is sure to help students recall details from a story! To begin, divide your class into groups of five students. In each group, assign each student a different part of the story: characters, setting, beginning, middle, or end. After reading the story aloud, have students recall details about their assigned story parts with their group members; then, as a class, compare the details that were remembered. If desired, further challenge each group to organize its information on a class chart. Without a doubt, this is a great way to learn about details!

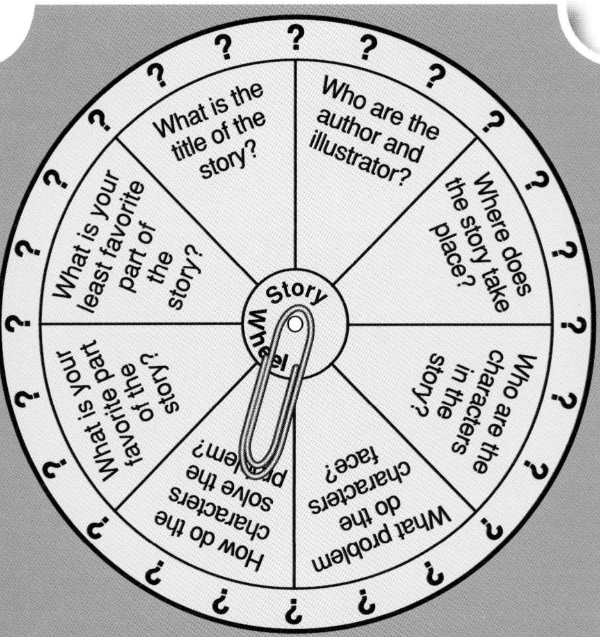
What is the title of the story?
Who are the author and illustrator?
Where does the story take place?
Who are the characters in the story?
What problem do the characters face?
How do the characters solve the problem?
What is your favorite part of the story?
What is your least favorite part of the story?
Story

Spin Up a Great Story!

Make four copies of the spinner from page 42 onto construction paper. Cut out each spinner. Then use a brad to attach a large paper clip to the middle of each spinner as shown. Next, divide the class into four groups. Read a story aloud, or have each group read one together. Distribute the spinners to the groups. In turn, have each group member rotate the paper clip on the spinner and recall details from the selected story part.

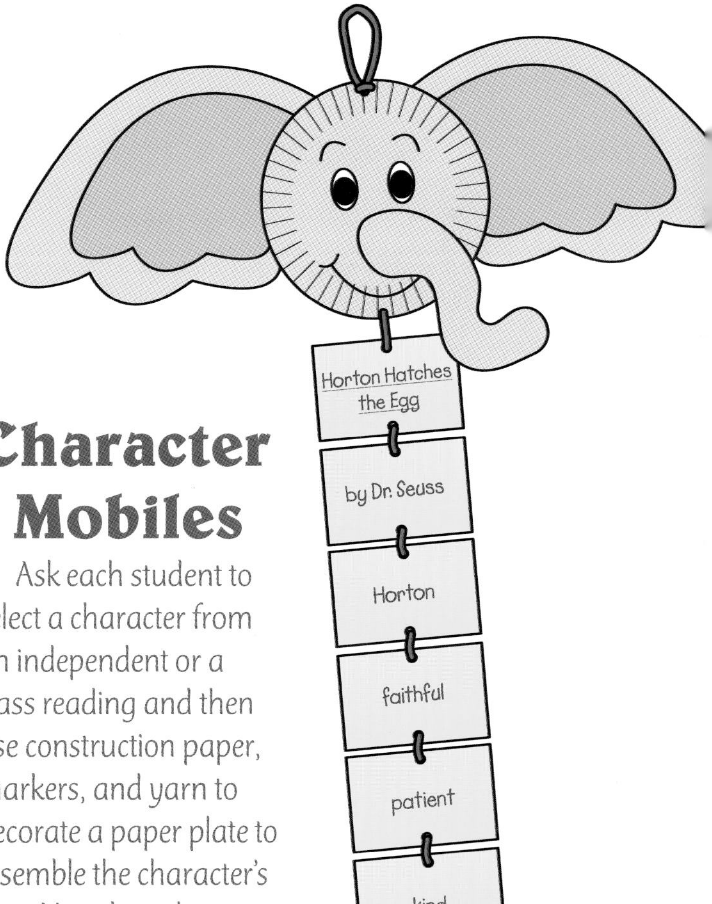
Horton Hatches the Egg
by Dr. Seuss
Horton
faithful
patient
kind

Character Mobiles

Ask each student to select a character from an independent or a class reading and then use construction paper, markers, and yarn to decorate a paper plate to resemble the character's face. Next, have him write the title, author's name, and character's name on separate index cards. On three additional cards, instruct him to write three different traits about his character. After the student has hole-punched his paper plate and cards, help him use yarn lengths to connect the cutouts as pictured. Suspend the completed mobiles from the ceiling for a dazzling display.

Story Wheels

Ask students to name the beginning, middle, and ending events from a given story. List their responses (in the order they occurred in the story) on the board. Then have each student illustrate the events on a story wheel. To make a story wheel, a student uses a pencil and a ruler to divide each of two paper plates into four sections. She writes the title and author of the story in the top right quadrant of one plate. Then she rotates the plate one-quarter turn clockwise, labels the top right quadrant "Beginning," and draws a picture of a corresponding event there. In a similar manner, she labels the next quadrant "Middle" and illustrates the problem of the story. Then she labels the final quadrant "Ending" and illustrates the ending of the story. To make a wheel cover, she draws a large dot in the center of the second plate where the four lines intersect. Next, she carefully cuts away one section of the plate, leaving the dot intact. Then she erases the pencil marks remaining on the plate and personalizes it as desired. Then, using a brad, she attaches the wheel cover atop the wheel.

Boomer's Big Day By Constance W. McGeorge
This end up
Ending
Boomer's Big Day By Constance W. McGeorge
Middle
Beginning

To use the story wheel, the student turns her wheels so that the second event is showing. She tells what happened before and after the second event. To check her answers, she turns the wheel forward or backward to reveal the other events. Continue having students turn their wheels to a determined event and having them tell what happened before or after the event shown.

First
Little Red Riding Hood sets off for her grandmother's house.
Next
She goes through the woods.
Then
A wolf is in Grandma's bed.
Finally
The hunter kills the wolf. Grandma and Little Red Riding Hood are OK.

Story Four-Square

After reading aloud a chosen story, have each student fold a sheet of drawing paper into fourths and open it. Starting in the upper left section, have her label the top of each section with one of the following words: *first, next, then, finally.* Instruct the student to retell the story in sequence by drawing a picture and writing a brief sentence in each square. Students who have trouble expressing themselves verbally will have the drawing as a visual prompt to help them organize their thoughts.

Airplane Pattern

Use with "High-Flying Stories!" on page 38.

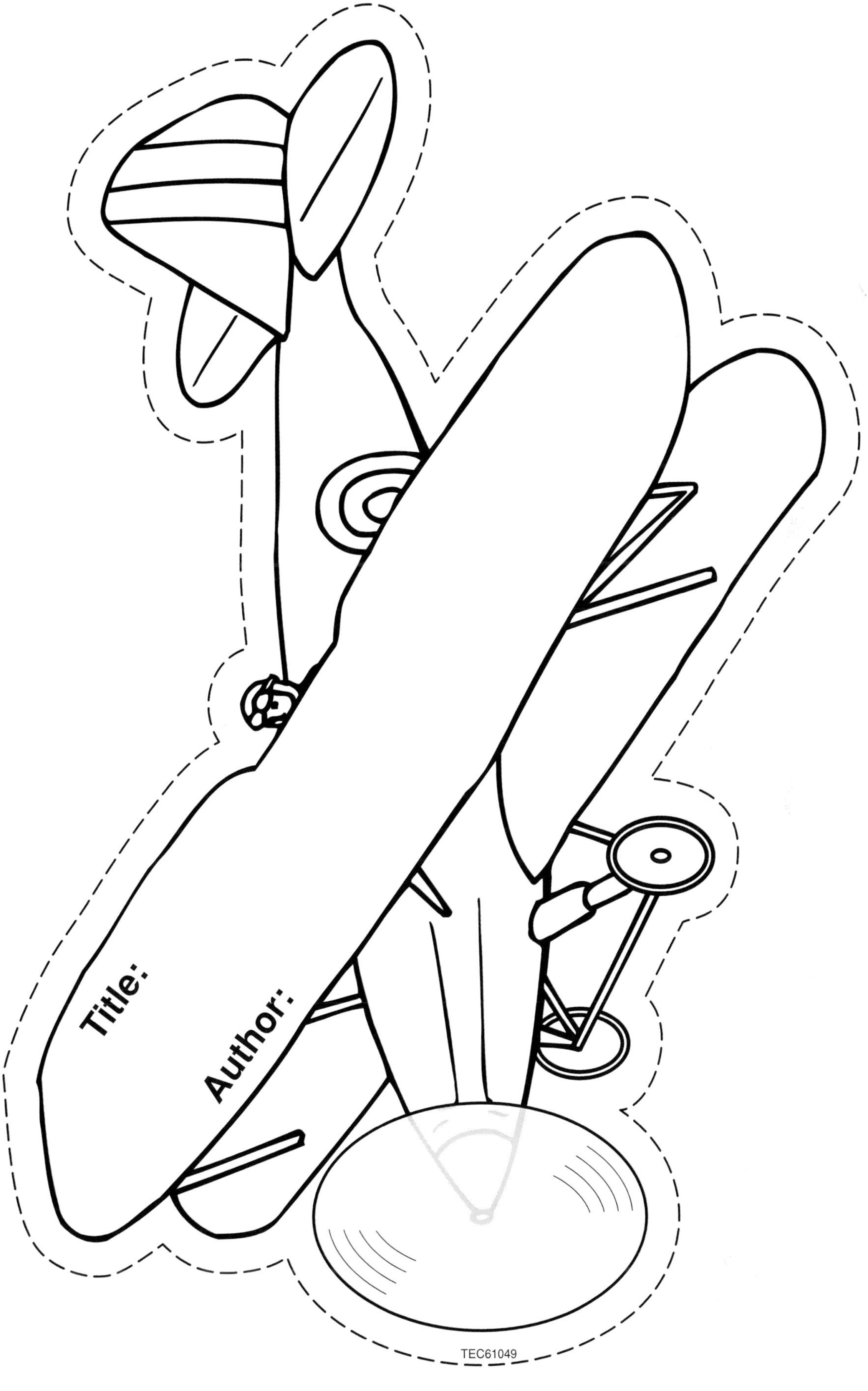
Title:
Author:
TEC61049

Story Wheel

Use the spinner with "Spin Up a Great Story!" on page 39.

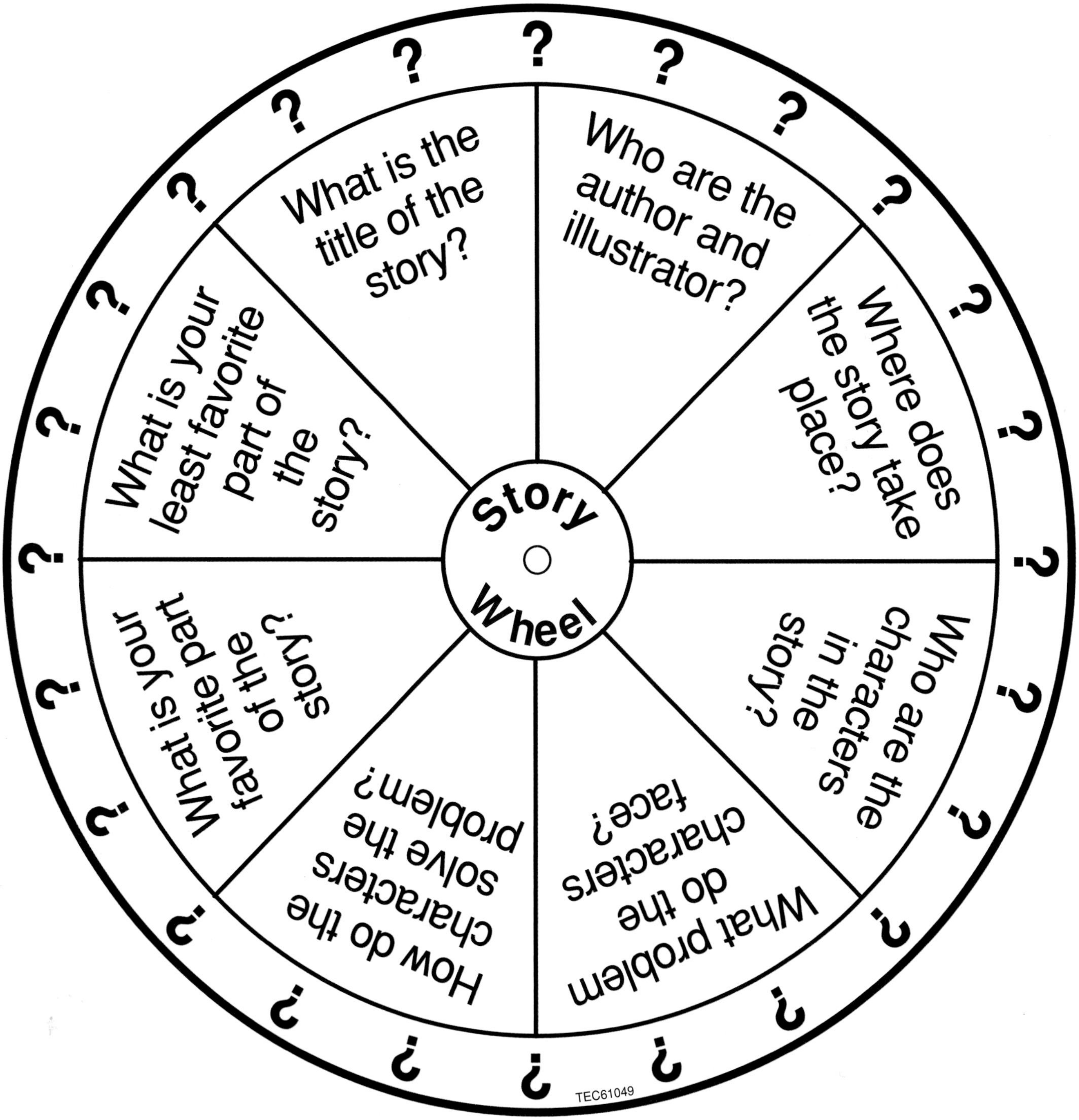
Story Wheel
What is the title of the story?
Who are the author and illustrator?
Where does the story take place?
Who are the characters in the story?
What problem do the characters face?
How do the characters solve the problem?
What is your favorite part of the story?
What is your least favorite part of the story?
TEC61049

Reports on File

To make a file folder report, a student writes the title of his chosen book on the tab of a colored file folder. Next, he completes a copy of the report form on page 45 with information about his book. At the bottom of his paper, he writes a question about the story on the lines provided. Then he draws a scene from the story on a sheet of drawing paper. Finally, he staples his completed form to the left side of the folder and his illustration to the right side. Store the folders in a file box for students to review during free time.

It's in the Bag

Have each student use markers, construction paper, and yarn to decorate a paper lunch bag to resemble a character from a favorite story. To report on the book, the student slips the puppet onto her hand and speaks about the story from the character's point of view. After the students have given their presentations, staple the puppets to a bulletin board. To complete the display, post a label near each puppet identifying the character and the story it's from.

Clifford

Handy-Dandy Reports

Have each student write the title and author of her book on a tagboard hand cutout. Next, on separate two-inch squares of white paper, have her illustrate two different characters, an item in the setting, and two objects that were important in the story. Have her cut out the pictures and then glue one picture to each finger of the hand cutout. Display the completed projects on a bulletin board titled "Give a Big Hand to These Books!"

If You Give a
Mouse a Cookie
Laura Joffe Numeroff
Name Sarah

A Dozen Other Ways To Share A Book

Book reports and literature sharing can be accomplished in a variety of ways. Copy the following activities onto poster board and post the chart in a prominent location. Then encourage students to share their favorite books using activities from the chart. Fun—and a better understanding of literature—will be had by all!

1. Use a marker to divide a sheet of construction paper into puzzle-shaped pieces. Draw or write about an event from or facts about the story in each section. Cut the puzzle pieces apart and store them in a resealable plastic bag.

Raisins
Dentist
Arthur's Tooth
by Marc Brown
Milk

2. Make a poster or an advertisement about a book. Use words and illustrations that will persuade others to read the book.

READ!
Arthur's Tooth
by Marc Brown
Will Arthur lose his tooth?

3. Create a collage of important events from the book. Use magazine pictures, your own drawings, and small objects that relate to the story.

4. Cover a shoebox and its lid with white paper. Use markers or crayons to decorate the shoebox with the book's title and author, and illustrations from the story. Then fill the shoebox with items or pictures of items that were important in the story or significant to the characters.

Dental Floss
Arthur's Tooth
by Marc Brown

5. Draw pictures from the beginning, middle, and ending of the book. Explain what is happening in each picture.

6. Construct a diorama showing an important scene from the book.

7. Create a character mobile from a wire coat hanger, string, and construction paper.

8. Design a book jacket with an illustration that summarizes the story. Include a brief description of the plot on the inside of the jacket.

9. Tape-record yourself reading aloud your favorite passage of the story.

10. Make a list of important words used in the story.

11. Find another book by the same author and compare the two stories.

12. Pretend you are one of the characters from the book. Write a letter to a friend telling him what happened to you in the story.

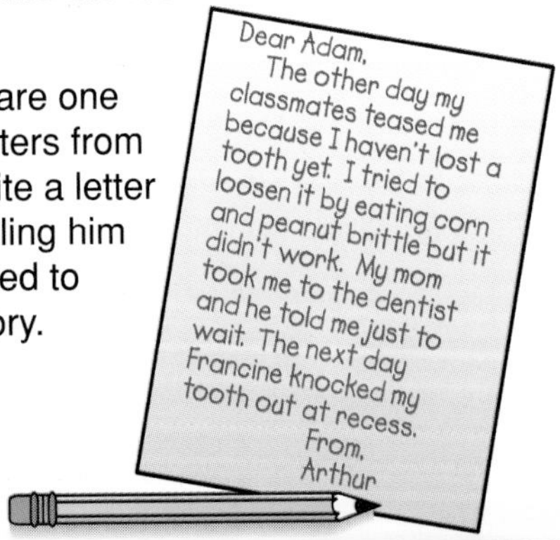
Dear Adam,
The other day my classmates teased me because I haven't lost a tooth yet. I tried to loosen it by eating corn and peanut brittle but it didn't work. My mom took me to the dentist and he told me just to wait. The next day Francine knocked my tooth out at recess.
From,
Arthur

Name ____________________ Book report

Report on File

Title: ____________________

Author: ____________________

Illustrator: ____________________

My favorite character:

____

My favorite part of the story:

____

____

____

Read the story to find the answer to this question:

____

____

____

____

Note to the teacher: Use with "Reports on File" on page 43.

Grammar and Sentence Skills

Capitalization Creations

Remind students that names, places, months, and holidays all need capital letters. Then provide each youngster with an old magazine and a sheet of construction paper. The student folds her paper to make three equal columns; then she labels the columns "Names," "Places," and "Months and Holidays" as shown. She cuts out words from the magazine that match those categories and have capital letters and glues each one in the appropriate column on her paper. If desired, have youngsters write additional words under each heading. Change the categories throughout the year for extra capitalization practice! Capitalization

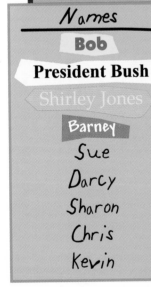

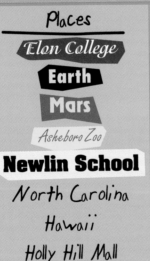

Names	Places	Months and Holidays
Bob	Elon College	June
President Bush	Earth	Father's Day
Shirley Jones	Mars	April
Barney	Asheboro Zoo	Easter
Sue	Newlin School	Halloween
Darcy	North Carolina	Christmas
Sharon	Hawaii	
Chris	Holly Hill Mall	
Kevin		

A Capital Idea

Cut out one short newspaper or magazine article for each student. Also obtain a class set of highlighter markers. To begin, tell students that they will be investigating the kinds of words that need capital letters. Next, give each student one article and one highlighter. The youngster highlights the words in his article that begin with capital letters; then he copies the words onto a separate sheet of paper. Next, he cuts the words on his list apart and sorts them into three categories: words at the beginning of sentences, names of people, and names of places. Pair students and have each child share her work with her partner. **Capitalization**

Capitalization Tools

This easy-to-make toolbox makes a handy student reference. Give each student a 6" x 12" piece of construction paper. Help her use her ruler to fold down a two-inch flap on the short side of the paper as shown. Next, help her use her ruler to fold up a five-inch flap on the bottom of the short side of the paper, creating a toolbox as shown. The child then uses construction paper scraps to make a handle and locks for her toolbox. Then she colors and cuts out a copy of the tools on page 55. She glues each tool on the inside of her toolbox. Encourage her to refer to her toolbox when she is writing for a reminder of the capitalization rules. Capitalization

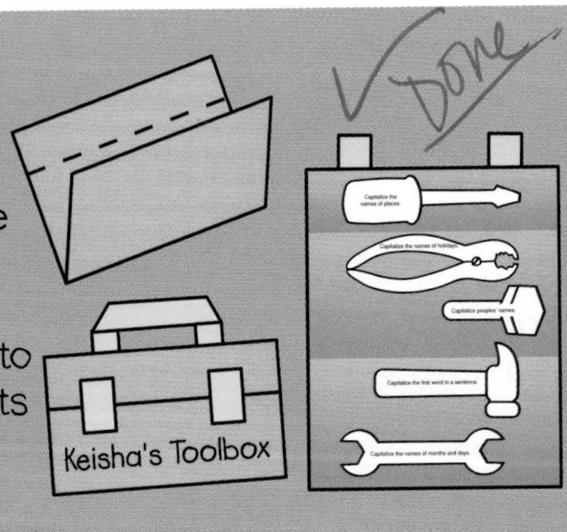
Keisha's Toolbox

Fishing for Capitals

Using only lowercase letters, program a supply of fish cutouts each with a different proper or common noun. Put a dot on the back of each fish with a proper noun for self-checking. Place the cutouts in a resealable plastic bag at a center along with a plastic fishbowl. A child sorts the cards by common or proper nouns and places those with proper nouns in the fishbowl. To check his work, he simply checks the back of the cutouts. **Capitalization**

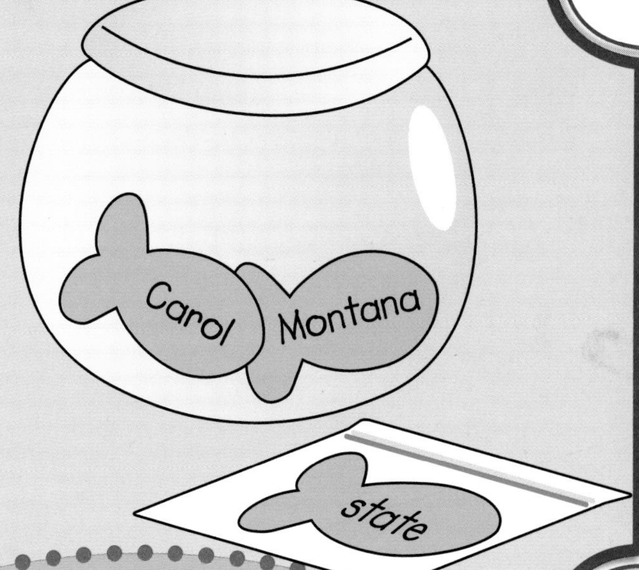
Carol
Montana
state

Keeping Capitals Colorful

Help students remember to capitalize the first word in a sentence by giving each child a sheet of colorful sticky dots. Each time she begins a new sentence, she places a sticky dot on her paper as shown. She writes the first letter of the first word in the sentence on the dot and then continues with the rest of the sentence. **Capitalization**

Today is our day
to visit the library.
I want to get two books.

Take a Chance!

This capitalization center begins with the roll of a die. Place a die at a center along with a supply of writing paper. A child rolls the die and then writes on his paper a sentence that contains the same number of capitalized words as the number showing on the die. He continues rolling and writing until he has written ten sentences. Capitalization

Is It a Sentence?

Explain to students that without a subject and a predicate, a group of words is a phrase, not a sentence. Next, have each student number a sheet of paper vertically from one to ten. Tell the youngsters that you will be reading aloud ten groups of words. Each student will have to decide whether each group of words is a sentence or a phrase. Read the first group aloud. The student writes *S* if it is a sentence or *P* if it is a phrase. Provide time for youngsters to discuss their answers. Continue in this manner until each group of words has been read. For an added challenge, have each youngster write an original sentence or phrase on a slip of paper. Then collect the slips and play the game again!
Subjects and predicates

How Does It End?

Write an equal number of each ending punctuation mark on a class set of blank cards, writing one mark on each card. To begin, tell students that punctuation marks help make the writer's meaning clear. Then involve students in this simple activity. Give each student one prepared card; then read aloud a sentence to the class. Have each youngster hold her card above her head if her ending punctuation mark is appropriate for that sentence. Engage students in a discussion about the results. Then repeat the activity with additional sentences.
Punctuation

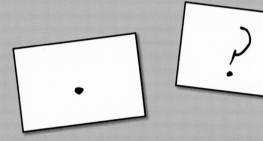

A Little Funny Business

Look to the comics section for a dialogue-writing activity that's guaranteed to tickle students' funny bones. Cut out a comic strip and use correction fluid to cover the original dialogue in the speech bubbles. Then make a copy of the strip for each pair of students. Instruct the partners to create new dialogue for the comic, reminding them to use context clues to write text that matches the pictures. Next, have each pair rewrite the text on a sheet of paper, adding quotation marks, other punctuation, and phrases such as "he said" and "she said" where needed. Allow time for each pair to share its work with the class before posting the strips on a bulletin board titled "Funny Business."
Punctuation

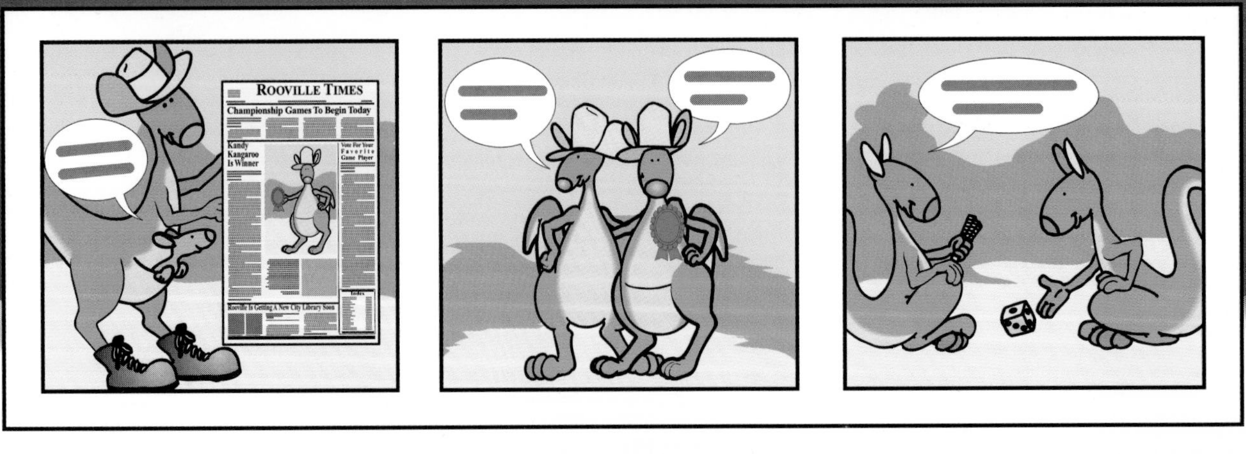
ROOVILLE TIMES
Championship Games To Begin Today
Kandy Kangaroo Is Winner
Vote For Your Favorite Game Player
Rooville Is Getting A New City Library Soon

Colorful Sentences

Reinforce basic sentence skills with this colorful idea! Ask students to share sentences; then help them identify the subject and the predicate. Next, invite a student volunteer to write the subject of a sentence on the board. Then ask another student to finish writing the sentence with a different color. Challenge students to name the subject and predicate. Have additional youngsters write sentences on the board until every child has had a turn. Next, using two different-colored crayons, each student writes a sentence in a similar manner on a sheet of construction paper. Then he illustrates it. Provide time for each youngster to share his sentence with his classmates. **Subjects and predicates**

The hairy monster hid in my closet.
Josh

Sensible Sentences?

Have each youngster write a complete sentence on a 3" x 24" strip of paper. The student draws a line on her strip between the subject and the predicate; then she cuts the strip apart along the line. Collect the parts. Place the subject parts in one box and the predicate parts in another; then label each box accordingly. Invite a youngster to draw a part from each box and read the new sentence aloud to the class. Have students decide whether the sentence is silly or makes sense. Then select another student to draw two new parts. Continue the process until every youngster has had a turn. Then return the parts to the appropriate containers and play the game again! Subjects and predicates

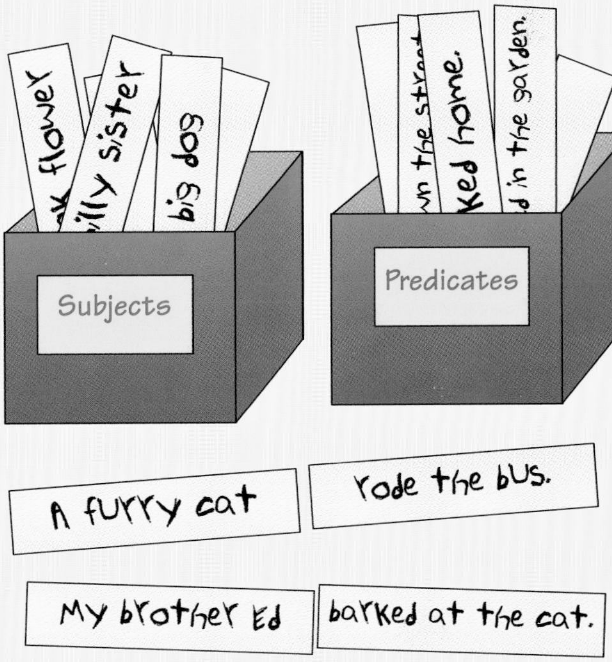
big dog
Subjects
Predicates
A furry cat
rode the bus.
My brother Ed
barked at the cat.

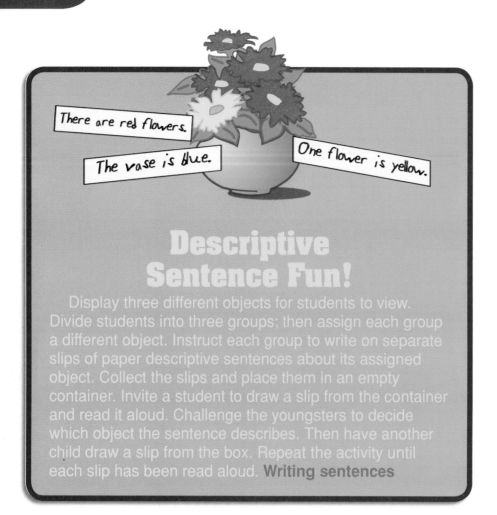

There are red flowers.
The vase is blue.
One flower is yellow.

Descriptive Sentence Fun!

Display three different objects for students to view. Divide students into three groups; then assign each group a different object. Instruct each group to write on separate slips of paper descriptive sentences about its assigned object. Collect the slips and place them in an empty container. Invite a student to draw a slip from the container and read it aloud. Challenge the youngsters to decide which object the sentence describes. Then have another child draw a slip from the box. Repeat the activity until each slip has been read aloud. **Writing sentences**

Picture This!

Cut four pictures from magazines and glue each one onto a separate piece of construction paper; then mount the pictures on a wall or bulletin board with the title "Picture This!" Next, assign an equal number of students to each picture. Have each student write a complete sentence about his assigned picture on a sentence strip. Collect the strips; then display them under the corresponding pictures. Replace the pictures and sentence strips weekly to keep youngsters on their toes with sentence skills. **Writing sentences**

Who? the dog
What? chased a cat
Where? up a tree
When? yesterday
Why? because the cat was in the yard

Super Sentences

Display a picture large enough for students to view easily. On the board, write the words *who, what, where, when,* and *why.* Explain that the answers to these questions can be used to write a super sentence that tells about the picture. Model the technique using the example shown at the left. Then display a different picture and have each student try his hand at using the five Ws to write a sentence about it. For additional reinforcement, encourage student volunteers to share their sentences with the class. When students are familiar with the technique, have them use their own drawings as the basis for super sentences. Before long, your students will be able to write super sentences for science, social studies, and other writing activities. Writing sentences

The ABCs of Nouns, Verbs, and Adjectives

Cover a large section of a wall with paper; then tape construction paper alphabet letters from A to Z to the paper, leaving space beneath each letter. Add the title "The ABCs of the Parts of Speech." Next, challenge each youngster to cut out pictures from old magazines that represent nouns, verbs, and adjectives. For example, a picture of a runner could represent the verb *running* or a picture of a red car could represent the adjective *red*. Have him label each picture with its name and part of speech; then mount each one under the appropriate letter. Challenge your students to add pictures to the display throughout the year. **Parts of speech**

Parts-of-Speech Lotto

Provide each child with a blank lotto board. Instruct him to randomly program the 16 squares with four nouns, four pronouns, four verbs, and four adjectives. As students are programming their cards, program an equal number of construction paper cards with the words *noun, pronoun, verb,* and *adjective* and place the cards in a container. Also give each child 16 paper markers. To play the game, draw a part of speech from the container. Read the card aloud and have each youngster cover the correct square of his choice. The first student to cover four words horizontally, vertically, or diagonally calls out, "Lotto!" To win the game, he must read each word aloud and state its part of speech for verification. If desired, award the winning student with a sticker or another small prize.
Parts of speech

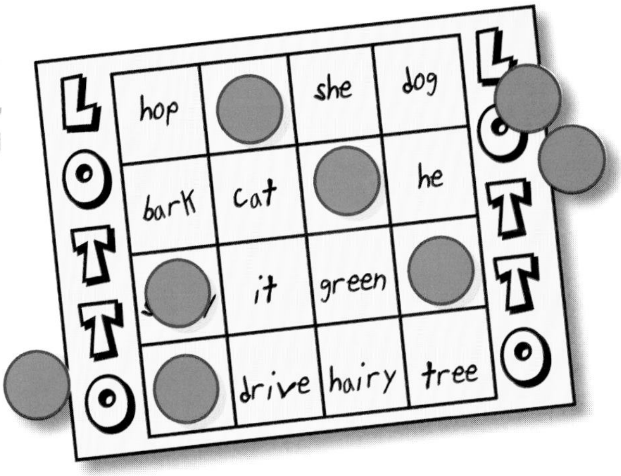
LOTTO
hop
she
dog
bark
cat
he
it
green
drive
hairy
tree
LOTTO

hairy
dog
barked
The hairy dog barked at the cat.
William B.

Marvelous Mobiles!

Have your youngsters make banana split mobiles to review the parts of speech! Cut three templates from tagboard: a scoop of ice cream, a banana, and a bowl. Place the templates, scissors, glue, and crayons at a center with the following construction paper pieces: white, brown, and pink squares (for the scoops), yellow strips (for the bananas), and purple strips (for the bowls). To make a mobile, a student traces the templates on the appropriate pieces of construction paper and cuts them out. Then he writes an adjective on his white scoop, a noun on his brown scoop, and a verb on his pink scoop. Next, he writes a sentence on his banana cutout using all three words; then he writes his name on his bowl cutout. He then attaches his cutouts to a length of yarn as shown.
Parts of speech

I Can...

Have students name examples of action verbs as you list their ideas on the board. Pair students; then assign each pair a different verb from the list, keeping each assignment secret from the other pairs. Have each pair pantomime its verb for the class. Further challenge youngsters by having each student write and illustrate four verbs on a sheet of divided paper titled "I can..." (see the illustration). If desired, collect the pictures and bind them between two covers; then add the title "What Can You Do?" Place the booklet at a reading center for all to enjoy! Verbs

I Can...
read
walk
run
jump
Hannah

Silly Sentences

After reviewing nouns and verbs, write a student-generated list of each on the board (enough to have one noun and one verb for each student). Distribute cards; then have each student choose a different noun and verb from the list and write each one on a separate card. Collect the cards and place each one into a corresponding container labeled "Nouns" or "Verbs." Each student draws a card from each container and then writes and illustrates a silly sentence using the words on the cards. Invite student volunteers to share their sentences and illustrations with their classmates. **Parts of speech**

Benjamin
skate
snake
The snake is skating down the street.

One-of-a-Kind Word Search

Divide students into four groups. Assign each group a different part of speech: nouns, pronouns, verbs, or adjectives. Then provide each group with a highlighter and a copy of a selected story or passage. Have the group read the story and highlight examples of its assigned part of speech. If desired, write the students' responses on the board. As students learn the parts of speech, provide additional sheets for individual youngsters to highlight. **Parts of speech**

A Picture for Every Verb

Here's an activity that reinforces the concept of verbs! Instruct each youngster to cut a picture from an old magazine; then have her glue it to the middle of a sheet of construction paper. Next, have the student list verbs around her cutout that relate to the picture. Challenge her to write a story that incorporates the verbs on another sheet of paper. Have each youngster tape her story to the bottom of her picture. Display the finished projects on a wall or bulletin board. **Verbs**

Describe That!

To make a picture web, a student cuts a detailed picture from a newspaper or magazine; then she glues it onto the middle of a sheet of construction paper. She draws five lines extending from her picture and then writes an adjective that describes her picture at the end of each line. If desired, have her write a sentence for each adjective. **Adjectives**

Comparisons

Draw a Venn diagram on a sheet of paper and then make a copy for each student. The student chooses two different objects and writes their names at the top of the diagram as shown. Next, the student writes under the matching heading adjectives that describe each object. Further challenge students by having them write in the middle of their diagrams words that describe both objects. **Adjectives**

Spaghetti
Chocolate Ice Cream
Spicy
hot
red
white
meaty
yummy
messy
sticky
sweet
cold
smooth
brown
drippy
frozen
Julio

Sentences With Spunk!

Instruct each student to think of a noun and list adjectives to describe it on a sheet of scrap paper. Next, on another sheet of paper, have her write a sentence that includes the noun and adjectives. Challenge students to see who can come up with the longest, most descriptive sentence. To enhance the activity, have students copy and illustrate their sentences on sheets of paper. Mount the completed drawings on a bulletin board titled "Sentences With Spunk!" **Adjectives**

Look at that smelly dog run!
The brown, smelly, hairy dog ran quickly down the crowded street.

dish
-s
-es
-ies
cat
party

Plural Noun Fun!

Write different singular nouns on separate 3" x 5" cards. Also label three berry baskets as shown. Show students pictures of a kiss, a cow, and a bunny. Have students name the plural form of each noun as you write it on the board. Explain the different endings plural nouns may have. Then distribute the programmed cards. Ask each student to place his card into the corresponding basket. As a class, check to be sure each card is in the right basket. **Plural nouns**

More Than One?

From old magazines cut pictures that represent several nouns (both singular and plural). Mount the pictures on construction paper; then laminate them for durability. After a review of nouns, ask students to sort the pictures into two categories: one and more than one. With students' help, write the name of each picture on the board. Lead students to determine that plural nouns name more than one thing and are usually formed by adding *-s, -es,* or *-ies* to the end of a singular noun. Then have each student write and illustrate a different noun in both its singular and plural forms on provided paper. Display the pictures on a bulletin board entitled "More Than One?"
Plural nouns

-s
-es
-ies
lunches
wishes
Rebecca's
Wallet

Wonderful Wallets!

To make a wallet, a student folds a sheet of construction paper in half lengthwise; then she creases the folded paper into thirds. Next, she staples her paper along each crease and outside edge, as shown, to create a wallet. She labels the compartments "-s," "-es," and "-ies." To fill her wallet, the student writes a plural noun on a card and places it into the appropriate compartment. Challenge your youngsters to fill their wallets with a variety of nouns throughout the year. **Plural nouns**

Check out the skill-building reproducibles on pages 56–64.

Name ____________________ Capitalizing the first word in a sentence

GARDENING GORILLA

If the sentence is capitalized correctly, color the tulip.

1. Gus is going to plant a garden.
2. first, he drives to the garden store.
3. He chooses lots of plants and seeds.
4. He also buys soil and garden tools.
5. at home, Gus pours soil onto the ground.
6. He digs a hole for each plant.
7. he places a plant in each hole.
8. Next, he plants the seeds.
9. Gus carefully waters his garden.
10. next year, Gus will try to plant bananas!

On the lines below, correct and rewrite each sentence that is not correct.

Moving Day

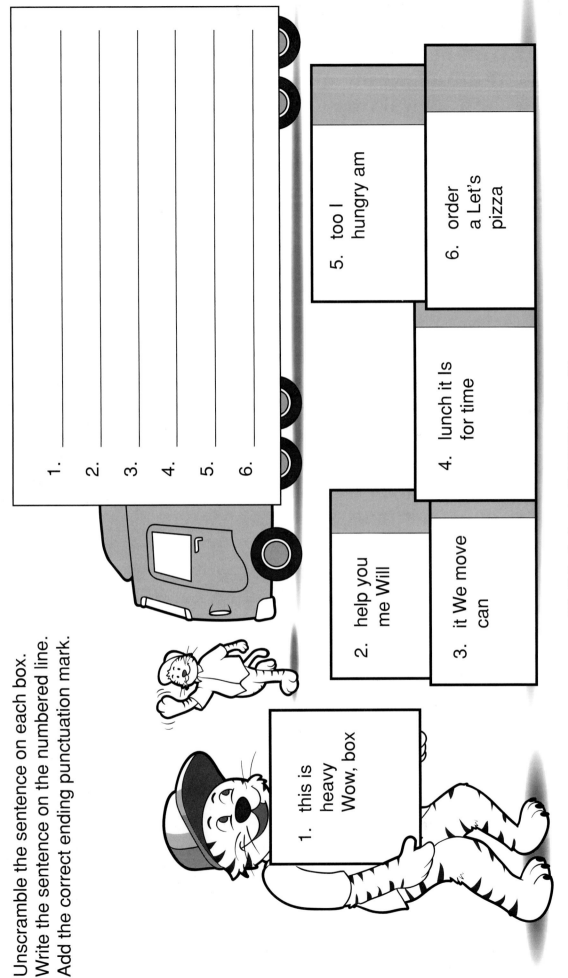

Unscramble the sentence on each box.
Write the sentence on the numbered line.
Add the correct ending punctuation mark.

1. ____________________
2. ____________________
3. ____________________
4. ____________________
5. ____________________
6. ____________________

1. this is heavy Wow, box
2. help you me Will
3. it We move can
4. lunch it Is for time
5. too I hungry am
6. order a Let's pizza

Name ______________________________

In the Huddle

Pair each subject with a different predicate.
Write the sentences on the lines between the goalposts.

Subjects
The coach
One player
That hot dog
The football
The crowd
Predicates
is on the ground.
is cheering.
is yelling.
tastes good.
threw the ball.
32
26

Loading Luggage

Cut apart the word cards below.
Sort out the words that are nouns.
Glue each noun on the matching cart.

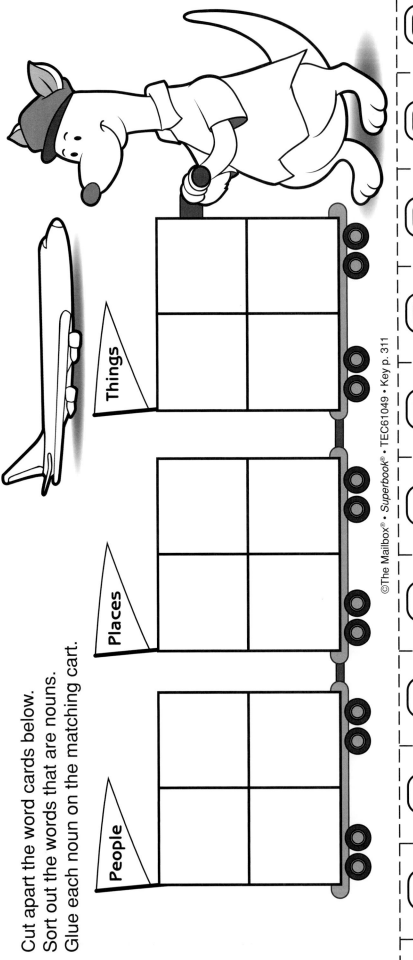

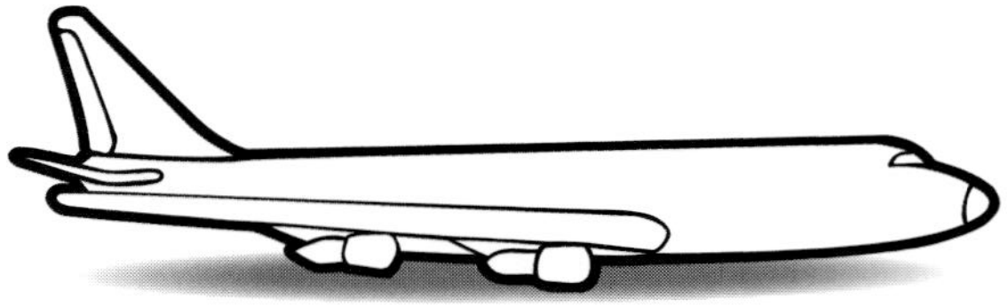

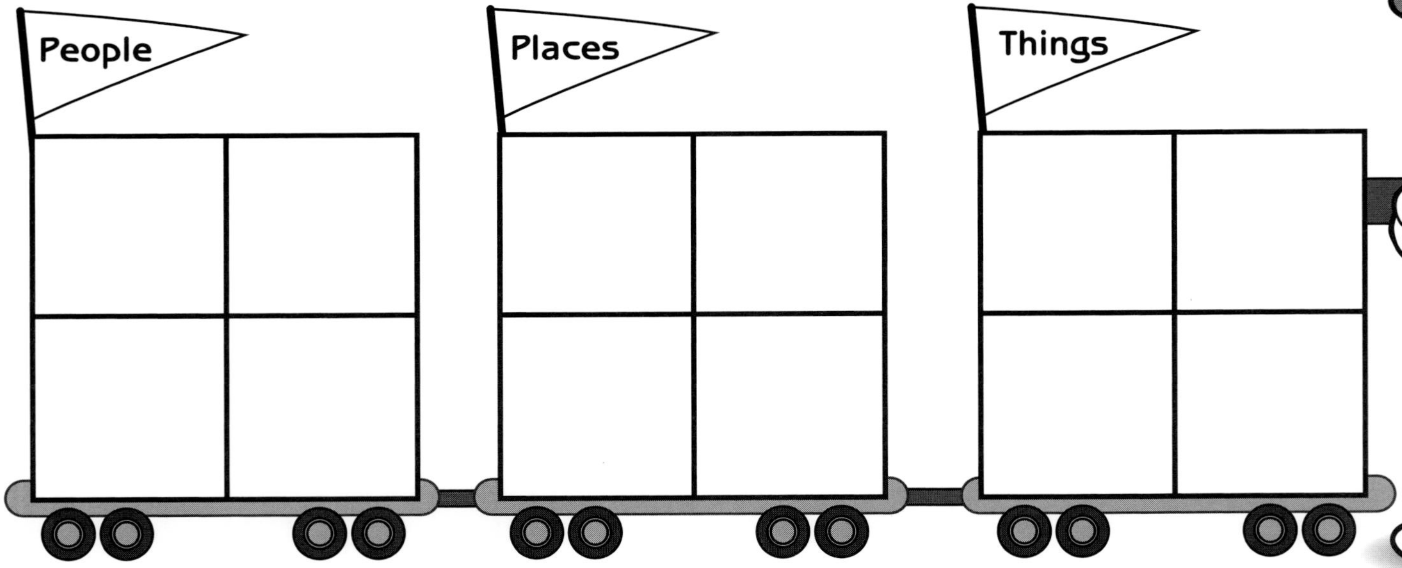
People
Places
Things

lately	cities	bottles	my	apples	under	states	farmers	is	doctors
babies	phones	were	men	schools	slowly	cooked	our	pencils	rooms

Name ______

PIZZA PARTY

Add *-s* or *-es* to each singular noun.
Write each new word on a pizza box in the matching stack.

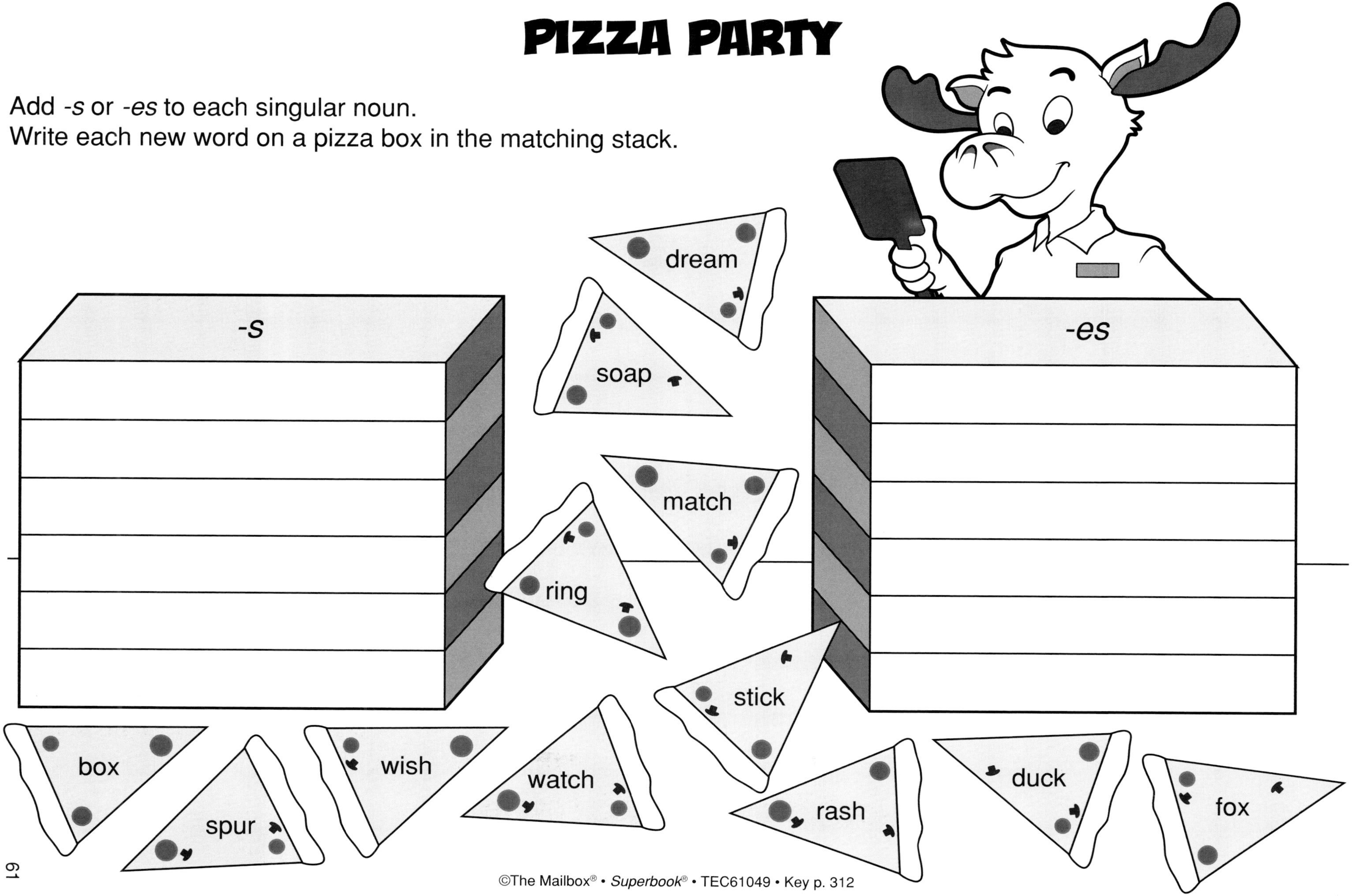
-s
-es
dream
soap
match
ring
stick
box
spur
wish
watch
rash
duck
fox

A TOOL WITH TEETH

Color each log that is below an action verb.

1. Billy is building a new house.
   T P
2. He chews each tree down with his teeth.
   E B
3. Billy's friend Bert walks by.
   R M
4. Bert shows Billy what he is carrying.
   E S
5. Bert bought a new saw!
   R I
6. Billy laughs at Bert's saw.
   I R
7. Bert starts to cut down a tree.
   S E
8. Billy watches and begins to chew.
   ! E
9. Bert finishes and saws down another!
   B !
10. Billy stops chewing and borrows Bert's saw!
    T P

Which month is Billy's favorite?

To solve the riddle, write the colored letters above on the numbered lines below.

" ___ ___ ___ - ___ ___ ___ ___ ___ ___ ___ "

7 2 10 1 6 3 9 4 5 8

Name ______________________________

Bonnie's Bakery

Underline the verb in each sentence.
Color the cakes by the code.

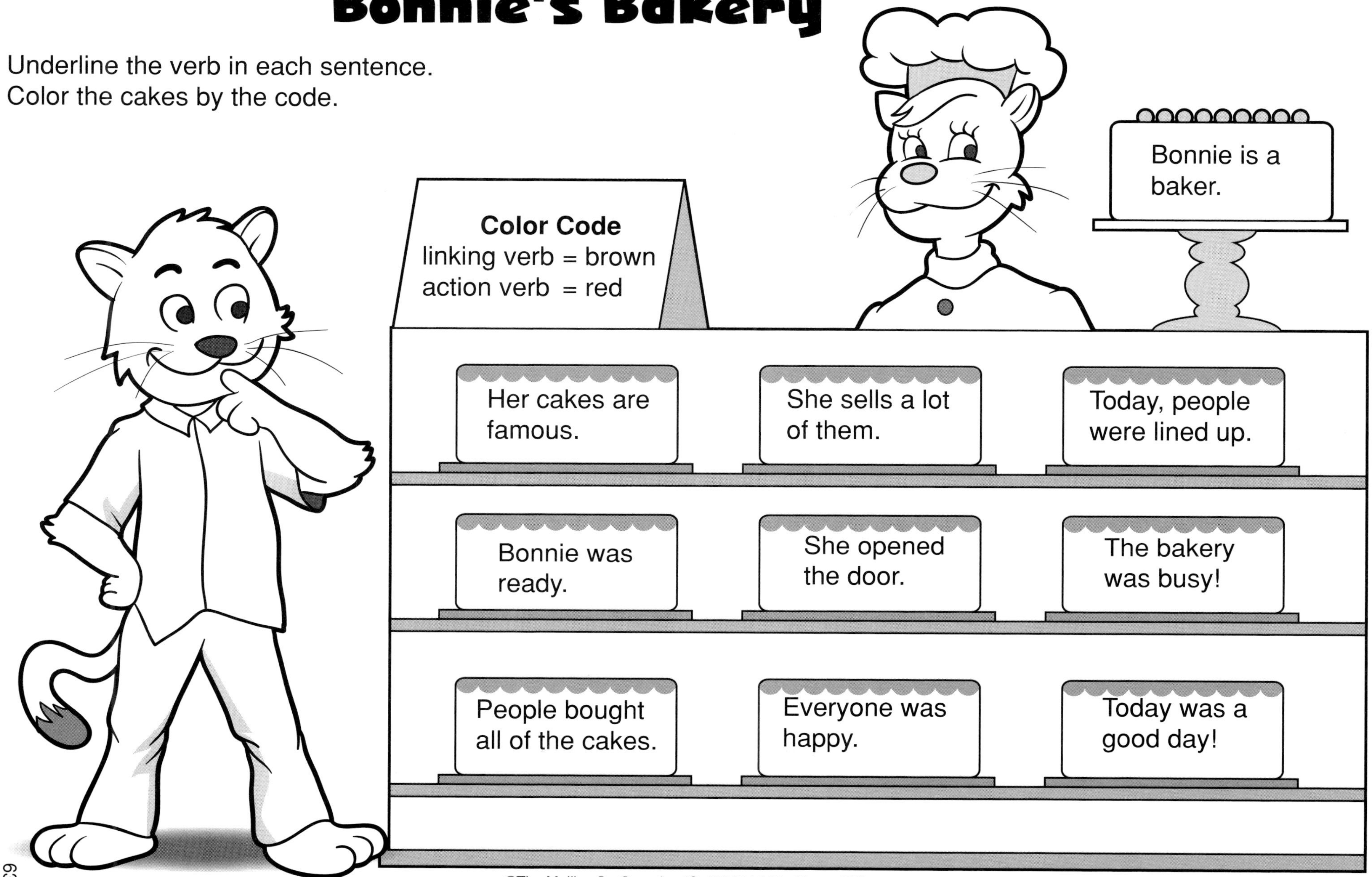
Bonnie is a baker.
Color Code
linking verb = brown
action verb = red
Her cakes are famous.
She sells a lot of them.
Today, people were lined up.
Bonnie was ready.
She opened the door.
The bakery was busy!
People bought all of the cakes.
Everyone was happy.
Today was a good day!

 Key p. 312

Name ____________________

Shopping for Adjectives

On the lines below the items, write two adjectives that describe them. Remember that an adjective describes a noun.

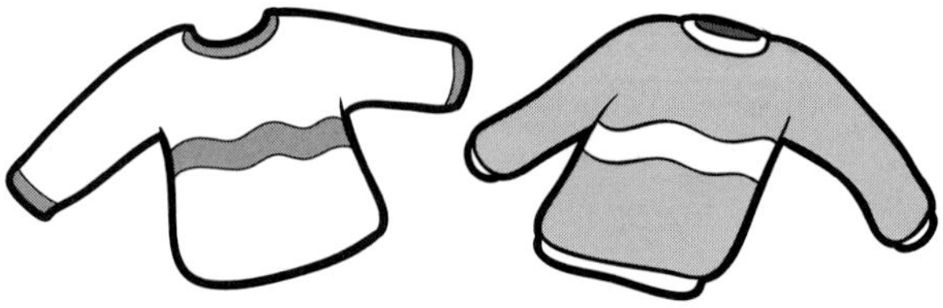

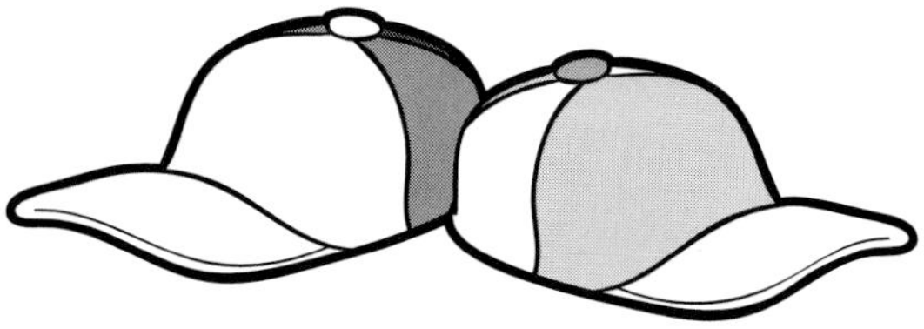

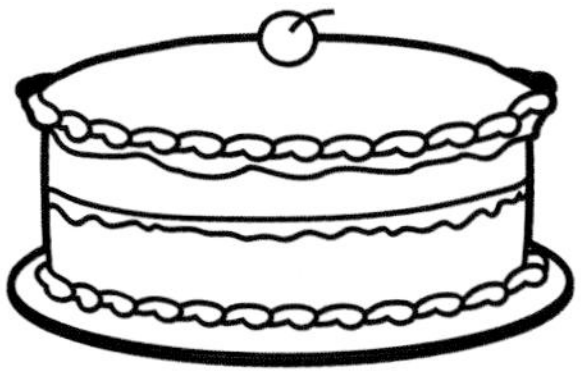

WORD SKILLS

won't
will not

Contraction Match

This large-group game helps youngsters master contractions lickety-split! For every two students, program an index card with a different contraction; then, for each contraction, label an index card with the words that make up the contraction. To play, randomly distribute the game cards. Each student reads the word(s) on his card and searches for the classmate who has the corresponding word(s). When two students discover that their game cards match, they sit down. After each student has found his match, collect and shuffle the cards; then play the game again! **Contractions**

On the Lookout

Encourage students to look for contractions with this activity. Have each student cut ten different contractions from old magazines or newspapers. The student then glues the contractions to a sheet of paper. Then, beside each contraction, he writes the two words that make up the contraction. Invite each student to share the contractions he found with his classmates. **Contractions**

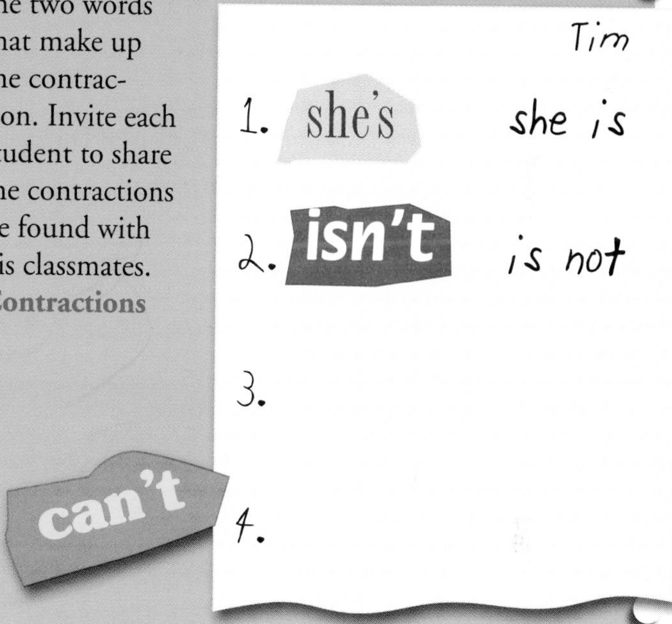
Tim
1. she's she is
2. isn't is not
3.
4.
can't

he is
we will
he's
we'll
he is
we will
she will
Bryan

Pasta Punctuation

How do you make reviewing contractions more fun? Try adding a little pasta! Place a box of elbow macaroni, glue, a supply of index cards programmed with word pairs that form contractions, and sheets of blank paper at a center. A student folds one sheet of paper into fourths, then unfolds it so that the paper is visually divided into four sections. He selects a programmed index card and copies the words onto one section of his paper. Next he writes the contraction made from the word pair, gluing a piece of macaroni in place of the apostrophe. He repeats this process with the remaining three sections. **Contractions**

Class Thesaurus

Reinforce synonyms with this daily activity. Each morning write a word on a sheet of drawing paper. Post the paper in a prominent location. Challenge students to brainstorm as many synonyms for the word as possible. Write students' responses under the word. Then hole-punch the paper and have a student place it in alphabetical order in a three-ring binder titled "Our Class Thesaurus." Place the thesaurus in the writing center for students to use in their writing activities. Synonyms

run

race
hurry
sprint
dash
speed
flee

Synonyms

afraid–scared
jump–leap
happy—glad
cold–chilly
friend–pal

Chart It!

Keep an ongoing class chart to record synonym pairs. Title a sheet of chart paper "Synonyms" and display it within students' reach. When a student identifies a new synonym pair while reading, have him write it on the chart. Periodically review the chart with youngsters to increase their vocabulary skills. Synonyms

Seeing Synonyms

For this center, cut from construction paper a pair of two-dimensional sunglasses similar to the ones shown. Also cut out a supply of construction paper lenses sized to fit the glasses. Label each pair of lenses with a synonym pair; then label the back of each pair with matching symbols for self-checking. (See page 75 for a list of synonyms.) Place the lenses, the prepared sunglasses, and a pair of real sunglasses at a center.

When a student visits the center, she dons the sunglasses and arranges the lenses faceup. After she finds a synonym pair, she places the lenses on the sunglasses and flips them to check her work. If she is correct, she sets the lenses aside; if she is incorrect, she searches for the matching lens. The child continues in the same manner until each pair is matched. **Synonyms**

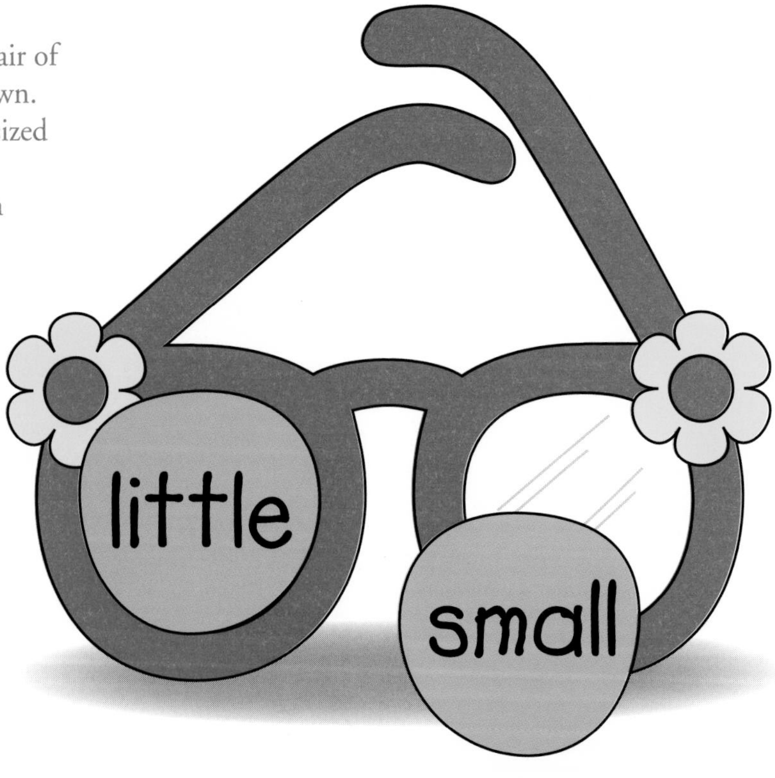
little
small

Fishing for Antonyms

Two players will be fishing for matching antonyms with this adapted version of Go Fish. Write pairs of antonyms on index cards, one word per card. (See page 75 for a list of antonyms.) Place the cards in a resealable plastic bag at a center. To begin, one student deals seven cards to himself and seven to the other player; then he places the remaining cards face-down to form a draw pile. Each player places all his matching pairs of antonyms on the table. Player 1 begins by asking Player 2 for an antonym to match one that he is holding. If he receives the match from Player 2, he places the pair on the table and takes another turn. If Player 2 does not have the card Player 1 requested, Player 2 says, "Go fish," and Player 1 draws a card from the pile. If he draws the card he requested, he may lay down the pair and take another turn. If he does not draw a match, he keeps the card and Player 2 takes a turn. Any time a player lays his last card on the table, he takes one card from the draw pile. When the draw pile is gone, the game ends. The player with more pairs wins the game! The cards can also be programmed for synonyms or homophones. Antonyms

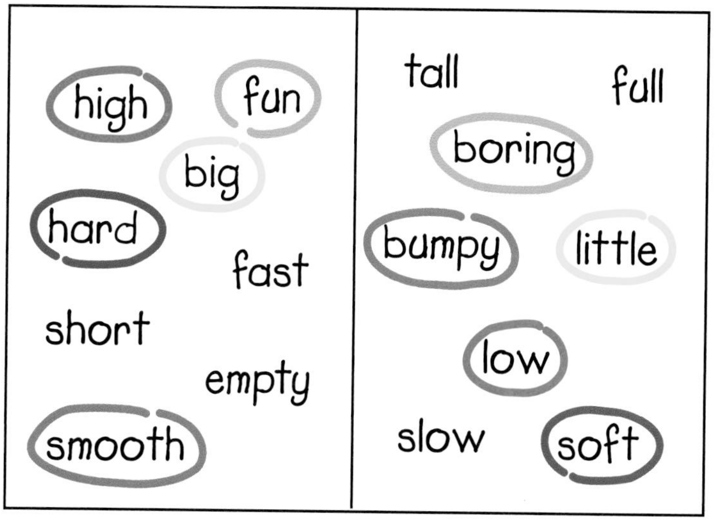
high
fun
big
hard
fast
short
empty
smooth
tall
full
boring
bumpy
little
low
slow
soft

Search and Circle

This partner activity helps students write and read antonyms. Have each child fold a sheet of blank paper in half, open it, and then trace over the crease. Direct each student to write one word of an antonym pair on the left side of his paper and the other word in a random location on the right side. Have him repeat this process until he has written eight antonym pairs. Next, instruct each student to trade his paper with a partner. Ask each child to use a crayon to circle one word on the left side of the paper and its antonym on the right side. Then have him choose a different color of crayon to circle the next pair. After each child has found all the pairs, have him return the paper to his partner to be checked. **Antonyms**

Antonym March

Use this catchy chant to help students review antonyms. Have students march in place as you lead them in the chant shown. Then designate one student as the leader and have her insert a different antonym pair where indicated. (See page 75 for a list of antonyms.) Repeat the chant until each child has had a chance to be the leader. Antonyms

Leader and Class: We know antonyms. Yes, we do!
Leader: Listen and repeat as I ask you to.
When I say, "[high]," you say, "[low]."
[High].
Class: [Low].
Leader: [High].
Class: [Low].
Leader and Class: We know antonyms. Yes, we do!

Helpful Homophone Chart

Help students learn to spell troublesome homophones with this whole-group activity. Make a list of homophones on a sheet of poster board. (See page 75 for a list of homophones.) Have each student select a different word from the list. Then have him illustrate the word on a small square of white paper. Glue each illustration near its corresponding word. Then post the completed project on a classroom wall. Encourage students to use the list in their writing. Homophones

Helpful Homophones
eight
ate
write
right
pair
pear
flower
flour

Have you heard the tale of the dog with the very long tail? His tail was so long that it wrapped all the way around his body. You'd better watch out when this dog wags his tail!

Silly Stories

Students use creative thinking to incorporate homophone word pairs into a short story. Assign each child a homophone pair. (See page 75 for a list of homophones.) Have him use both words in a story and then draw a corresponding picture. After each child has shared his work, compile the completed papers in a class book titled "Just-Right Writing." **Homophones**

Homophone Matchup

For this class activity, gather a class supply of blank cards. Label each card with one word from a homophone pair. (See page 75 for a list of homophones.) Give each child a card to read and then have her hold her card facing out. On your signal, instruct each student to find her homophone match. When all students are paired, direct the twosomes to identify the meaning of each word. Invite partners to share their homophones and definitions with the class. If desired, redistribute the cards for another round of play. **Homophones**

Suffixes:

-able, -ible, -fy, -ful, -er, -est, -ance, -ence, -ing, -less, -ly, -ment, -ness, -y, -ey, -like, -ion, -sion, -tion

Prefixes:

a-, bi-, de-, extra-, dis-, im-, in-, ir-, non-, pre-, pro-, re-, un-, super-, tele-, over-, mis-

Affix of the Day

This activity gives each student the opportunity to teach a prefix or suffix to her classmates. Assign each child a prefix or suffix (see the list above for suggestions). Then have her look through books to find a word with her assigned affix. Have her determine the meaning of the word. Then have her write on a sentence strip a sentence incorporating the word. In turn, ask each child to share her assigned affix, the word she found, and her sentence. If desired, display the sentence strips for students to use as references. **Suffixes and prefixes**

Charades, Anyone?

Try an exciting game of charades to help your students understand affixes. Write words with prefixes or suffixes on separate slips of paper and place them in a container. Write the same words on the board and read them aloud to your students. To begin the game, divide students into two teams. Have one member of Team 1 draw a word from the container and silently act it out. Challenge Team 2 to determine the word from the list on the board. If Team 2 guesses correctly, erase the word from the board and let a student from Team 2 draw a word and silently act it out for Team 1. If Team 2 guesses incorrectly, invite another student from Team 1 to help his classmate act out the word. Play continues with the teams alternating turns until all the words have been mimed. **Suffixes and prefixes**

- cheerful
- misspell
- repaint
- unpack
- untie
- jumper
- teacher
- cleaner
- sickness
- sadness
- quietly
- happily

un
tie
hope
ful

Prefix and Suffix Books

These flip books are guaranteed to help your students uncover many new words! Divide students into small groups and assign each group a different suffix or prefix. Have one student from each group write the assigned affix on either the beginning (if it's the prefix) or the end (if it's the suffix) of a 3" x 9" construction-paper strip. Then have each group brainstorm base words that can combine with the affix. For each group, assign a student to record each base word on a separate 3" x 5" card. After a predetermined amount of time, have each group stack its cards and staple them on the paper strip (as shown) to make words. Ask each group to share its completed flip book with the class; then place the books in the writing center for students to refer to in their writing. **Suffixes and prefixes**

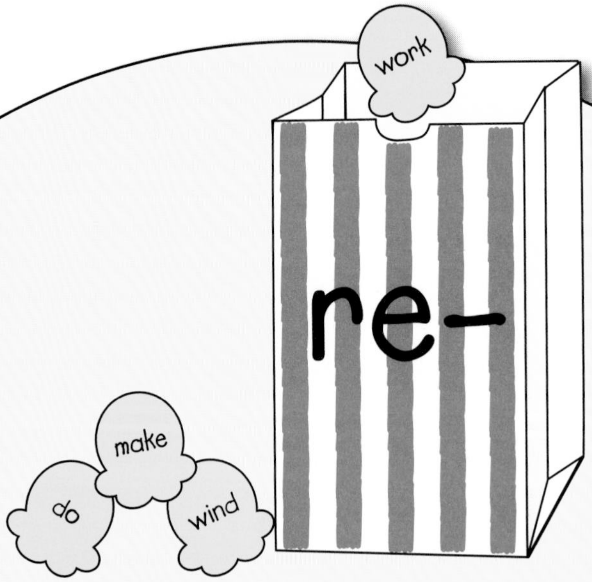
work
re-
make
do
wind

Freshly Popped Practice

Whet students' appetites for suffix and prefix practice with this tempting idea! Have each child label a white paper lunch bag with an assigned prefix or suffix. Then invite her to decorate the bag to resemble a popcorn bag. Next, direct her to cut from yellow construction paper several popcorn shapes. On each shape have her write a different base word for her affix. As she places a popcorn cutout into the bag, direct her to combine the affix with the base word and name the new word. After reading each word, have each student trade bags and popcorn with a partner for more practice. **Suffixes and prefixes**

Prefix or Suffix?

Use this tip to help students remember the difference between a prefix and a suffix. Ask students to recite the alphabet and determine which letter comes first; *p* as in *prefix* or *s* as in *suffix*. After they determine that *p* comes first, lead them to realize that a prefix comes before a word and a suffix comes after a word, just like the order in the alphabet. **Suffixes and prefixes**

All Aboard the Affix Train

Students are sure to get on board with prefixes and suffixes with this idea, which doubles as a classroom display! Trim a sheet of construction paper to resemble a train engine. Label the engine with a desired prefix or suffix. Invite a student to name a word that has the chosen affix. Then have him write the word on a construction paper rectangle and add paper wheels to resemble a train car. Continue in the same manner for several words; then display the engine and train cars in a prominent location. Repeat the process for other prefixes and suffixes. **Suffixes and prefixes**

-ful
thankful
hopeful
careful
thoughtful
joyful

Spelling Football

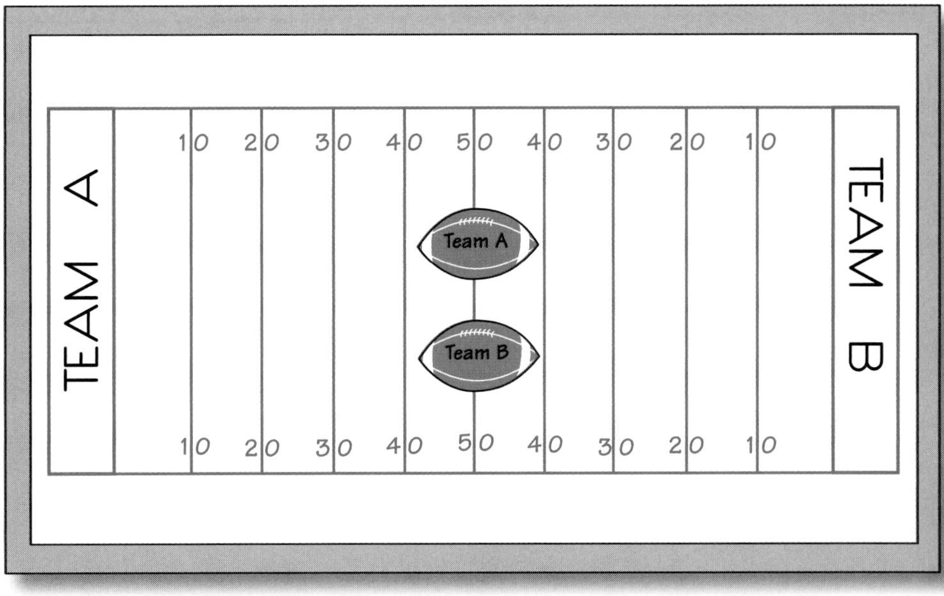
TEAM A
10 20 30 40 50 40 30 20 10
Team A
Team B
10 20 30 40 50 40 30 20 10
TEAM B

Draw a large football field on the board, marking off the yard lines as shown. Also tape two brown construction paper footballs, one labeled "Team A" and the other labeled "Team B," on the 50-yard line. Divide students into two teams and have each team stand in a straight line. Assign and label a goal line for each team. To begin play, announce a spelling word to the first member of Team A. If he spells the word correctly, he moves the ball ten yards toward his team's goal line. If he misspells the word, the ball remains at the 50-yard line. Then provide the first member of Team B a chance to spell the same word. If he spells it correctly, he moves his team's ball ten yards toward his team's goal. Continue in this same manner, alternating turns. The team that reaches its goal line first wins a point. Play resumes with both balls on the 50-yard line. The team with more points at the end of the designated game time wins! **Spelling**

Down the Line

You can count on this fast-paced spelling game being a class favorite! Group students into four teams and have each team sit in a straight line. Give the first person in each row a small white board and a wipe-off marker. To begin play, announce a spelling word. The first player in each row writes the first letter of the word on the board and then passes it to the second player. The second player writes the second letter of the word on the board, and so on until the entire word has been spelled. The player who writes the final letter of the word stands up. The first team that has a member standing with a correctly spelled word wins a point. Before beginning play again, the first player of each team moves to the back of the line. The team with the most points at the end of game time wins! **Spelling**

Stop and Go

Reinforce several weeks' worth of spelling words with this partner center. Write at least 30 spelling words on individual index cards. Also program six index cards with stop signs. Place the cards at a center. To play, a student shuffles the cards and places them facedown on the playing surface. To begin, one player (the caller) draws a card from the deck and announces the word. He listens carefully as his partner spells the word for him. If a correct spelling is given, he draws another card and reads the word aloud. If an incorrect spelling is given, the caller repeats the word and the two partners spell it together. The caller places the spelled words in a discard pile. Play continues in this manner until the caller draws a "stop" card. The partners then change positions, and the activity is repeated. Since this game has no winners or losers, students are eager to participate in this spelling review! **Spelling**

ā
ĕ
acorn
bed

The Long and the Short of It

These nifty booklets will encourage students to look for long and short vowels. For each student, staple five 6" x 9" sheets of paper inside a folded 9" x 12" sheet of construction paper. To make a booklet, a student writes "Long and Short Vowels" on the front cover. Next, she writes each short vowel on the front of a separate page and each long vowel on the back. She then searches through old magazines for a picture that contains each vowel. To complete the booklet, she glues each picture to its corresponding page and labels it. Students can use their vowel booklets as a review or as a reference for future vowel activities. **Vowels**

Real-Life Phonics

To reinforce phonetic concepts, try this real-life approach! Ask each student to bring to school a wrapper or an empty box from a food product. Mount the wrappers and boxes on a large sheet of bulletin board paper. Then use the names of the products to create your phonics lessons. For example, have students brainstorm words with the *ch* sound found in Cheerios cereal or the *oo* sound found in Kool-Aid mix. As students contribute to each discussion, form a list of words from their responses. At the conclusion of each lesson, post each list near its corresponding product. **Phonics**

Scavenger Hunt

This scavenger hunt phonics review is sure to receive rave student reviews! After introducing or reviewing several phonics concepts, have students search the classroom or their homes for items that contain the featured sounds. Instruct students to write the words on a sheet of scrap paper. Then have students copy the words from their papers in the corresponding columns on a chart similar to the one shown. For an added challenge, have each student complete a copy of the reproducible on page 76. No doubt students will be on the lookout for phonics everywhere! **Phonics**

bl	cl	pl	fl
blender	clock	plaid	flag
blanket	clothes	plate	float
blue	cleaning supplies	plant	flannel

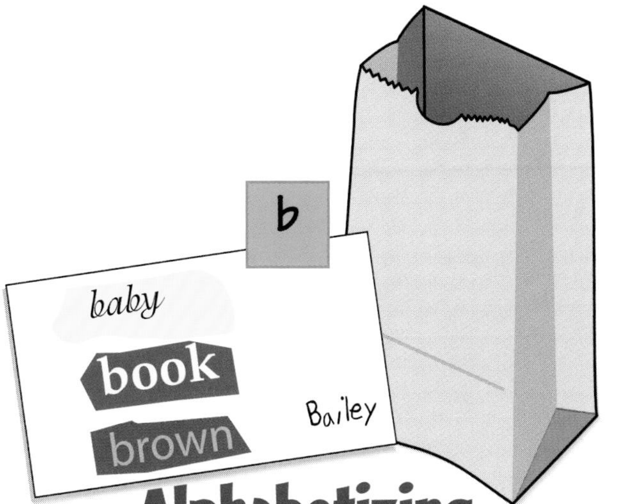
b
baby
book
Bailey
brown

Alphabetizing Alert

Alphabetizing skills are in the bag with this nifty activity. Program two-inch tagboard squares with different letters of the alphabet, excluding hard-to-find letters such as *q, v, x, y,* and *z.* Then place the resulting cards in a paper lunch sack. Each student, in turn, draws a card. From old magazines or newspapers, she cuts three words that begin with her chosen letter and have different second letters. Then the student glues the words in alphabetical order on a blank card. After checking each student's work, enlist students' help in compiling the cards in alphabetical order. If desired, punch the top left corner of the cards and bind them with a metal ring. Then place the cards at a center for students to review. **ABC order**

ABC!

This small-group game proves that three heads are better than one! For each group of three students, label ten index cards with grade-appropriate vocabulary words. Place each set of cards in a resealable plastic bag. To play, give each group a bag. When you say, "Go," each group places its cards in alphabetical order as quickly as possible. The first team to complete the activity calls out, "ABC!" To win the round, a group member must read aloud the words on the group's cards in alphabetical order for verification. Repeat the activity daily, making sure that each group gets a new bag of cards. **ABC order**

ABC Classroom

Students will take stock of their classroom with this alphabetical-order activity. Write each letter of the alphabet on chart paper (each letter on a different line). Ask students to name items in the classroom that begin with each letter. Write students' responses beside the corresponding letters. Then assign each student a different letter and have him write the words listed for that letter in alphabetical order on a sheet of paper. Staple the completed pages in alphabetical order between two construction paper covers. Label the front cover "The ABCs of Our Classroom." Then place the book in the classroom library for everyone to enjoy. **ABC order**

A apple, alphabet chart, art center
B book, beanbag, bathroom
C closet, computer, chalk, crayons
D desk, door, dictionary
E eraser, egg timer
F fish, friend, flowers, fan
G glue, garbage can
H headphones, handwriting book
I index card, ink pen
J juice box, jar, jackets
K keys, kids
L lights, letters, loudspeaker
M math book, map, magnet
N newspaper, number chart
O oval, orange crayon

Guide Word Game

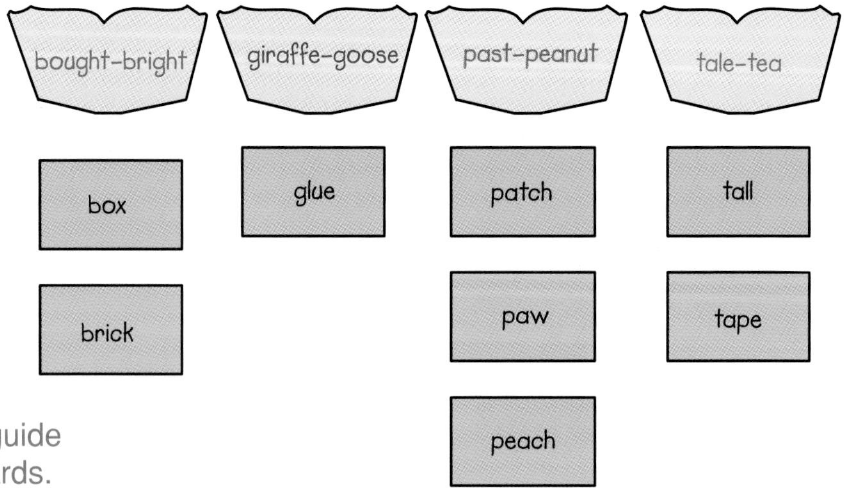
bought–bright
giraffe–goose
past–peanut
tale–tea
box
brick
glue
patch
paw
peach
tall
tape

To prepare for this center, use a marker of a different color to label each of four blank book cutouts with a different pair of guide words. For each guide word pair, program four corresponding word cards and color-code the backs for self-checking. Place the word cards and book cutouts at a center. A center visitor sorts each card below the book with the corresponding guide words. To check his work, he flips the cards. Change the guide words and cards as desired for more practice. **Guide words**

Search and Learn

Give each pair of students a dictionary and a slip of paper. Have the partners search the dictionary, looking for a word they do not know. Ask one student from each pair to write the word on the paper slip and place it in a container. When each pair has contributed a word, draw a slip from the container and write the word on the board. Instruct each twosome to find the word in its dictionary and silently read the definition. Then invite a child to share the definition aloud. Continue in the same manner for each remaining word. **Dictionary skills**

Oo
oppose

Dictionary Detectives

Are you looking for a way to reinforce dictionary skills? Then turn your students into dictionary detectives! Post a list of spelling words, content-related words, or vocabulary words at a center. Place several dictionaries, pencils, and copies of page 77 at the center. A student looks up each word on the list; then, on her paper, she records the word as well as the guide words and the page where the word was found. If desired, provide an answer key at the center so that students can check their work after looking up the words. In no time at all, your students will be on the trail of good dictionary skills! Dictionary skills

Check out the skill-building reproducibles on pages 78–81.

Ready Reference

Synonyms

Synonyms are words that have similar meanings.

above—over
afraid—scared
aid—help
alike—same
angry—mad
auto—car
begin—start
below—under
big—large
chilly—cold
correct—right
cry—weep
end—finish
false—untrue
fast—quick
find—discover
fix—repair
friend—pal
glad—happy
go—leave
grin—smile
hard—difficult
home—house
hot—fiery
jog—run
jump—leap
keep—save
kind—nice
late—tardy
look—see
loud—noisy
neat—tidy
rip—tear
road—street
shout—yell
skinny—thin
small—little
soggy—wet
story—tale
stroll—walk
throw—toss

Antonyms

Antonyms are words that have opposite meanings.

above—below
add—subtract
alike—different
asleep—awake
backward—forward
bad—good
beautiful—ugly
begin—end
big—small
buy—sell
catch—throw
clean—dirty
close—open
cold—hot
come—go
cry—laugh
day—night
down—up
dry—wet
early—late
enemy—friend
false—true
fancy—plain
fast—slow
fat—thin
few—many
float—sink
forget—remember
found—lost
frown—smile
give—take
happy—sad
hard—soft
hot—cold
in—out
left—right
lose—win
mean—nice
more—less
noisy—quiet
old—new
over—under
peace—war
play—work
polite—rude
poor—rich
right—wrong
rough—smooth
save—spend
short—tall
sour—sweet
whisper—yell

Homophones

Homophones are words that sound alike but have different spellings and meanings.

ate—eight
be—bee
bear—bare
beet—beat
blew—blue
bored—board
break—brake
buy—by—bye
cell—sell
cents—scents
course—coarse
creak—creek
deer—dear
do—dew
eye—I
feat—feet
flour—flower
forth—fourth
great—grate
groan—grown
hair—hare
hear—here
hole—whole
hour—our
knead—need
knew—new
knight—night
knot—not
know—no
knows—nose
made—maid
male—mail
meat—meet
one—won
pail—pale
pair—pear
pane—pain
piece—peace
plane—plain
red—read
road—rode
sale—sail
sea—see
sew—so
sight—site
soar—sore
some—sum
son—sun
stare—stair
steak—stake
tail—tale
there—their
through—threw
to—too—two
wait—weight
waste—waist
way—weigh
week—weak
would—wood
write—right

Name ______________________ Phonics review

On the Lookout

Look through newspapers, books, or magazines for words that contain the sounds shown below. Write each word in the correct box.

Vol. XXI	**In the News**	25 cents
ai	**ay**	**ea**
ee	**oa**	**oo**
sh	**th**	**wh**

 Note to the teacher: Use with "Scavenger Hunt" on page 72.

Name ____________________

Wise About Words

Word	Page	First Guide Word	Second Guide Word

Note to the teacher: Use with "Dictionary Detectives" on page 74.

Name ____________________

Boat Race

Color the boats by the code.

Color Code
synonyms = orange
antonyms = green

1
easy
simple
2
narrow
wide
3
hard
soft
4
fast
quick
5
jump
leap
6
kind
nice
7
old
new
8
end
finish
9
early
late
10
go
leave
11
clean
dirty
12
false
true

Name ______________________________

A PAIR OF BEARS

Circle the homophone that completes each sentence.
Write each circled word on the line.

Bare Essentials
Country Store

1. Betty and Beth ______________ like to eat.
   would/wood

2. There is ______________ food in the cabinets.
   know/no

3. They go to the store to ______________ honey.
   by/buy

4. The store is ______________ down the road.
   right/write

5. Is honey on ______________ today?
   sail/sale

6. The honey costs 50 ______________.
   cents/scents

7. Beth and Betty ______________ a big jar of honey.
   choose/chews

8. That ______________ of cake looks tasty!
   peace/piece

9. They buy the jar of honey and ______________ cake.
   some/sum

10. They ______________ all the food before walking home!
    eight/ate

Name ______________________________ Prefixes: *re-*, *un-*

Sweet Serenade

Add the prefix *re-* or *un-* to each base word.
Write the new word on the correct log.

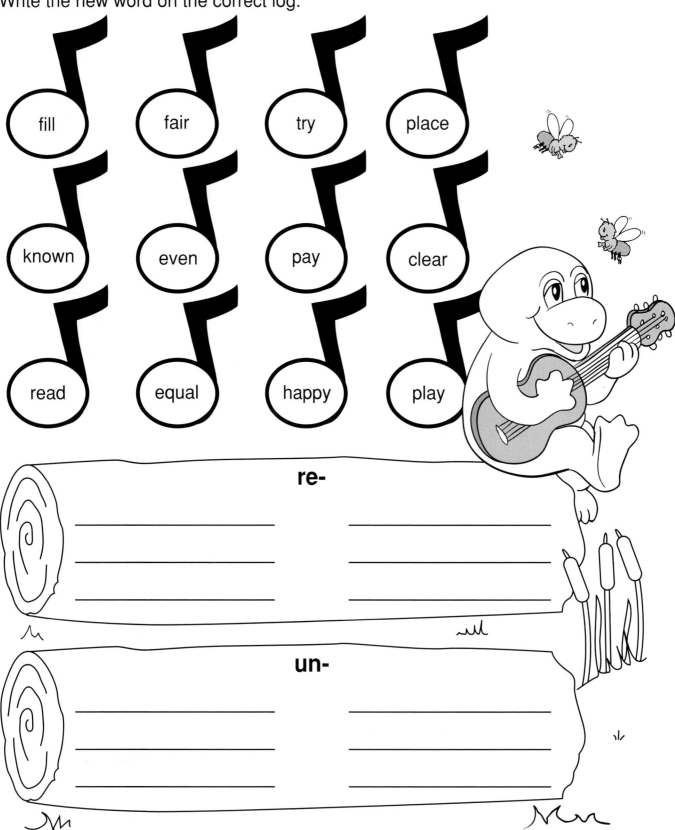

fill	fair	try	place
known	even	pay	clear
read	equal	happy	play

re-

______________ ______________
______________ ______________
______________ ______________

un-

______________ ______________
______________ ______________
______________ ______________

Name ______________________

Cow Call

Add the suffix *-less* or *-ness* to each base word.

1. shy ____________
2. hope ____________
3. home ____________
4. sad ____________
5. soft ____________
6. help ____________
7. dark ____________
8. calm ____________
9. color ____________
10. end ____________

Write each new word below its meaning.

11. state of being calm

_ _ _ _ (_) _ _ _

12. without a home

_ (_) _ _ _ _ _ _

13. without hope

_ (_) _ _ _ _ _ _

14. state of being shy

_ _ _ (_) _ _ _

15. state of being soft

_ _ _ (_) _ _ _ _

16. without color

_ _ _ _ (_) _ _ _ _

17. state of being sad

(_) _ _ _ _ _ _

18. without help

(_) _ _ _ _ _ _ _

19. without an end

_ _ (_) _ _ _ _

20. state of being dark

_ _ _ (_) _ _ _ _

Why did the cow ring its bell?

To solve the riddle, match the circled letters above to the numbered lines below.

Because its _ _ r _ _   _ o _ ' _   w _ _ _ !

(18 12 r 14 17 — 19 o 11 ' 15 — w 13 16 20)

Writing

Every Picture Tells a Story

This story-starter activity will inspire students to use their imaginations! Label four brown paper bags, each with one of the following categories: "people," "places," "animals," and "objects." Have students cut out pictures from old magazines and place them in the corresponding bags. After a class supply of each type of picture has been collected, have each student randomly select a picture from each bag. Next, have each student glue his pictures to a sheet of construction paper; then have the student write a story incorporating the pictures into the story line. Display the pictures and completed stories on a bulletin board. **Writing process**

Branching Out

Students won't be stumped for writing ideas with this "tree-mendous" idea. Make a brown paper tree with three branches and label each branch as shown. Post the tree in an easy-to-see location and place a supply of paper leaf cutouts nearby. Encourage each student to visit the tree when she has a story idea. Have her write her idea on a leaf and place it on the matching branch. Or periodically designate time to have every child brainstorm and post ideas on the tree. When a student needs an idea for her writing, she can refer to the tree. **Writing process**

Plot
Setting
Characters
monkey
learning to play the piano

Prewriting Plan

Are your students having trouble getting started with story writing? Provide each student with two copies of the prewriting form on page 96. Initially, use the form as a whole-group activity. Direct students, as a group, to decide on a topic for a story and write it in the topic web on one of their forms. Have students brainstorm descriptive and related words for the topic and write them on the blanks around the topic. Next, have students think of possible characters and settings for the story and add that information to the form. Finally, have students write topic sentences for the beginning, middle, and end of the story.

As students become accustomed to putting their writing plan on paper, have them complete their second forms individually. Provide writing paper for students to use in transferring the information on their prewriting forms into story format. Remind students that their planning sheets are for generating ideas, and the final story may differ slightly from the original plan. For a final touch, give a sheet of drawing paper to each student so that he can illustrate his story. Invite students to share their completed works with the class, or display them for students to read during free time. **Writing process**

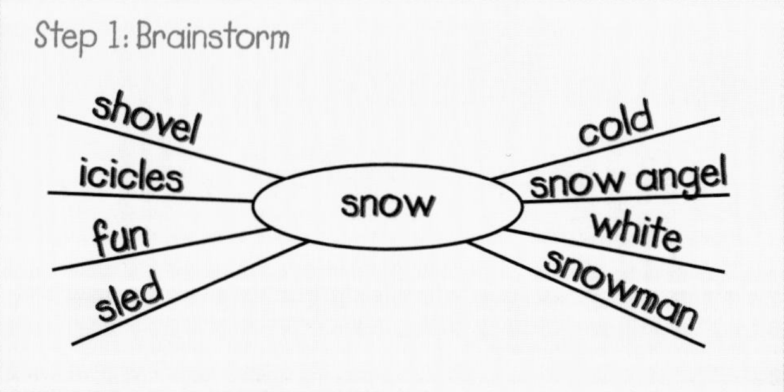
Step 1: Brainstorm
shovel
icicles
fun
sled
snow
cold
snow angel
white
snowman

Four-Star Sentences

Put students in charge of their own proofreading with this star-studded reproducible. Give each child a copy of page 97 before he starts writing a rough draft to remind him what to include in his work. Then, after he has written his draft, have him check each sentence for the skills listed. He colors the matching star for each skill he included. When all sentences have been checked, he corrects any skills that were missing from his draft. Now when you review his writing or an adult volunteer or a peer editor reviews his work, he can be proud of his stellar writing. **Writing process**

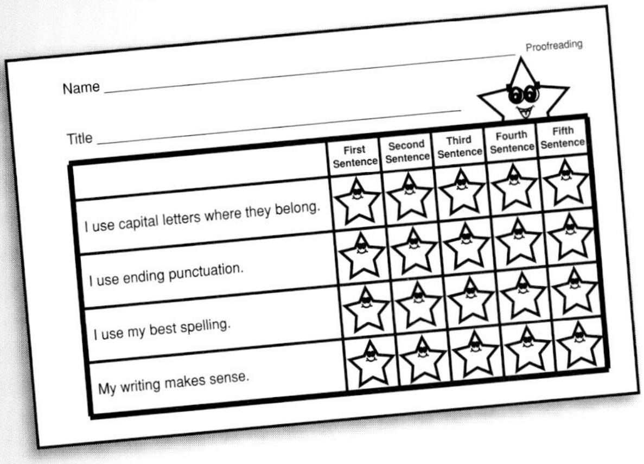
Proofreading

Name ____________________

Title ____________________

	First Sentence	Second Sentence	Third Sentence	Fourth Sentence	Fifth Sentence
I use capital letters where they belong.	☆	☆	☆	☆	☆
I use ending punctuation.	☆	☆	☆	☆	☆
I use my best spelling.	☆	☆	☆	☆	☆
My writing makes sense.	☆	☆	☆	☆	☆

Editors in Training

Enlarge the train patterns on page 98, making one locomotive and three different-colored cars. Label each car as shown. Then, on a piece of matching construction paper, list examples of the idea shown on each car. Mount the train display in a prominent location and have students refer to it when they are ready to edit their writing. Add more examples or replace the cars with new ones as the school year and students' skills progress. **Writing process**

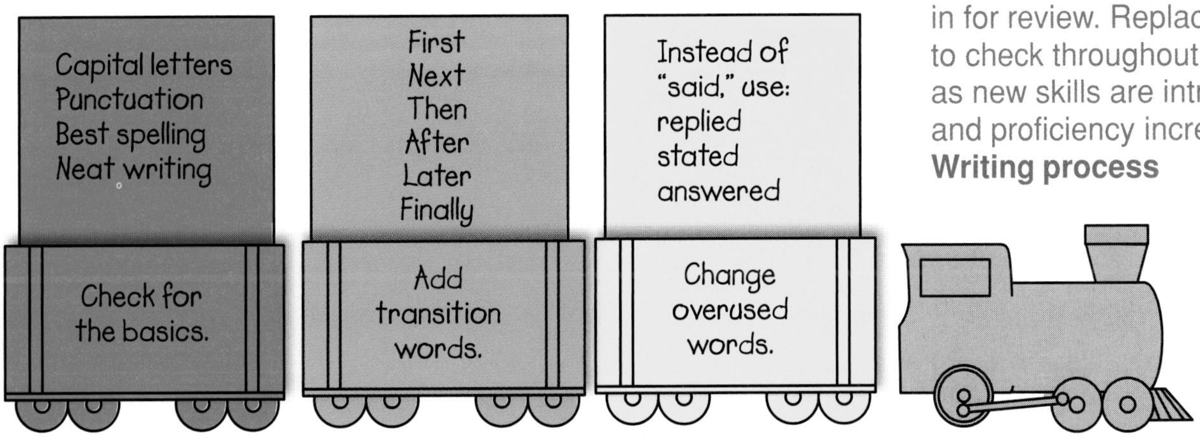
Capital letters
Punctuation
Best spelling
Neat writing
Check for the basics.
First
Next
Then
After
Later
Finally
Add transition words.
Instead of "said," use:
replied
stated
answered
Change overused words.

Red = Capital letters at the beginning of sentences
Yellow = Capital letters to start names of people
Green = Punctuation at the end of each sentence

Crayon Corrections

Post on the board a key, like the one shown, with three things that students should look for in their writing. As he reviews his work, have each student start with the item listed next to the color red. He circles every example of that item with a red crayon. He continues the process with the item next to yellow and then green. After he has completed these proofreading steps, he can have a partner review his work or turn the paper in for review. Replace items to check throughout the year as new skills are introduced and proficiency increases. **Writing process**

The Joy of Journals

Begin the school year by having your students write, write, write! Include on your school supply list a notebook for each student. Have the students keep the notebooks at their desks to use as journals. Then begin each day by writing a journal assignment on the board. Include timely assignments, such as "Today there is a chance of rain. Do you like rainy days? Write a journal entry explaining your answer." By the time students have completed their assignments, you'll be finished with your morning routine. **Journal writing**

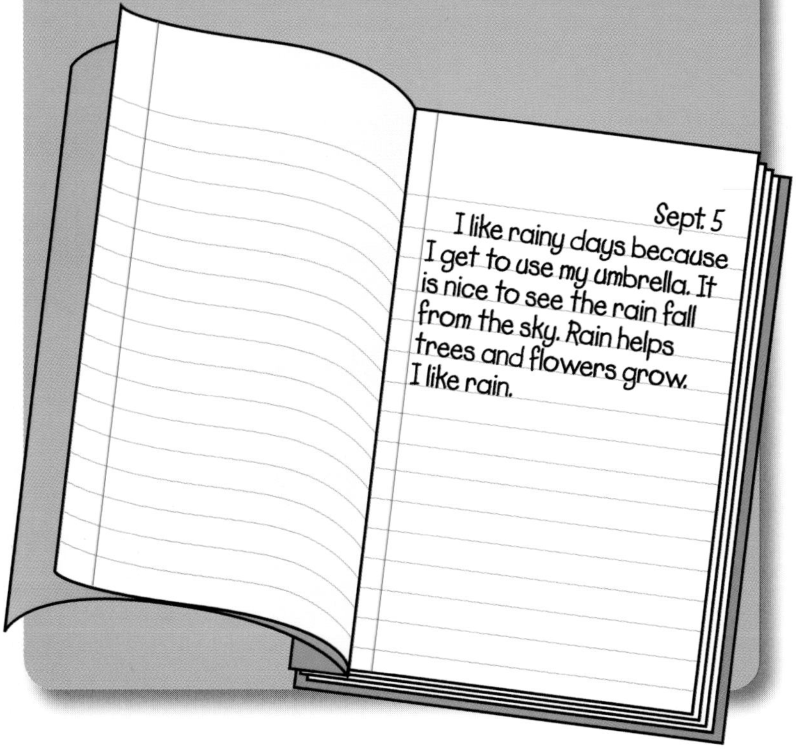
Sept. 5
I like rainy days because I get to use my umbrella. It is nice to see the rain fall from the sky. Rain helps trees and flowers grow. I like rain.

The Classroom Journal

Model journal-writing techniques with your class by keeping a big-book account of weekly activities. At the end of each week, ask students to recall the events of the past few days—what they learned, class birthdays, guests visiting, and other special happenings. List the responses on the board. After a list has been generated, transfer each event to chart paper in chronological order, using a complete sentence. Use transition words—such as *first, next, then,* and *last*—to help with the flow of ideas. Then have your students read the completed entry aloud with you. This is a good way to model effective writing with the added bonus of having a weekly account of your school year. **Journal writing**

This has been an exciting week! First, we had a visitor from the fire department. Then we had class pictures taken. On the last day of the week, we painted.

Positive Ponderings

Use the last few minutes of each day as a time for students to reflect on the good things that happened at school. Ask each student to write a sentence or two about positive feedback he received about his work, a nice thing someone said to him or did for him, or a way he was helpful to another student. If time allows, ask student volunteers to share their entries. You'll end the day in a positive way, and students will be eager to share the good things about their day with their parents. **Journal writing**

Dear Secret Pal,
What do you like to do for fun?

Secret-Pal Journals

Arrange with another teacher to buddy up classes for this writing activity. Without revealing identities to the students, pair each child in your class with a student in the other classroom. Instruct each student to write a question in his journal, such as "Do you have any pets?" or "What is your favorite book?" Gather your students' journals and trade them with the other class. Provide time for each student to answer the question in his secret pal's journal and include a question of his own before you return the journals to their original owners. Continue the secret-pal activity for the remainder of the grading period; then have a pal-revealing celebration in which each student discovers his writing partner's identity. You may decide to let the pals continue writing to each other or to switch to a new set of secret pals for another round of journal-writing fun. **Journal writing**

All About Me

If the thought of journal writing is a little overwhelming to your students, begin the writing process by providing topics that are personal and familiar. Twice a week, have your students write about an assigned topic from the list below. The students will feel more comfortable writing about themselves and their own experiences. Keep each child's completed papers in a separate folder. At the end of the semester, help each student compile her journal pages into a booklet. Provide construction paper covers for the booklet and have the student add the title "All About Me." These booklets will be treasured keepsakes when displayed at open house, and they will serve as good journal-writing practice for students. **Journal writing**

All About Me

- Tell about your family.
- Describe your favorite meal.
- Write about the things in your room.
- Write about a special toy.
- Tell about a friend of yours.
- Describe your favorite place to go.
- Share a story about a vacation or trip.
- Tell about your pet or a pet you would like to have.
- Describe some of your favorites (color, food, TV show, book).

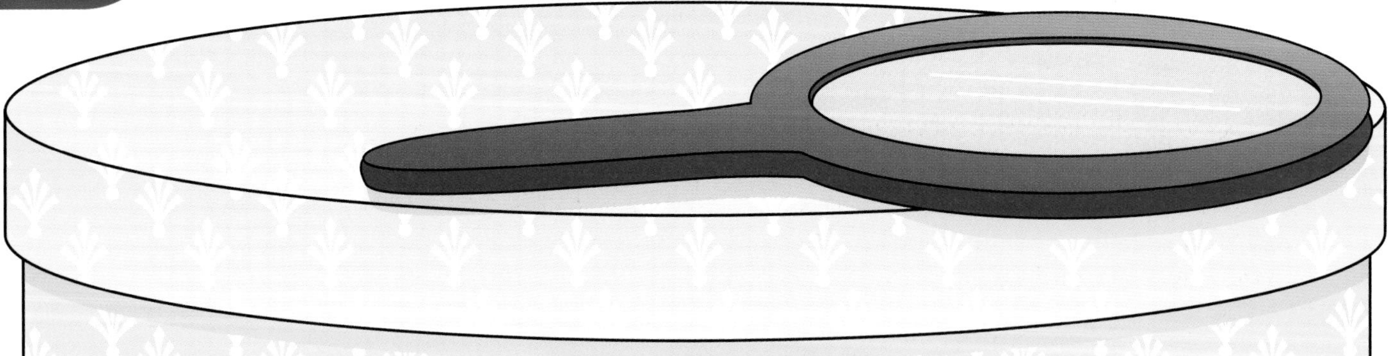

The Clue Box

Use a favorite class event—show-and-tell—to launch a daily writing activity. All you need to start the activity is a sturdy, easy-to-carry box (a hatbox works well) and an object to place inside. (If desired, use a seasonally appropriate item or an object relating to a current unit of study.) Without the students observing you, place the object in the box. Write three clues about the object on an index card, listing the most general clue first. Present the box to your students and read the clues aloud. The first student to identify the object gets to take the box home. Take the object out of the box and show it to the class. Inside the empty box, put a note to the student's parents explaining that their child is to select an object to place in the box and write three clues about it. Provide time during the following day for the student to read her clues to the class. The classmate who identifies the object gets to take the box home that night. Continue the activity until each student has had an opportunity to present the clue box. Students will have so much fun taking the box home that they won't realize they're using deductive-reasoning, public-speaking, and sentence-writing skills! **Descriptive**

1. Almost every time you look at this, you see something different.
2. You probably have one at home.
3. It reflects light.

Fish Stories

Children love to enhance the ordinary—why not capitalize on this to develop imaginative sentences? Begin by discussing the concept of exaggeration; then explain that some exaggerated tales are called fish stories because of the way fishermen may enhance tales about the size of fish they catch. As a class, complete some of the sentences below with an exaggerated idea. Then provide each student with a copy of the fish pattern on page 99. Instruct the student to copy onto her fish a sentence starter from the list below and then complete the sentence with her own exaggerated idea. Finally, have students color and cut out their fish. Staple the fish stories onto a bulletin board covered with blue bulletin board paper. Now who told the biggest fish story in the class? **Descriptive**

- It was thundering so loudly that…
- The quarterback threw the ball so far that…
- The kangaroo jumped so high that…
- The bird flew so fast that…
- It was so cold that…
- The stars were so bright that…
- The sun was so hot that…
- It rained so hard that…
- The opera singer hit a note so high that…
- I was so tired that…

Promoting Paragraph Writing

Use a picture prompt to introduce the concept of a paragraph. Select from a coloring book a page that features two characters and a simple background. Copy a class supply. Provide time for each student to color his page; then have him think about the objects in the picture. Next, give a sheet of writing paper to each student, and have him write a paragraph about the picture using the following formula:

- Write one sentence identifying the picture's characters and setting.
- Write one sentence about the first character.
- Write one sentence about the second character.
- Write one sentence about the setting.
- Write one sentence telling how the picture makes you feel.

By using this formula, the student develops the topic sentence, supporting details, and summary sentence. Use the completed writing samples to point out each of these elements of a paragraph. Your students will have a clear picture of what a paragraph is all about! **Descriptive**

Picture This

Use students' artwork to inspire creative writing. Give each student a sheet of drawing paper. Have her fold down a one-inch section across the top of her paper as shown. Instruct the student to draw a picture of a seasonal character—such as a scarecrow, an elf, or a leprechaun—on the paper. Encourage her to add several details and colors to her illustration. Have her decide on a name for her character and write it on the folded section so the name is hidden from view. Next, provide each student with a sheet of writing paper, and instruct her to write a paragraph describing and naming the character in her picture. Display the completed drawings and paragraphs on a bulletin board. Students read each paragraph and match it to one of the illustrated characters. To check their guesses, the students flip up the folded section on each drawing to reveal the character's name. **Descriptive**

LUCKY LOUIE

Training Tips

To help students over their story-writing hurdles, give each student a copy of page 100. Have him fold the copy to make a tent, as shown, and then glue or tape it together. He places the tent on his desk so that the "Beginning" hurdle faces him. He refers to the hurdle as he writes, using it to guide his story. When he is ready, he turns the tent to reveal the "Middle" hurdle and continues writing his story. He turns the tent one more time to show the "End" hurdle and completes his story. **Narrative**

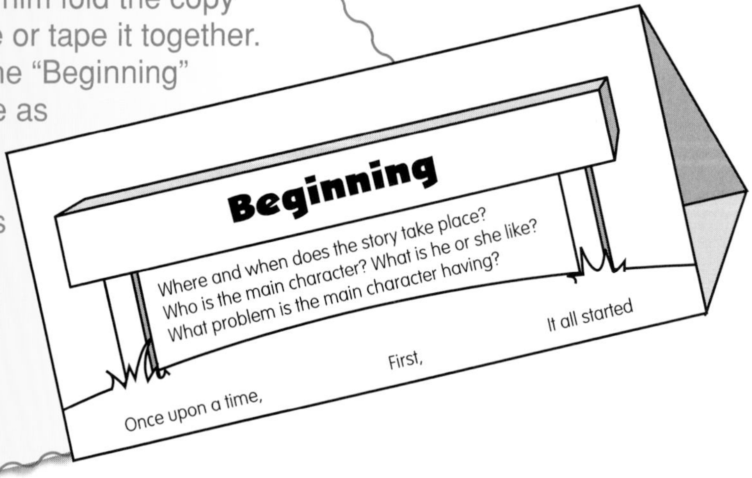
Beginning
Where and when does the story take place?
Who is the main character? What is he or she like?
What problem is the main character having?
Once upon a time,
First,
It all started

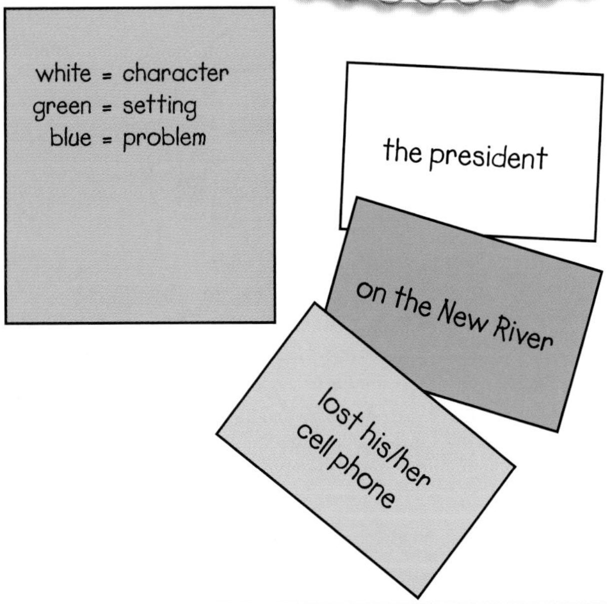
white = character
green = setting
blue = problem
the president
on the New River
lost his/her cell phone

In the Cards

Play these cards right, and students will have story ideas in no time! Copy the key shown onto the board and give each student an index card of each color. Have her write an idea for the corresponding story element on each card. Collect the cards, place them in like-colored piles, and shuffle the piles. Then have each child choose one card from each pile. She uses the ideas to generate a story. After the story is written, have each student return her card to its pile. Repeat the process at a later date, allowing each student to choose new cards. **Narrative**

What's the Story?

Place a collection of wordless picture books at a center with writing paper and pencils. Label a folder with each book's title and then place the folders with the books. A student chooses a book and reviews its contents. Then he copies the title onto his paper and uses the illustrations to write a story. He places the completed story in the folder with the same title. After all the students have visited the center, share and compare the different stories based on the each book. Narrative

Winter Adventure
It was a cold winter day. Charlie played in the park. Then he got bored. He sat on a rock, wondering what to do.

Stories in Season

Bring in a seasonal object and place it in an accessible area. Allow time for each child to use her senses to observe it. As a class, brainstorm words related to the object and record students' responses on the board. Then have each student write a story from the object's perspective, referring to the board to add descriptive details. **Narrative**

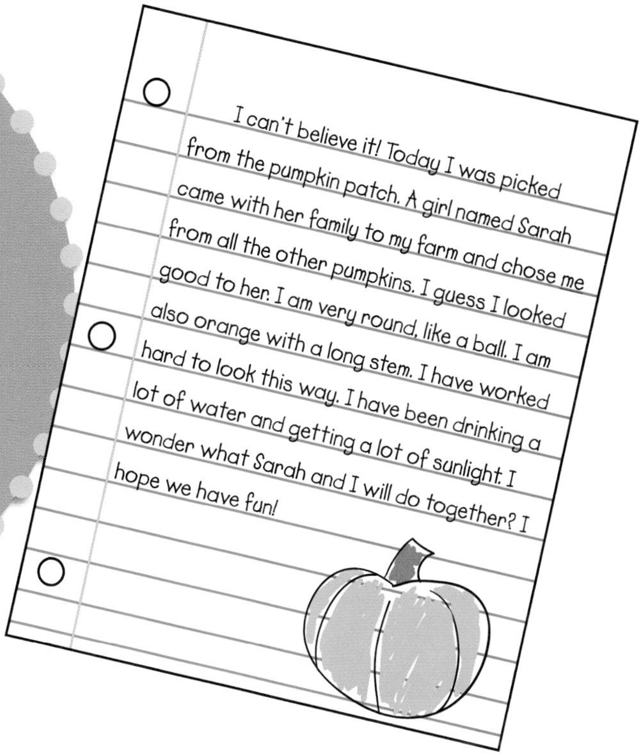
I can't believe it! Today I was picked from the pumpkin patch. A girl named Sarah came with her family to my farm and chose me from all the other pumpkins. I guess I looked good to her. I am very round, like a ball. I am also orange with a long stem. I have worked hard to look this way. I have been drinking a lot of water and getting a lot of sunlight. I wonder what Sarah and I will do together? I hope we have fun!

Pizza
Pizza Palace
After soccer game
Mom and Dad
To celebrate the win

Serving Up Stories

To feed students' appetites for story ideas, cut out pictures of recognizable foods from magazines or grocery store circulars. Glue each cutout to a paper plate and write the food's name near the cutout. Have each child choose a plate and list words or phrases that tell where and when he ate the food, who he was with, and why he ate it. Then have him use the ideas to write a story about his personal or imaginary experience with that food. Post the completed stories with the plates on a display titled "Now Serving Special Stories." **Narrative**

Newsworthy Events

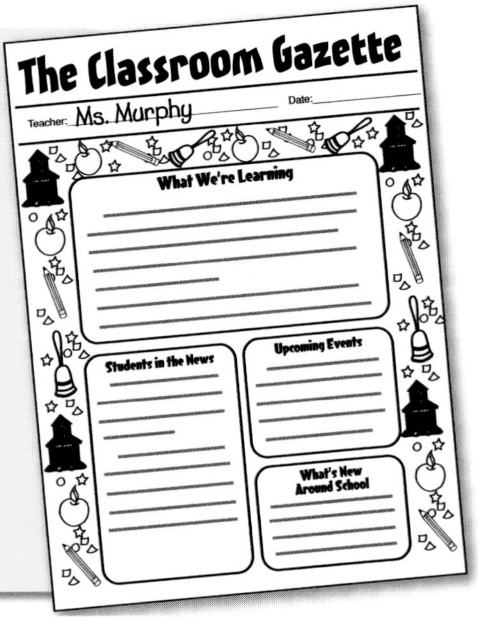
The Classroom Gazette
Teacher: Ms. Murphy
Date:
What We're Learning
Students in the News
Upcoming Events
What's New Around School

A newsletter is the perfect tool for letting parents know all the happenings in your classroom. Use the newsletter form on page 101 combined with the writing talents of your students to produce a periodical for parents to enjoy. Each week assign each newsletter topic to a different student. Encourage the student to interview classmates, talk with the school secretary, or confer with school staff members to gather information about his topic. After editing each student's article, have him, in turn, copy the information onto a newsletter form. Then make and distribute classroom copies for students to take home and share with their families. Expository

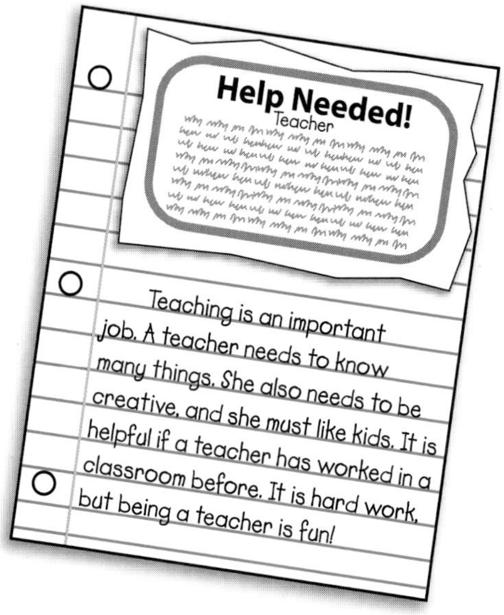
Help Needed!
Teacher
Teaching is an important job. A teacher needs to know many things. She also needs to be creative, and she must like kids. It is helpful if a teacher has worked in a classroom before. It is hard work, but being a teacher is fun!

On the Job

Writing about community helpers will be a snap with the help of your local newspaper. To prepare, cut out a variety of easy-to-read help-wanted ads from a newspaper. Place the ads with paper and pencils at a center. A child chooses an ad and glues it to her paper. Then she reads the want ad and uses its information to write a paragraph about the job. She includes information in her paragraph about the experience and special skills needed for the position. Then she draws a picture of a worker carrying out her duties on the job. **Expository**

Important People

This easy organizer helps students write well-organized biography reports. Have each student choose an important person to study and help him locate research materials. Then give each child a large sheet of construction paper. Have him fold the paper into four equal sections and label each section as shown. Using his research materials, he writes words and phrases or glues pictures in each section of the organizer. Then he uses these notes to write his report on a sheet of lined paper. If desired, have him use his organizer as a visual aid when he shares his report aloud. **Expository**

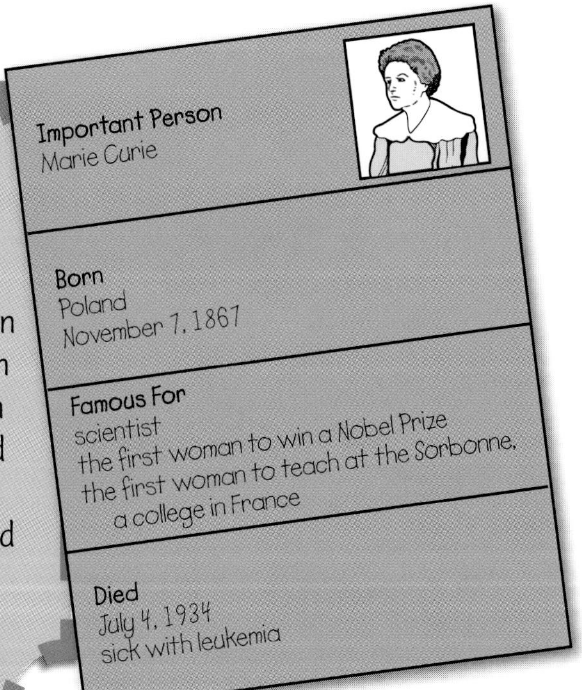
Important Person
Marie Curie
Born
Poland
November 7, 1867
Famous For
scientist
the first woman to win a Nobel Prize
the first woman to teach at the Sorbonne, a college in France
Died
July 4, 1934
sick with leukemia

Informative Writing

Announce a general topic for writing, such as rain forests or weather. On the board, write a student-generated list of words that relate to the topic. Have each student select a word from the list and use complete sentences to tell three things about it. If desired, have him add an illustration to his page. Enlist students' help in arranging the completed papers in alphabetical order according to their topic words. Add a construction paper cover and bind the pages into a booklet. The result will be a classroom dictionary of words about your unit of study. **Expository**

wind
Wind is moving air. It can be gentle. It can also be dangerous.

rain
Rain falls from the clouds. It makes puddles. Plants need rain.

Ice cream is good to eat. **There are lots of flavors.** You can add different toppings.
I like vanilla with chocolate sprinkles.

Round-Robin Writing

Try round-robin writing to help keep the ideas flowing. Give a sheet of writing paper to each student and instruct her to write a topic sentence on the page. (You can provide topic sentences for students to copy, or, if appropriate, have them develop sentences on their own.) Have each student then pass her paper to the classmate sitting to her right. Each student adds a related sentence to the new paper before passing it again to the right. Continue having students pass the papers, adding new sentences, until five or six sentences are written on each page. Provide time for each student to read aloud the paper she ends up with. Students will enjoy hearing the completed paragraphs developed from their original topic sentences in this open exchange of ideas! **Expository**

Shake on It

A simple handshake is all it takes to help students remember the five parts of a friendly letter. After reviewing the date, greeting, body, closing, and signature with students, discuss the purpose of a friendly letter. Compare it to a handshake—both reach out to others with caring and kindness. Also share with students that a handshake starts with five fingers, just as a friendly letter has five parts. Encourage students to think of a handshake when writing a friendly letter. **Letter writing**

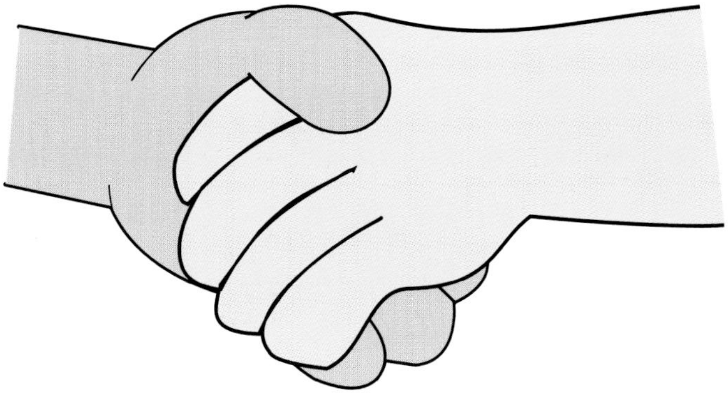

Stamp It

Get students on their feet and on their way to remembering the parts of a letter. Post a chart, like the one shown, where students can see it. Then start at the heading and complete the movements. Name parts of the letter while completing the corresponding body motions. Start slowly and then speed up as students become more familiar with naming the parts of the letter. **Letter writing**

Heading = Touch head.
Greeting = Wave at shoulder level.
Body = Put hands on waist or hips.
Closing = Clap hands in front of knees.
Signature = Use foot to write signature on the floor.

Secret Admirers

Turn unused student valentines into memorable stationery. To prepare, write the name of a different student on the back of each valentine. A student chooses a card and reads the name on the back. He writes a letter to that student, naming at least one thing that makes that child special. Then he glues the card to the paper. Collect the letters and distribute them to the intended recipients. **Letter writing**

Dear Kylie,
May 9
I think that you are very nice. I liked it when you shared your snack with me. You're lucky to have a dad who makes such good brownies! I hope that you have a nice day.
Your friend,
Andy

Dear Teacher

Personalize student feedback with this noteworthy idea. At the end of a unit of study, have each student reflect on that unit's activities. Have each child write a friendly letter to you, telling you what she liked or disliked about the unit, what was easy or hard, or simply what she learned. For extra motivation, give students themed stationery on which to write their letters. Students practice letter-writing skills, and the resulting letters will help you plan future units and get to know your students better. **Letter writing**

March 10
Dear Mr. Foster,
I loved our community unit. I was glad we invited community helpers to our room. I learned a lot about their jobs. I also liked when we toured the fire station and grocery store. It was neat to compare them. I can't wait to learn more from you this year!
Your student,
Anna

A Fitting End

Students will have no problem choosing an appropriate closing with this simple idea. To prepare, label large sheets of construction paper with greetings for different letter recipients, such as a grandma, teacher, friend, pen pal, or favorite author. Next, give each child a sentence strip with a letter closing written on it. Have the child post his closing on a matching construction paper chart, placing the closing on the right side of the chart. Keep charts posted for students to refer to when writing letters. **Letter writing**

Dear Grandma,
Your grandchild,
Love,

Special Delivery

Surprise one or two students each week with a special journal assignment. Before class, write a letter to the chosen student in her journal. Then, after the student finds your letter, tell her that her journal task for that day is to write a letter back to you. Be sure to keep track of who you've written to so that everyone gets a surprise. Then, when everyone has received a letter, start the process over again. What a fun way to keep in touch and have students look forward to their journal-writing tasks! **Letter writing**

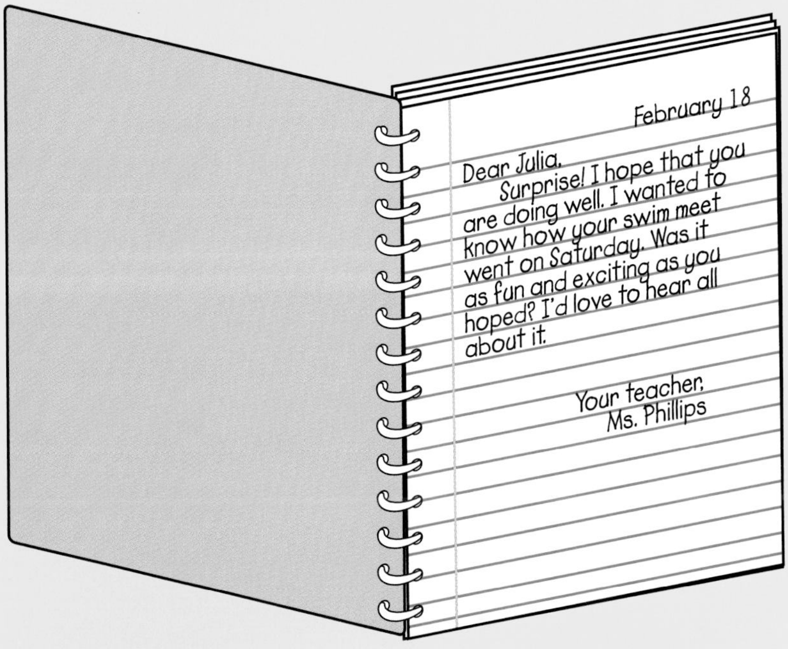
February 18
Dear Julia,
Surprise! I hope that you are doing well. I wanted to know how your swim meet went on Saturday. Was it as fun and exciting as you hoped? I'd love to hear all about it.
Your teacher,
Ms. Phillips

Acrostic Poems

Build vocabulary and reinforce descriptive words with acrostic poetry. Announce a topic, such as dinosaurs, rainbows, or firefighters. Have each student write the topic on his paper vertically. Instruct him to use each letter in the word for the initial letter of an adjective or a phrase that describes the topic. **Poetry**

Dangerous
Interesting
No longer alive
Outrageous lizards
So big!
All kinds
Unusual animals
Roar!
Searched for food

Shape Poems

Even the most reluctant poets will enjoy writing shape poetry! In a shape poem, words are written around the outline of a picture of the subject. The words may define, describe, or analyze the subject. Make copies of a simple shape, or provide a stencil for each student to trace on her paper. Then encourage your young poets to list words or phrases about the subject around its outline. **Poetry**

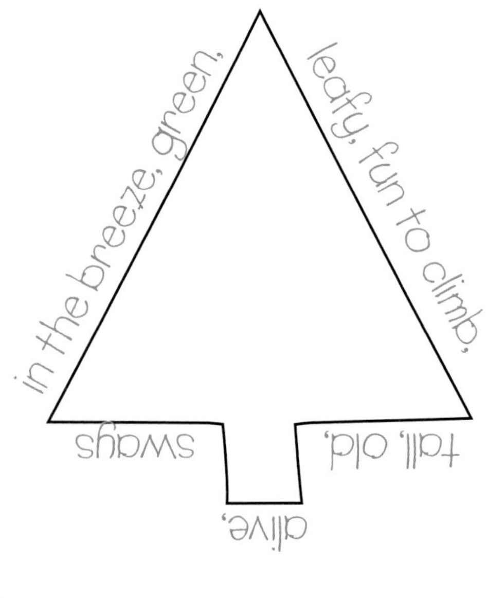
leafy, fun to climb,
tall, old,
alive,
sways
in the breeze, green,

The Five Ws

A simple and fun poem for children to write is the five Ws verse. Each line of this poem answers one of the five Ws of questioning: who, what, where, when, and why. Brainstorm a list of topics with your class; then model the poem as follows:

Who is the subject?
What does he do?
Where does he do it?
When does he do it?
Why does he do it?

The puppy
Chases its tail
In the yard
Every morning
Because it's silly!

Have students write a version of their own. **Poetry**

Diamonte Poems

Reinforce the parts of speech with this seven-line diamond-shaped poem. The student selects a topic and then completes the poem with related information in this format shown below. **Poetry**

Line 1: Topic (noun)
Line 2: Two adjectives
Line 3: Three action words
Line 4: A four-word phrase
Line 5: Three action words
Line 6: Two adjectives
Line 7: Topic repeated

Ants
Black, red
Running, building, digging
Always in a hurry
Moving, lifting, crawling
Tiny, busy
Ants

Syllable Cinquains

In a syllable cinquain, the student creates a five-line poem using a specific number of syllables in each line. Model the format of a syllable cinquain as shown below. **Poetry**

Line 1: Topic	2 syllables
Line 2: Description of topic	4 syllables
Line 3: Action about the topic	6 syllables
Line 4: Feeling about the topic	8 syllables
Line 5: Synonym for the topic	2 syllables

Sunshine
Rays of bright light
Making the earth so warm
Sunny days make me feel happy
Golden

Sensory Poems

Students combine the five senses with similes and metaphors to create this expressive type of poetry. Have your students brainstorm a list of possible topics while you record their responses on the board.Instruct each student to select a topic and complete the following sentences to create a sensational verse. **Poetry**

Topic
A (topic) looks as _______ as _______.
A (topic) sounds as _______ as _______.
A (topic) smells as _______ as _______.
A (topic) tastes as _______ as _______.
A (topic) feels as _______ as _______.
A (topic) is _______________.

Lemon
A lemon looks as yellow as the sun.
A lemon sounds as quiet as a mouse.
A lemon smells as fresh as clean sheets.
A lemon tastes as sour as a pickle.
A lemon feels as smooth as a rock.
A lemon is a mystery.

Check out the skill-building reproducibles on pages 96–101.

Name ____________________

Prewriting Plan

Topic Web

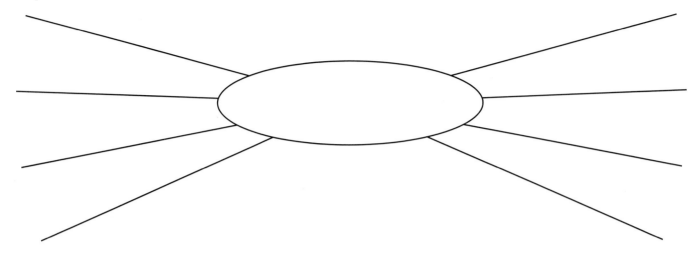

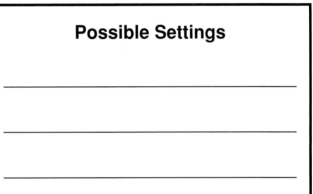

Possible Characters

Possible Settings

Topic Sentence for the Beginning of the Story:

Topic Sentence for the Middle of the Story:

Topic Sentence for the End of the Story:

 Note to the teacher: Use with “Prewriting Plan” on page 82.

Name ____________________

Title ____________________

	First Sentence	Second Sentence	Third Sentence	Fourth Sentence	Fifth Sentence
I use capital letters where they belong.	☆	☆	☆	☆	☆
I use ending punctuation.	☆	☆	☆	☆	☆
I use my best spelling.	☆	☆	☆	☆	☆
My writing makes sense.	☆	☆	☆	☆	☆

Name ____________________ Proofreading

Title ____________________

	First Sentence	Second Sentence	Third Sentence	Fourth Sentence	Fifth Sentence
I use capital letters where they belong.	☆	☆	☆	☆	☆
I use ending punctuation.	☆	☆	☆	☆	☆
I use my best spelling.	☆	☆	☆	☆	☆
My writing makes sense.	☆	☆	☆	☆	☆

©The Mailbox® • *Superbook®* • TEC61049

Note to the teacher: Use with "Four-Star Sentences" on page 83.

Train Patterns

Use with "Editors in Training" on page 83.

TEC61049

TEC61049

Fish Pattern

Use with "Fish Stories" on page 86.

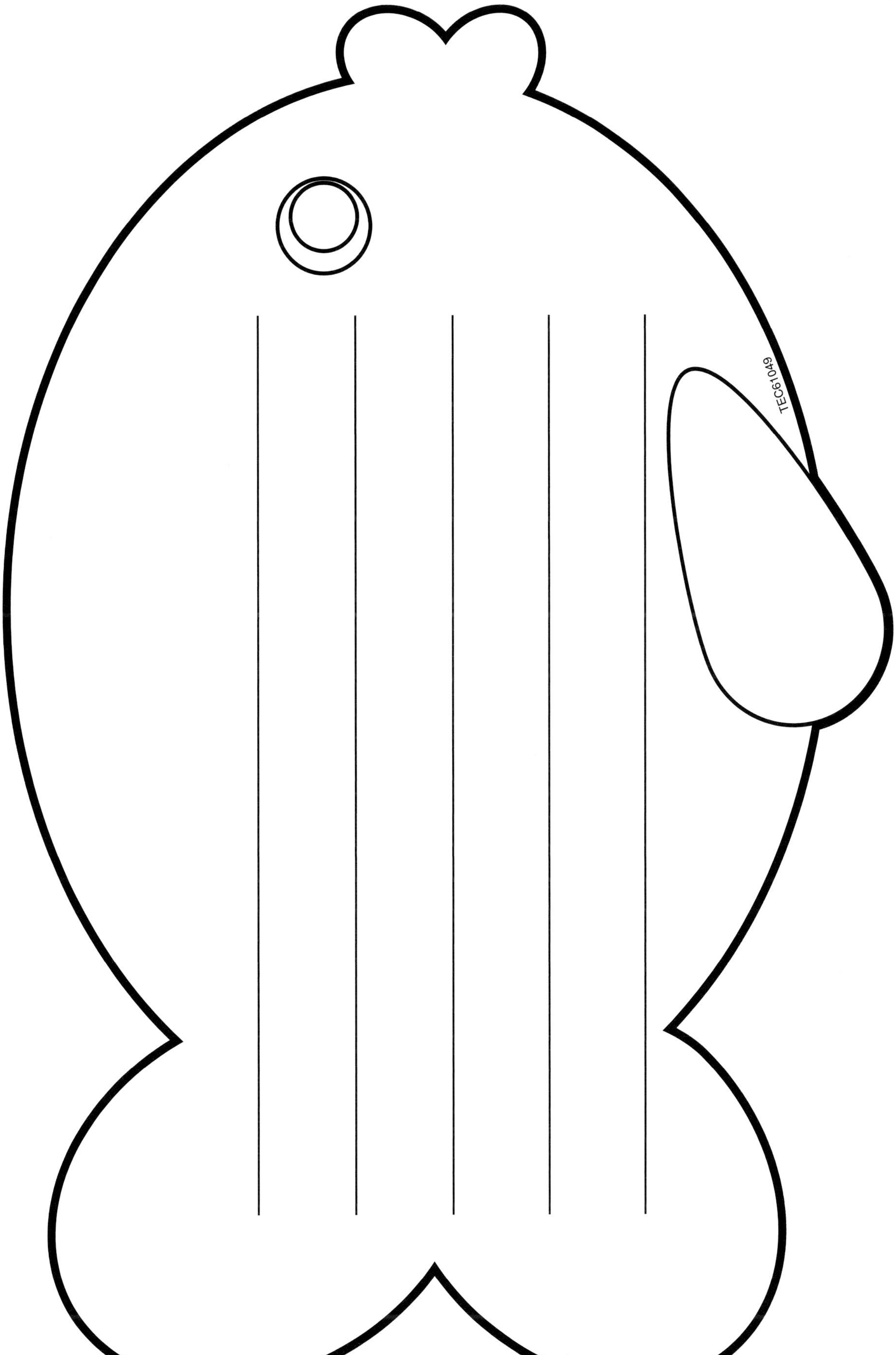
TEC61049

Beginning

Where and when does the story take place?
Who is the main character? What is he or she like?
What problem is the main character having?

Once upon a time, **First,** **It all started**

Middle

How does the main character try to solve his or her problem?
(Try to name several ways.)

Next, **Then** **Later,** **After that,** **All of a sudden,**

End

How is the problem finally solved?
What happens to the main character?

By now, **Finally,** **In the end,**

 Note to the teacher: Use with "Training Tips" on page 88.

The Classroom Gazette

Teacher: ______________________________ Date: ____________________

What We're Learning

Students in the News

Upcoming Events

What's New Around School

Note to the teacher: Use with "Newsworthy Events" on page 90.

Name ______________________________ Open reproducible

____
title

 Note to the teacher: Use with the poetry ideas on pages 94 and 95.

Number Concepts and Place Value

A Daily Dose of Place Value

Give your students a daily dose of place value with a readily available source: the date! Each day, have a selected student use manipulatives to demonstrate the date in tens and ones. Have the following materials handy in your calendar center for students to use with the daily demonstration:

- craft sticks, individuals and bundles of ten

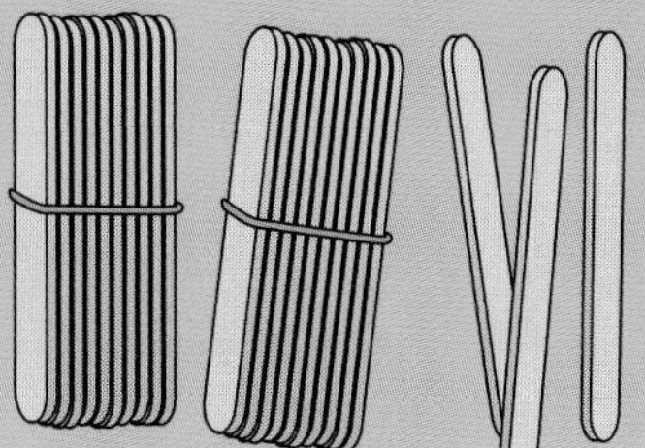

- dried beans, individuals and resealable bags of ten

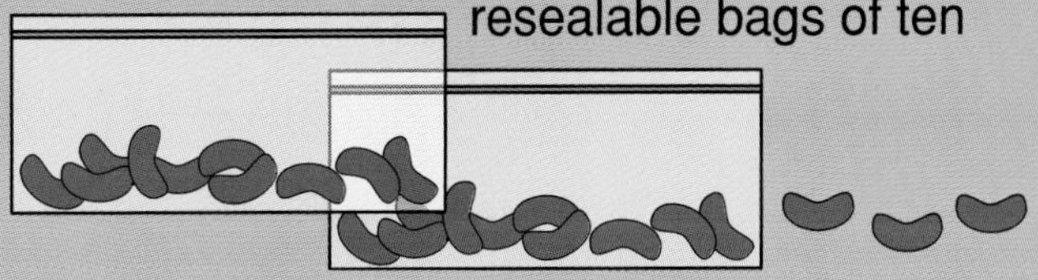

- handprint cutouts, individuals with some fingers extended, and pairs stapled together (see example)

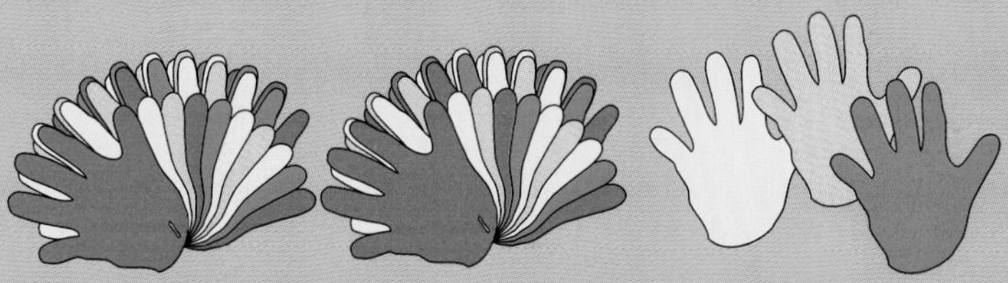

- pennies and dimes

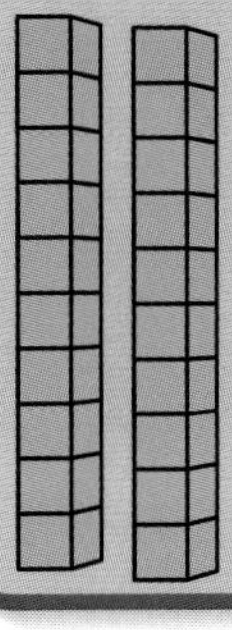

- Unifix cubes, individuals and stacks of ten

- beads, individuals and strings of ten

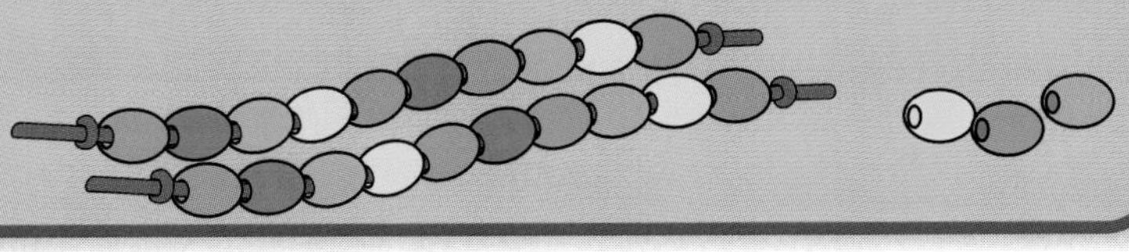

Domino Place Value

Give each student a domino. Instruct the student to count the dots on the right side of her domino as ones and the dots on the left side of her domino as tens. Ask each student to identify the two-digit number her domino represents; then ask students to compare to see who has the largest and smallest numbers. Collect the dominoes, redistribute them, and repeat the procedure. For an added challenge, have the students line up in numerical order according to the value of their dominoes.

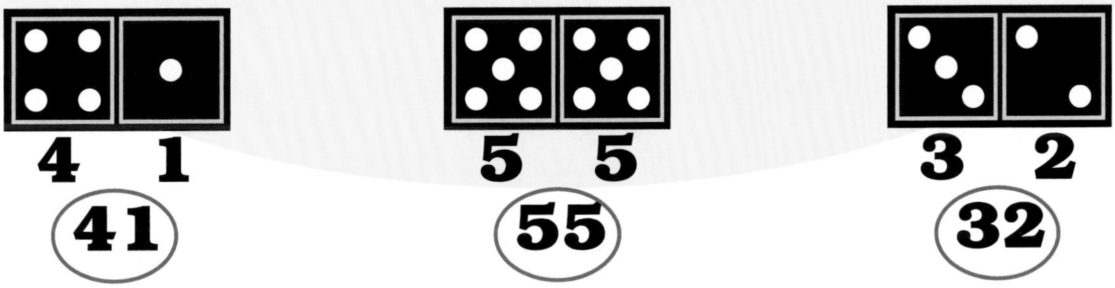
4 1
41
5 5
55
3 2
32

Court sup
affirmative action ban
NE RECORD
City's Annual Budget Exceeds Million
Index
53
269
$115
421

Place Value in the News

Write a list of guidelines for numbers on the board for students to find in old newspapers. For example, have students look for a number with a 3 in the ones place, a number with a 6 in the tens place, or a number with a 4 in the hundreds place. Instruct each student to cut out the numbers he finds and glue them to a sheet of paper. After the students have completed the activity, have them compare their results.

Daily Count

This daily counting activity helps your students reinforce number concepts. Display a hundred chart where all students can easily see it, or provide each student with a copy of the chart on page 105. Each day, ask a student volunteer to use a pointer to touch each number on the chart as the class counts out loud. Vary the counting activity each day with instructions such as the following:

- Count by fives to 50.
- Count by tens to 100.
- Say the even numbers to 20.
- Say the odd numbers from 21 to 33.
- Count from 45 to 65.
- Count backward from 90 to 80.

Daily Number Drill

Incorporate an ongoing number-concept review into your daily routine. Program slips of paper each with a number from 1 to 20 and place them in a cup. At the start of each math lesson, randomly draw a number from the cup. Have your students answer the following questions about the number:

1. Is the number odd or even?
2. What number is one less?
3. What number is one more?
4. What are two numbers that can be added together to total the number?
5. If the number were doubled, what would the sum be?

Check out the skill-building reproducibles on pages 106–108.

Hundred Chart

Use with "Daily Count" on page 104.

1	2	3	4	5	6	7	8	9	10
11	12	13	14	15	16	17	18	19	20
21	22	23	24	25	26	27	28	29	30
31	32	33	34	35	36	37	38	39	40
41	42	43	44	45	46	47	48	49	50
51	52	53	54	55	56	57	58	59	60
61	62	63	64	65	66	67	68	69	70
71	72	73	74	75	76	77	78	79	80
81	82	83	84	85	86	87	88	89	90
91	92	93	94	95	96	97	98	99	100

Name ____________________

Mmmm...Cookies!

Write >, <, or = in each ◯.

A. 36 ◯ 47	H. 70 ◯ 69
B. 14 ◯ 14	I. 63 ◯ 43
C. 71 ◯ 77	J. 29 ◯ 31
D. 24 ◯ 10	K. 62 ◯ 62
E. 82 ◯ 28	L. 94 ◯ 46
F. 34 ◯ 48	M. 3 ◯ 13
G. 12 ◯ 9	N. 45 ◯ 54

Name ______________________________

Walking the Line

Write the number that comes before, after, or between.

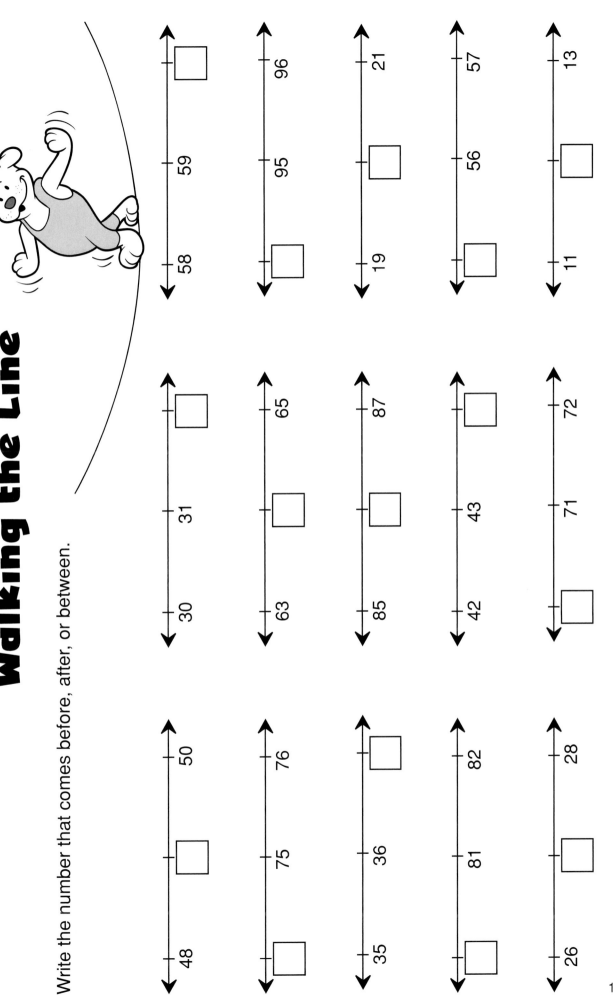

48 ☐ 50	30 31 ☐	58 59 ☐
☐ 75 76	63 ☐ 65	☐ 95 96
35 36 ☐	85 ☐ 87	19 ☐ 21
☐ 81 82	42 43 ☐	☐ 56 57
26 ☐ 28	☐ 71 72	11 ☐ 13

Name ______________________________ Expanded notation

Burgers and Drinks

Cut out the cups below.
Glue each cup next to the matching burger.

A. 300 + 60 + 2

B. 100 + 30 + 9

C. 800 + 60 + 4

D. 500 + 70 + 3

E. 700 + 10 + 5

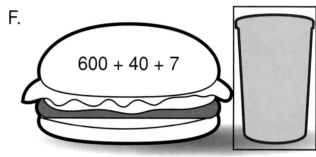

F. 600 + 40 + 7

G. 200 + 90 + 1

H. 400 + 50 + 6

647 | 456 | 715 | 573 | 139 | 362 | 864 | 291

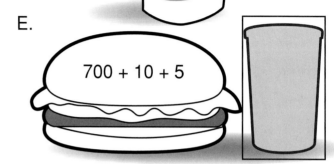

+ Addition & Subtraction –

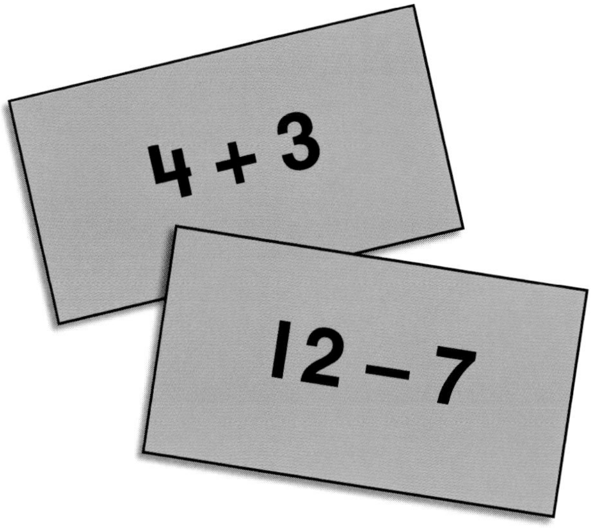
4 + 3
12 – 7

Number Line Concepts

Use a number line to review and reinforce basic math facts. Make an interactive number line on your classroom floor with a strip of masking tape. (Or if weather permits, draw a number line in chalk on the sidewalk outdoors.) Program the line with the numerals 1 to 18. Then program a set of task cards with addition or subtraction problems to 18. Have each student, in turn, take a card and demonstrate how to solve the problem by stepping through it on the number line. **Basic facts**

Math in Motion

Get students moving with some math fact practice! Label several open areas of the classroom with different numbers. Invite small groups of students to stand in each of the designated areas. To begin, play lively music or clap as groups rotate to each location in a predetermined path. When you stop the music, announce a math problem to which the answer is one of the labeled numbers. Students silently solve the problem. The group that is standing at the corresponding answer announces the sum or difference out loud. Continue in the same manner for several problems. If desired, periodically change the posted numbers for more fact practice. **Basic facts**

Empty the Basket

Put basic fact practice and strategic thinking into play with this partner center! Prepare two sets of ten apple cutouts, making each set a different color. Number each set of apples from 1 through 10. Also trim two sheets of brown construction paper to each resemble a basket. Place the baskets, the apples, and two dice at a center.

When a twosome visits the center, each child takes a basket and places a set of apples faceup above it. To take a turn, a player rolls the dice. She decides whether to add or subtract the two numbers and announces the corresponding math fact; then she removes the apple with the sum or difference and sets it aside. If there are no apples that she can remove, then her turn is over. Players alternate turns in the same manner. The winner is the first player to remove all of the apples from her basket. **Basic facts**

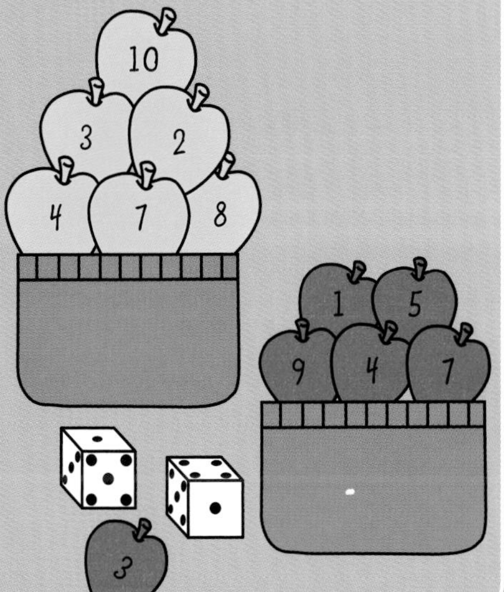
10
3
2
4
7
8
1
5
9
4
7
3

MUSICAL MATH

To prepare for this game, create a class supply of math problems of the desired skill level on separate blank cards. Write the problem on one side of the card and the answer on the other side. Next, have students move their chairs to create a circle and place a problem on each chair. To begin, play some lively music and have students march around the circle of chairs. When the music stops, each student grabs the math problem on the chair in front of him and says the answer out loud. To check his answer, he looks on the back of the card. Continue in this manner for a desired amount of time. Since there is a chair for each student, no one sits out or misses a turn, and everyone gets plenty of practice! **Basic facts**

13 – 4 =

Math Around the Room

This fast-paced game will help students practice basic facts. Have students sit in a circle on the floor. Select one student to start the game and have him stand behind the student seated to his left. Display a flash card for both students to see. If the standing student is first to call out the correct answer, he moves behind the next student to his left. If he is incorrect or does not call out the answer first, he takes the place of the seated student, who then stands behind the student to his left. The game continues until one student moves around the circle and travels back to his original spot. Students will be eager to brush up on their facts in an effort to be the first to travel all the way around the circle! **Basic facts**

Quick Draw

Students can use an ordinary deck of playing cards for this addition version of the game of War. To simplify the game, remove the face cards and let the aces have a value of one. Pair students and supply each pair with a prepared deck of cards. Instruct the partners to divide the cards equally into two piles and to place one pile facedown in front of each player. On the count of three, each player turns over her top card. The first player to correctly add the two numbers together takes the cards and adds them to the bottom of her pile. Play continues until one partner acquires all the cards. If time is a factor, have students count their cards at the end of the time period. The partner with more cards in her pile wins the game. **Addition**

13!
7
6

Subtraction Action

Your students will be on a roll with this mental-math game! To prepare, write a number between 6 and 20 on the board. Have your students sit in a circle on the floor, and hand a die to the first student. Instruct her to roll the die and then subtract the resulting roll from the number on the board. She announces the difference before passing the die to the next player. The students continue to roll and subtract from the designated number until each student has had a turn. If time allows, write a different number on the board for students to subtract from. Everyone gets a chance to participate as the facts keep rolling along! **Subtraction**

20
- 6
14
20
- 4
16
20 minus 4 is 16!

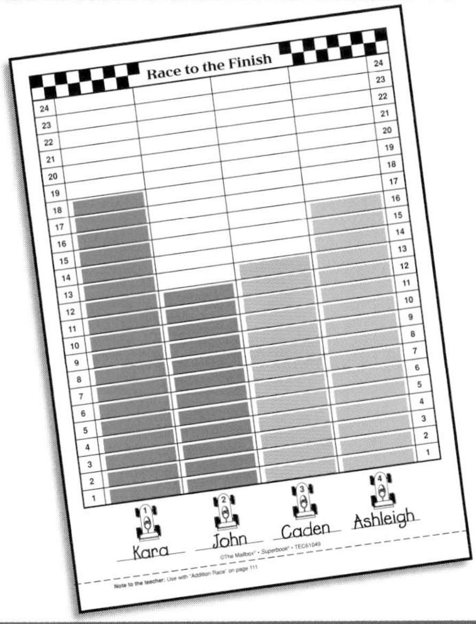
Race to the Finish
Kara
John
Caden
Ashleigh

Addition Race

Give each group of four students a copy of the gameboard on page 114 and a die. Each child writes her name below a different car on the gameboard and chooses a different color of crayon. To begin play, each student, in turn, rolls the die. She colors the corresponding number of spaces in her column. On each remaining turn, she rolls the die, adds the number rolled to her number on the gameboard, and then colors up to the corresponding sum. For example, if she is on 12 and she rolls a six, she adds 12 and six to get 18 and then colors up to 18. Play continues until a player reaches the finish line by the exact count. **Addition facts**

Triple Scoops

To prepare for this center, cut from colorful construction paper several ice-cream scoops. Label each scoop with a number from 1 through 9, repeating numbers as desired. Store the ice-cream scoops in an empty, clean ice-cream carton. Also trim a sheet of brown construction paper to resemble an ice-cream cone. Place the cone, the ice-cream carton, and a supply of paper at a center. When a child visits the center, he randomly chooses three ice-cream scoops and places them above the cone. Then he writes the corresponding addition problem on a sheet of paper and finds the sum. He returns the scoops to the carton and continues in the same manner as time allows. **Addition with three addends**

4
9
3
Tony
5
8
+ 8
21
4
9
+ 3
16

Sum Fun!

This supersimple partner game provides students with plenty of addition practice! Give each pair of students four dice and two sheets of paper. To play, each child rolls two dice to form a two-digit number. Then each student writes the two numbers as an addition problem and finds the sum. After partners compare answers to check for accuracy, they roll again for another round. Play continues in the same manner as time allows. **Two-digit addition**

Chris
43
+ 51
94
Courtney
43
+ 51
94

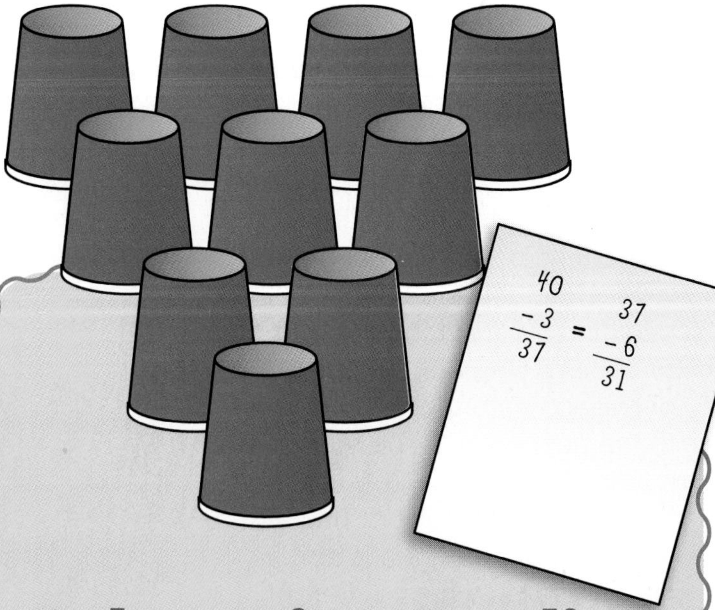
40
- 3
37
=
37
- 6
31

Subtraction Bowling

The object of this game is to get a score of zero! In an open area, place ten large plastic cups upside down. Write on the board a desired two-digit number for students to subtract from (score).

To play, a child gently rolls a soft ball toward the cups and then counts the number of cups he knocked down. Next, he writes the number on the board under the score to form a subtraction problem. The difference becomes the new score. After he replaces the cups, the next student rolls the ball and subtracts the number of knocked-down cups from the new score. Students take turns in the same manner until the score reaches zero. **Two-digit subtraction**

Toss It!

For this partner game, give each twosome a hundred chart and two base ten cubes. (Or for an easier version, cut the hundred chart in half and give the students the chart up to 50.) To play, each child gently tosses a cube onto the chart. Each player writes the two numbers on a sheet of paper to form a subtraction problem and solves the problem. Then they count back on the hundred chart to check their answers. Partners continue in the same manner as time allows. **Two-digit subtraction**

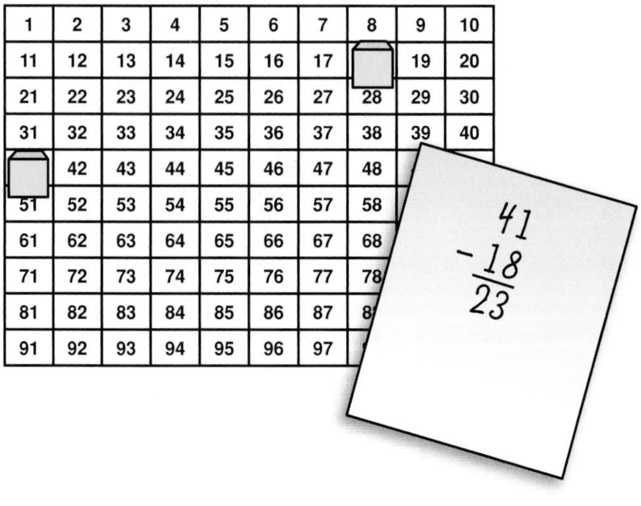
1 2 3 4 5 6 7 8 9 10
11 12 13 14 15 16 17 19 20
21 22 23 24 25 26 27 28 29 30
31 32 33 34 35 36 37 38 39 40
42 43 44 45 46 47 48
51 52 53 54 55 56 57 58
61 62 63 64 65 66 67 68
71 72 73 74 75 76 77
81 82 83 84 85 86 87
91 92 93 94 95 96 97
41
- 18
23

To Regroup or Not to Regroup

Program a class supply of blank cards with different two- or three-digit addition or subtraction problems, choosing some problems that require regrouping and some that do not. In the top row of a pocket chart, place two cards labeled as shown. Give each child a problem card and have her copy and solve the problem on a sheet of paper. After each child has solved her problem, invite her to place her card under the corresponding header in the pocket chart. After confirming the placement of the cards, redistribute the cards for another round. **Two- or three-digit addition or subtraction**

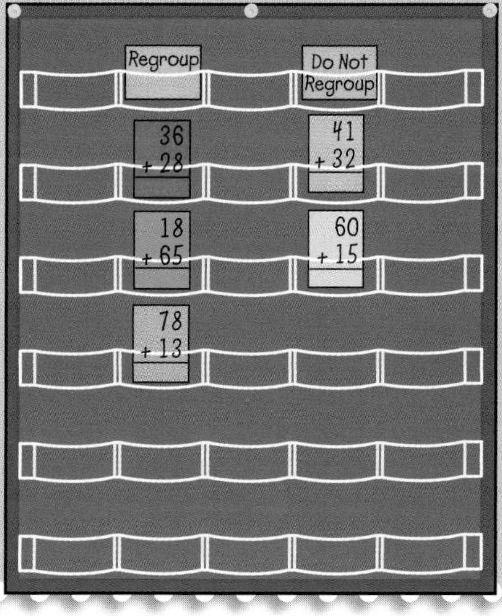
Regroup
Do Not Regroup
36 + 28
41 + 32
18 + 65
60 + 15
78 + 13

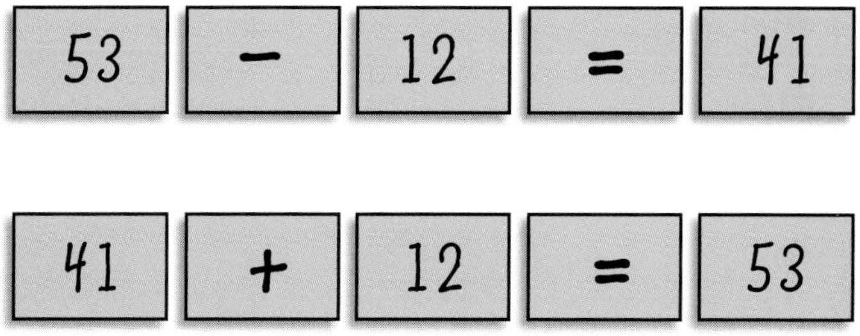
53 − 12 = 41
41 + 12 = 53

Switcheroo!

For hands-on practice with relating addition and subtraction, try this! Assign each student a different two-digit subtraction problem and give him six blank cards. Direct each child to program each card with one of the following: a subtraction symbol, an addition symbol, an equal sign, the subtrahend, the minuend, and the difference. Have the student arrange his cards to model the subtraction problem. Direct each student to rearrange his cards to make the corresponding addition problem when you announce, "Switcheroo." Then have students trade cards and continue in the same manner. **Relating addition and subtraction**

Place Your Order!

What's on the menu at this center? Plenty of practice with adding or subtracting money amounts! Cut out food pictures from magazines or grocery store circulars. Glue each picture to a tagboard sheet and add money amounts to resemble a menu. Place the menu and a supply of paper at a center. For adding practice, a student chooses two or more items from the menu and adds the values together on a sheet of paper. For subtracting practice, label the papers with a starting money amount. A student chooses one item from the menu and subtracts its value from the amount on his paper. Students continue in the same manner, choosing different combinations of menu items each time. **Adding or subtracting money**

PRIMAK'S CAFÉ
sandwich $3.50
pizza $2.80
ice cream $1.99
steak $7.45
cheese $4.10
$2.80 pizza
+ $1.99 ice cream
$4.79
$10.00
$10.00
− $ 4.10 cheese
$5.90

Check out the skill-building reproducibles on pages 115–118.

Race to the Finish

24					24
23					23
22					22
21					21
20					20
19					19
18					18
17					17
16					16
15					15
14					14
13					13
12					12
11					11
10					10
9					9
8					8
7					7
6					6
5					5
4					4
3					3
2					2
1					1

1
2
3
4

__________ __________ __________ __________

 Note to the teacher: Use with "Addition Race" on page 111.

Name____________________

Under the Big Top

Add or subtract.
Color by the code.

Color Code
0–5 = red
6–11 = yellow
12–18 = orange

12 − 8
4 + 2
6 + 7
8 − 8
17 − 9
9 + 8
11 − 8
6 + 4
9 − 8
7 + 4
9 + 9
11 − 9
14 − 7
6 + 6
13 − 8
15 − 7
3 + 2
18 − 9
9 − 4
3 + 8

Name ______________________________ Two-digit addition without regrouping

Hot Dog Stop

Add.

Hoppy's
Hot Dogs

15 + 34 = ___ **A**	50 + 19 = ___ **Y**	73 + 21 = ___ **H**	24 + 23 = ___ **T**	31 + 66 = ___ **I**
40 + 45 = ___ **L**	17 + 11 = ___ **I**	34 + 24 = ___ **D**	48 + 31 = ___ **A**	28 + 10 = ___ **L**
32 + 12 = ___ **W**	65 + 22 = ___ **G**	83 + 16 = ___ **C**	56 + 33 = ___ **O**	42 + 25 = ___ **S**

Why did the kangaroo put hot sauce on his hot dog?

To solve the riddle, match the letters above to the numbered lines below.

Because __ __   __ __ __   __   __ __ __ __ __ __   __ __ __!

97 47   44 49 67   79   99 94 28 38 85 69   58 89 87

Locked Lockers

Add.
Color the key with the matching answer.

A. 36 + 5 Keys: 31, 41	B. 62 + 8 Keys: 70, 60	C. 49 + 22 Keys: 71, 81	D. 56 + 38 Keys: 85, 94
E. 75 + 15 Keys: 90, 80	F. 23 + 58 Keys: 75, 81	G. 27 + 27 Keys: 54, 40	H. 19 + 38 Keys: 47, 57
I. 88 + 8 Keys: 96, 80	J. 37 + 14 Keys: 43, 51	K. 43 + 49 Keys: 82, 92	L. 55 + 28 Keys: 83, 73

Name ____________________

Super Skaters

Subtract.
Help Sammy get to the skate park.
If the answer is **less than 50,** color the space orange.

		33 − 16	74 − 16
31 − 27	73 − 26	56 − 28	91 − 12
60 − 55	93 − 15	70 − 14	85 − 28
67 − 38	82 − 45		

Multiplication Readiness

Learning in a Flash

Provide multiple learning opportunities with these easy-to-use array flash cards. Place small stickers in rows and columns on an index card. Label the back of each card with its matching multiplication facts. Use the cards with the whole class as flash cards. After students are familiar with the cards, place them at a center. A student reviews the cards with a partner or independently. Then she flips the cards over to check her work.

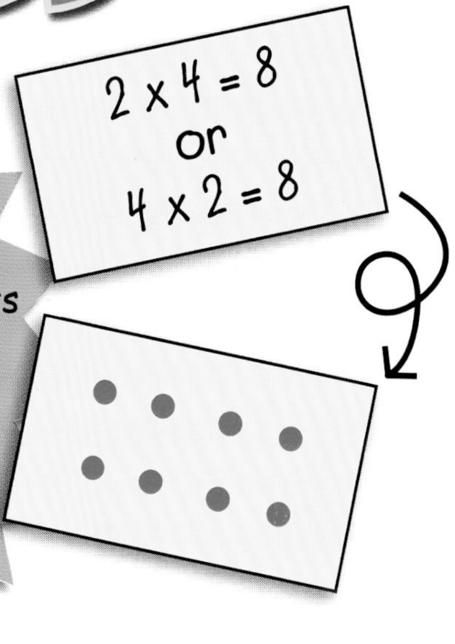
2 x 4 = 8
or
4 x 2 = 8

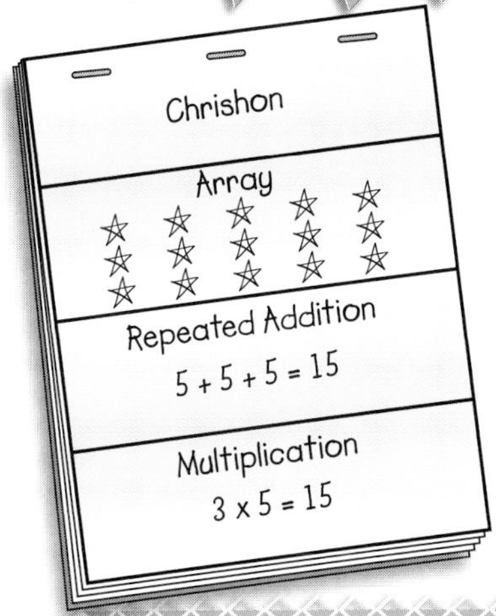
Chrishon
Array
Repeated Addition
5 + 5 + 5 = 15
Multiplication
3 x 5 = 15

Hip, Hip, Array!

Celebrate a greater understanding of arrays with this project. Have a child fold a sheet of paper in half vertically two times, making four equal rows. Next, he writes his name in the top section and labels the remaining rows as shown. He chooses a multiplication fact and draws its array in the second section. Then he writes the repeated addition sentence in the third section and the multiplication sentence in the last section. Bind the completed pages in a class book titled "Hip, Hip, Array!" and place it in your classroom library.

Neat to Repeat

Give students a hands-on understanding of the relationship between repeated addition and multiplication with this center activity. Choose a number between 1 and 9 and write it repeatedly on a supply of index cards. Add puff paint dots to match the number on each card. Allow the paint to dry; then place the cards in a resealable plastic bag. Repeat with different numbers and amounts of cards. Place the bags at a center with paper and pencils. A child chooses a bag and lays the cards in a row across her workspace. She uses the cards to write a repeated addition sentence and a matching multiplication sentence. Encourage the child to skip-count or count the dots to find the total if needed. She returns the cards to the bag, chooses another, and repeats the process.

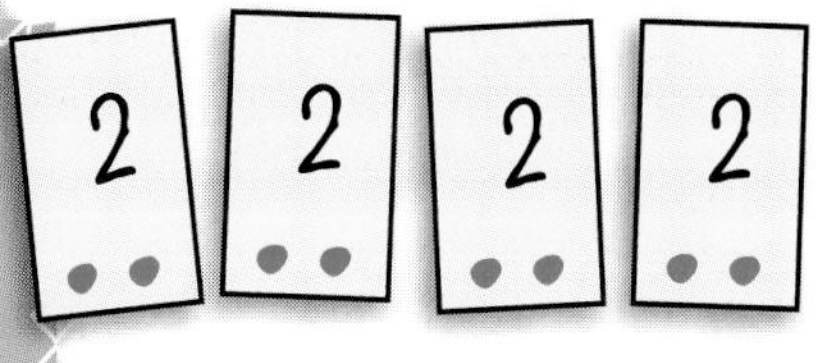
2
2
2
2

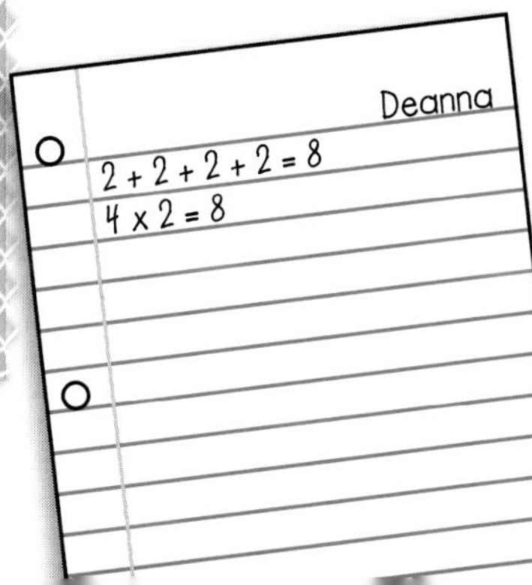
Deanna
2 + 2 + 2 + 2 = 8
4 x 2 = 8

Mat Work

Keep manipulative practice under control with this simple solution. Give each child two plastic six-pack rings and a paper cup full of cereal. Have each student model and solve a multiplication problem, using the rings to hold his sets of cereal. He draws the model and writes the multiplication problem on a sheet of paper. Then he returns the cereal to his cup before repeating the process with another problem.

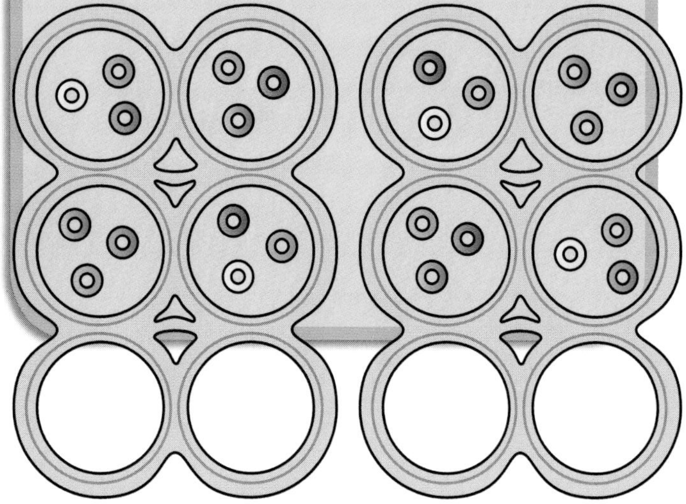

Take a Break

Break out your linking cubes to build students' understanding of multiplication strategies. Provide each child with a supply of cubes. Assign each cube a value, such as two, and ask students to link seven cubes. Guide them to understand that the cubes now represent 2 x 7 = 14. Next, have each student remove two cubes from the end of her link to make its own set; then ask if the total number of cubes has changed. Explain to students that adding the products of two smaller facts can help them solve problems with larger numbers. Demonstrate this and then have students use their cubes to explore other multiplication facts using this strategy.

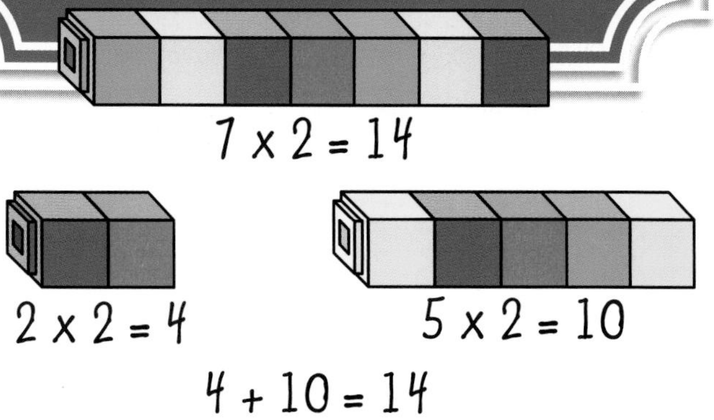
7 x 2 = 14
2 x 2 = 4
5 x 2 = 10
4 + 10 = 14

Under the Sea

Prepare a display by posting a sheet of blue bulletin board paper. Copy and cut out a supply of the sea patterns on page 121. Post one set of the same kind of item in a row (for example, four starfish). Next, skip count as a class by the number the item represents (5, 10, 15, 20). Then post facts under the pictures, as shown, for a visual reference. After students are familiar with a set, add another to the display. Review previous sets as well as those most recently posted and students will be familiar with their twos, fives, and tens facts in no time!

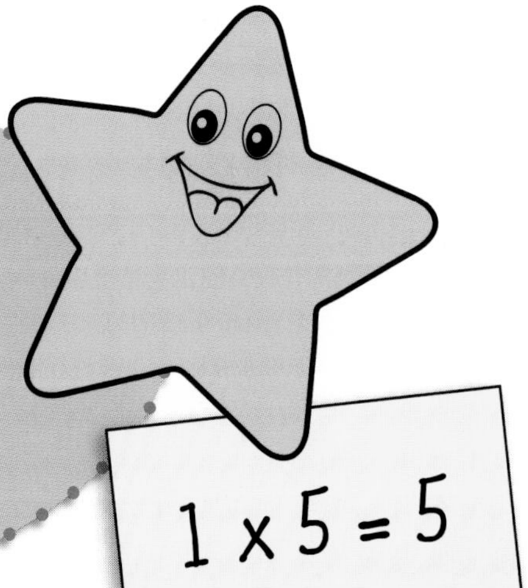
1 x 5 = 5

Check out the skill-building reproducible on page 122.

Sea Patterns

Use with "Under the Sea" on page 120.

twos

TEC61049

fives

TEC61049

tens

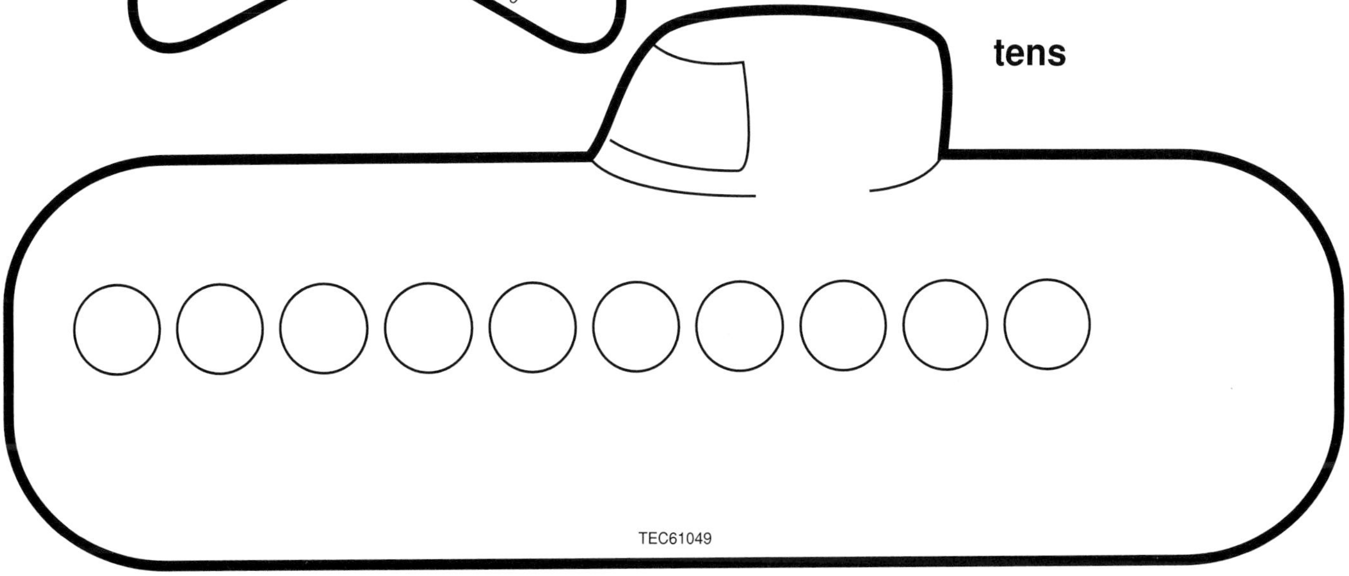
TEC61049

Name____

Shaping Up

Use a rubber band to make each shape below on the Geoboard.
Write a multiplication sentence to show your work.

A. Make two different rectangles with 12 pegs inside. _____ x _____ = 12 _____ x _____ = 12	B. Make a square with 16 pegs inside. _____ x _____ = 16 Make a rectangle with 16 pegs inside. _____ x _____ = 16
C. Make a square with 25 pegs inside. _____ x _____ = 25	D. Make two different rectangles with 24 pegs inside. _____ x _____ = 24 _____ x _____ = 24
E. Make a square with 36 pegs inside. _____ x _____ = 36 Make a rectangle with 36 pegs inside. _____ x _____ = 36	F. Make two different rectangles with 30 pegs inside. _____ x _____ = 30 _____ x _____ = 30

Note to the teacher: Make a class supply of this page. Place the copies at a center with a Geoboard and rubber bands. Have students work alone or with a partner to complete the activities.

Fractions

A Fraction Connection

Stock a center with linking cubes and drawing paper. In addition, program a set of index cards each with a different fraction such as 1/8, 3/8, 6/8, 1/4, 2/4, 1/3, and 1/2. Each visitor to the center chooses a card and then uses the linking cubes to model the fraction he has chosen. Next, he draws his model on his paper and labels the illustration as shown.

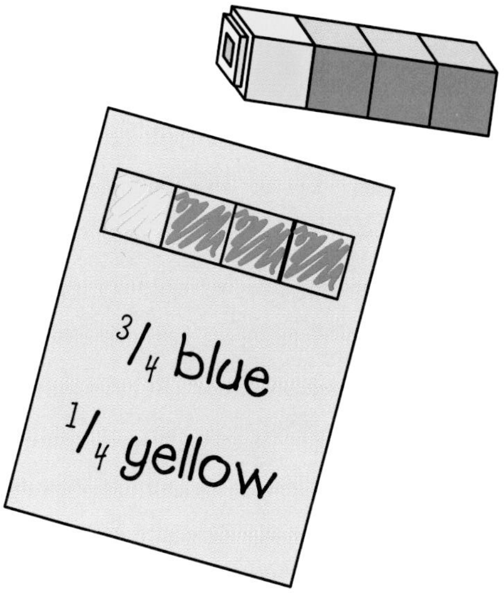
3/4 blue
1/4 yellow

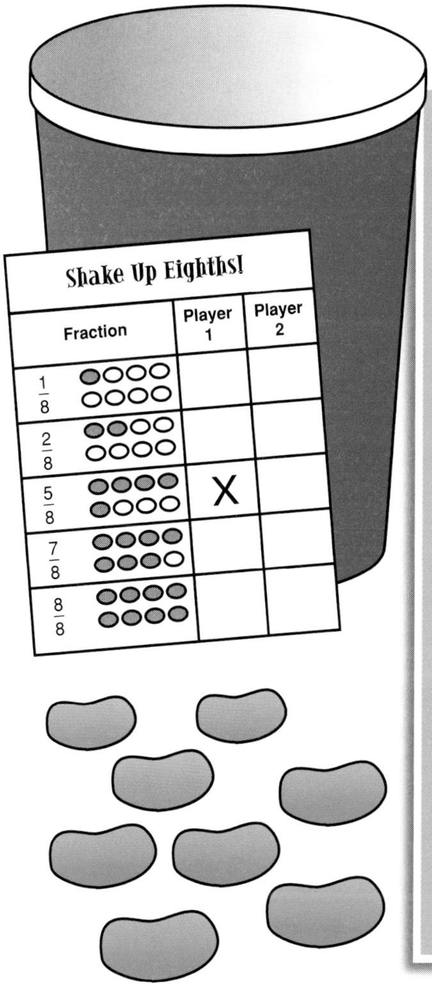
Shake Up Eighths!
Fraction
Player 1
Player 2
1/8
2/8
5/8
X
7/8
8/8

Shake-Up!

Give each pair of students the listed materials. Then guide the pair through the directions to play the game.

Materials for each pair: 8 dry lima beans (painted on one side), plastic cup, copy of the "Shake Up Eighths!" game card on page 125.

Directions for Each Pair:

1. Player 1 puts the beans in the cup. He shakes the beans and then pours them onto the playing surface. He looks at the beans to see whether he can make one of the fractions on the game card. If he can, he puts an X in the matching row and column and his turn is over. If he cannot, his turn is over.
2. Player 2 takes a turn in the same manner. If a player makes a fraction that he has already marked off, he does not make another mark and his turn is over.
3. Players continue taking turns until one player has made an X in all five squares in his column and is declared the winner.

Shake up the game by having students play with ten beans! Follow the directions above, but replace the "Shake Up Eighths!" game card with the "Shake Up Tenths!" game card also found on page 125.

Fraction Fishing

To prepare this center, place six red counters and six blue counters in a paper lunch sack. Place the sack at the center along with a copy of the spinner on page 125. A pair of students visits the center together. To begin, one partner uses a pencil and paper clip to spin the spinner and, without looking, fishes into the bag to remove the number of counters indicated on the spinner. He shows the counters to his partner and then gives the fractions for the counters he has pulled.

I pulled three-fifths red counters and two-fifths blue counters.

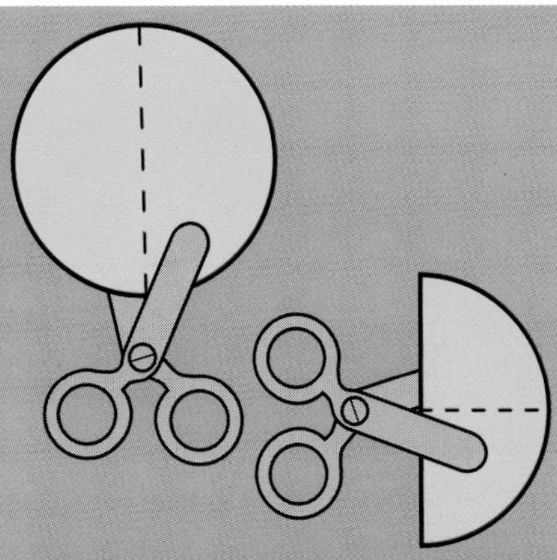

"Flowerful" Fractions

Give each student the materials listed below. Then guide her through the directions to create her own colorful, "flowerful" masterpiece!

Materials for each student: 4½" construction paper squares in assorted colors, 9" x 12" sheet of colorful construction paper, 12" x 18" sheet of light-colored construction paper, access to 4" circle templates, scissors

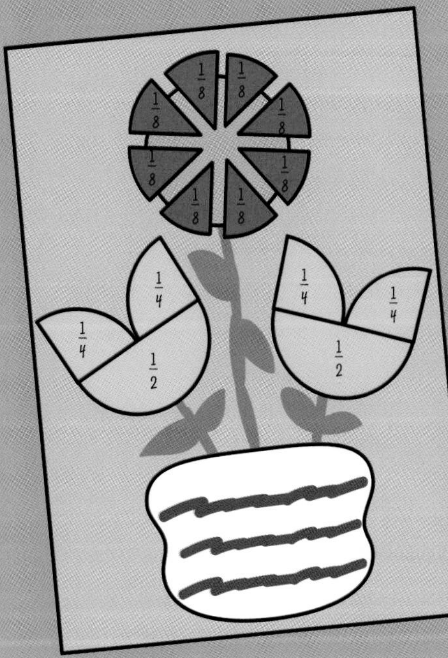

1/8
1/4
1/2

Directions for each student:

1. Use a template and scissors to make several circular cutouts from the construction paper squares.
2. **To make a tulip:** Fold one circle in half; then fold it in half again. Unfold the circle. Cut on one fold line so that the circle is cut in two halves. Fold one half in half and then cut it on the fold line. Glue the pieces so that they form a tulip as shown.
3. **To make a carnation:** Fold one circle in half three times. Unfold the circle and cut it on each fold line so that the circle is cut into eighths. Arrange the cut pieces on a whole circle so that they form a carnation as shown.
4. Cut a vase out of construction paper and glue it onto the paper. Glue the flowers onto the paper. Use crayons to label each piece of each flower with its fractional part. Then use crayons to add details to the picture.

Check out the skill-building reproducible on page 126.

Game Cards

Use with "Shake-Up!" on page 123.

Shake Up Eighths!		
Fraction	**Player 1**	**Player 2**
$\frac{1}{8}$		
$\frac{2}{8}$		
$\frac{5}{8}$		
$\frac{7}{8}$		
$\frac{8}{8}$		

Shake Up Tenths!		
Fraction	**Player 1**	**Player 2**
$\frac{1}{10}$		
$\frac{3}{10}$		
$\frac{4}{10}$		
$\frac{7}{10}$		
$\frac{9}{10}$		

Spinner Pattern

Use with "Fraction Fishing" on page 124.

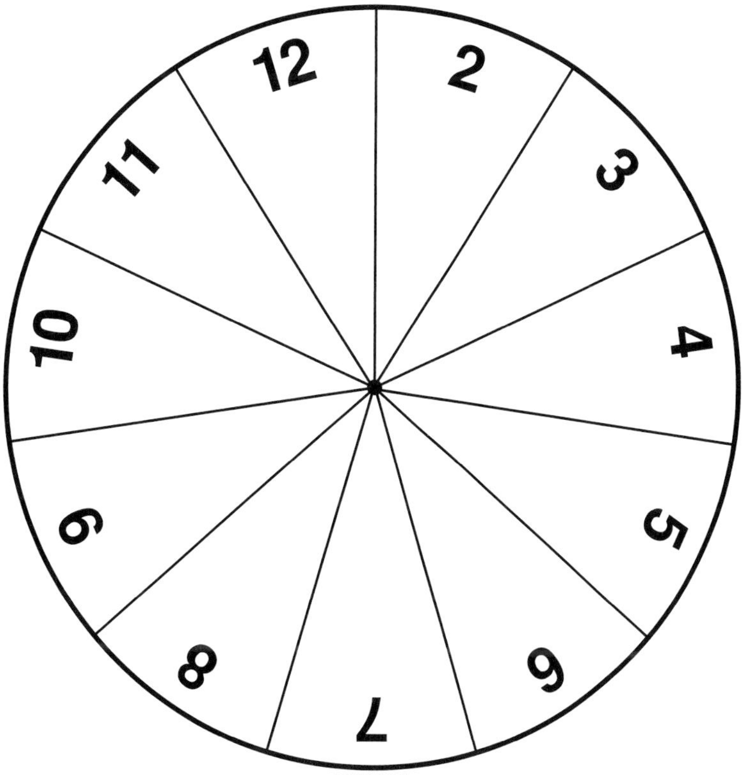
12
2
3
4
5
6
7
8
9
10
11

TEC61049

Name ______________________________

Ice Cream by the Scoop

Write a matching fraction on each line.
The first one has been done for you.

A.

$\frac{1}{3}$ = shaded

$\frac{2}{3}$ = not shaded

B.

______ = shaded

______ = not shaded

C.

______ = shaded

______ = not shaded

D.

______ = shaded

______ = not shaded

E.

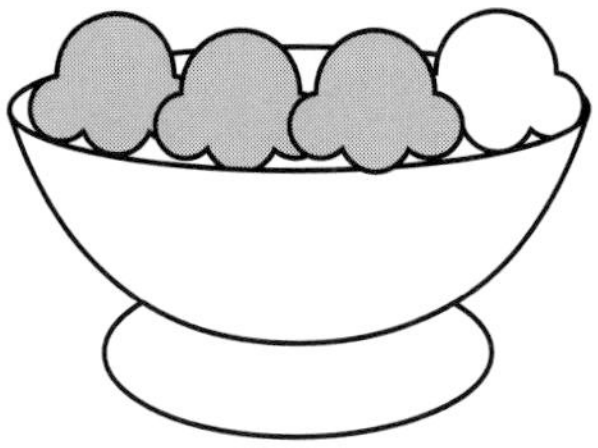

______ = shaded

______ = not shaded

F.

______ = shaded

______ = not shaded

G.

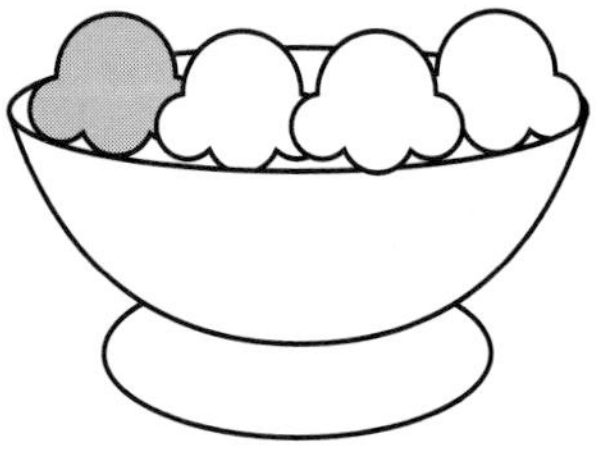

______ = shaded

______ = not shaded

H.

______ = shaded

______ = not shaded

I.

______ = shaded

______ = not shaded

MEASUREMENT

Nonstandard Measurements

To introduce the concept of measurement, have each student choose a nonstandard unit of measure from objects available in the classroom. Instruct him to predict the width of his desk in terms of the size of the object. How many board erasers would fit across his desk? How many crayons? Demonstrate how to measure with each object by placing it flush against one side of the desk, making an erasable mark where the end of the object rests, and then moving the object so that it is flush with the mark. Continue moving the object until it has spanned the width of the desktop. Have him count the number of times the object was placed on his desk; then have him compare the results with his predictions. Ask each student to share his results. Did everyone get the same answer? Guide students to decide whether this is a good way for people to take measurements. Then try the activity at the right to reinforce the need for standard units of measure.

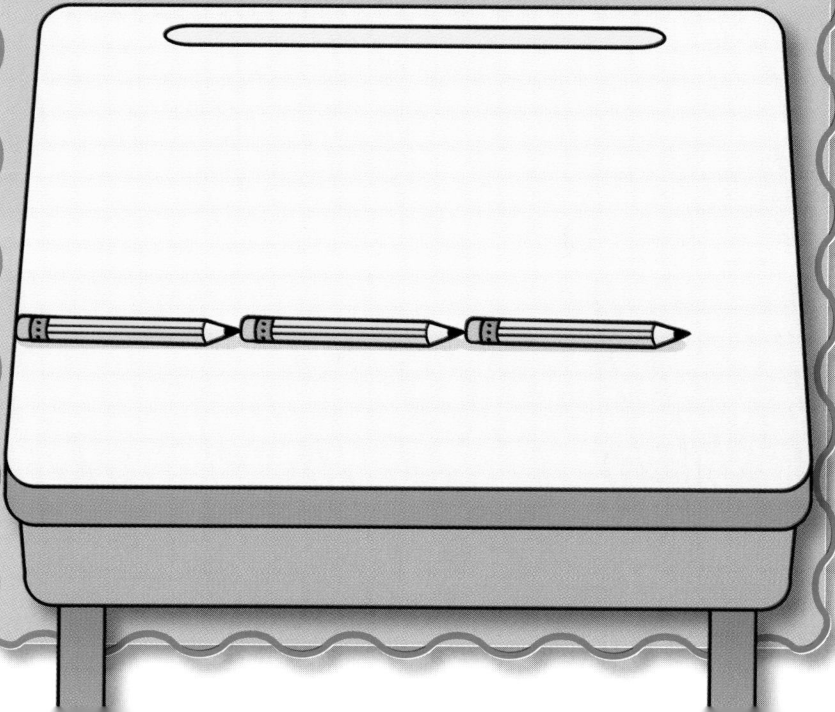

Get in Step With Measurement

How accurate can we be using nonstandard units of measure? Have your students find out as they get in step with this activity. Have each student stand with her back against one wall in the hallway. Tell her to walk across the width of the hall heel to toe, using her footsteps as a unit of measure. Remind each student to count silently as she measures. When all students have completed the activity, compare their results. Ask students to determine why there are so many different answers; then discuss the need for a standard unit of measure. Give a copy of the reproducible on page 133 to each student, and have her practice measuring and drawing line segments with the ruler cutout included on the page. If desired, laminate each student's ruler and save it for use with additional measurement activities. When it comes to measurement, your students will be right in step!

Measurement Masterpieces

Use measurement and addition to inspire works of art in your classroom. To prepare for this art project, have students use rulers and scissors to cut a supply of construction paper strips into a variety of lengths ranging from one to eight inches. Instruct each student to select several construction paper strips and measure each one with a ruler, writing the length on the strip. Next, have him add the lengths of his pieces. After he determines the total length, have the student glue his pieces onto his construction paper to make a picture or design. To complete the project, the student names his masterpiece with a title that incorporates the total length of his pieces. Display the finished projects on a bulletin board titled "Measurement Masterpieces."

The 30-Inch House
3
6
6
5
5
5
by Kyle
3
3
3
1
3
3
3
5
The 24-Inch Flower
by Aiden

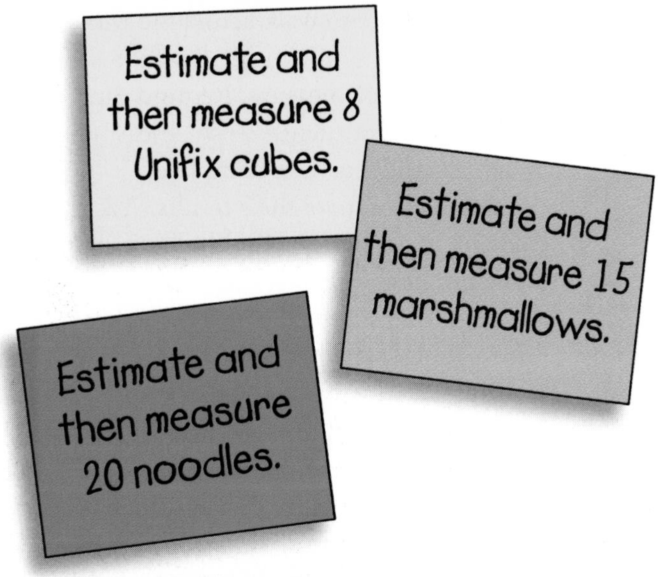
Estimate and then measure 8 Unifix cubes.
Estimate and then measure 15 marshmallows.
Estimate and then measure 20 noodles.

Measurement Task Cards

This learning-center activity improves both estimation and measurement skills. Program task cards with directions for estimating the lengths of a desired number of manipulatives, such as dried beans, toothpicks, cotton balls, and paper clips. Place the task cards, the manipulatives, and a ruler at a center. A student reads a task card and selects the specified number of manipulatives. Then he lines up the manipulatives end to end and estimates their length. To check his answer, he measures the length with the ruler. Add new manipulatives and task cards to the center periodically to promote practice of these important skills.

On the Lookout for Lengths

Send students on a classroom scavenger hunt by challenging them to find objects of specific lengths. Place students in small groups and assign each group a different length from 1 to 12 inches. Supply each student with a ruler; then send him off in search of objects of his designated length. After a specified time period, have each student group meet and discuss its findings. Then provide materials for the group to use to create a poster illustrating the objects it found. Display the posters in the hallway with the title "Look How Our Room Measures Up!"

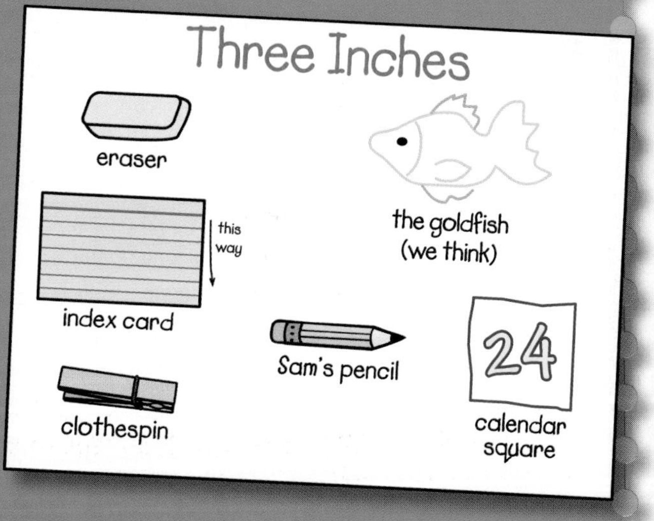
Three Inches
eraser
the goldfish (we think)
this way
index card
Sam's pencil
24
clothespin
calendar square

Time to Take a Card!

Prepare a two-player game by making two copies of the cards on page 131. Program each digital clock with a different time. Next, program the analog clocks with times that match the digital clocks. Cut apart the cards.

To play the game, stack the cards facedown in the center of the playing surface. Each player draws seven cards, removes any matching pairs from his hand, and places them faceup in front of him. Then Player 1 asks Player 2 for a card that matches one in his hand. If Player 2 has the cards, she gives it to Player 1. Player 1 places the matching pair in front of him and his turn is over. If Player 2 does not have the card, she says, "Time to take a card!" and Player 1 draws a card from the pile. If he draws the card he asked for, he removes the matching pair from his hand and his turn is over. If he does not get the card he asked for, he adds the card to his hand and his turn is over. Play continues until there are no more cards in the draw deck. The player with more matches wins.

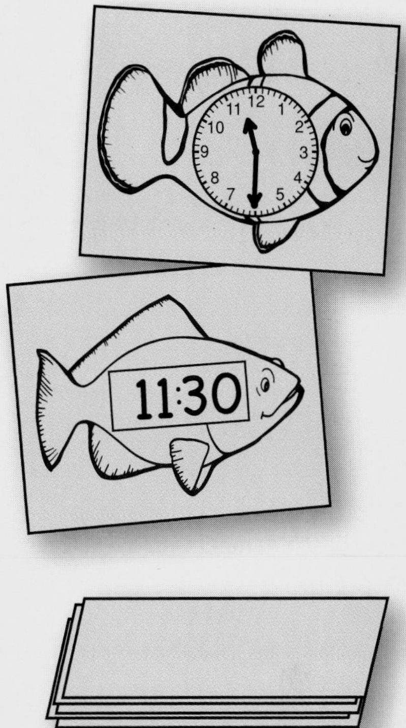
11:30

1. 8:30
2. 10:00
3.
4.
5.
6.
7.
8.
9.
10.

What Time Is It?

Have students practice their time-telling skills throughout the day with this simple activity. At the beginning of the day, have each student number a piece of paper from 1 to 10. At ten various hour and half-hour times throughout the day, ask, "What time is it?" Instruct students to stop what they are doing and write the time on their papers, being sure to record the times yourself. After the tenth time check, announce the list of times that should be listed on students' papers. How's that for a "time-ly" activity?

Rockin' Around the Clock

For a rockin' review of time-telling skills, put the practice to music! Find an upbeat recording, such as "Rock Around the Clock" by Bill Haley and the Comets. Give a manipulative clock face to each student. (Or make a class set of clocks with the patterns provided on page 132.) To begin, play the music for 15 to 20 seconds; then turn it off and announce a time for students to display on their clocks for your approval. A quick glance can assess students' efforts. Repeat the activity as time allows. Collect the clocks and keep them for students to use during the next rockin' review.

Making Sense of Temperature

Give each child a copy of the thermometer pattern on the bottom of page 132 and a 1" x 8" strip of red construction paper. Direct the child to cut out the thermometer. Next, help her carefully cut a slit on the pattern where indicated. Then show her how to slip her red strip through the slit as shown.

Ask students questions such as those listed below. After each question, instruct each student to place her thermometer on her desk, slide the strip to the appropriate temperature, and then hold the thermometer up to display her answer.

- Which temperature would be best for a day at the beach, 86°F or 41°F?
- Which temperature would be best for building a snow fort, 91°F or 38°F?
- Which temperature would be best for a football game, 72°F or 11°F?

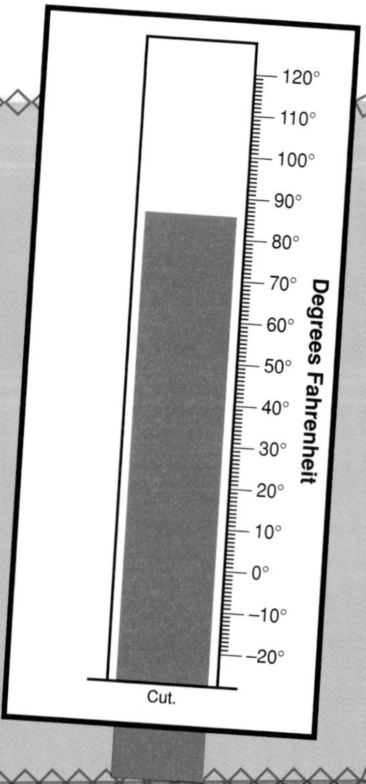
120°
110°
100°
90°
80°
70°
60°
50°
40°
30°
20°
10°
0°
–10°
–20°
Degrees Fahrenheit
Cut.

Cup for Cup

To prepare this center, fill a variety of lidded containers that are both smaller and larger than one cup of popcorn kernels. Label each container with a different letter and place them at a center along with an empty bowl, a measuring cup, and paper. At the center, a student draws a chart as shown. He examines the first container, decides whether he thinks it is larger or smaller than one cup, and records his guess in the first column. Next, he uses the measuring cup and bowl to measure the popcorn. He records the actual measurement and returns the popcorn to the original container. Have the child repeat the steps for each remaining container.

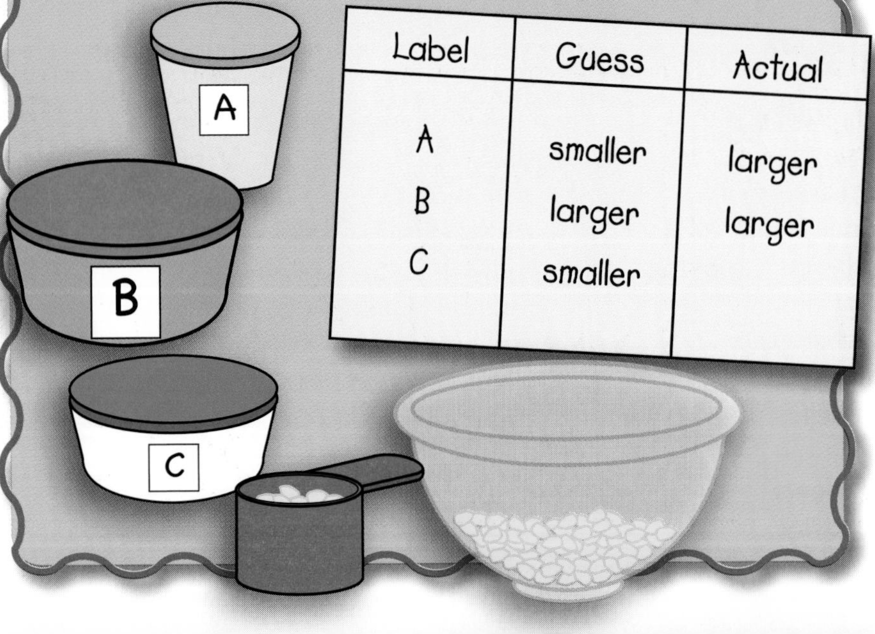
A
B
C

Label	Guess	Actual
A	smaller	larger
B	larger	larger
C	smaller	

Weighty Guesses

Gather a variety of common objects with different weights. Hold up an object and have each child write an estimate of the object's weight on a scrap piece of paper. Next, have a student volunteer weigh the object. Lead students in a discussion of their predictions and the actual results. Repeat the process with each of the remaining objects. With each object, students' guesses—and their understanding of weight—will become more on target!

Playing Cards

Use with "Time to Take a Card!" on page 129.

12
1
2
3
4
5
6
7
8
9
10
11
TEC61049

Clock Pattern
Use with "Rockin' Around the Clock" on page 129.

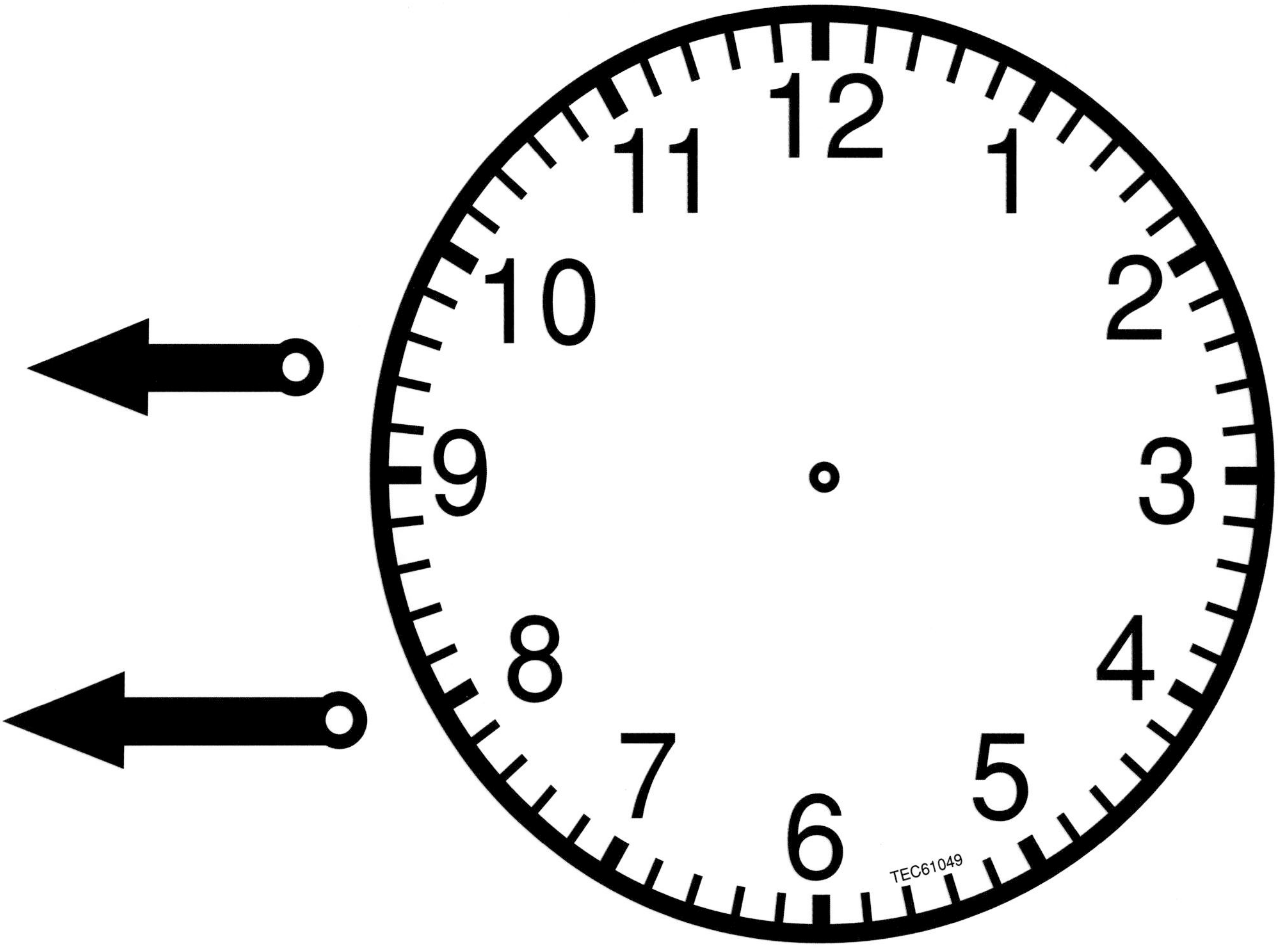
12
1
2
3
4
5
6
7
8
9
10
11
TEC61049

Thermometer Pattern
Use with "Making Sense of Temperature" on page 130.

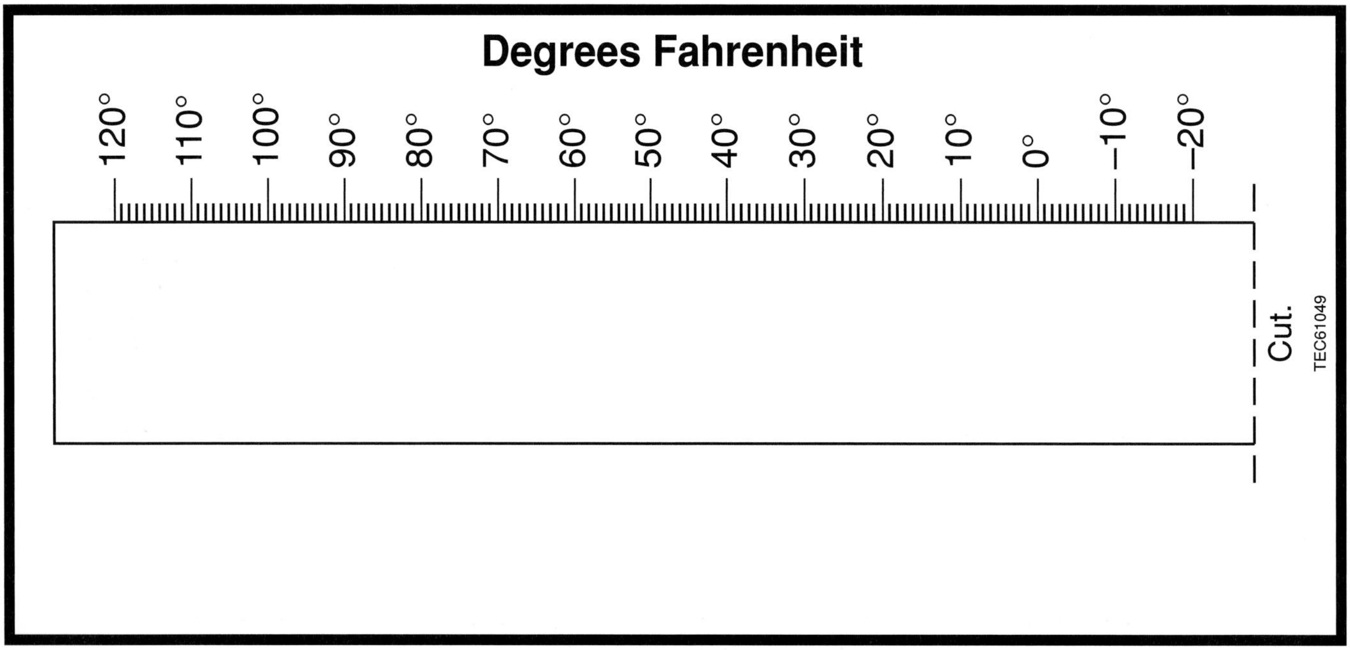
Degrees Fahrenheit
120°
110°
100°
90°
80°
70°
60°
50°
40°
30°
20°
10°
0°
–10°
–20°
Cut.
TEC61049

Name ____________________

Ready, Set, Measure!

Use the ruler to measure each line segment.
Then, under each segment, draw a line one inch longer than the segment.

1.  _______ inch(es)

2. 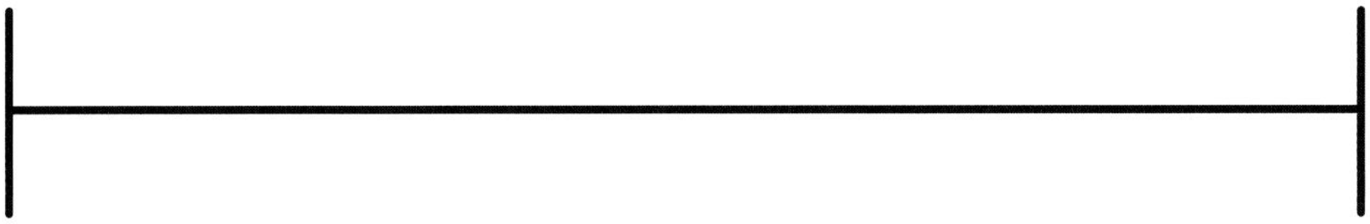 _______ inch(es)

3.  _______ inch(es)

4.  _______ inch(es)

5.  _______ inch(es)

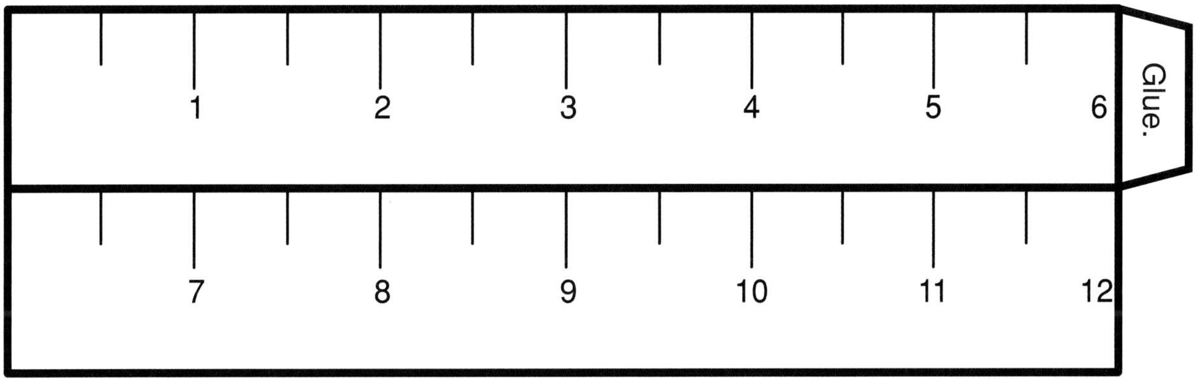
1
2
3
4
5
6
Glue.
7
8
9
10
11
12

Note to the teacher: Use with “Get in Step With Measurement” on page 127.

Using Scales at School

Cut apart the cards below.
Decide whether it would be easier to measure each item in ounces or pounds.
Glue each item in the matching box.

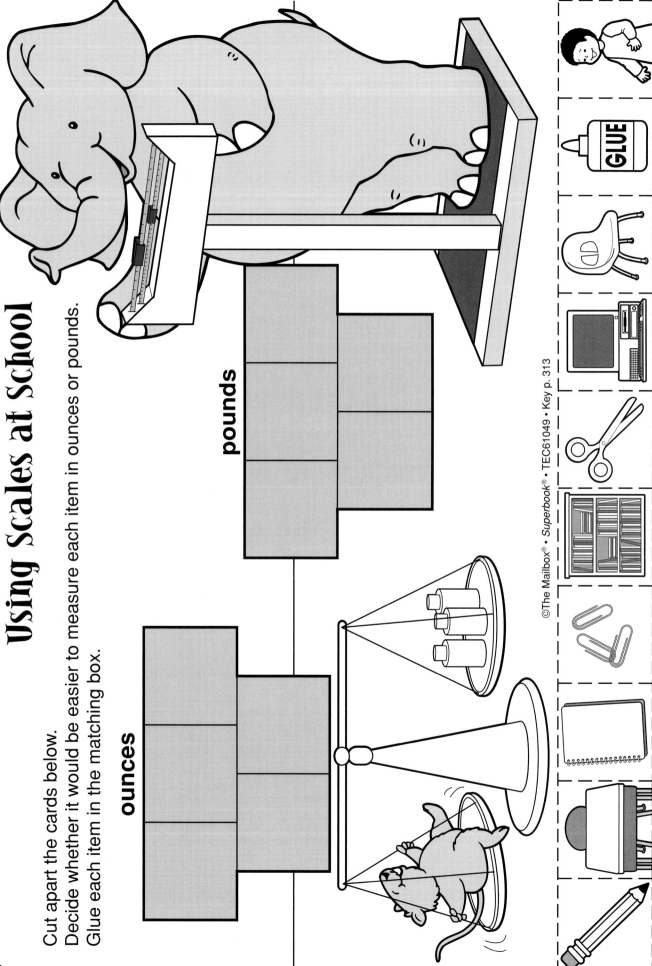

ounces

pounds

GLUE

Geometry

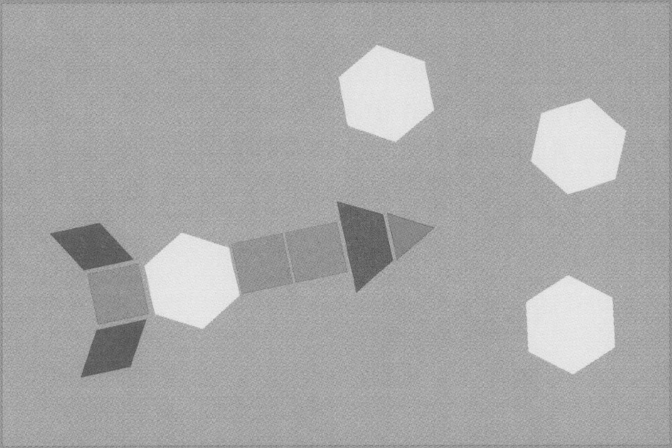

Shapely Designs

Provide each student with a copy of page 138. Review the name and attributes of each shape; then direct students to color and cut out the pieces. Next, have each student glue the shapes onto a sheet of construction paper to create a picture or design. If desired, extend the lesson by having each student write a story about her completed project incorporating the shapes into the story.

Shape Scavenger Hunt

Review with your class the names and attributes of several shapes; then lead your class on a walk around the school grounds in search of objects that feature these different shapes. Record the objects your students observe on separate cards. After you return to the classroom, post the cards on a bulletin board. Next, enlist students' help in creating shape categories for the objects on the list. Write each category on a strip of paper and post it on the board. Finally, have student volunteers move the cards under the appropriate categories.

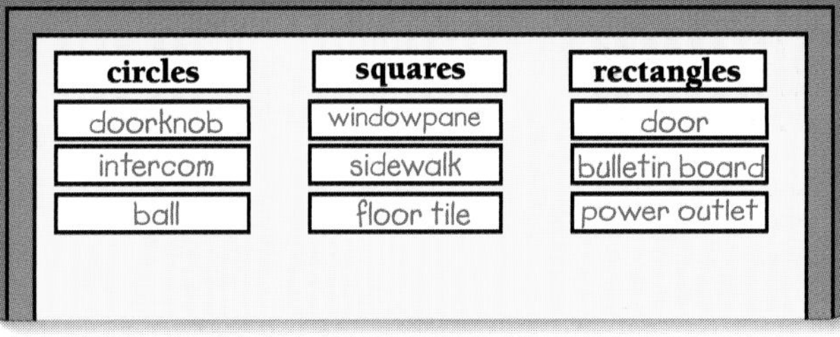
circles
doorknob
intercom
ball
squares
windowpane
sidewalk
floor tile
rectangles
door
bulletin board
power outlet

Small-Group Organizing Tip

Reinforce congruent figures by using them as a means of dividing students into small groups. Create a set of construction paper congruent figures for the number of students you want in each group. Place the figures in a bag; then have each student draw one. Have all students holding congruent figures work together for the group activity.

Shaping Up With Symmetry

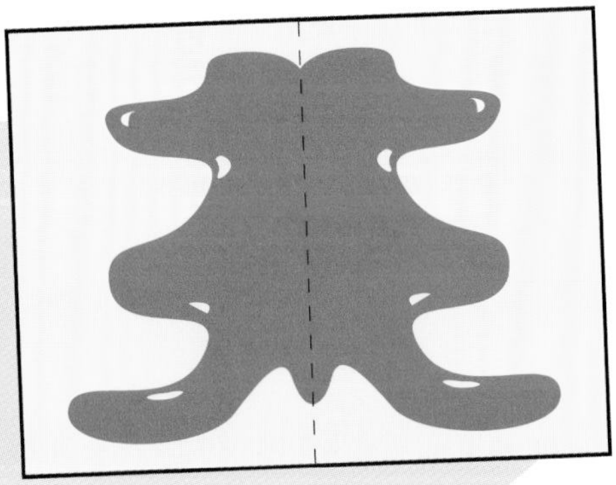

To introduce the concept of symmetrical figures, have students use tempera paint to create symmetrical shapes of their own. To begin, have each student fold a sheet of construction paper in half and reopen it. Then pour a small amount of tempera paint onto one half of the folded paper. Tell her to gently refold the paper and press down on the top half of the paper, spreading the paint between the two sheets. Have students unfold their papers and examine the resulting symmetrical figures, taking note of how the right and left sides of the figures are mirror images of each other. Set the projects aside to dry; then bind the pages into a class book and place it in the classroom library.

Solid-Figure Show-and-Tell

Enhance a study of solid shapes by presenting students with a homework challenge. Ask them to find items at home with each of these solid shapes: a pyramid, a cone, a cylinder, a cube, a rectangular prism, and a sphere. After students bring the objects to school, provide time for them to share the objects. Next, divide students into small groups, and have each group place its objects on a separate table. Then have the group sort the objects according to their shapes. After each group finishes sorting, have students rotate clockwise to other tables to observe the work of other groups.

Celebrate With Shapes

Hold a special snack celebration during your study of shapes. Send a note home prior to the event asking parents to supply snack foods that come in the following shapes: circles, squares, rectangles, triangles, and any other shapes you have studied. The day of the event, arrange the snacks on a large table. Have students form a line near the table; then give a plate and a napkin to each student. A student fills his plate with foods from the table, identifying the shape of each treat before he puts it on his plate. What a tasty way to reinforce shape recognition!

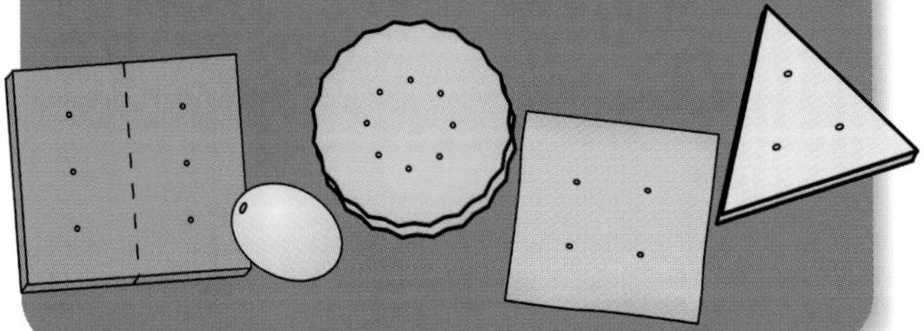

Take Sides!

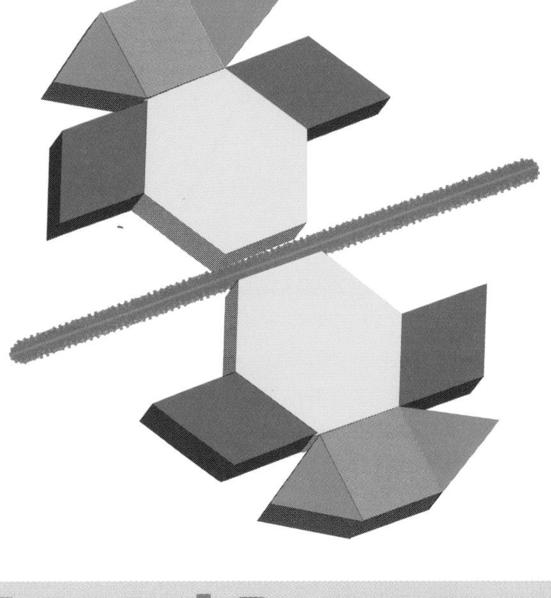

Give each pair of students a supply of pattern blocks and a pipe cleaner. The partners sit side by side with the pipe cleaner positioned vertically on the desk in front of them. One partner selects a pattern block and places it beside the pipe cleaner. The other child places a similar block in the same position on her side of the pipe cleaner as shown. After students have taken several turns in this manner, have them stop working. Lead them in a discussion of the design they have created. Guide them to conclude that they have created a design that is symmetrical. If desired, challenge students to carefully remove the pipe cleaner and then reposition it below the design. Then have them use the pipe cleaner as a new line of symmetry as they create a new design.

Journal

Shapely Journal Prompts

- Imagine that you are a square and it's your job to write a poem for a second-grade classroom. You'll want to tell the students what makes you different from other shapes. You also need to let the second graders know what makes you special.
- You've just been appointed to the Shape Police Squad! On your first day at work, one of the shapes is missing! You need to write an advertisement to let people know what to look for. Tell them how this shape is different from the others. Tell them where they might be able to find this shape. You can draw pictures of this shape to help people find it.
- Pretend that you are a circle. Write to tell all of the ways you are different from a triangle. Be sure to tell all of the things you can do that a triangle can't. Where will people use circles that they can't use triangles?

Matchup Game

For this partner game, program ten pairs of index cards, each with the same congruent shape. The partners arrange the cards facedown in rows on a playing surface. One partner takes a turn by selecting two cards and turning them over. If the revealed shapes are congruent, the student keeps the cards and takes another turn. If the shapes are not congruent, he replaces the cards and his turn is over. His partner takes a turn in the same manner. Play continues until all of the cards have been matched. Players count their matches, and the player with more pairs is declared the winner.

Check out the skill-building reproducibles on pages 139–140.

Shape Patterns

Use with “Shapely Designs” on page 135.

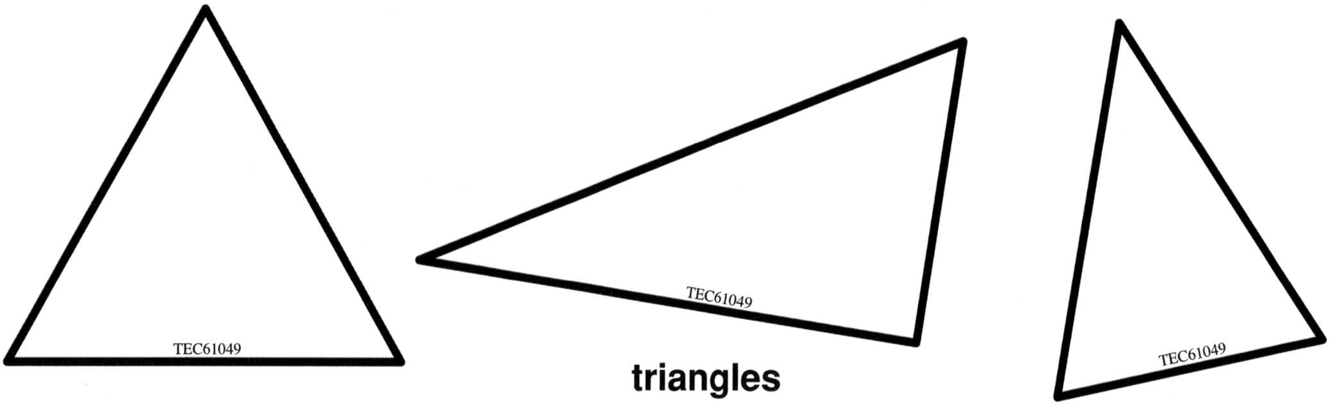
TEC61049
TEC61049
TEC61049

triangles

TEC61049

square

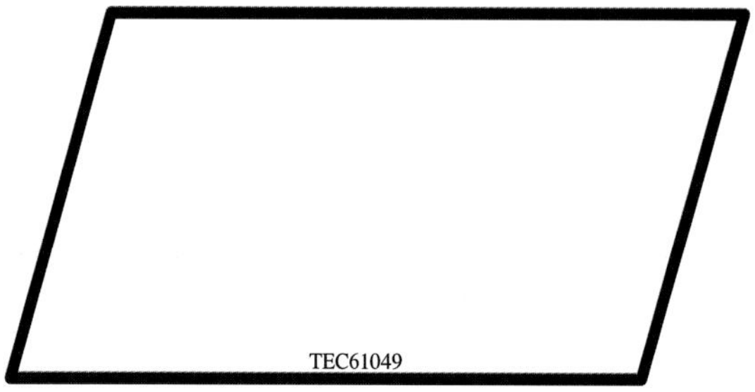
TEC61049

parallelogram

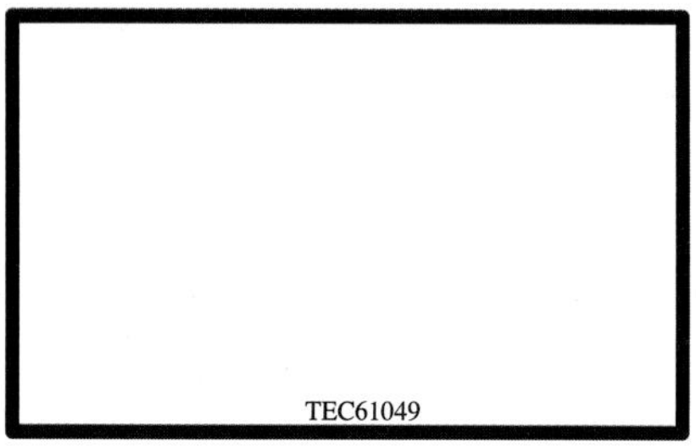
TEC61049

rectangle

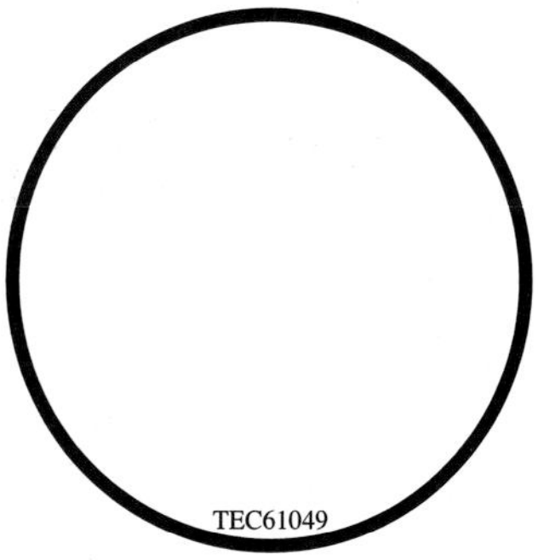
TEC61049

circle

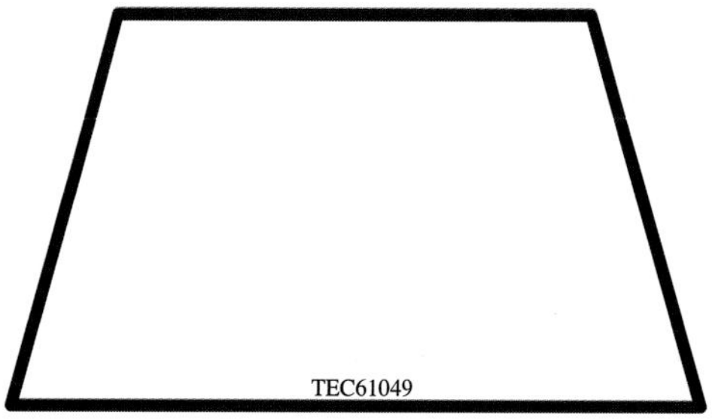
TEC61049

trapezoid

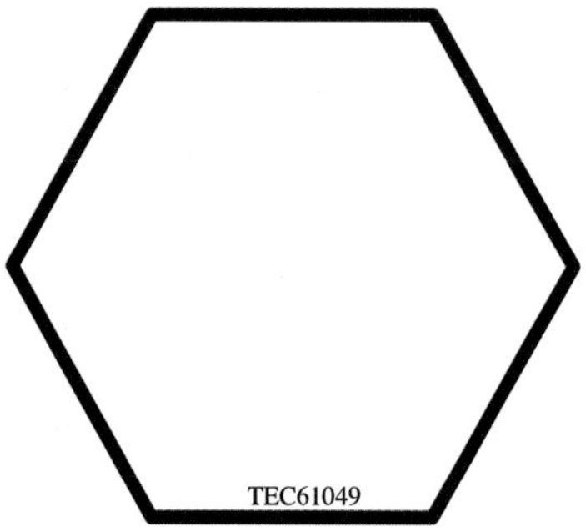
TEC61049

hexagon

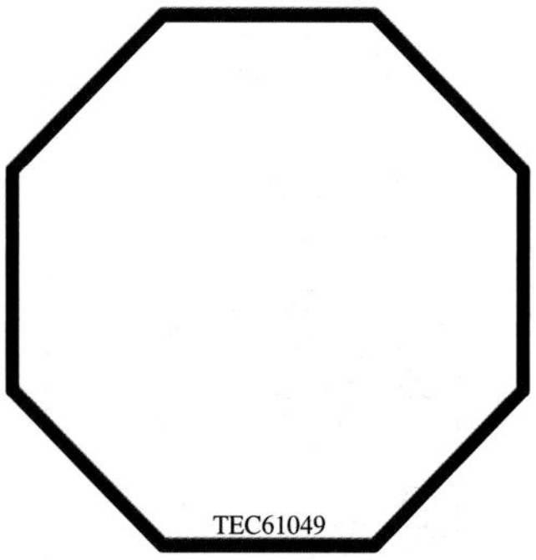
TEC61049

octagon

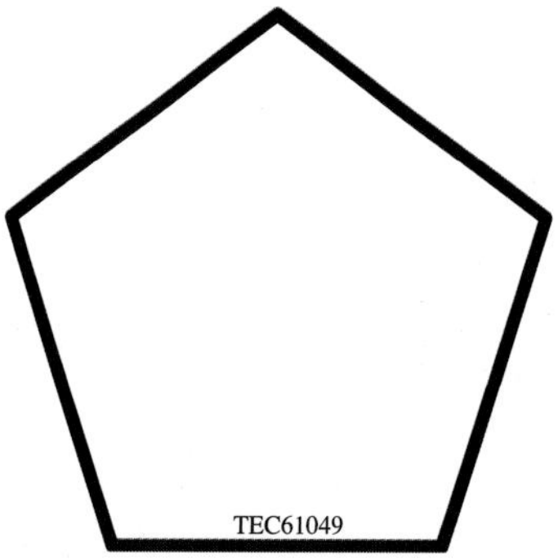
TEC61049

pentagon

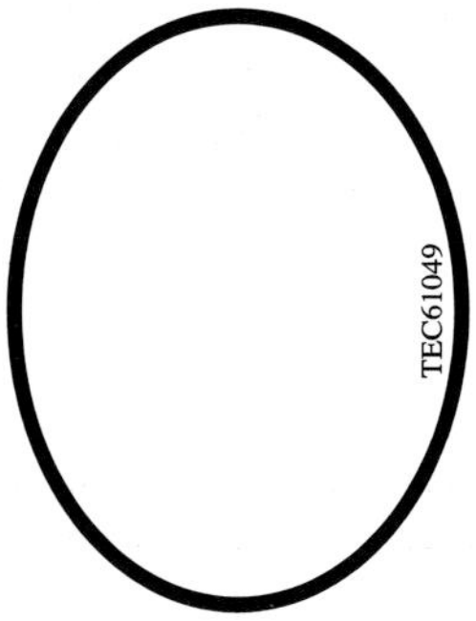
TEC61049

oval

Name ______________________________

Searching for Shapes

Cut apart the cards below.
Glue each one next to the matching shape.

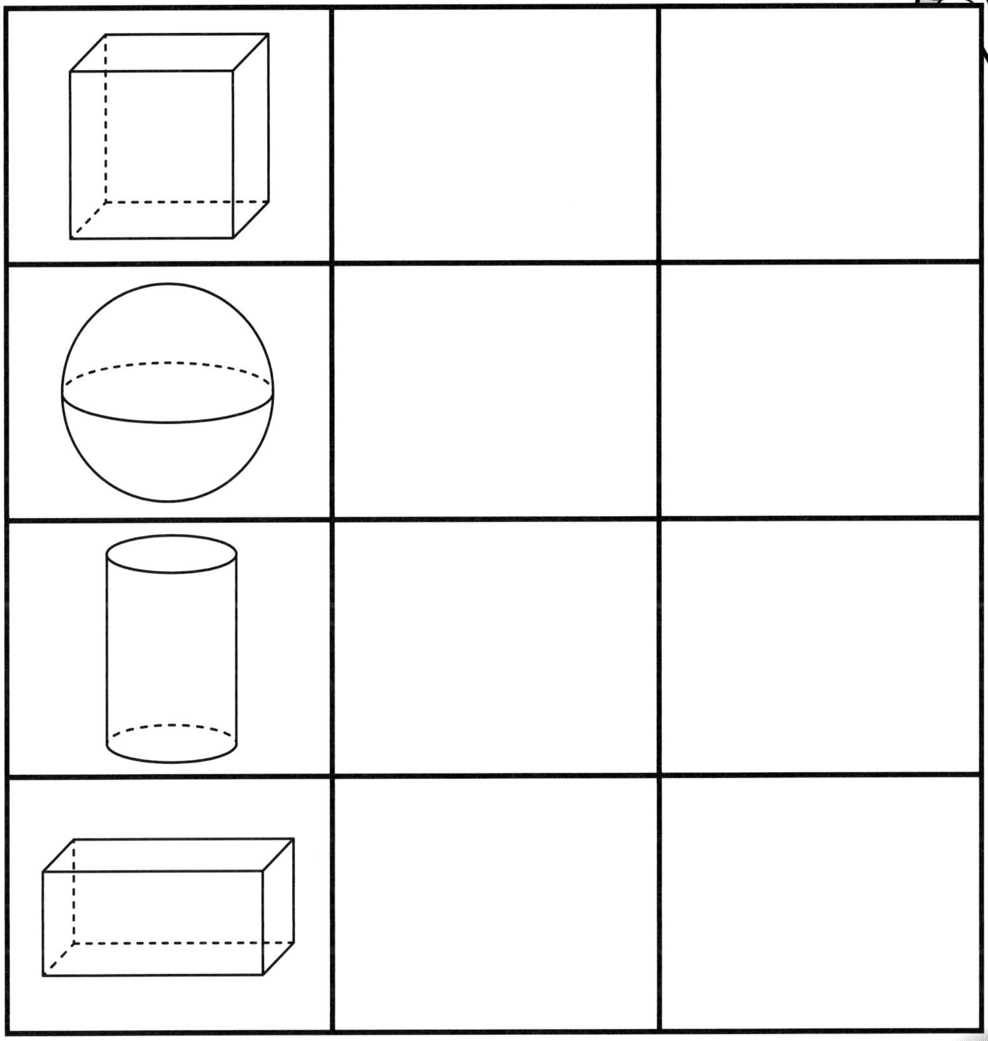

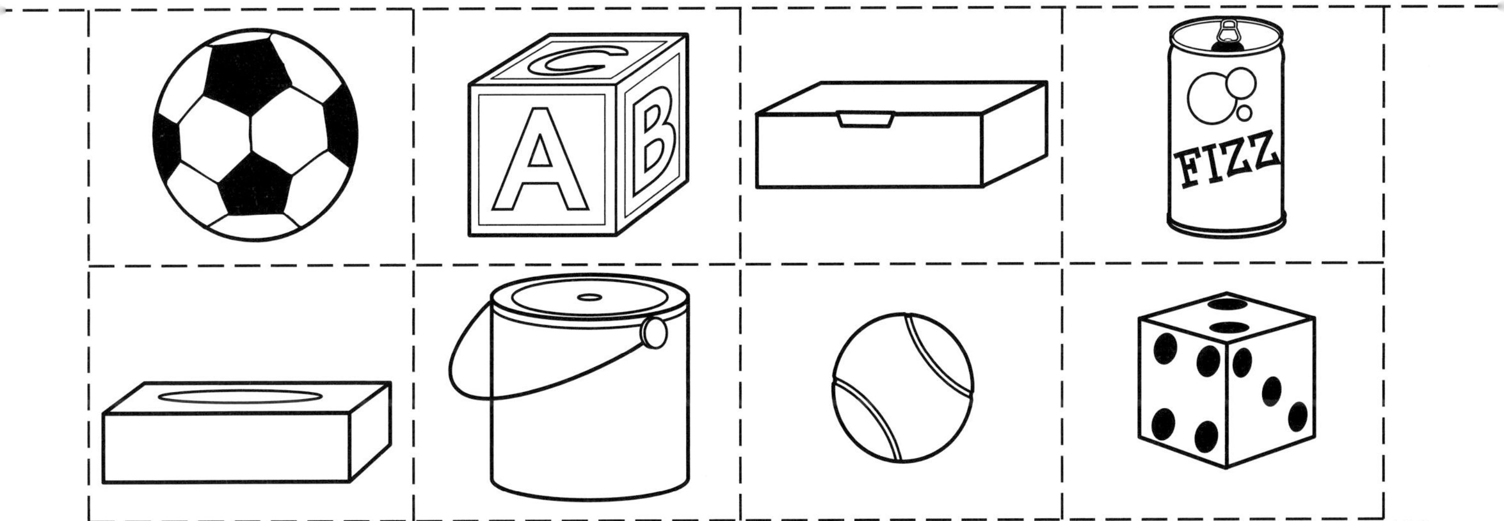
A
B
C
FIZZ

Name ______________________________

Shapely Riddles

Write the name of each shape.
Use the clues to help you.

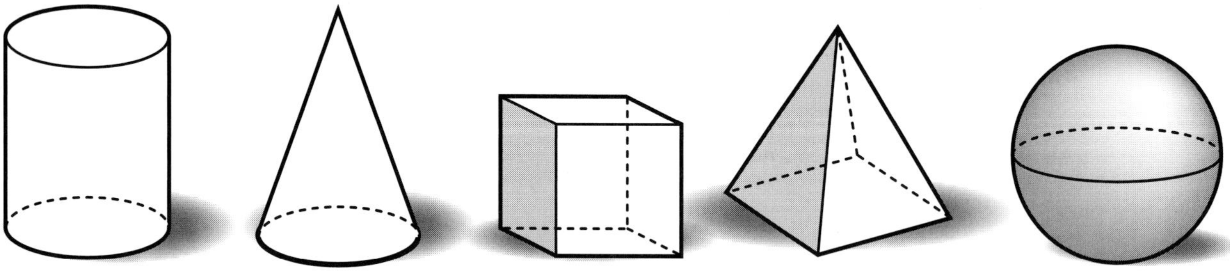

cylinder cone cube pyramid sphere

1. I have 6 faces.
   I have 8 corners.
   I can be stacked.
   ____

2. I have 0 faces.
   I have 0 corners.
   I cannot be stacked.
   ____

3. I have 5 faces.
   I have 5 corners.
   I cannot be stacked.
   ____

4. I have 2 faces.
   I have 0 corners.
   I can be stacked.
   ____

5. I have 1 face.
   I have 0 corners.
   I cannot be stacked.
   ____

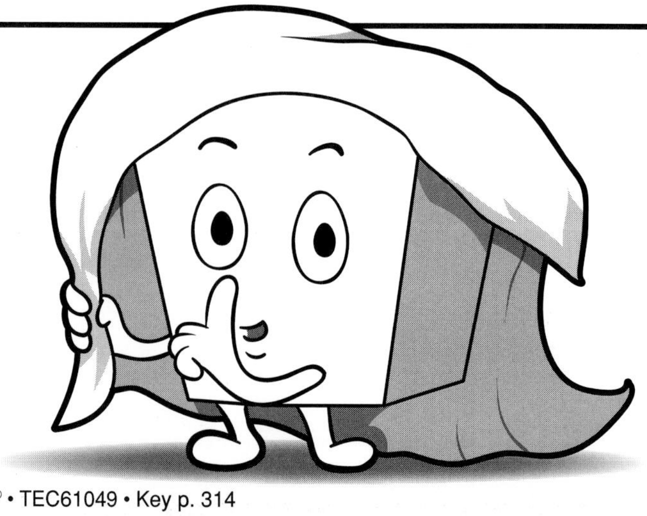

Graphing and Probability

Use Your Noodle!

Fill a class supply of resealable plastic bags with an assortment of dried pasta pieces. Give a bag and a copy of the bar graph on page 143 to each student. Have each student sort his pasta by shape and then glue a different shape under each column at the base of the graph. Next have him record his results by coloring the appropriate number of squares in each column. Mount the completed graphs on a bulletin board; then have students glue pasta pieces to a precut border. Staple the border to the board and add the title "Now That's What We Call Using Our Noodles!" **Bar graphs**

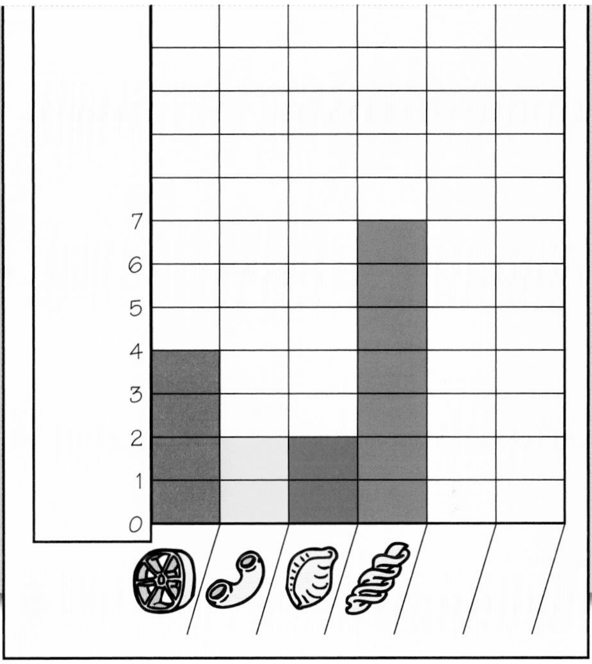
7
6
5
4
3
2
1
0

Spin-a-Graph

Make a spinner by dividing a paper plate into four sections, coloring each section a different color. Use a brad fastener to attach a tagboard arrow to the center of the plate. Give a copy of the bar graph on page 143 to each student. Instruct each student to label the columns of his bar graph to correspond with the colors used on the spinner. Next, have a student volunteer come to the front of the room and spin the spinner. Announce the result of the spin and have each student color a square in the corresponding column on his graph. Repeat the activity until all students have had a chance to spin the spinner. Then discuss the results of the completed graph by asking questions such as those below. **Bar graphs**

- Which column has the most colored squares?
- Which column has the fewest colored squares?
- How many colored squares are in the first column?
- How many colored squares are in the second and third columns combined?
- How many more colored squares are in the highest column than in the lowest column?
- How many colored squares are in the highest and lowest columns combined?
- Order the columns from highest to lowest.
- How many colored squares are represented on the graph in all?

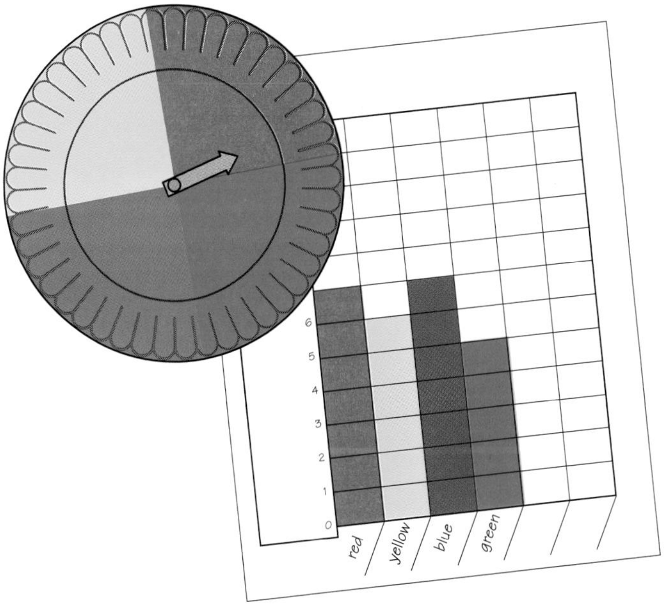
6
5
4
3
2
1
0
red
yellow
blue
green

Graphs in a Jar

This unique approach to graphing will also reinforce measurement skills. Select several identical clear, empty jars. Pose a question to the class, such as "What is your favorite school subject?" Label each jar with a corresponding category. Have each student input his data by measuring a designated amount of water and pouring it into the correct jar. After each child has added his data, have the class observe the water level in each jar to determine which categories have the most and least water. Enlist students' help in arranging the jars from least amount of water to greatest amount. Then encourage students to make statements about the results, such as "More people prefer math than prefer spelling" and "The same number of people enjoy reading and science." **Graphs**

math
reading
science
social studies

Hieroglyphic Graphs

A hieroglyphic graph, or "glyph," is a form of picture writing that conveys information. To create a glyph, collect data for a predetermined topic and create a legend to represent each component of information. Have your class create the clown glyph outlined at the right with information about themselves. **Glyphs**

CLOWN GLYPH

red nose—I am a girl.
blue nose—I am a boy.

yellow hat—I am an only child.
green hat—I have at least one brother or sister.

dots on hat—I have always lived in this state.
stripes on hat—I have lived outside this state.

freckles—I own a pet.
no freckles—I do not own a pet.

curly hair—I ride the bus.
straight hair—I do not ride the bus.

Fruit Salad

On the board, list the words *certain, likely, unlikely,* and *impossible.* Give each student a copy of page 144 and direct her to cut apart the fruit cards at the bottom. Guide her to imagine that the cards have all been placed in a bag. Direct students' attention to the board and then have student volunteers share whether it would be certain, likely, unlikely, or impossible to pull an apple card out of the bag. After several students share their predictions and the reasons behind them, repeat the question with a different fruit card. To follow up, give each student a brown paper bag, have her put her cards in it, and then have her complete the top of page 144. **Probability**

Check out the skill-building reproducible on page 145.

Name ______________________________ Open bar graph

____

title of graph

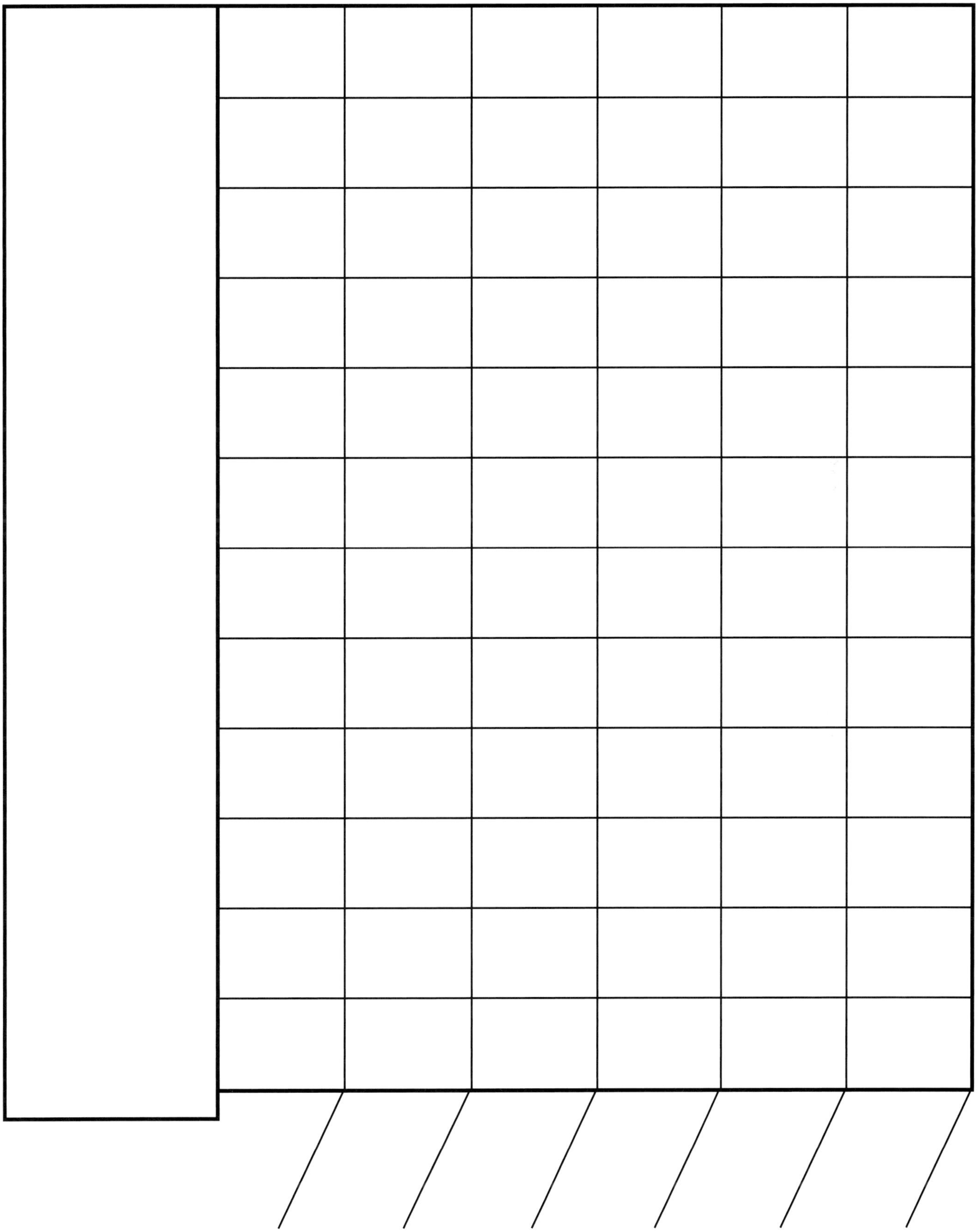

Note to the teacher: Use with "Use Your Noodle!" and "Spin-a-Graph" on page 141.

Name ________________________________

Fruit Salad

Think about your fruit cards.

Predict.

1. Which fruit is most likely to be drawn?

   ____

2. Which fruit is least likely to be drawn?

   ____

Test.

1. Draw a card.
2. Make a tally mark on the chart to show which fruit was drawn.
3. Keep drawing and making tally marks until you have made 20 marks.

Fruit	Tally Marks
apple	
orange	
banana	
cherry	

Think.

1. Which fruit was drawn the most? ______________________
2. Why do you think this happened? ______________________

   ____

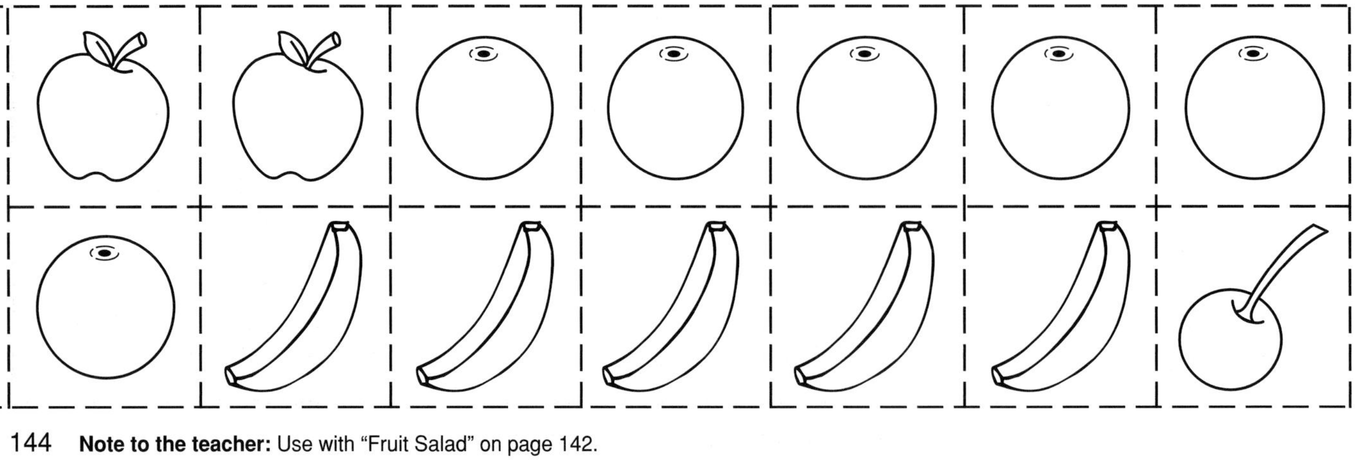

 Note to the teacher: Use with "Fruit Salad" on page 142.

Name ____________________

Fishy New Pets

Color the bags with pet combinations that are **possible** to find in the aquarium.
Cross out the bags with pet combinations that are **impossible** to find in the aquarium.

Sorting, Patterning, and More

Petal by Petal

Give each pair of students a copy of the patterns on page 148 and several pieces of scrap construction paper. Each partner uses the patterns to make a flowerpot, a flower center, a stem, and several petals. He assembles his flower as shown. Next, he writes the beginning of a number pattern on the first few petals of his flower before exchanging flowers with his partner. Each partner completes the pattern his partner started and then writes the rule for his pattern on the center of the flower he is holding. Collect the completed flowers and display them on a bulletin board titled "Pretty Petal Patterns." Number patterns

3
6
9
12
15
18
21
24
Add 3.

Three in a Row!

Materials for each pair of students: copy of the gameboard on page 149, copy of the game cards on page 149, set of pattern blocks, 1 red crayon, 1 blue crayon

To play:

1. One player cuts out the gameboard and puts it on the playing surface between the two players. The other player cuts apart the game cards, shuffles them, and places the deck facedown next to the gameboard.
2. Player 1 draws a card and uses the pattern blocks to make a pattern matching the description on the card. He repeats the pattern at least twice. Player 2 confirms his pattern. If correct, Player 1 colors in a matching square on the gameboard red. If incorrect, or if all of the matching blocks have already been colored, his turn is over.
3. Player 2 takes a turn in the same manner, using the blue crayon to color a matching square.
4. Play continues until one player colors three blocks in a row or until all the blocks are colored. The player with more colored blocks wins.

Geometric patterns

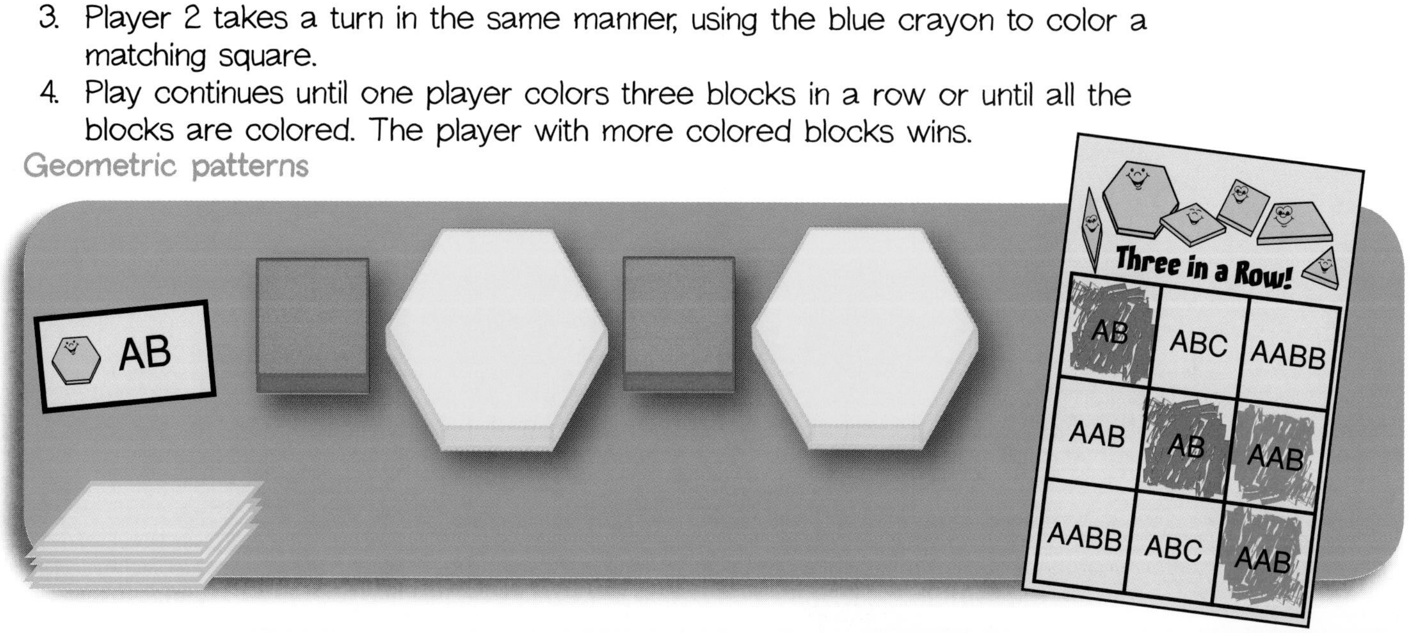
AB
Three in a Row!
AB
ABC
AABB
AAB
AB
AAB
AABB
ABC
AAB

Picture Sort

To prepare this center, ask each student to bring a current photograph of herself to school. (If desired, protect each picture by placing it in a resealable plastic bag.) Also, prepare sets of index cards by programming each one with different headings, such as those shown. Place the bagged pictures and the prepared cards, along with several blank cards, in a center. Students use the sets of headings to sort the pictures. Once they have sorted the pictures in several different ways, challenge students to come up with their own descriptors, write them on the blank cards, and use them to sort the pictures in a new way. **Sorting**

brown hair
blonde hair
red hair
black hair
glasses
no glasses
straight hair
curly hair
boy
girl

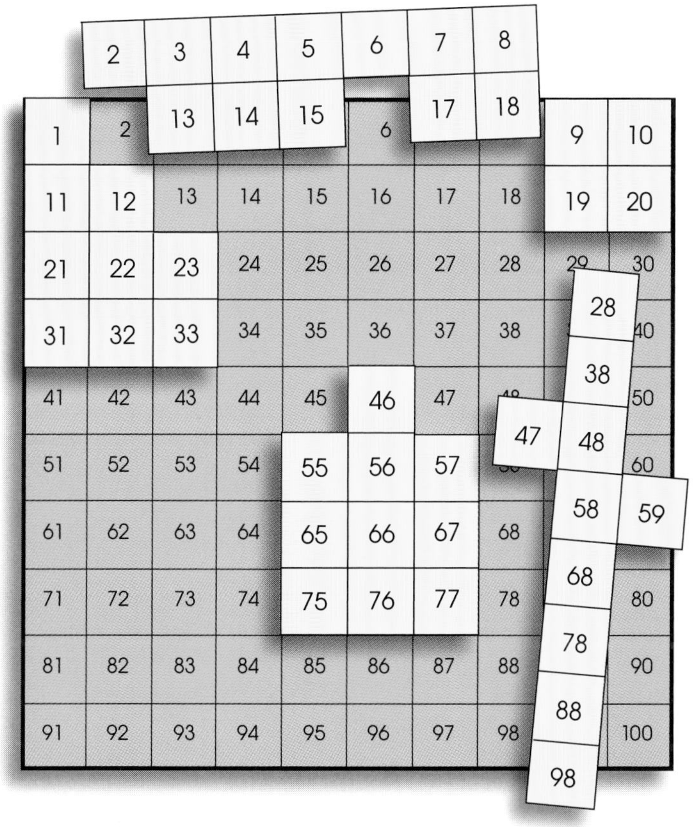

By the Hundreds!

For a quick and easy center, make several copies of a hundred chart (see page 105) on different colors of paper. Laminate the copies and then cut each one into puzzle pieces as shown. Place each puzzle in a different resealable plastic bag and then display the bags at a center. Place a whole copy of the hundred chart next to each bag for students to use as a frame. To use the center, a child assembles the puzzle in each bag. For an even greater challenge, have students assemble the puzzles without the frames. **Patterns**

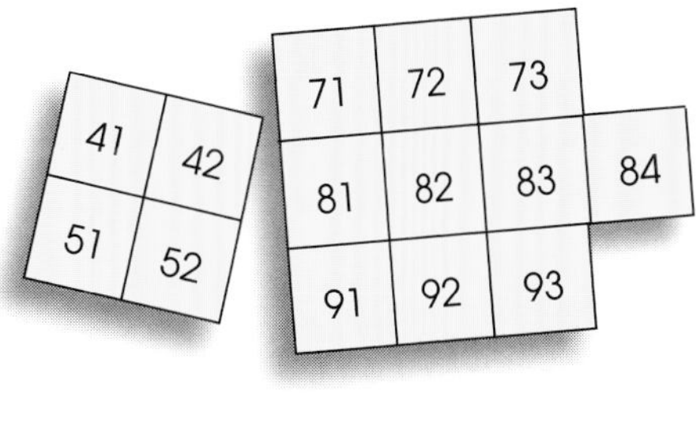

Flower Part Patterns

Use with “Petal by Petal” on page 146.

center

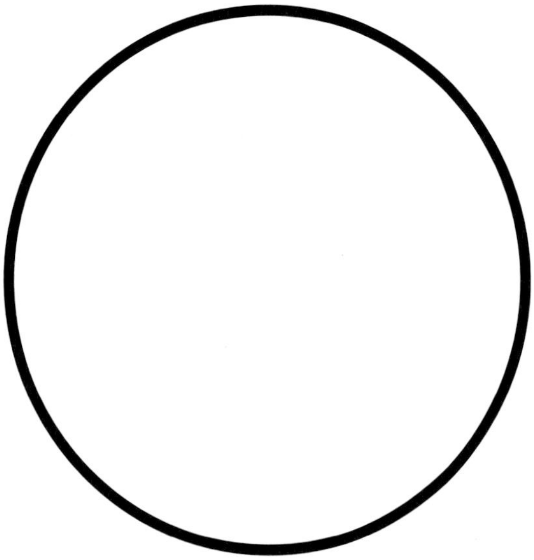

petal

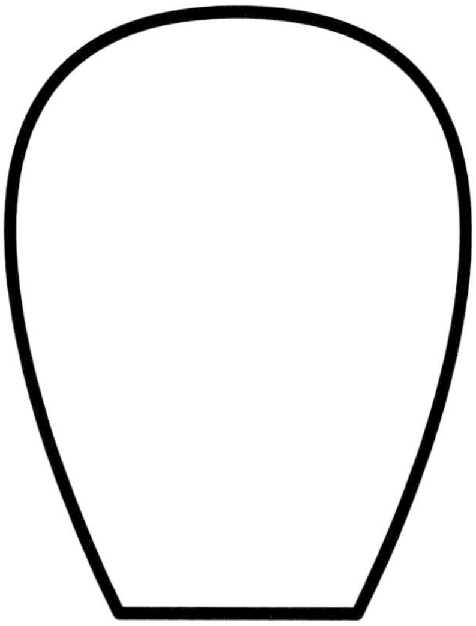

flowerpot

TEC61049

stem

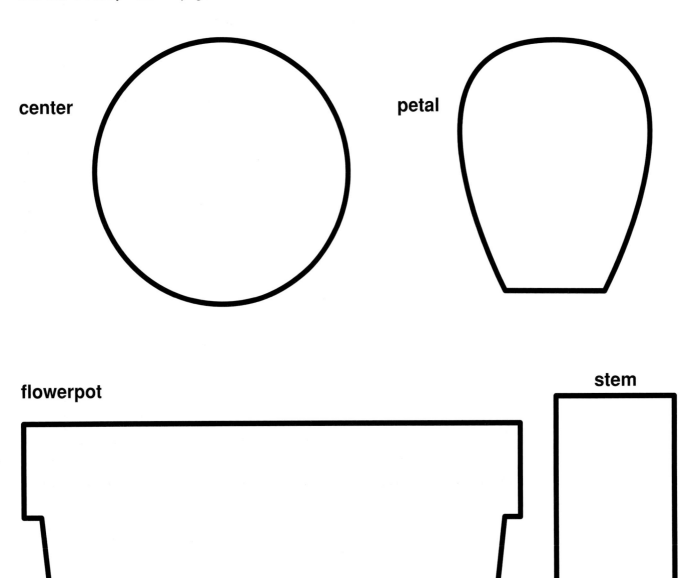

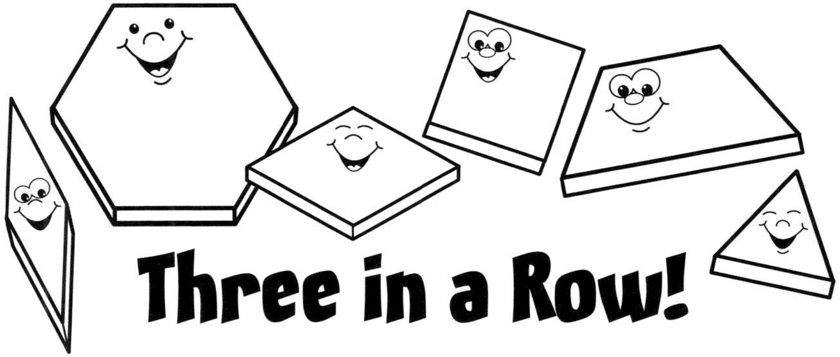

Three in a Row!

AB	ABC	AABB
AAB	AB	AAB
AABB	ABC	AAB

AB TEC61049	AB TEC61049
AB TEC61049	ABC TEC61049
ABC TEC61049	ABC TEC61049
AABB TEC61049	AABB TEC61049
AABB TEC61049	AAB TEC61049
AAB TEC61049	AAB TEC61049

PROBLEM SOLVING

Catch a Big One!

For this whole-class game, collect a supply of word problems that vary in difficulty. Label the problems or sort them into categories: guppy (least difficult), bass, and shark (most difficult). Assign a point value to each category and write it in a chart on the board as shown. To begin, divide your class into two teams. Have one member from each team stand. In turn, each player chooses a category and attempts to solve the problem that is read aloud to him. If he answers it correctly, his team gets the appropriate number of points. If he answers incorrectly, no points are earned. After each team has answered a question, ask another member from each team to stand; then repeat the procedure. Continue as time allows. The team with more points at the end of the game wins.

guppy = 1 point
bass = 3 points
shark = 5 points

Act It Out!

Demonstrate the act-it-out strategy with this simple activity. Gather several small items—such as a glue stick, a pencil, a crayon, and an eraser—and have your students do the same. Secretly arrange the items from left to right. Announce clues about the position of the items, such as, "The crayon is not next to the glue stick," and, "The pencil is not at the end." Have students move the objects on their desks to determine the correct order and solve the problem.

GLUE STICK

Pick a Problem

For this easy-to-make center, cut a supply of word problems from old workbooks or worksheets. Label each problem with a letter. Place the problems in a plastic jar at a center along with paper and pencils. If desired, provide an answer key for self-checking. To use the center, a child selects five problems from the jar. He records each problem letter on his paper and then solves the problems. When he's finished, he places the problems back in the jar and turns in or checks his work.

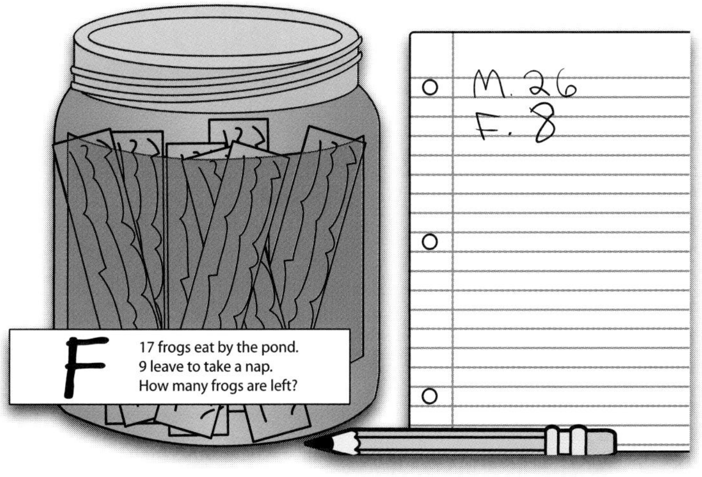
M. 26
F. 8
F
17 frogs eat by the pond.
9 leave to take a nap.
How many frogs are left?

Three Scoops, Please

Students practice the make-a-list strategy with this cool idea. Give each pair of students 18 Unifix cubes—six each of pink, white, and brown—to represent strawberry, vanilla, and chocolate ice-cream scoops. Challenge students to determine the different ways there are to stack three scoops of ice cream on a cone. Have them stack the cubes to help them solve the problem and then record their results in an organized list.

You Take It!

This partner game is perfect for practicing logical reasoning. Give each pair of students 11 beans or other manipulatives. To play, the partners place the beans in the center of the playing surface. Partners take turns removing one, two, or three beans from the pile. The winner is the player who forces his partner to take the last bean. After playing several rounds and taking turns going first, students share their strategies for winning. Then have students change partners and play a few more rounds.

Check out the skill-building reproducibles on pages 152–154.

Name ______________________________

Flower Power

Cut out the flowers below.
Read the clues on each lily pad.
Find the two flowers that show the correct numbers.
Glue the flowers in place.

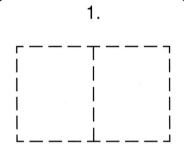

1.

- The sum of the numbers is 10.
- The difference is 4.

2.

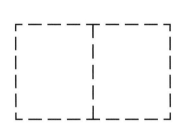

- The sum of the numbers is 13.
- The difference is 3.

3.

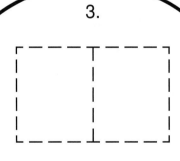

- The sum of the numbers is 11.
- The difference is 5.

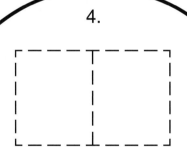

4.

- The sum of the numbers is 10.
- The difference is 2.

3 4 5 7 6 8 3 8

Name ______________________________

Racer Rankings

Read the clues and complete the logic chart.
Put a ✔ in each box that is true and an X in each box that is not true.

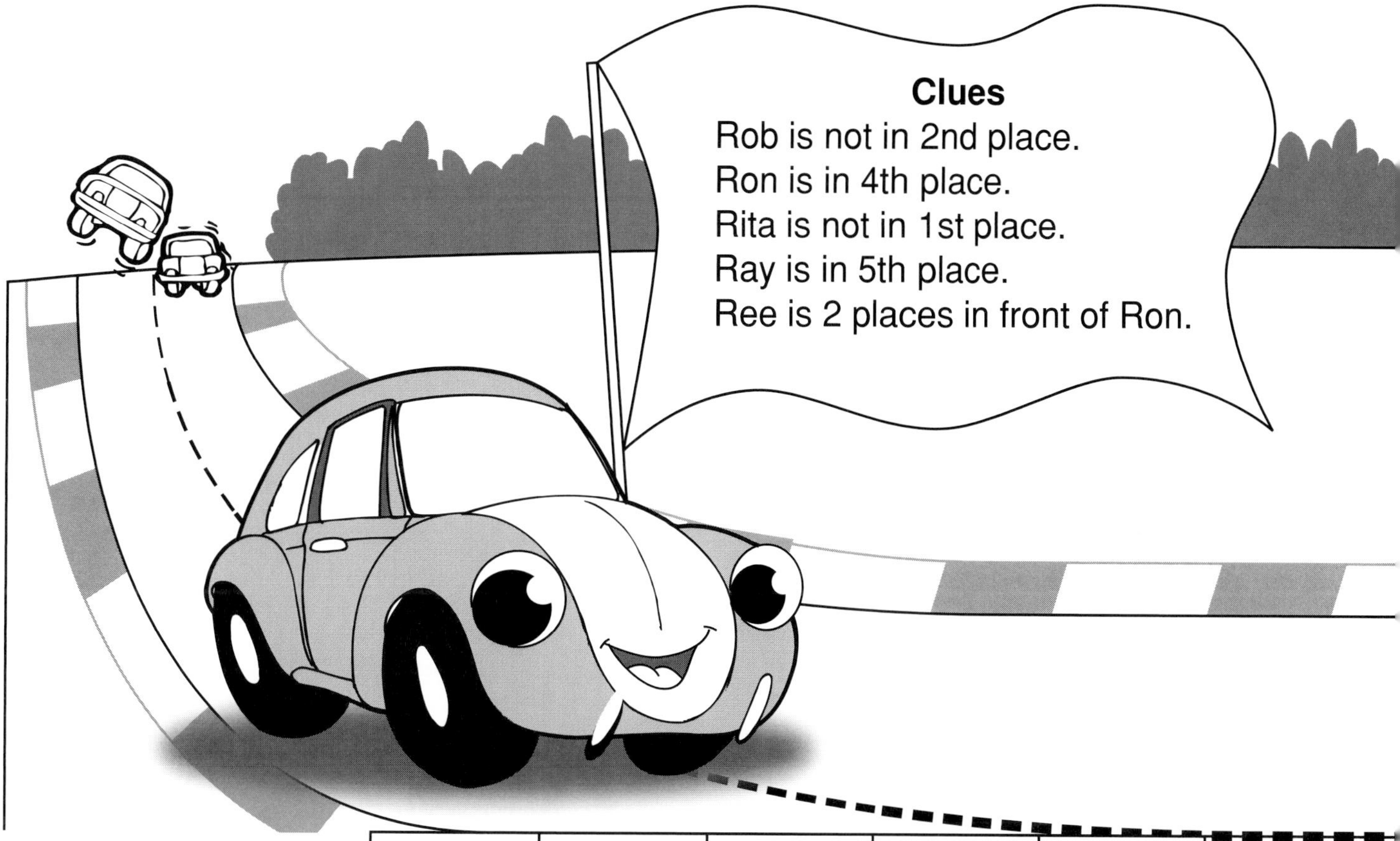
Clues
Rob is not in 2nd place.
Ron is in 4th place.
Rita is not in 1st place.
Ray is in 5th place.
Ree is 2 places in front of Ron.

	1st Place	2nd Place	3rd Place	4th Place	5th Place
Ray					
Rita					
Ron					
Ree					
Rob					

Name ____ Finding a pattern

FEEDING THE PACK

Look for a pattern.
Complete the table.

Amount of Dog Food Needed for One Month									
Number of dogs	1		3			6		8	
Pounds of dog food	10	20			50				

Use the table to answer the questions.

1. How many pounds of dog food are needed each month for 2 dogs?

   __________ pounds

2. How many dogs can be fed for one month with 50 pounds of dog food?

   __________ dogs

3. How many pounds of dog food are needed each month for 9 dogs?

   __________ pounds

4. There are 70 pounds of dog food. There are 8 dogs. Is there enough food for one month?

   ☐ Yes ☐ No

Living & Nonliving Things

What's in the Bag?

air	water	food	shelter	clothing
in a balloon	rain	apple	tent	hat
in a bag	snow	orange	house	coat
	pond	bread	apartment	pants
	lake		condo	shirt
	stream			socks

Introduce the needs of living things by creating a mystery bag. Fill a paper lunch sack with items that represent the needs of living things: an uninflated balloon, a bottle of water, a sock, a piece of wood or a brick, and an apple. One by one, pull the objects out of the mystery bag. (Inflate the balloon to represent air after pulling it out of the bag.) Ask students to guess what these items signify. After a few responses, explain to your students that these objects represent the needs of living things—air, water, food, and some type of shelter. People also need clothing to help keep them warm. Nonliving things don't have these needs. For a fun follow-up, have each student name examples of needs as you record them on a chart similar to the one shown. Keep the chart on display during your study. Do your students understand the needs of living things? The answer is in the bag!

Mystery Bag

Student Study

Emphasize that living things grow and change by having your students keep records of the differences that occur in themselves during the school year. Copy the recording sheet on page 157 and give one to each student. On the top row, have each student write the date, draw a self-portrait, write his favorite things, and sign his name in the corresponding columns. Then measure each student's height and have him record his height in the remaining column. Collect the papers and store them in a secure location. Then, at three additional times during the year, distribute the same recording sheets and have students repeat the recording process. If desired, keep the completed papers in your students' portfolios to document the growth and progress they have experienced in second grade. Your students will be amazed at the changes that occur in only a year's time!

People, Pets, and Plants

Most students have had experience with pets, either at home or in the classroom. Capitalize on students' knowledge of these animals to look at the different needs of living things. Have your students brainstorm a list of things that pets need in order to stay healthy. Responses might include pet food, water, a shelter or cage, chew toys, exercise, and vaccinations. Write students' responses on the board. Then repeat the activity having students brainstorm a list for people. Use the information from the lists to make a Venn diagram on the board. Ask students to help you determine where each item on the lists should be placed. To reinforce the concept of living things and their distinct needs, repeat the activity comparing pets and plants. For an added challenge, create a three-way Venn, and have students assist you in plotting the information for people, pets, and plants. Then provide time for students to discuss how they help take care of these living things at home.

Classification Relay

Use teamwork to help students classify living and nonliving things. Post a length of bulletin board paper on a wall, visually divide the paper in half, and label one half "Living Things" and the other half "Nonliving Things." From old magazines and newspapers, have each student cut out a separate picture of a living thing and a nonliving thing. Collect the pictures and put an equal number in two large brown paper bags. Divide the class into two teams. Line up each team behind a bag of pictures. At your signal, the first player on each team randomly draws a picture from the bag, walks to the chart, and tapes it to the correct side. He walks back to his team and gently tags the next player, who repeats the procedure. The game continues until all players have had a turn. After the activity, review the chart with your students. Keep the chart on display and encourage students to bring more pictures from home to add to it.

Needs Change Through Time

Take a look into the past to see how our needs have changed through time. Highlight three different periods of time: cave times, Colonial times, and modern times. Discuss the different ways people in each period satisfied their needs. Then enlist students' help in making a chart to compare the needs of the different groups. To make a chart, write headings on a large piece of bulletin board paper as shown. Pair students and have each pair illustrate a different category on a sheet of drawing paper. Next, have each pair glue its picture in its corresponding place on the chart. Use the completed chart as a springboard for a discussion of the importance of taking care of natural resources so that our needs will continue to be met in the future!

Cave Times
Colonial Times
Modern Times
Air
Water
Food
Shelter
Clothing

Name______________________________

I Grow and Change

Complete.

Date	Self-Portrait	Height	Favorite Things (books, games, foods)	Signature

Note to the teacher: Use with “Student Study” on page 155.

Life Cycles

Which Came First?

This activity is "eggs-actly" what you need for an introduction to animals that come from eggs. Begin your study by sharing *An Extraordinary Egg* by Leo Lionni. After reading the story aloud, give each student a plastic egg filled with a small plastic or paper chicken, frog, alligator, or turtle. Ask each child to think about what might be inside his egg; then have him record his guess on a copy of page 160. Next have him crack open the egg to see what is waiting inside and record the animal's name in the corresponding box on the reproducible. Then have him write guesses for the next three statements before setting his paper aside. To complete the activity, help students research facts about each animal's life cycle; then have students use the information to complete their reproducibles.

Home Movie Featuring Life Cycles

These individual tachistoscopes provide students with reinforcement of the life cycle of any species. To begin, share information with your students about a specific life cycle. Ask students to recall what they've learned. List their ideas on the board. Then have each student use the information to create a tachistoscope. To make a television tachistoscope, a student labels and illustrates each stage of the animal's life cycle on a separate index card. She tapes her cards together in sequence to create one strip; then she tapes a blank card on each end of the strip. Next she opens a business envelope, holds it upside down, and cuts out a 3" x 4½" section from the envelope front as shown. She trims the sides of the envelope, seals the remaining flaps on the back, and then colors the front (still upside down) to resemble a television set. She then inserts the strip into the television. To use her tachistoscope, the student moves the strip to view the stages of the animal's life cycle.

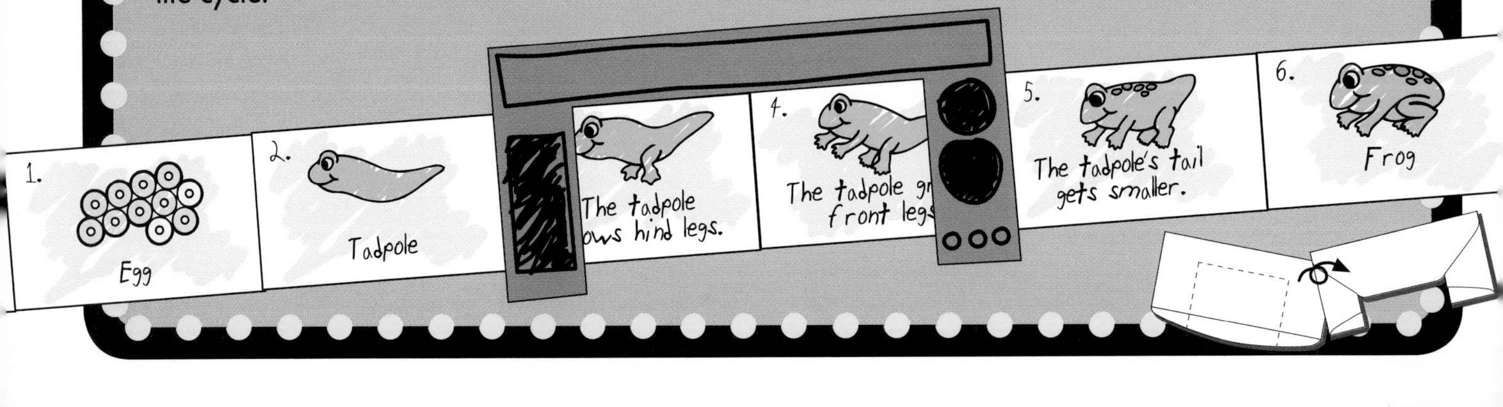
1.
Egg
2.
Tadpole
4.
5.
The tadpole's tail gets smaller.
6.
Frog

Seeds and Their Cycles

Your students can get an "underground" look at new plants emerging by placing layers of wet paper towels around the insides of clear, plastic cups. Give a dry lima bean or pinto bean to each student, and instruct her to place it between the paper towels and the cup. Have her store the cup away from direct sunlight and observe the changes every day. (If the paper towel becomes dry, have her add a little water to the cup for the towel to absorb.) Within a few days, a root and tiny plant will begin to grow. If desired, have the students carefully remove the plant from the cup, throw away the paper towel, and fill the cup with soil. Help each student gently place the new plant in her soil. Move the cups to a sunny location and watch your classroom garden grow!

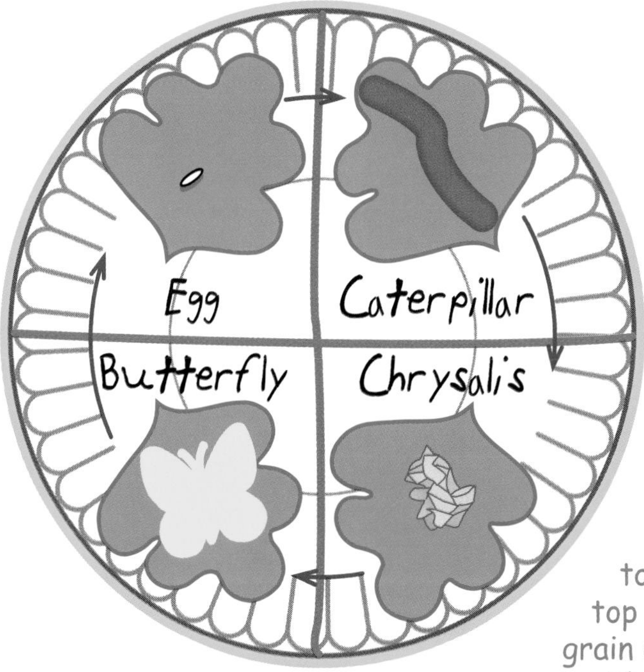
Egg
Caterpillar
Butterfly
Chrysalis

Metamorphosis Models

This tactile project will help youngsters understand the changes a butterfly experiences from an egg to adult insect. To make a metamorphosis model, a student uses a pencil and a ruler to divide a paper plate into four equal sections. Next she glues a construction paper leaf to each section of the plate. She then labels the top left quadrant of the plate "Egg" and glues one grain of uncooked white rice to the leaf to represent an egg. Then she labels the top right quadrant "Caterpillar" and glues a three-inch pipe cleaner piece to the leaf. In a similar manner, she labels the bottom right quadrant "Chrysalis" and glues a wadded piece of tissue paper to the leaf. Then she labels the final quadrant "Butterfly" and glues a construction paper butterfly to the leaf. Display the completed projects on a bulletin board for students to observe during your study of insects.

Name ____

An Extraordinary Egg

Complete.

	Guess	Check
Inside the egg is a(n) ______________.		
It takes ______________ days/ months to hatch.		
When it hatches it will look like this:		
When it is an adult it will look like this:		

More facts about how the animal grows:

____

____

____

____

____

____

 Note to the teacher: Use with "Which Came First?" on page 158.

Plants

Plant Chant

Write the following chant on a sheet of chart paper. Have students practice reciting the chant as they point to each part of a plant on a large plant diagram. Post the chant where students can refer to it as they complete their plant studies.

We are the **roots.**
This is our toil:
We take water and minerals
Out of the soil.

I am the **stem.**
I keep the plant tall.
Soil, rocks, and water—
I rise above them all.

We are the **leaves.**
The plant stays alive
Because we make the food
That helps it thrive.

We are the **flowers.**
We're pretty, you see.
Our job is to attract insects,
And so we need to be.

We are the **seeds.**
We thought you should know
We are the part
From which a new plant will grow.

Plant Parts and Their Purposes

To create a class book that goes along with plant study, divide the class into five groups. Assign each group one verse from the plant chant on this page. Direct the group to make a book page by copying, and then illustrating, its verse on a sheet of drawing paper. Gather the completed pages, stack them in order between two colored construction paper pages, and bind them into a book titled "Plant Parts and Their Purposes."

Plant
Parts and
Their
Purposes

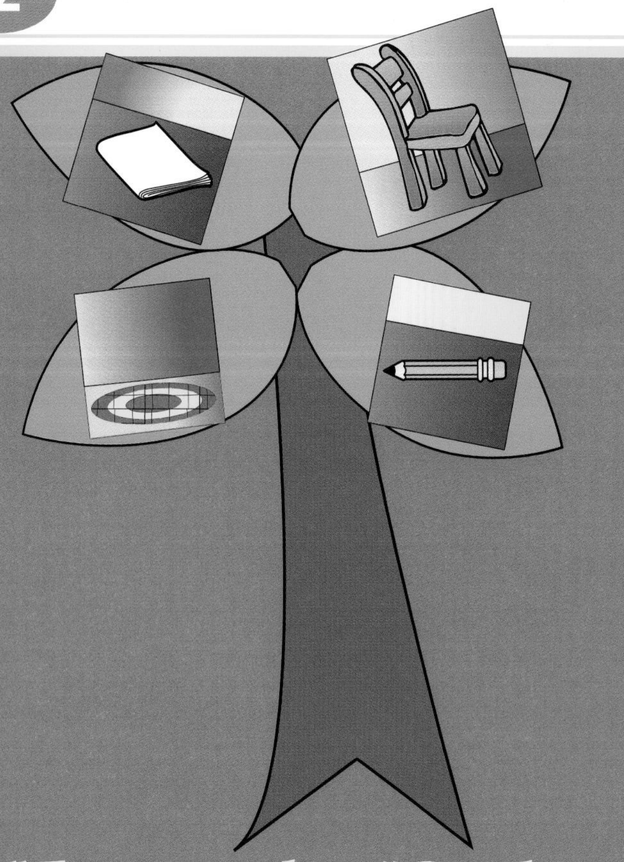

"Tree-mendous" Products

Create a display by cutting a large tree shape out of brown bulletin board paper and posting it on a wall or bulletin board. Next, direct students to search through old magazines to find pictures of items that come from plants or trees. Guide their search by suggesting that they look for items such as paper products, wood products, or products made from herbs and leaves. Have each child cut out the pictures he finds and glue each one on a leaf-shaped cutout. Then help him glue his leaves on the tree display for a visual reminder of all the things we depend on that come from plants.

A Plant Investigation

Divide the class into groups and give each group a cherry tomato plant and a copy of the investigation sheet on page 163. Assign each group a different question such as "What will happen if we stop watering the plant?" or "What will happen if we put the plant in a dark place?" Have the group conduct its investigation, recording information on its sheet as it works. After five days, provide time for each group to share its findings with the class.

Name ______ Investigation

A Plant Investigation

Write about your investigation.

Question: ______

Our prediction: ______

Day 1: Our plant looks ______

Day 2: Our plant looks ______

Day 3: Our plant looks ______

Day 4: Our plant looks ______

Day 5: Our plant looks ______

Our conclusion: ______

It Takes All Kinds of Seeds!

birdseed
sunflower seeds
pumpkin seeds
kidney beans
flower seeds
popcorn kernels

Stock a center with a bowl of different types of seeds (see the list for suggestions). Also place a spoon, several small bowls, glue, and a class supply of page 164 at the center. A child places a spoonful of seeds in a small bowl. He uses his bowl of seeds to complete the reproducible.

Name ______________________________________

A Plant Investigation

Write about your investigation.

Question: ______________________________________

____

Our prediction: ______________________________________

____

Day 1: Our plant looks ______________________________________

____

Day 2: Our plant looks ______________________________________

____

Day 3: Our plant looks ______________________________________

____

Day 4: Our plant looks ______________________________________

____

Day 5: Our plant looks ______________________________________

____

Our conclusion: ______________________________________

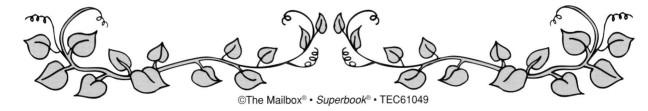

____

____

Note to the teacher: Use with "A Plant Investigation" on page 162.

Name ______________________________

It Takes All Kinds of Seeds!

Read each description.
Glue a matching seed in each circle.

a small seed

a large seed

a long, thin seed

a short, fat seed

a seed that is more than one color

my favorite seed

 Note to the teacher: Use with "It Takes All Kinds of Seeds!" on page 162.

WEATHER

Fictional Forecasters

Introduce your unit on weather with a journey through an imaginative forecast! To begin, have your students brainstorm a list of weather words while you record their responses on the board. After a list has been generated, ask each student to choose one type of weather and then close his eyes and think of the sights, sounds, smells, and types of clothing that are associated with his choice. Then turn off the lights and have each child, in turn, describe his chosen weather. The other students may close their eyes, put their heads on their desks, and imagine the type of weather that is being described. After everyone has had a chance to participate, your students will feel as though they have changed from raincoats to bathing suits to mittens and parkas!

Wild Conditions

When it comes to weather, there's no shortage of ways to describe it! Share with your students these idioms about weather. Then have each student choose one expression to illustrate. Display the completed drawings on a bulletin board titled "Watch Out for Wild Weather!"

- It's raining cats and dogs.
- The fog is as thick as pea soup.
- It's hot enough to fry an egg on the sidewalk.
- Jack Frost is nipping at your nose.
- The wind is howling.
- April showers bring May flowers.
- It's pouring down in buckets.
- It's 92° in the shade.

It's raining cats and dogs.

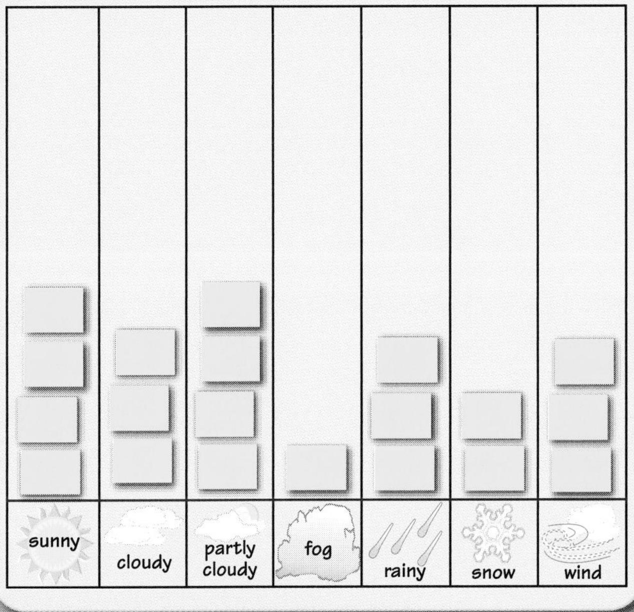
sunny
cloudy
partly cloudy
fog
rainy
snow
wind

Weather Watchers

A weather unit is the perfect opportunity to incorporate a graphing activity. To create a weather graph, visually divide a sheet of poster board into columns as shown. Each morning have a student volunteer look out the window and announce the current weather conditions. Have him place a self-stick note in the appropriate column of the graph. At the end of the observance period, use the resulting graph to ask students questions such as "Were there more rainy days or sunny days?" or "How many windy days were there all together?" Your class will be weather-wise and graphing-great!

1. It is moving air.
2. It blows leaves.
3. It can make a kite fly.
What's the Weather?
The Wind!
What's the Weather?

Weather Riddles

Your students will enjoy making and solving this guessing-game bulletin board. Have each student fold a sheet of white construction paper so that a two-inch strip is visible at the bottom. Across the strip, have her use a crayon to write "What's the Weather?" Next have her choose a weather condition and write three clues about it on the top flap of her paper. Then have her unfold the paper, and illustrate and label the weather condition in the resulting space. Staple the completed projects to a bulletin board so the clues are visible but the pictures are concealed by the flaps. Provide time for students to read the clues and try to predict the weather conditions waiting inside.

Seasonal Symphony

Incorporate music into your study of the seasons. Find recorded music that suggests the sound of rain, thunder, wind, or other weather conditions. Have the students close their eyes while they listen to the recording. Then give each student a sheet of drawing paper and crayons. Play the music a second time while students illustrate the weather scenes they imagine the music is portraying. Invite student volunteers to display their drawings and explain why they depicted the weather as they did.

Take a Seasonal Tour

This small-group project is the perfect culmination for a study of the seasons. Divide the class into four groups and assign each group a different season. On a large piece of white bulletin board paper, have each group use markers to design a mural about its assigned season. Instruct the students to draw a landscape that shows an appropriate scene of their season. Next have each student complete a copy of the seasonal tour brochure (page 167) for her season. On the back of the brochure, have her draw a scene for her season. Then instruct each student how to fold the brochure into thirds. Tape the completed murals to a classroom wall. Then have each group use its brochures as it gives a guided tour of its season for the class. Encourage each group to dress in seasonally appropriate clothes for the occasion. What a whirlwind tour of a changing year!

WELCOME TO SUMMER

Welcome to Our Season!

Check out the skill-building reproducible on page 168.

Welcome to Our Season!

The name of our season is ________________.

There are many things to see and do during this season.

To dress for our season,
you should wear
______________, ______________,
and ______________.
Here is a picture of something to wear during our season.

In our season you can ___________,
___________________, and
______________.

Here is a picture of something to do during our season.

In our season you can see
______________, ______________,
and ______________.

Here is a picture of something to see during our season.

Note to the teacher: Use with "Take a Seasonal Tour" on page 166.

Name ______________________________

Tools of the Trade

Write the best word for each sentence.
Use the word bank to help you.

Word Bank

anemometer

rain gauge

thermometer

weather balloon

weather vane

Channel 4 Weather High: 72° Low: 59°

1. A _ _ _ _ _ _ _ _ _ _ _ measures the air temperature.

2. An _ _ _ _ _ _ _ _ _ _ measures wind speed.

3. The direction wind is blowing from is shown using a _ _ _ _ _ _ _ _ _ _ _ _.

4. A _ _ _ _ _ _ _ _ _ measures how much rain has fallen.

5. A _ _ _ _ _ _ _ _ _ _ _ _ _ _ measures weather high in the sky.

Sun and Moon

Light Show

Demonstrate how the moon shines with this quick experiment. Have students examine a reflector or a mirror in a dark room. Then use a flashlight to shine light on the object. Students will observe that the object does not create its own light; it only reflects the beam from the flashlight. Explain that this is similar to the way the moon reflects the light of the sun.

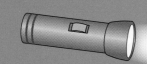

Moonlight in the Sky

(sung to the tune of "The Wheels on the Bus")

The way the moon appears occurs in a cycle,
In a cycle,
In a cycle.
The way the moon appears occurs in a cycle,
All through the month.

The moon reflects light and we see its phases,
See its phases,
See its phases.
The moon reflects light and we see its phases,
All through the month.

There's new and quarter and full and crescent,
Plus there's gibbous,
Plus there's gibbous.
There's new and quarter and full and crescent
All through the month.

A Constant Cycle

Help students visualize the phases of the moon. After reviewing the moon's phases, give each child a copy of page 171. Have her use a black crayon to shade each moon shape to represent the phase named. Next, have her cut out the strips and glue them together, attaching the new moon below the waning crescent. Then help her score two 3½-inch lines two inches apart on a 6" x 9" black construction paper rectangle. She uses a white crayon to title her project as shown. Then she feeds the strip through the scored lines and glues the two ends together. She gently pulls the strip to reveal the phases of the moon.

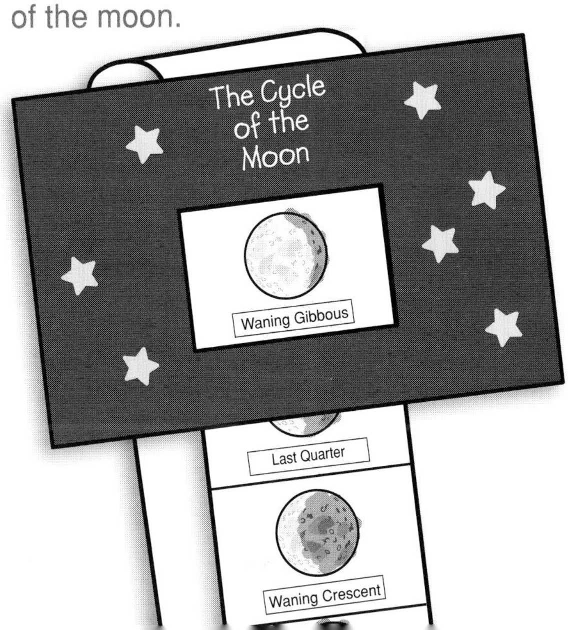
The Cycle of the Moon
Waning Gibbous
Last Quarter
Waning Crescent

Handling the Heat

Demonstrate the power of the sun's rays with this simple activity. Place an equal number of ice cubes inside two separate paper cups. Tell students that you will place one cup in the sunlight and the other in a dark place. Ask them to predict which cup of ice will melt first. Then give each child a copy of page 172 to record his prediction. Place the cups in their designated locations and have each student use the recording sheet to track the progress of the ice. Follow up the activity with a discussion of how the sun provides heat to Earth.

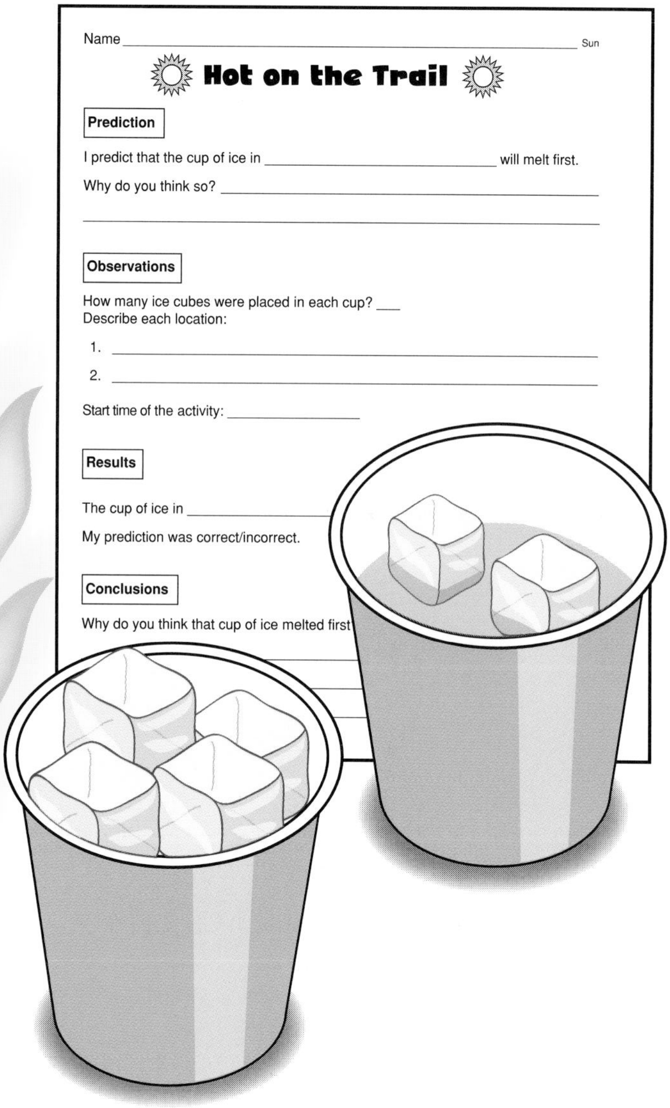
Name ____________________ Sun

Hot on the Trail

Prediction

I predict that the cup of ice in ____________________ will melt first.

Why do you think so? ____________________

Observations

How many ice cubes were placed in each cup? ___
Describe each location:

1. ____________________
2. ____________________

Start time of the activity: ____________

Results

The cup of ice in ____________

My prediction was correct/incorrect.

Conclusions

Why do you think that cup of ice melted first

Solar Provider

This easy-to-make booklet shows the importance of the sun to life on Earth. Review how living things use and need the sun's rays. Then give each student three 9" x 12" sheets of yellow construction paper. He stacks and folds two sheets of paper and then cuts them into a circular shape as shown. Next, he places the circular pages on top of the other sheet of paper and draws rays around it. He cuts around the rays and staples the pages to the center of the rays along the top fold. After trimming the pages as shown, he writes a sentence on each page telling how the sun's rays are used. Finally, he illustrates each page.

The Sun
It gives Earth heat and light.
The light helps feed the plants.
People eat the plants. They also eat animals that eat plants.

Booklet Pages

Use with “A Constant Cycle” on page 169.

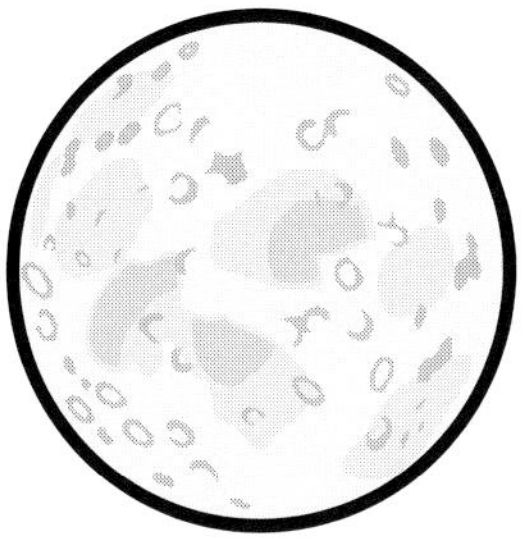

Full Moon

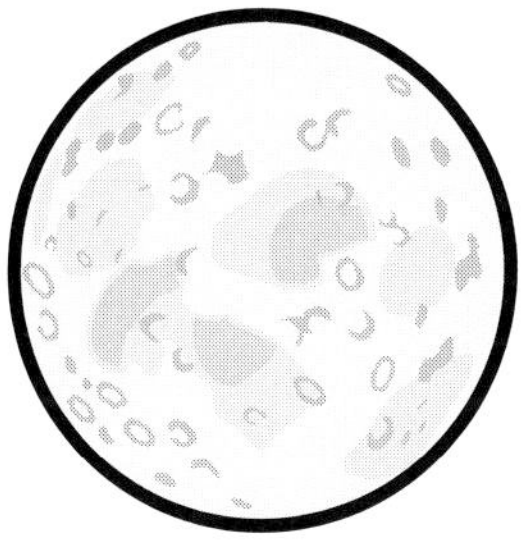

Waning Gibbous

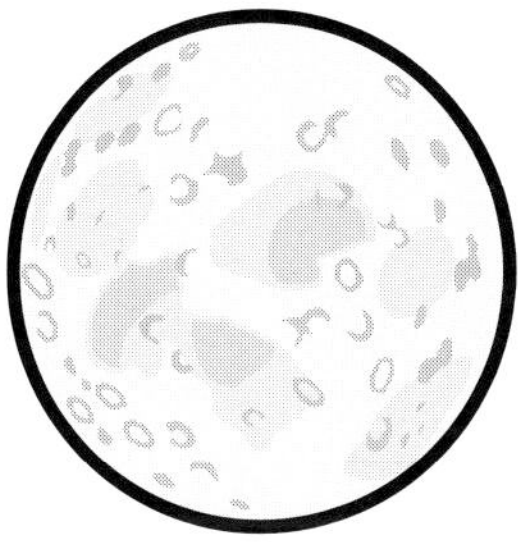

Last Quarter

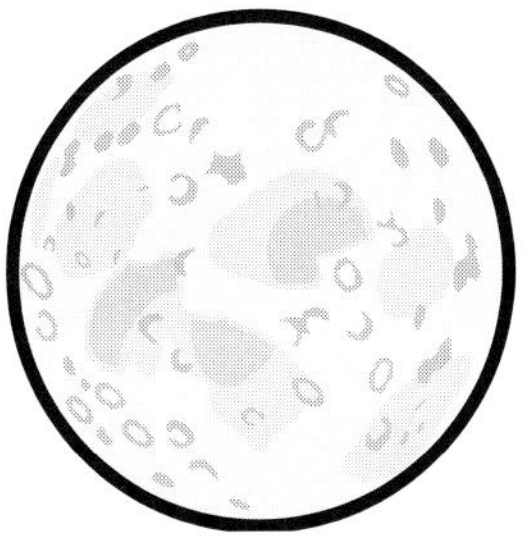

Waning Crescent

Glue.

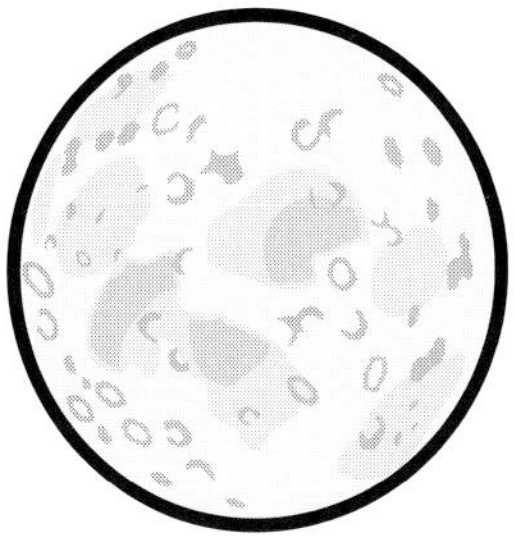

New Moon

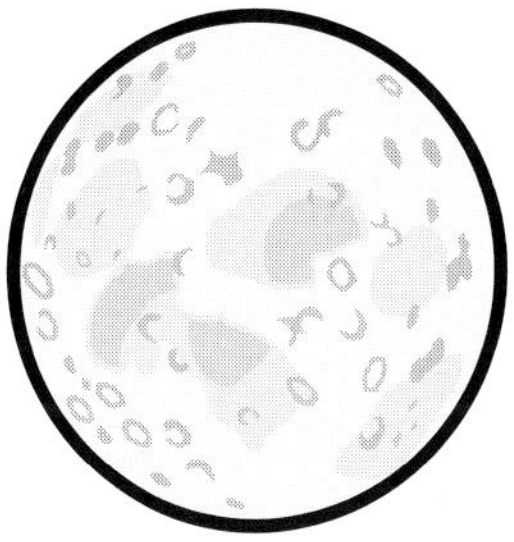

Waxing Crescent

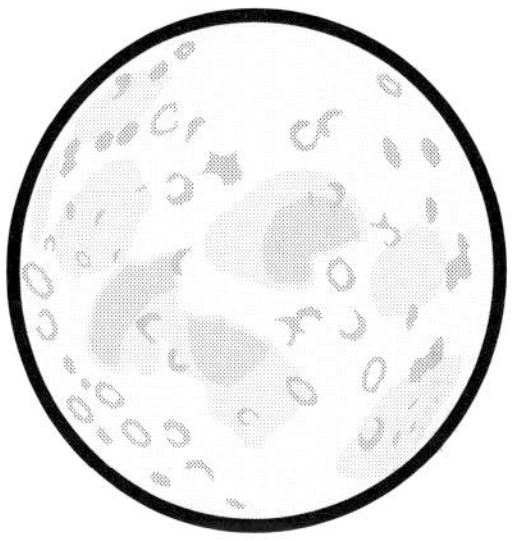

First Quarter

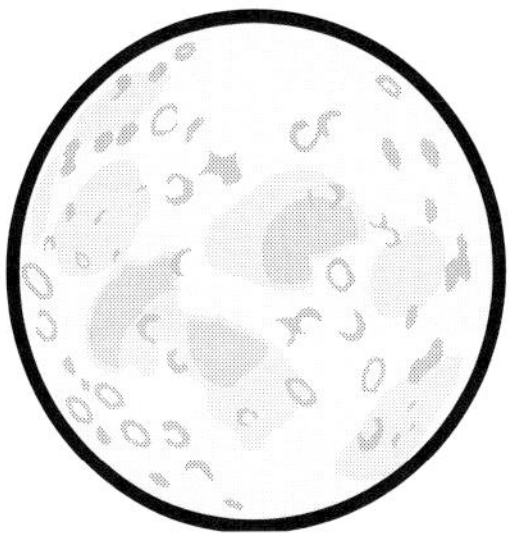

Waxing Gibbous

Glue.

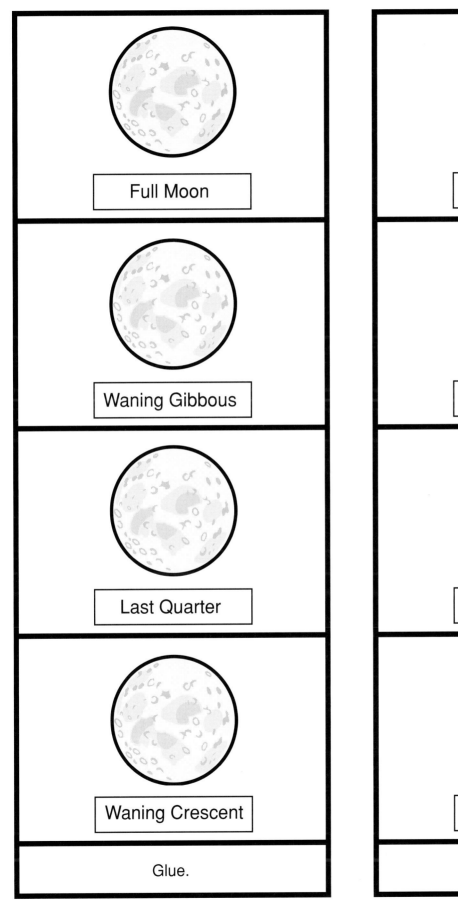

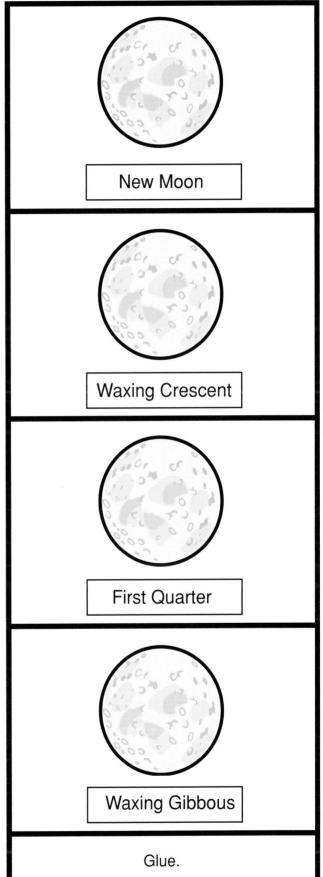

Name ____ Sun

Hot on the Trail

Prediction

I predict that the cup of ice in ______________________ will melt first.

Why do you think so? ____________________________________

____

Observations

How many ice cubes were placed in each cup? ___
Describe each location:

1. ____

2. ____

Start time of the activity: ____________

Results

The cup of ice in ________________ melted first.

My prediction was correct/incorrect.

Conclusions

Why do you think that cup of ice melted first?

____

____

____

 Note to the teacher: Use with "Handling the Heat" on page 170.

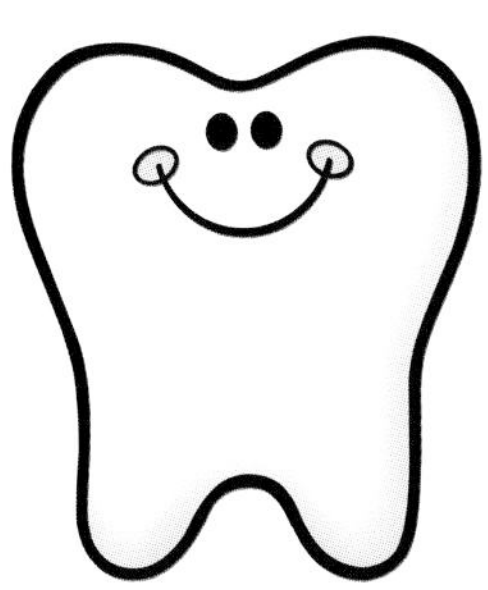

Dental Health

Toothy Terminology

Help students identify the parts of a tooth with this "tooth-rific" idea! Make one enlarged copy of the tooth pattern on page 174 for each student. Prepare a class chart that identifies the parts of a tooth (as shown). Refer to the chart as you share the information with the class.

Cementum: lies over the dentin of the tooth's root
Crown: the part of the tooth that you can see
Dentin: a yellow substance, harder than bone, that makes up most of the tooth
Enamel: a hard substance that covers the tooth and lies over the dentin
Nerves: enter the tooth through the pulp
Pulp: the innermost layer of the tooth
Root: the part that holds the tooth to the bone

Next, have each student make a two-dimensional tooth model. To make a model, a student cuts out her tooth pattern and glues it to a sheet of construction paper. Next, she draws, colors, and labels each part of the tooth (cementum, crown, dentin, enamel, pulp, and root) as shown. She then glues various lengths of white dental floss inside the pulp cavity to represent the nerves of the tooth. To complete her project, she draws a pink gum line next to the tooth. Collect the projects and mount them on a bulletin board with the title "Toothy Terminology."

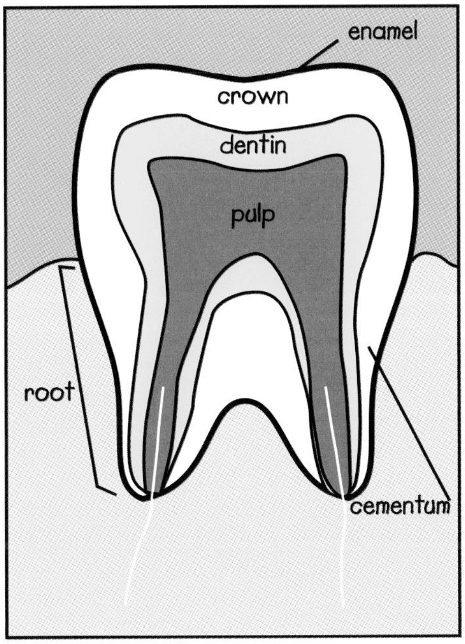
enamel
crown
dentin
pulp
root
cementum

Three-Dimensional Dentures

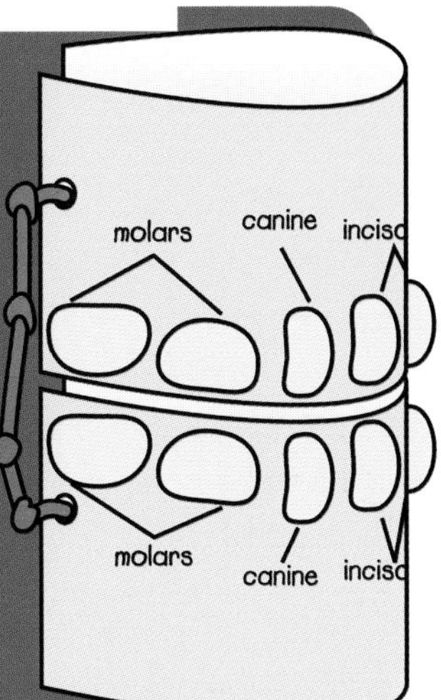
molars
canine
molars
canine

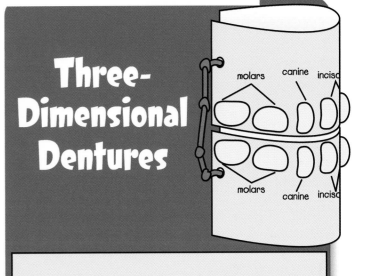

lima beans
navy beans
lima beans

Youngsters will love to make these three-dimensional dentures as they learn about the placement of their teeth. Cut two 2" x 5" strips of tagboard and obtain 12 navy beans and eight lima beans for each student. After reviewing the different kinds of teeth, have each youngster make a three-dimensional model of a child's mouth. First, a student colors the strips pink to represent the gums. Next, he glues the lima beans (molars) and the navy beans (incisors and canine teeth) along the bottom of each strip as shown. When the glue has dried, he labels each tooth with its appropriate name. He then punches a hole above the molars at the ends of both strips. Holding the strips so the teeth touch, thread a length of yarn through the holes on one side of the mouth model and tie the top jaw to the lower jaw; then repeat the procedure on the other side. Now that's an activity any youngster will want to sink his teeth into!

Tooth Attack

Conduct a class experiment to determine why brushing is so important. Tell students that dentists recommend brushing your teeth after each meal. Then show students a hard-boiled egg. Explain that the hard shell protects the egg the same way enamel protects their teeth. To begin the experiment, pour two cups of vinegar into a large jar. Place the egg in the jar, add a lid, and put the jar in a safe location for student observation. Ask youngsters to predict what they think will happen to the egg. Write the students' responses on a sheet of chart paper. When two days have passed, gently remove the egg from the jar. Ask students to examine the egg and compare their predictions with the results. Tell the students that the vinegar caused the shell of the egg to break down and become soft, the same way tooth enamel is damaged by acid and bacteria in the mouth. Brushing every day is the only way to keep this from happening. If desired have each student write about the experiment. You can count on plenty of toothbrushing from now on!

Molar Mobiles

Brush your teeth after each meal.
Eat healthful foods.

Make four copies of the tooth pattern below on white construction paper for each student. After a review of dental health, a student writes and illustrates one dental-health tip on each tooth pattern; then she cuts out the patterns. She staples the top corners of the cutouts together as shown. Next, the student punches a hole at the top of each tooth; then she ties a 12-inch length of dental floss at each punched hole. To complete the project, she gathers the four strings at the top and ties the strings together. If time allows, have each youngster share her mobile with her classmates. Then suspend the mobiles around the room for all to enjoy!

Tooth Pattern

Use with "Toothy Terminology" on page 173 and "Molar Mobiles" on this page.

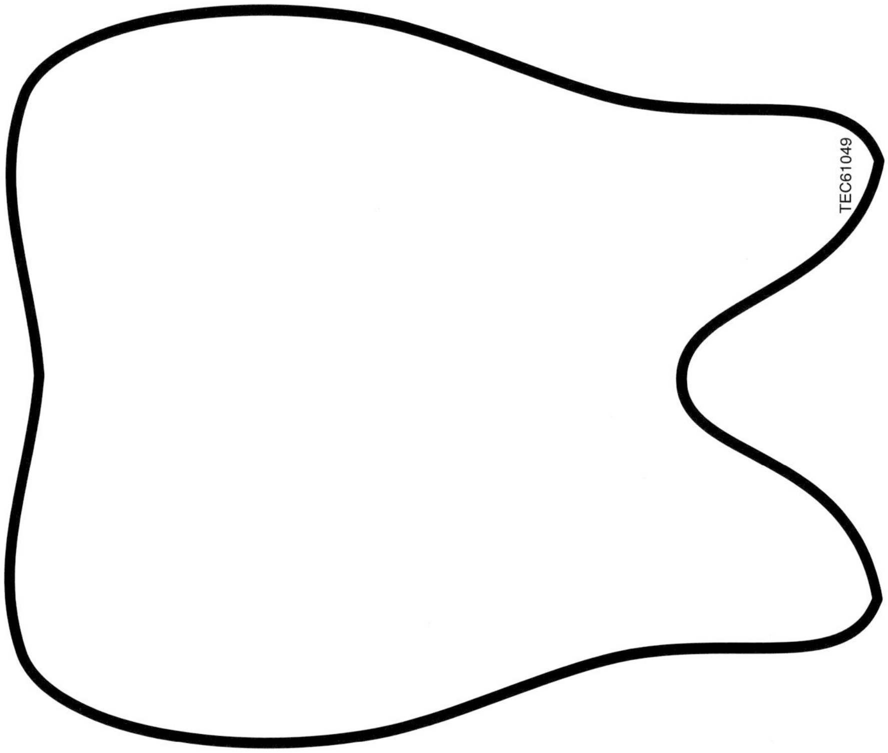
TEC61049

Nutrition

Blast Off With
Good Nutrition!
Team 1
Team 2
Team 3
Team 4

Blast Off With Good Nutrition!

Encourage students to eat nutritious, healthful meals with this far-out idea! Make four copies of the rocket pattern on page 176; then label each one with a different name: "Team 1," "Team 2," "Team 3," and "Team 4." Cover and decorate a bulletin board like the one shown; then use a marker to draw evenly spaced sections (the same size as the rockets) between Earth and the moon. Place the rockets in the four sections closest to Earth. Next, assign each student to one of the four teams. Every day have each student list one nutritious meal that she has eaten in the last 24 hours on a piece of paper. Challenge her to name the food group for at least three items on her list. Move each team's rocket one section for each team member who ate a nutritious meal. Continue moving the rockets until each team has reached the moon. Then reward students with a nutritious snack.

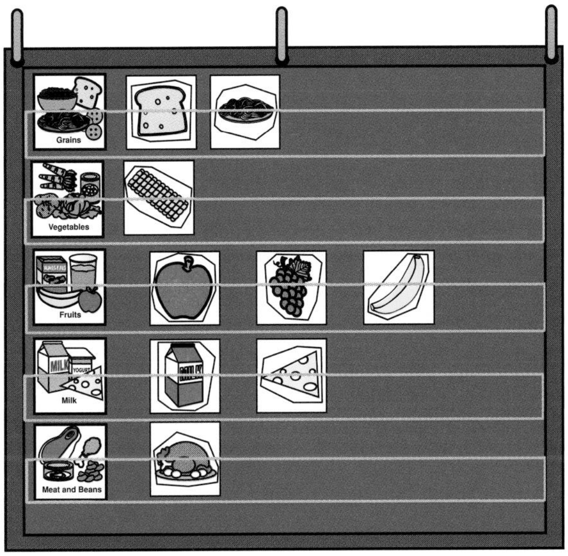
Grains
Vegetables
Fruits
Milk
Meat and Beans

Which Group?

Introduce the five food groups with this pocket-chart activity. To prepare, enlist students' help in cutting out several pictures of foods from grocery store circulars, being sure to include foods from each food group. Glue the pictures on tagboard for durability. Also, color and cut out a copy of the food group cards on page 176. Place each food group card in a different row of a pocket chart and set the picture cards nearby.

To begin, read each displayed food group card, in turn, and identify the examples pictured on the card. Next, have a volunteer take a picture card, name the food, and place it in the corresponding row. After confirming the placement, continue as described until all of the pictures are displayed.

Rocket Pattern

Use with “Blast Off With Good Nutrition!” on page 175.

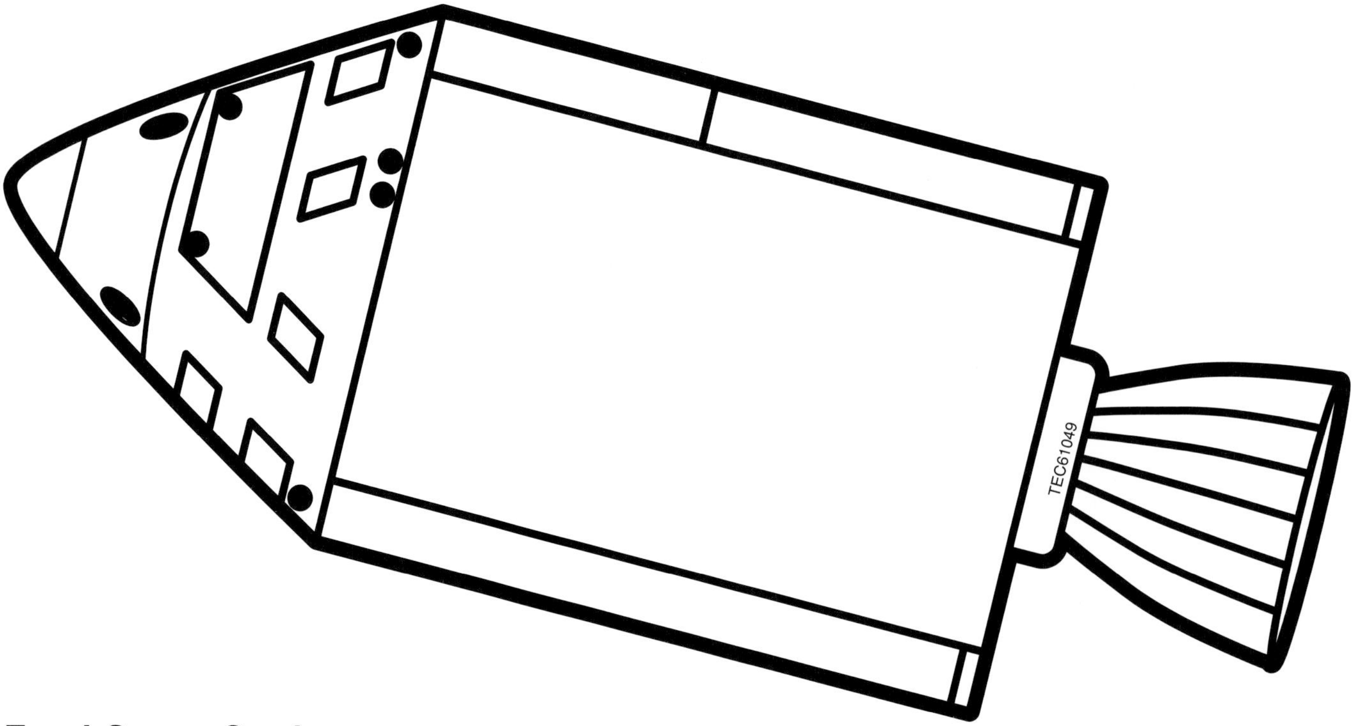
TEC61049

Food Group Cards

Use with “Which Group?” on page 175.

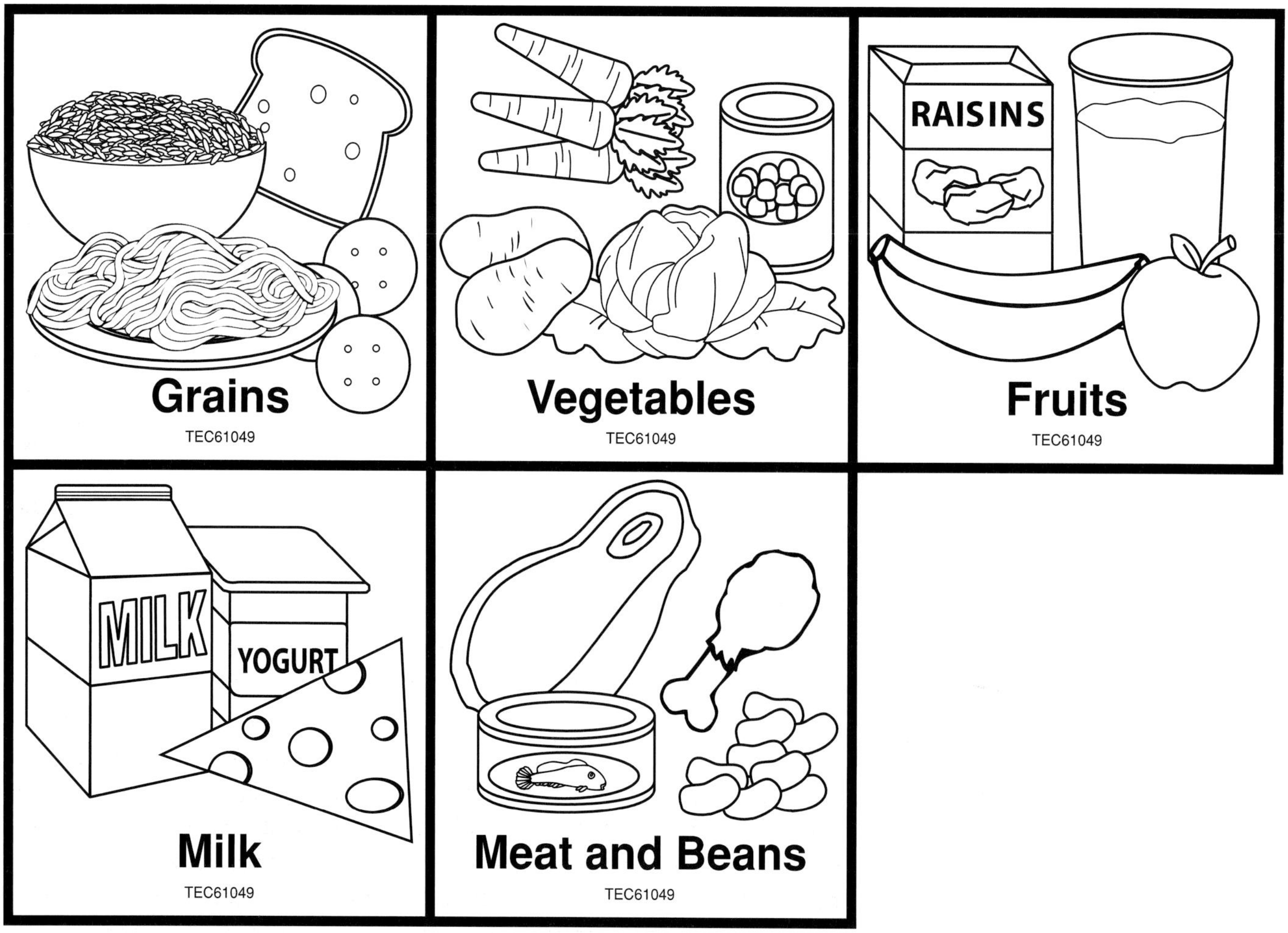
Grains
TEC61049
Vegetables
TEC61049
RAISINS
Fruits
TEC61049
MILK
YOGURT
Milk
TEC61049
Meat and Beans
TEC61049

COMMUNITIES

A Look at the Past

How did your community begin? Long ago, communities began near water because boats were a main form of travel. Communities near water were easy to reach. When the railroads appeared later, communities sprang up around them too. Display a large U.S. map. Have your students observe the areas in which there are clusters of cities. Lead your class in a discussion of what may have caused different communities to form. Point out that the colonists settled along the East Coast close to where their ships landed, the gold rush in California attracted people to the West Coast, and the abundance of oil in Texas drew people south. Ask your students to think of resources in their area that may have caused their community to grow. Then have each child draw a picture of something that is important to the community today. If desired, bind the completed pictures between two construction paper covers and place the booklet in the classroom library for all to enjoy.

Illustrate Your Community

What is a community? It's a place where people live, work, and play. Many of the jobs, dwellings, and recreational events in a community depend on the resources found in the area. Ask your students to think about the many types of workers, homes, and activities in your community. Divide the class into three groups. Provide each group with crayons and a sheet of poster board. Ask the first group to list the different types of jobs, the second to list the types of homes, and the third to list the forms of entertainment in the community. Provide time for each group to share its completed poster with the class. Then display the projects on a bulletin board titled "Welcome to Our Community!"

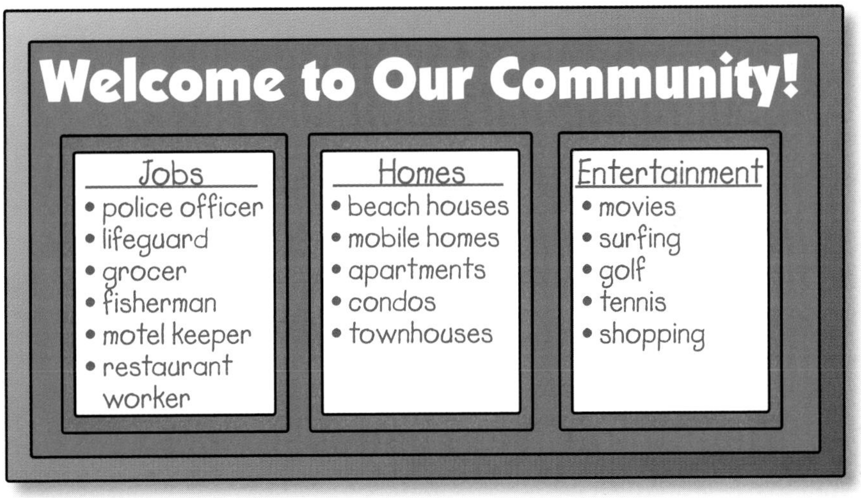
Welcome to Our Community!
Jobs
• police officer
• lifeguard
• grocer
• fisherman
• motel keeper
• restaurant worker
Homes
• beach houses
• mobile homes
• apartments
• condos
• townhouses
Entertainment
• movies
• surfing
• golf
• tennis
• shopping

Community-Helper Pantomime

People depend on many helpers to keep their community happy and healthy. Point out to your students that a community relies on an assortment of workers. A community needs workers to help keep it safe, to keep people healthy, to provide transportation, and to help maintain communications. A community also needs people who provide sources of food, clothing, and shelter. Have your students list the types of workers who provide these things in your community while you record their responses on the board. Then have each student secretly select a helper to pantomime in front of the class. Can the children correctly identify all the important workers?

Signs of a Safe Community

Explain to students that signs are important ways to maintain order and safety. Often a sign will have a symbol to help convey a law or to provide information. Ask students to name situations where safety is a concern, such as when crossing the street, playing outdoors, or driving through a construction zone. Next, have your students think of times when a sign provides valuable information, such as showing the way to an airport, indicating a bus stop, or marking a no-smoking area. Reinforce the significance of signs and symbols by having each student make a poster of this important community information. Give each student a copy of the signs on page 180. Discuss the correct color for each sign; then have each student color and cut out her signs and glue them to a sheet of white construction paper. To make sure each student understands the meaning of each sign, have her write a sentence under each one telling the safety or information message the sign conveys. Have your students take their completed posters home to share with their families and friends.

STOP
Stop your car.
Watch for a stoplight ahead.
R R
Be careful of the railroad tracks.
Watch out for schoolchildren crossing the street.
Don't smoke here.
Look out for people riding bikes here.

Caring for the Community

Remind your students that a community provides people with places to live, work, and play. It is up to each member of the community to keep it clean, well cared for, and safe. Have student groups participate in skits showing responsible community behavior in the following situations:

- Two children are walking down the street. One child offers the other a stick of gum, and they must dispose of the wrappers.
- A child notices a woman having difficulty opening the door to the library because her arms are full of books.
- A group of children wants to play jump rope and one child insists that there is more room to play in the middle of the street.
- While walking home from school, a child finds a wallet on the sidewalk.
- A neighbor comes home from the hospital with a broken leg and expresses concern that he will not be able to walk his dog.
- The neighborhood park is becoming run-down and covered with litter.
- Two children are playing ball and one child accidentally hits the ball through a window.

A Community of Many Groups

Once your students understand that they are part of a community, have them take a look at the other groups to which they belong. Define *group* as a number of people who have something in common. Groups meet together to have fun, to learn, or to get a job done. Ask students to think about things they do, places they go, or people they meet with to focus on a special interest. List students' responses on the board. Remind students that they are also part of larger groups, such as American citizens, state residents, and community members. Then have each student create a mobile showing all the different groups to which he belongs. To make a mobile, a student illustrates each group he belongs to on a separate card. If desired, also provide each student with a small construction paper outline of your state and the United States. The student then hole-punches the top of each card and map and ties them to a coat hanger with a length of yarn.

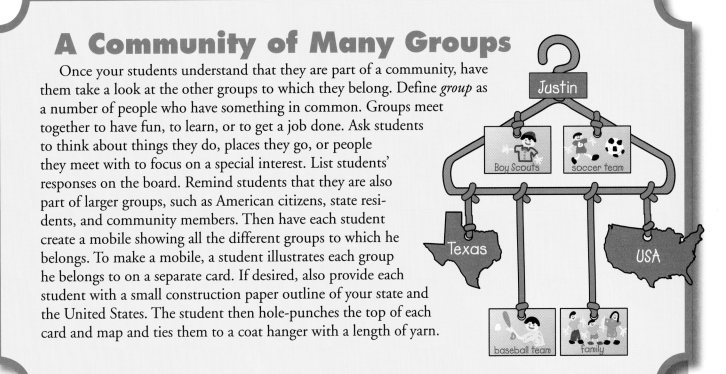

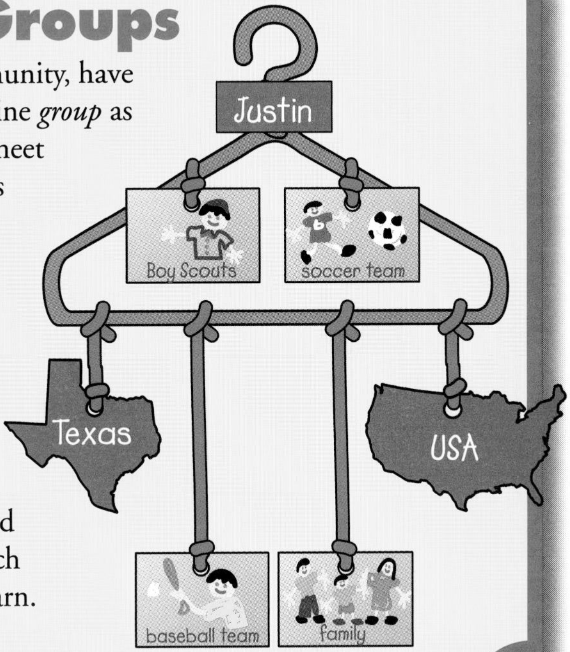
Justin
Boy Scouts
soccer team
Texas
USA
baseball team
family

Communities of the Past

What were communities like long ago? Ask your class to think about the places in your community now. Where do your students go to get items such as clothes, food, and toys? What do their parents do when the car breaks down, the roof leaks, or the TV is broken? Tell your students to close their eyes and imagine the community before their grandparents were born. Where would people get their clothes, food, and toys? Did they need the same types of repairs that we do today? Challenge students to name something that has changed in the community before the time their grandparents were growing up. Then have each student draw a picture showing how the community might have looked long ago. Provide time for students to share their drawings with the class.

Communities of the Future

After discussing communities of the past, challenge your class to think of changes the future might bring. What will the needs of the community be like? How will people travel? What will they do for entertainment? What type of clothing will they wear? Have each child share her thoughts on the subject by creating an advertisement for a futuristic newspaper. To make an ad, a student decides on a product or service that might be offered in a community of tomorrow. Then she draws an ad for it on a sheet of construction paper. Post the completed ads on a bulletin board display titled "Coming Soon in a Community of the Future!"

Underwater cell phones! Don't miss a call while you're swimming.

Check out the skill-building reproducible on page 181.

Sign Patterns

Use with “Signs of a Safe Community” on page 178.

STOP

stop sign

traffic light warning

bike crossing

R
R

railroad crossing

no smoking

school crossing

Name____________________

Comparing Communities

Cut apart the strips below.
Glue each strip on the matching building.

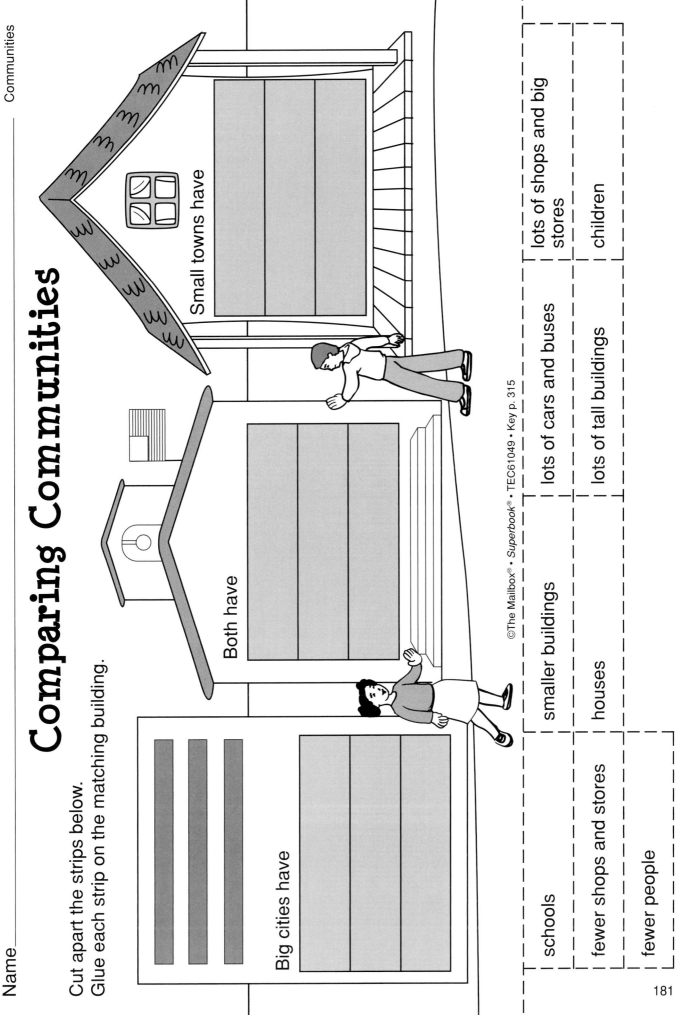

Big cities have
Both have
Small towns have

schools	smaller buildings	lots of cars and buses	lots of shops and big stores
fewer shops and stores	houses	lots of tall buildings	children
fewer people			

Rules and Laws

My Citizenship Book
Brendan

Citizenship Booklets

Here's a flag-waving idea for understanding citizenship! Ask your youngsters to brainstorm examples of good citizenship in the classroom. List their ideas on the board. Then have students create these citizenship booklets. To make a booklet, a student staples four sheets of white construction paper along the left edge. He then glues a 2" x 15" strip of dark blue tagboard atop the staples as shown. He writes the title "My Citizenship Book" on the front cover; then he decorates the cover to resemble a flag. To complete his booklet, he copies, completes, and illustrates the phrase "Citizenship is" on each remaining booklet page. Invite youngsters to take their booklets home to share with their families.

Rules and Laws in the Community

Reinforce the need for maintaining order in the community with a discussion of rules and laws. Explain to students that a rule is a good guideline created for the protection and respect of people and property. A law is a command that everyone must obey to ensure safety and fairness. Guide students to give eamples of each. To make sure your students have an understanding of these two concepts, give a copy of the reproducible on page 183 to each child. Instruct her to write and illustrate a rule and a law that are enforced in your community. Then compile the completed pages into a classroom booklet titled "We Follow Rules and Laws."

Name ______________________________

Rules and Laws

A community has rules and laws.
Rules and laws protect people.
Write one rule and one law in your community.
Draw a picture to go with each sentence.

Rule: ______________________

____

____

____

____

____

Law: ______________________

____

____

____

____

____

Note to the teacher: Use with "Rules and Laws in the Community" on page 182.

CONSTITUTION DAY

September 17

Free to Be...

Put important freedoms on display with this easy-to-make class quilt. As a class, brainstorm a list of activities students have the freedom to do in their community. Next, explain to students that amendments to the Constitution name our freedoms and that these freedoms are important to our country. Then have each student pick a freedom that has meaning to her. She writes a sentence about it on an 8" x 8" paper square and then draws a matching picture. After each child shares her square, assemble them to make a class quilt.

I have the freedom to listen to any music I like.
Carrie

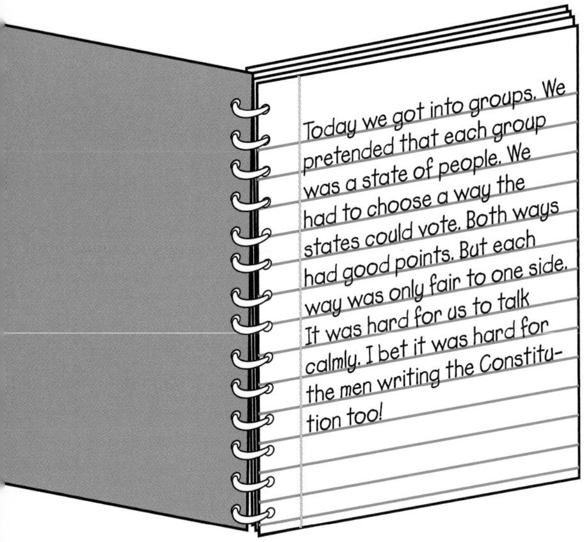
Today we got into groups. We pretended that each group was a state of people. We had to choose a way the states could vote. Both ways had good points. But each way was only fair to one side. It was hard for us to talk calmly. I bet it was hard for the men writing the Constitution too!

Decisions, Decisions

Help students understand an important decision the forefathers had to make with this whole-class activity. To start, divide students into several groups of different sizes. Next, tell students that they will vote on a class issue, such as a special snack or a free-time activity. Explain to students that they have two ways to conduct the vote: have each group get one vote per student or give each whole group one vote. Discuss the problems and benefits associated with each way to vote. If desired, have students try both methods. Then reveal to students that the writers of the Constitution had to make a similar decision, and the results settle the issue of representation in the U.S. Congress. Wrap up the activity by having students reflect on their experience in a journal entry.

Just Like That

Encourage students to make connections to history. First, explain to students that the delegates at the Constitutional Convention had many different ideas. They understood the importance of their job, and after arguing over many issues, they realized that they needed to compromise. Next, have each student reflect on a time when he had to compromise. Allow time for students to share their ideas in small groups. Then give each student a piece of drawing paper. He folds the paper in half and then writes a sentence telling how the delegates compromised and another telling about a time he compromised. Then he illustrates both sentences. Post the completed projects on a display titled "We're Just Like the Founding Fathers!"

They had to compromise when they decided how voting would work.
I had to compromise when my sister wanted to watch a show that I didn't want to watch.
Alex

Check out the skill-building reproducible on page 185.

Making Plans

Read the passage.

A group of men met in May 1787. They met in Philadelphia. These men wanted to make a better government.

The men wanted their meetings to be kept secret. They locked the doors and closed the windows so no one could listen in. These men also wanted someone to be in charge of the meetings. They chose George Washington to be in charge.

The men had a lot to talk about. They knew the job of the president was important. They needed a backup leader for the country. So the men chose to have a vice president too. The men did not want any person or group to have all the power. That is why they split the government into three parts.

These men made plans for our country. We still follow their plans today. We often call these men our Founding Fathers.

Read each cause statement.
Use the passage to write its effect.

1. **Cause:** The Founding Fathers wanted to keep their meetings secret.

   Effect: ______________________________

2. **Cause:** They wanted someone to be in charge of the meetings.

   Effect: ______________________________

3. **Cause:** The men wanted to have a backup leader for the president.

   Effect: ______________________________

4. **Cause:** They did not want all the power to go to one person or group.

   Effect: ______________________________

Economics

Needs
Wants

Learning About Wants and Needs

Reinforce needs and wants with this small-group activity. Have your class brainstorm a list of items that belong in each category. List students' responses on the board. Then have each group cut ten pictures of wants and ten pictures of needs from old magazines. After a determined length of time, have each group, in turn, share their pictures before gluing them in the corresponding column of a sheet of bulletin board paper labeled as shown. Display the resulting class poster in a prominent place.

Produced or Provided?

Show how goods and services take care of wants and needs with this partner activity. To make a spinner, give each student a tagboard copy of page 187. She illustrates three jobs that provide goods and three jobs that provide services; then she cuts out the wheel and arrow. She uses a brad to attach the arrow to the center of her wheel. Pair students and have them exchange spinners. One partner spins the arrow and names the job as either a good or a service. After verifying the answer, her partner then repeats the process on her spinner. Student pairs continue in this manner until each picture on both spinners has been identified.

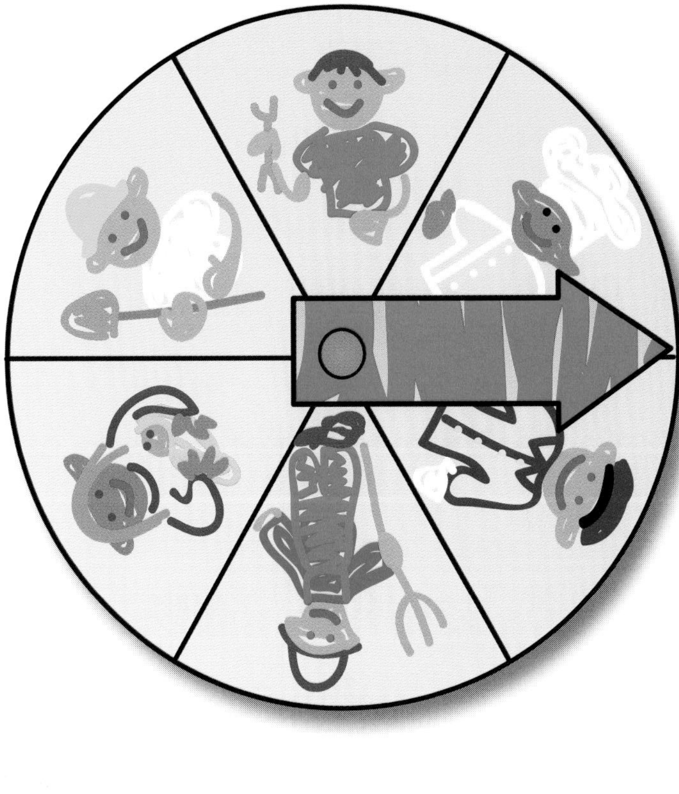

Spinner Patterns

Use with "Produced or Provided?" on page 186.

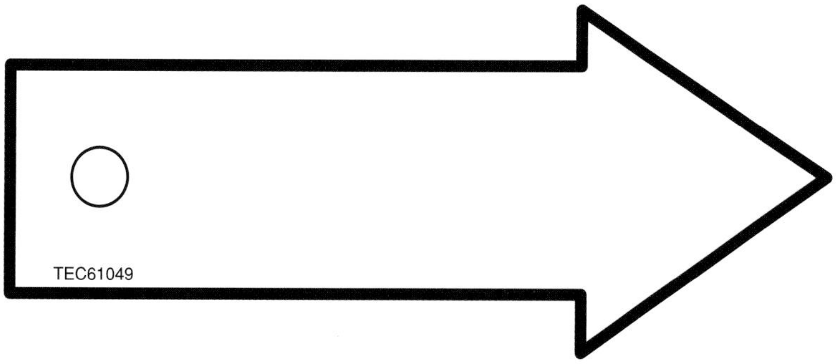
TEC61049

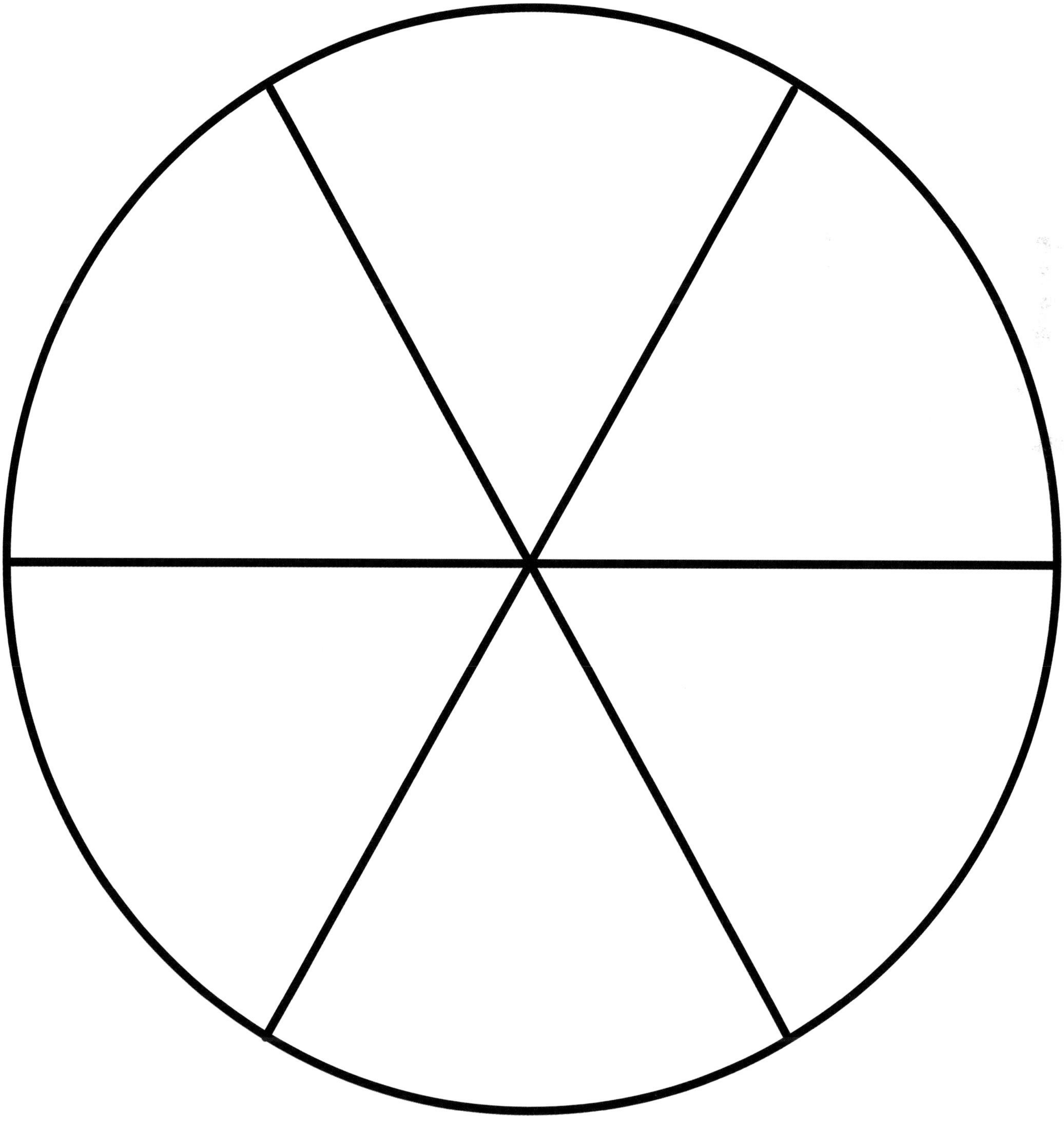

Map Skills

A Rose Is a Rose

Start your study of maps with one of the basics of map reading—the compass rose. Explain to your students that most maps have a symbol to show where the directions of north, south, east, and west are located. This symbol is called a compass rose. Use a classroom map to show your students what a compass rose looks like; then have each student create a model of a compass rose from a small paper plate. Have each student program his plate as shown. To show how the compass rose works, point to the north wall of the classroom. Have each student place his completed compass rose on the floor so that it is pointing to the north. Next, have him sketch a map of the classroom, making sure to include a compass rose to indicate the positions.

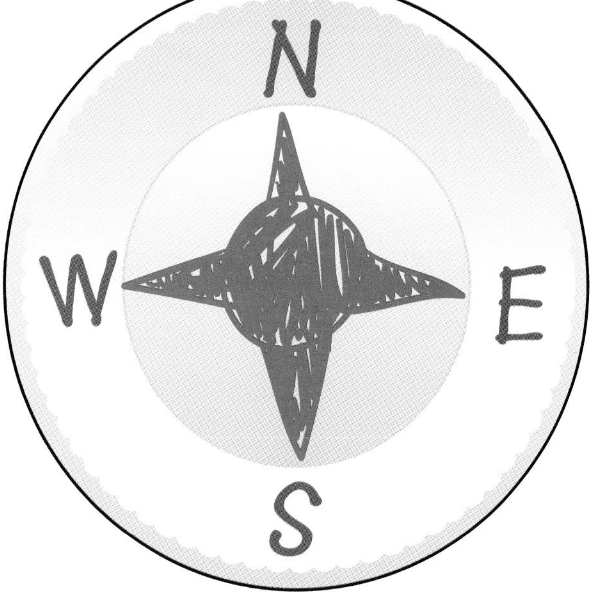
N
W
E
S

Map Key
desk
table
trash can
door

Super Symbols

Tell your students to refer to the classroom maps they made in the activity "A Rose Is a Rose." Ask students what symbols they used to represent the desks. Draw a large box on the board and write "Map Key" at the top of it. Then draw a square in the box and label it "desk." Explain that the square can be a symbol for a desk. Ask students what other symbols were included on their maps. What did they use to represent the door? The trash can? The table? Draw examples of their responses on your map key. Then have each student create a map key for his own classroom map. If time allows, have student volunteers show their maps and completed keys to the class.

Maps That Tell a Story

Share your favorite version of a well-known story with your class. After reading the story aloud, ask your students to describe the setting of the book. Then have each pair of students draw a picture of the setting on a large sheet of construction paper. Remind the pairs to include a compass rose and map key on their projects too! Provide time for students to share their completed maps with the class.

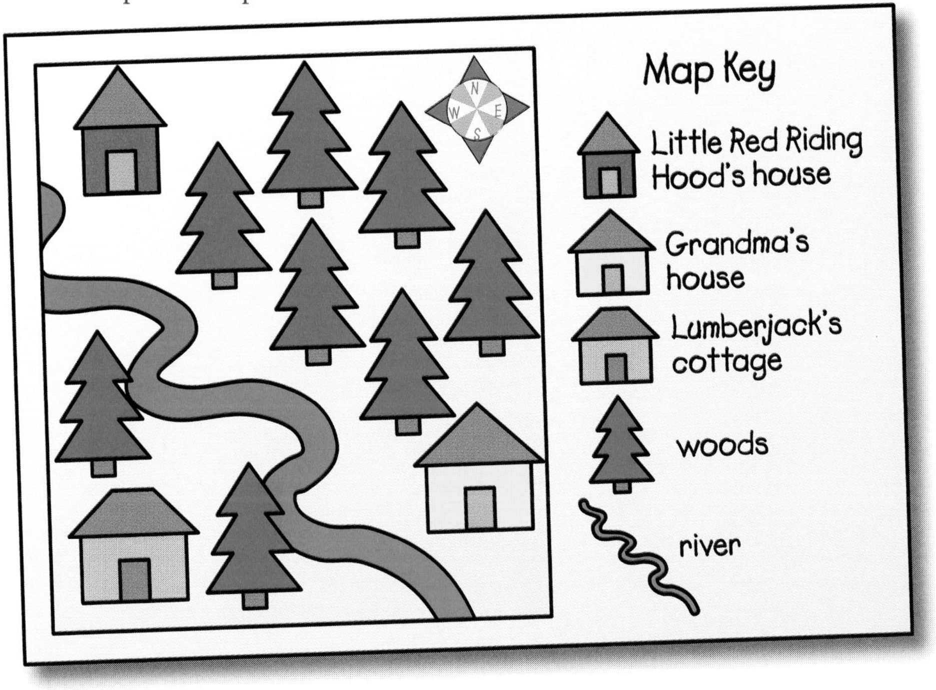
N
E
S
W
Map Key
Little Red Riding Hood's house
Grandma's house
Lumberjack's cottage
woods
river

Great Grids

Prepare a poster board grid with two-inch squares as shown. Also create a two-inch copy of your school mascot or another popular character. Laminate the grid and character for durability; then mount the grid on a small bulletin board. Pin the cutout to a square on the grid. Each morning select a student to move the cutout around the grid according to your oral directions. Give instructions such as "Move the character one square south and two squares east." Ask the class to listen and watch carefully to help monitor the student's work. Increase the difficulty of the instructions as students become more familiar with the cardinal directions.

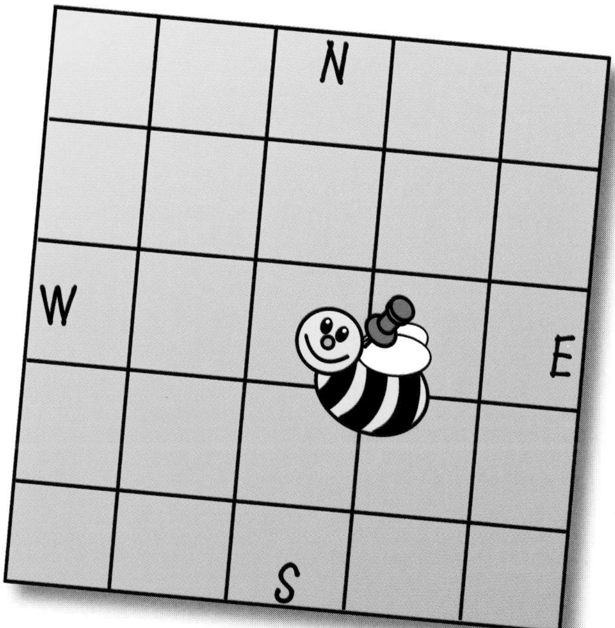
N
W
E
S

Giant Grid Game

Create a large grid by using a permanent marker to divide a plastic tablecloth into nine-inch squares. Draw a compass rose in the center square. To play the game, spread the grid on the floor. Have as many students as possible each stand on a different square on the grid. Ask the remainder of the students to sit around the edge of the grid and monitor the actions of the players. Announce a directional move for the students to follow, such as, "Move three squares north." If a student is unable to move that many squares in that direction, she must leave the grid and take a place with the seated students. Play continues until only one student remains and is declared the winner. Next, invite the second group of students to each take a place on the grid for another round of play.

Check out the skill-building reproducibles on pages 190 and 191.

Name________________________________

Sports Shopping

Cut out the boxes on the left.
Glue each one on the map.
Use the clues to help you.

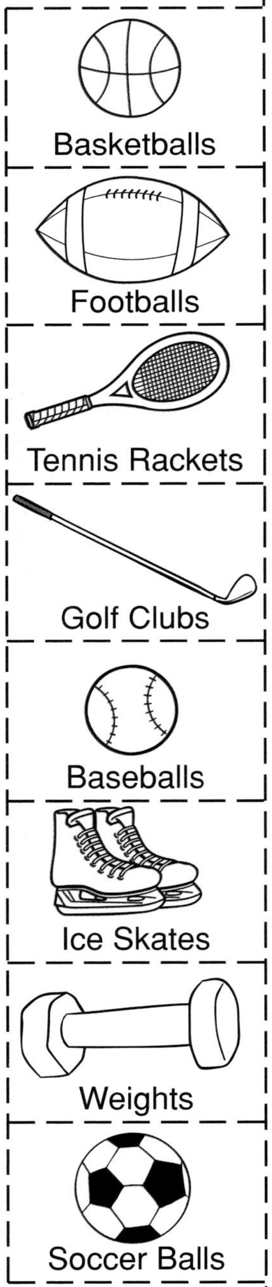
Basketballs
Footballs
Tennis Rackets
Golf Clubs
Baseballs
Ice Skates
Weights
Soccer Balls

Clues

- The basketballs are north of the cash register.
- The soccer balls are east of the cash register.
- The weights are west of the basketballs.
- The golf clubs are south of the cash register.
- The ice skates are north of the soccer balls.
- The footballs are east of the golf clubs.
- The baseballs are west of the cash register.
- The tennis rackets are south of the baseballs.

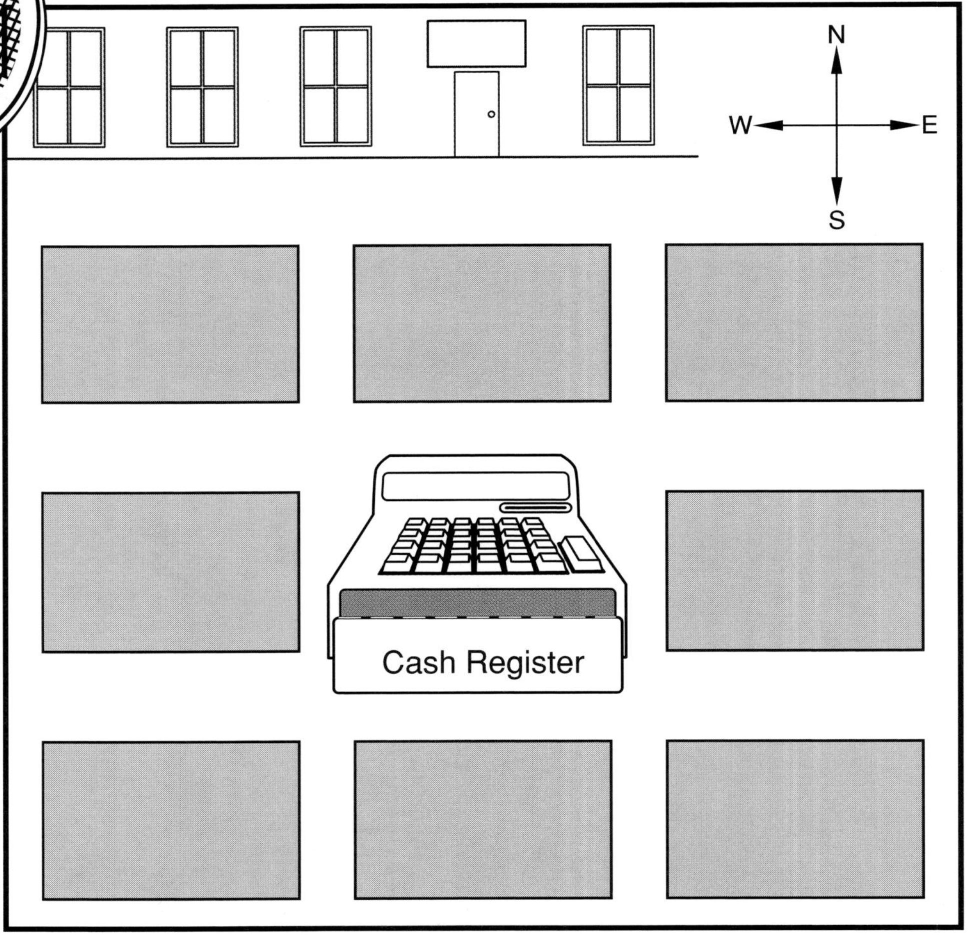
N
W
E
S
Cash Register

Name ____________________

Sofa City

Follow the directions to color each group of sofas.
Use the map key to help you.

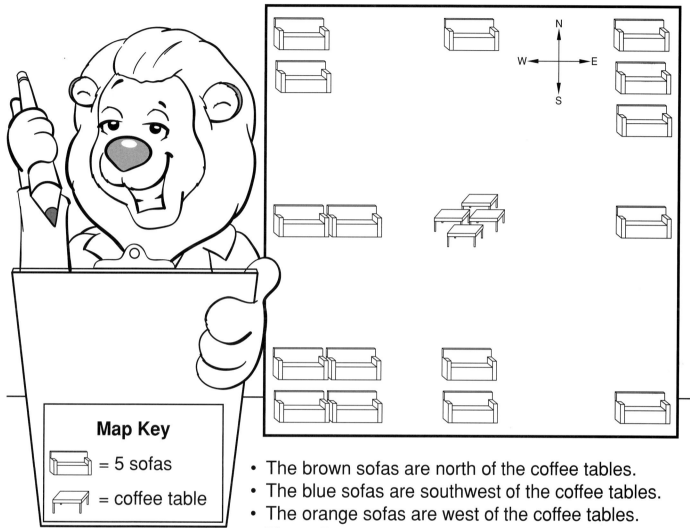

Map Key
= 5 sofas
= coffee table

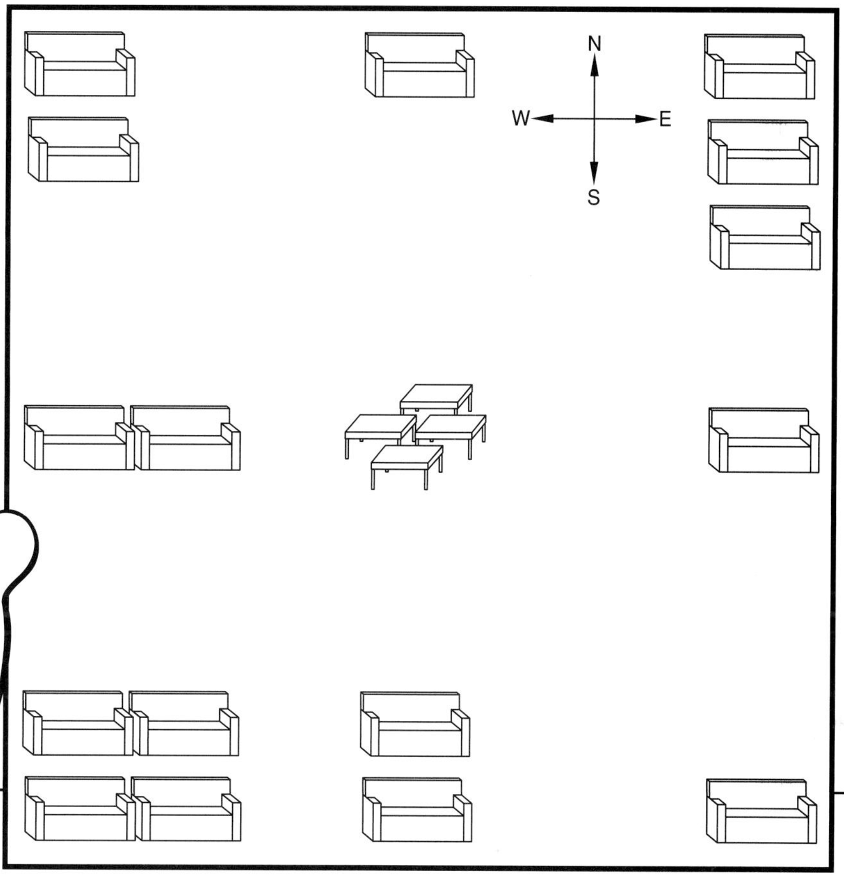
N
W
E
S

- The brown sofas are north of the coffee tables.
- The blue sofas are southwest of the coffee tables.
- The orange sofas are west of the coffee tables.
- The yellow sofas are northeast of the coffee tables.
- The black sofas are south of the coffee tables.
- The green sofas are southeast of the coffee tables.
- The purple sofas are northwest of the coffee tables.
- The red sofas are east of the coffee tables.

Write the number of sofas of each color.
Use the key to help you.

_______ red	_______ brown	_______ blue	_______ purple
_______ yellow	_______ black	_______ green	_______ orange

Graphic Organizers

Name
Beginning, middle, and end
Bus Stop
Title: The Vacation
Beginning
My family and I drove to Florida.
Middle
We visited my cousins. We went to the beach and collected seashells. We went on a boat tour in a swamp.
End
We came home. We made a scrapbook to help us remember our trip.

E Chart

Give each child a copy of the E chart on page 195. As she reads a paragraph, have her record the paragraph's main idea on the rake's handle. Then direct her to write each supporting detail on each of the rake's prongs. Provide time for each child to share her work with the class.

Beginning, Middle, and End

Use the beginning, middle, and end chart on page 194 as a prewriting sheet. When students are planning a narrative story, have each child write his title on his copy of the page. Next, have him complete the page. Then have him refer to the page as he writes his story.

Name
A Sandy Summary
Summarizing
Title:
Stellaluna
First,
an owl knocks Stellaluna out of her mother's arms.
Then
Stellaluna lands in a bird's nest. She eats what the birds eat and learns to live like a bird. She learns to fly.
Next,
After that,
Finally,

Summarizing Chart

To build students' understanding of summarizing, have them complete the chart on page 196. Before a child reads a picture book, he writes the book's title on the top of the sand castle. After he reads the book, he summarizes the events from the story in order on each layer of the sand castle.

Character Comparison Chart

Give each pair of students a copy of the character comparison chart on page 197. Read aloud a picture book and direct one partner to write the name of two characters on the chart. Next, have partners work together to write on the jar below each name words and phrases that show differences between the characters. Then have the partners write similarities between the characters in the space where the jars overlap.

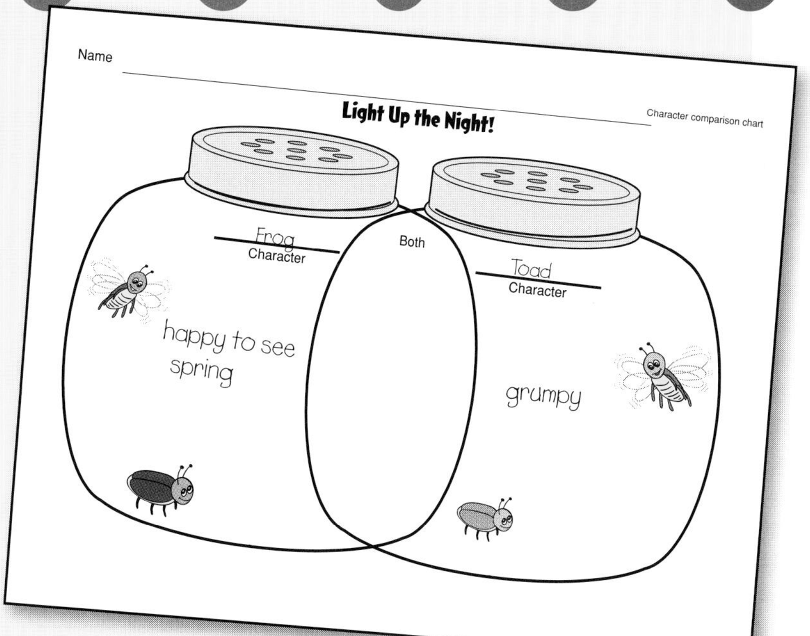
Name
Light Up the Night!
Character comparison chart
Frog
Character
Both
Toad
Character
happy to see spring
grumpy

Word, Definition, and Picture Chart

Use the word, definition, and picture chart on page 198 to increase students' vocabulary. Each child writes a vocabulary word across the top of the sunglasses. She writes the definition of the word on one lens and then draws a picture of the word on the other. On each of the keys, she writes a word that her word reminds her of.

Question-and-answer chart
Name
Packing for a Trip
Question:
Which part of the plant helps it make food?
Question:
What do the plant's roots do?
Answer:
Answer:
Question:
Question:
Answer:
Answer:

Question-and-Answer Chart

Before reading a nonfiction passage or article, give each child a copy of the question-and-answer chart on page 199. Guide the child to write questions about the topic in the top of each suitcase. After he reads the piece, direct the child to write the answer to each of his questions.

Name ____________________

Bus Stop

Title: ____________________

Beginning
Middle
End

Note to the teacher: Use with "Beginning, Middle, and End" on page 192.

Raking in the Details

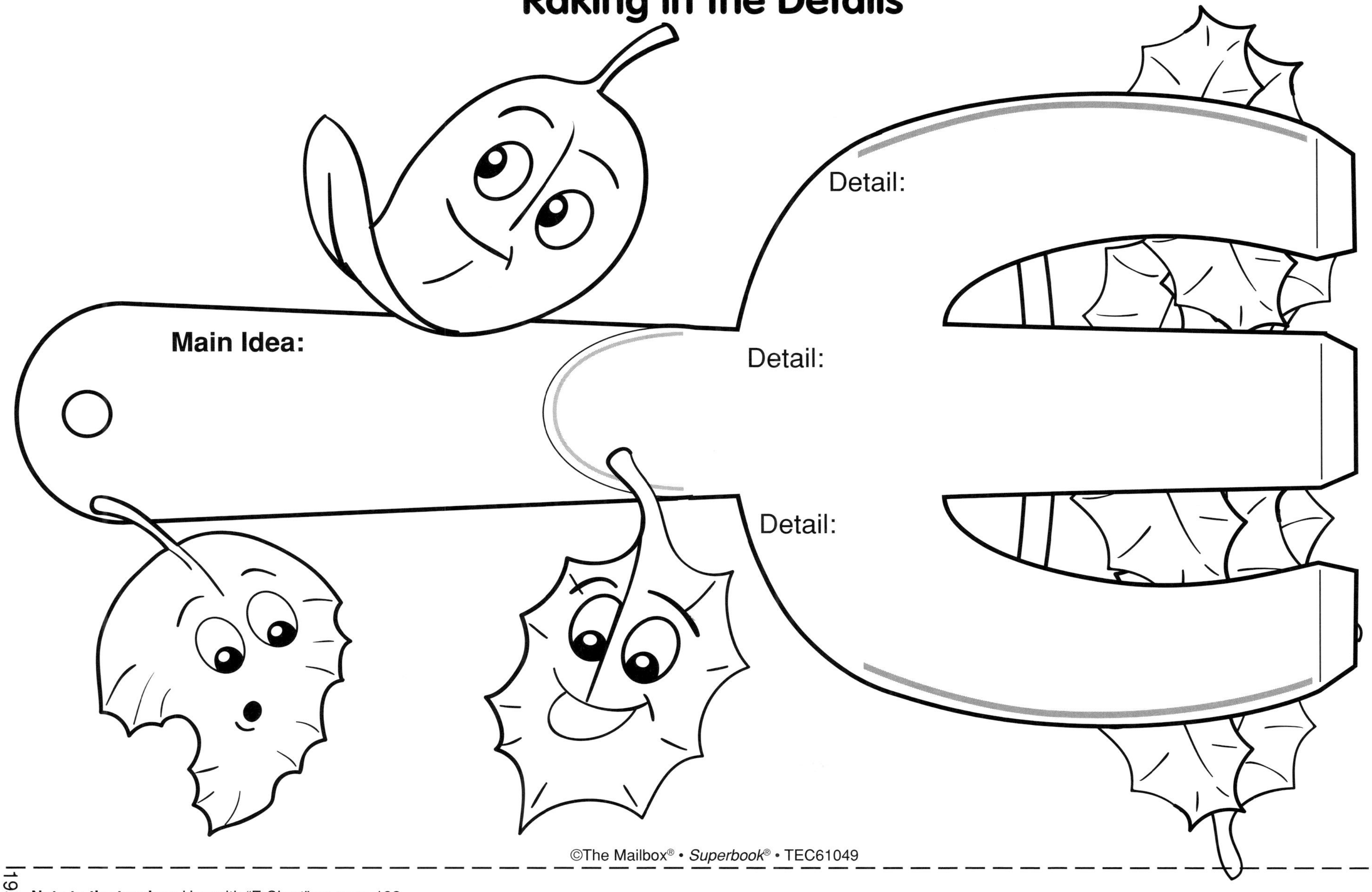
Main Idea:
Detail:
Detail:
Detail:

Note to the teacher: Use with “E Chart” on page 192.

Name ____________________

A Sandy Summary

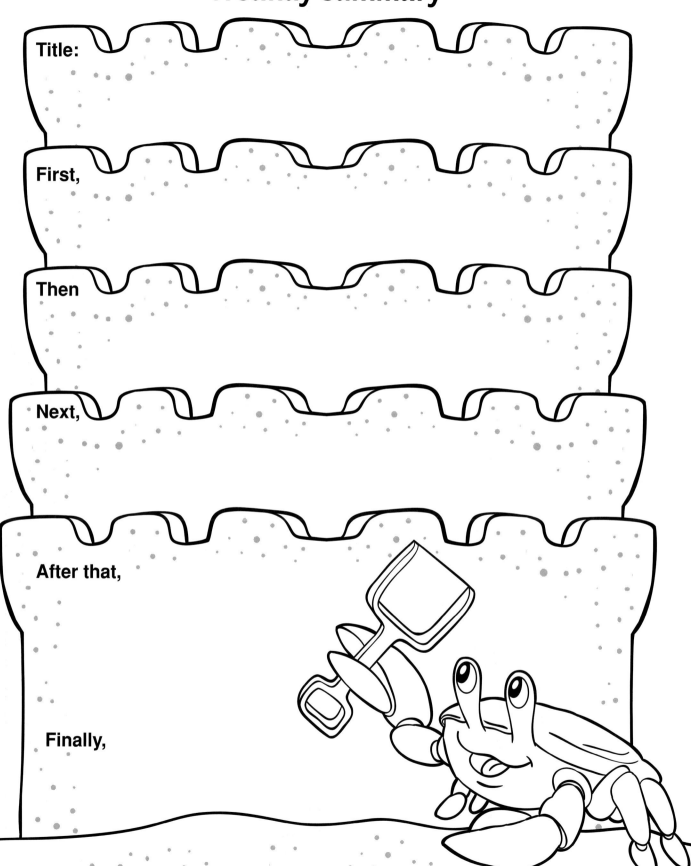

Title:

First,

Then

Next,

After that,

Finally,

 Note to the teacher: Use with “Summarizing Chart” on page 192.

Name ______________________________ Character comparison chart

Light Up the Night!

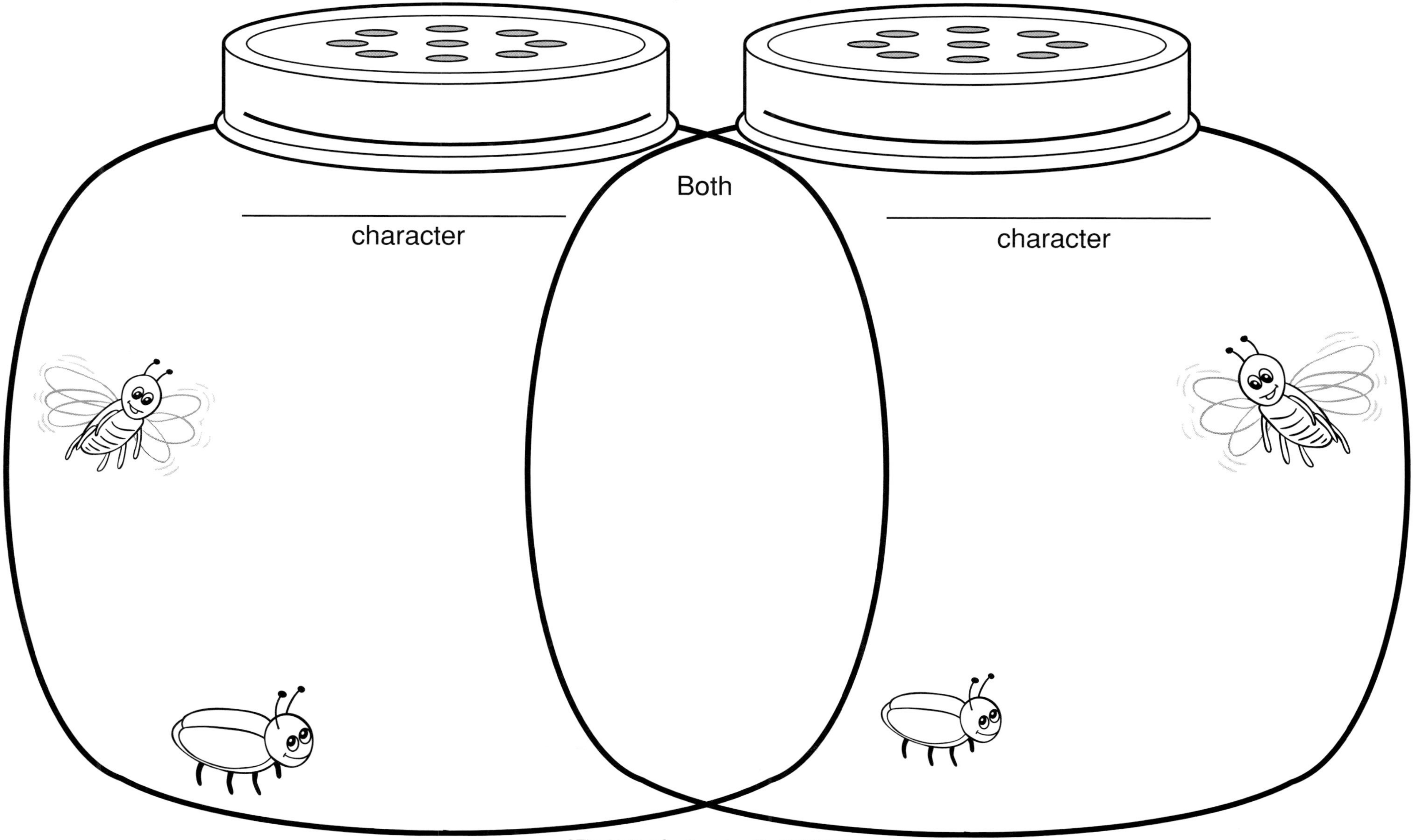
Both
character
character

Note to the teacher: Use with "Character Comparison Chart" on page 193.

Name ______________________ Word, definition, and picture chart

Time to Hit the Road!

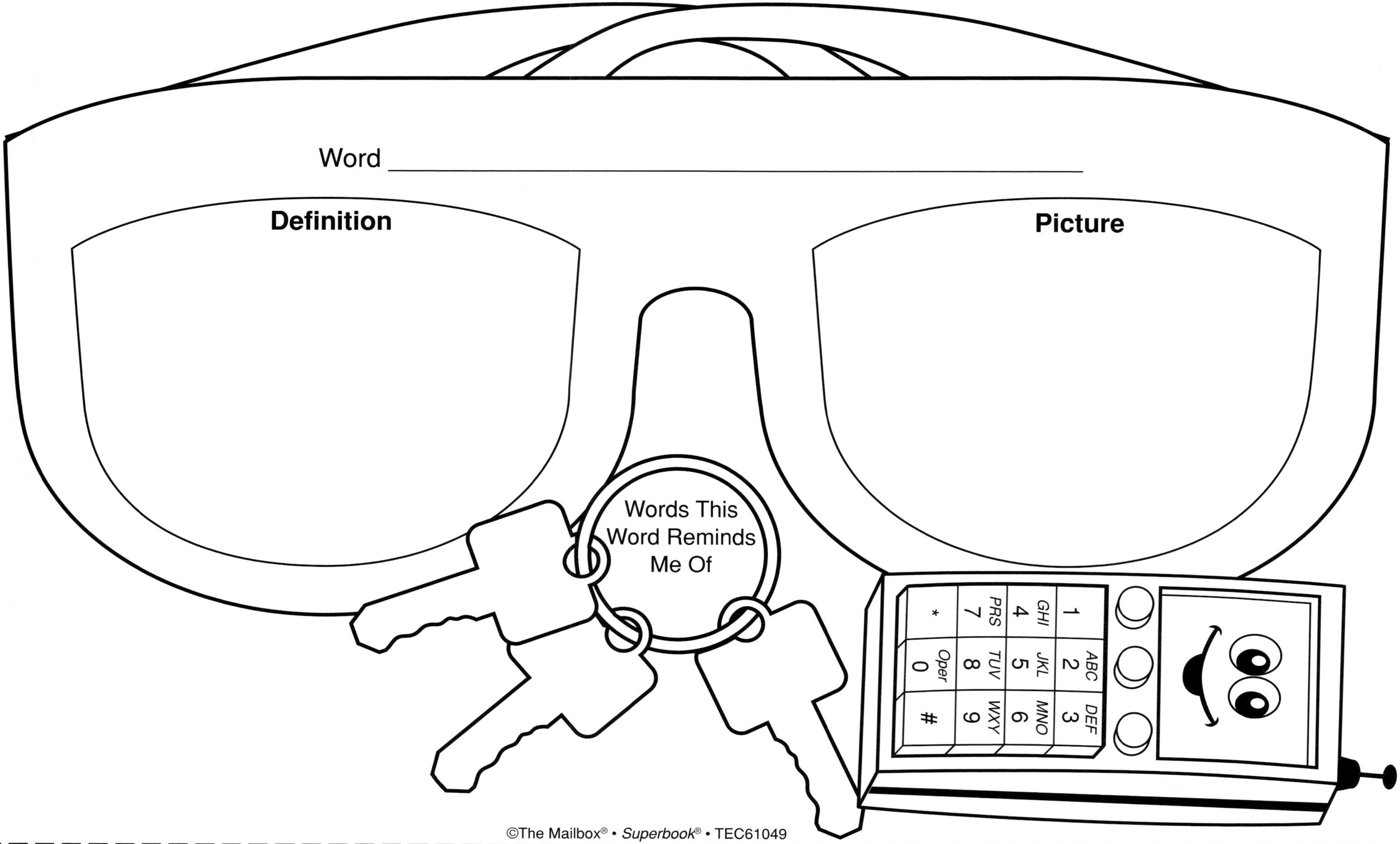
Word ______________________
Definition
Picture
Words This Word Reminds Me Of
1
ABC 2
DEF 3
GHI 4
JKL 5
MNO 6
PRS 7
TUV 8
WXY 9
*
Oper 0
#

Note to the teacher: Use with "Word, Definition, and Picture Chart" on page 193.

Name ____________________ Question-and-answer chart

Packing for a Trip

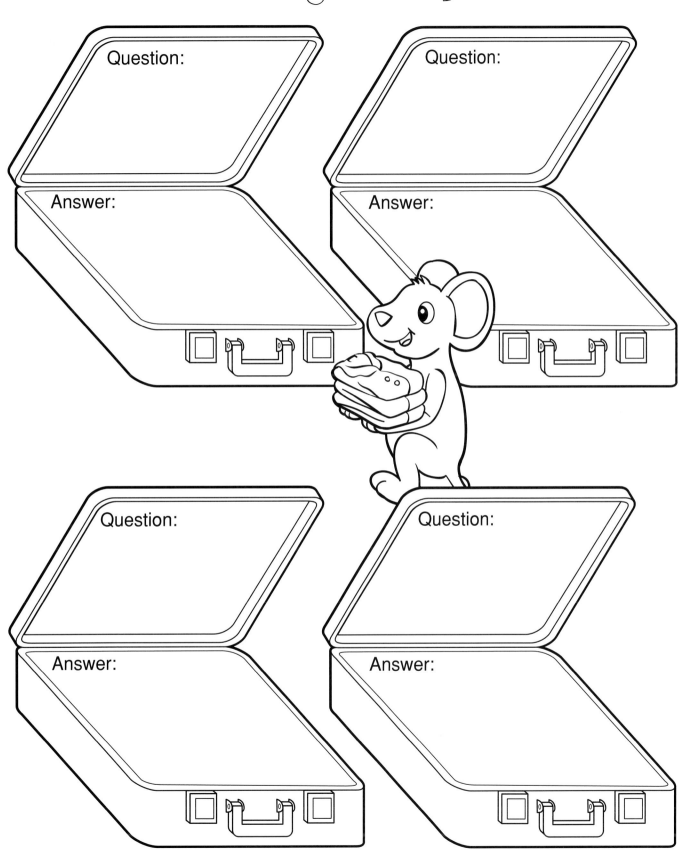

Question:

Answer:

Question:

Answer:

Question:

Answer:

Question:

Answer:

Note to the teacher: Use with "Question-and-Answer Chart" on page 193.

Language Arts Centers

bell
candle
gift
holly
present

What a Hang-Up!

For a fast and easy sequencing center, suspend a clothesline between two chairs. Program a set of seasonal shapes with desired vocabulary words or story events; then store the shapes in a bag. Also make an answer key for self-checking and place it in the bag. Place the bag and a supply of clothespins at the center. A student sequences the cutouts by suspending them on the clothesline in the correct order. Then she looks at the answer key to check her sequence. **Sequencing**

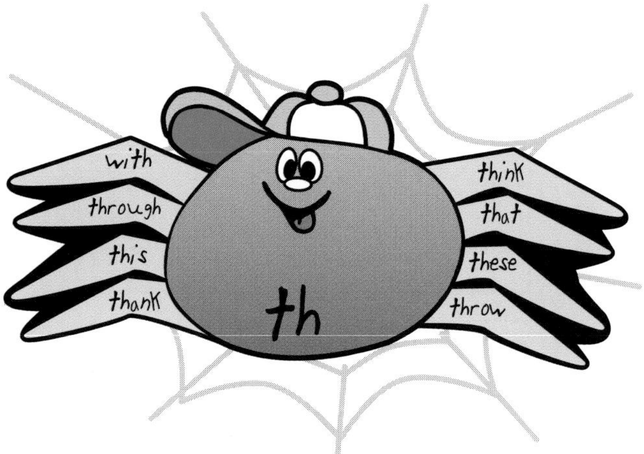
with
through
this
thank
think
that
these
throw
th

Word-Skill Web

Spin a center of word-skill reinforcement with the help of these super spiders. Make a class supply of the spider pattern on page 203, and place them at a center along with crayons, scissors, and markers. Post a sign showing a desired sound, letter blend, or vowel combination. A student labels a spider pattern with the featured letter(s), then writes a word containing the letter(s) on each of the spider's legs. She then colors and cuts out the spider. Display the completed projects on a bulletin board covered in artificial webbing material. **Phonics**

In the News

This versatile learning center will make headlines in your classroom! Post a list of skill-based tasks (similar to the ones shown) at a center. Also place at the center a supply of discarded newspapers, scissors, glue sticks, and sheets of blank paper. A student chooses a task from the list. Next, he searches for words in the newspaper to complete the task. He then cuts out the words and glues them to a sheet of paper. If desired, post a different skill each week to provide review or reinforcement. **Skill review**

- Find ten proper names. Glue them in alphabetical order.
- Find five nouns and five verbs.
- Find five words that contain the *sh* digraph.
- Find ten number words. Glue them in numerical order.
- Find five words that have the long *a* sound.
- Find a headline that contains a compound word.
- Find ten words that end in silent *e*.

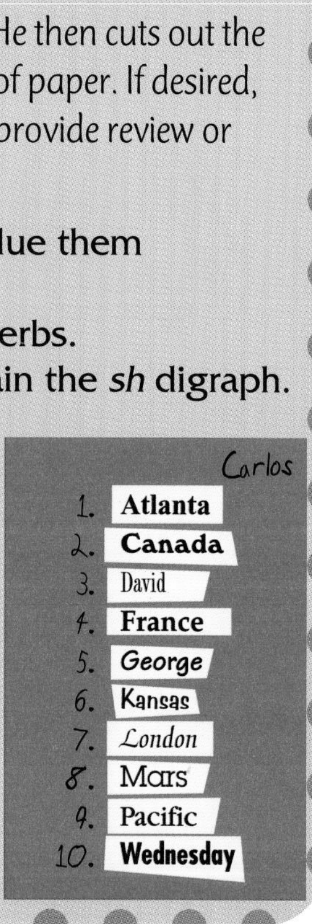
Carlos
1. Atlanta
2. Canada
3. David
4. France
5. George
6. Kansas
7. London
8. Mars
9. Pacific
10. Wednesday

Book-Report Recipe

Set up a book-report writing center featuring this easy-to-use recipe for literature reviews. Copy the recipe shown onto poster board, and decorate it to resemble a recipe card. Place the card, crayons, and supplies of writing and drawing paper at a center. A student follows the directions on the recipe to report on a desired book. Remind students to answer the questions with complete sentences. After a student answers the questions, he illustrates a favorite scene from the story. **Responding to literature**

Book-Report Recipe

1. Name the title and author of the book.
2. Tell when and where the story takes place.
3. Describe the main characters.
4. Write a sentence or two telling what the story is about.
5. Explain why you did or did not like the book.

red
sweet
delicious
eat
APPLES
juicy
crunchy
tasty
yummy

Student-Made Word Banks

This simple vocabulary-building activity will speak for itself! Draw and label a desired picture on a sheet of chart paper. Place the chart paper, dictionaries, and an assortment of colored markers in an easily accessible area. Invite students to write words to describe the picture along the sides of the chart paper. After a few days, display the completed word bank for students to refer to during writing assignments, journal time, or language activities. **Vocabulary**

Idea Factory

Complement any unit of study with this center that focuses on creative abilities and results in a class book. Decide on a topic for the learning center, either from a unit of study, a seasonal theme, or an area of student interest. Place a supply of writing paper, drawing paper, markers, colored pencils, and reference books at a center. Encourage each student to visit the center and complete a page about the designated topic. Students can write an informative paragraph, compose a poem, draw a picture, or relate information about the topic in another creative form. Compile the completed pages into a class book. Invite each student to take the book home overnight to share with her family. **Writing**

Vanessa
Dinosaurs
Dinosaurs lived a long time ago. Some ate meat. Some ate plants. Dinosaurs are extinct now.
Billy

Pocket Pals

I will see Mrs. Smith next week.
correct
correct
my favorite day is saturday.
incorrect
incorrect

Get students hopping with this capitalization review game. Make two copies of the kangaroo pattern on page 204. Color and cut out the patterns; then label one kangaroo's pocket "correct" and the other kangaroo's pocket "incorrect." Glue the kangaroos to the inside of a file folder as shown. Program five cards each with a correctly written sentence, and five cards with sentences containing capitalization errors. Label the backs of the cards for self-checking. Store the cards in a resealable bag clipped to the folder; then place the folder at a center. A student reads each card and places it on the corresponding kangaroo's pocket. She flips the card to check her work.

Reinforce other skills by creating additional folders and card sets for real/make-believe, correct/incorrect math problems, complete/incomplete sentences, or correct/incorrect punctuation. **Capitalization**

Three in a Row

For this lotto game, program several 3 x 3 grids with different combinations of periods, question marks, exclamation marks, and commas. Cut out a copy of the sentence cards on page 203 and program the back of each card for self-checking. Stack the cards faceup at a center along with the prepared gameboards and a supply of game markers.

When a small group of students visits the center, each child takes a gameboard. A volunteer takes a card and reads the sentence aloud. Players identify the correct punctuation, and the volunteer confirms their response by flipping the card. Then each player covers a matching gameboard space. Play continues until one player marks three spaces in a vertical, horizontal, or diagonal row and announces, "Three in a row!" **Punctuation**

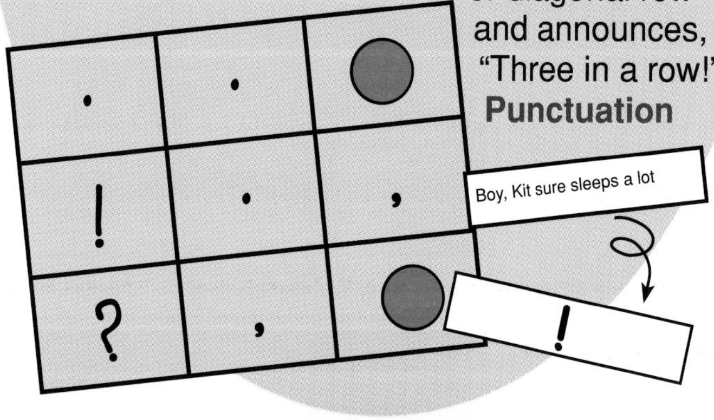
Boy, Kit sure sleeps a lot
!

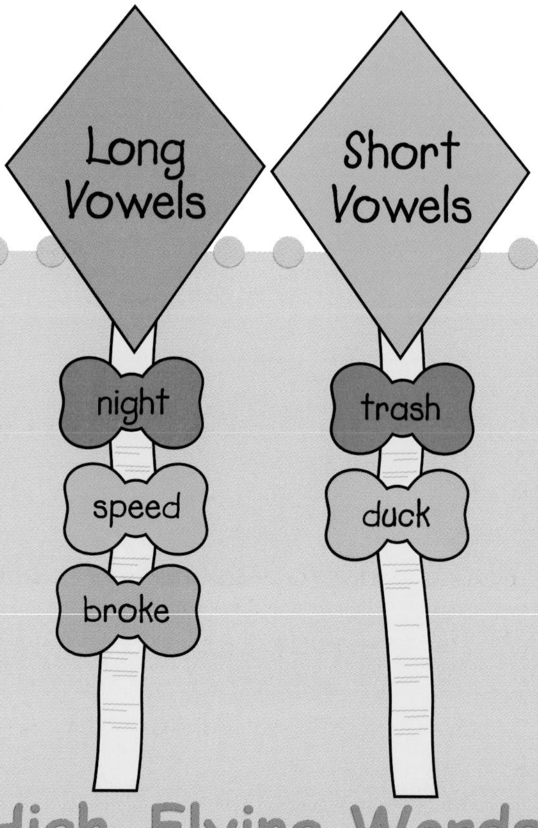
Long Vowels
Short Vowels
night
speed
broke
trash
duck

High-Flying Words

Students match bows to kites with this easy-to-prepare center! Cut from construction paper two kites and a supply of bows similar to the ones shown. Label one kite "Short Vowels" and the other kite "Long Vowels"; then attach a crepe paper tail to each kite. Program each bow with a different long- or short-vowel word. Place the bows and kites at a center. A child selects a bow, reads the word, determines whether the vowel sound is long or short, and places the bow on the corresponding kite tail. She continues in this manner for each remaining bow. **Vowels**

Spider Pattern

Use with "Word-Skill Web" on page 200.

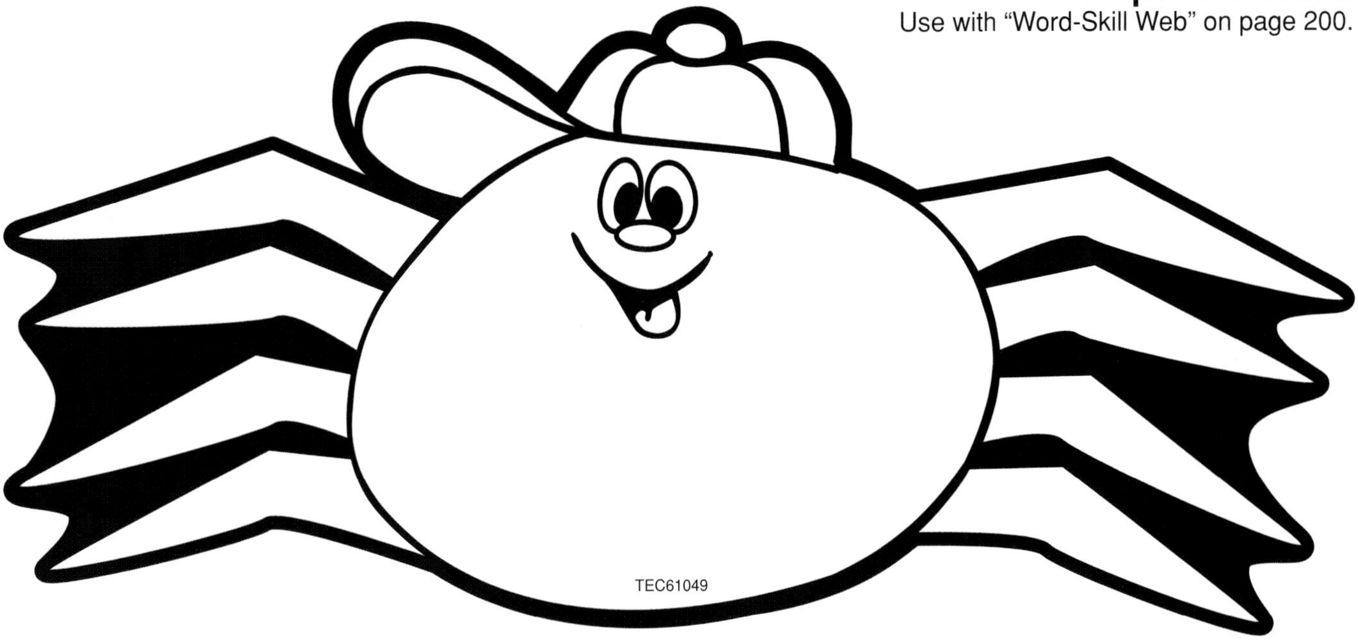
TEC61049

Sentence Cards

Use with "Three in a Row" on page 202.

Kit naps below the window TEC61049	Boy, Kit sure sleeps a lot TEC61049
Kit is a friendly cat TEC61049	Wow, Kit ate all the tuna fish TEC61049
Jen gives Kit some milk TEC61049	Oh no, the milk spilled TEC61049
Does Kit see the mouse TEC61049	Fish cheese, and beef are Kit's favorites. TEC61049
Why does Kit like the sun TEC61049	Kit was born on June 12 2000. TEC61049
When will Kit wake up TEC61049	Miami Florida, is Kit's hometown. TEC61049

Kangaroo Pattern

Use with “Pocket Pals” on page 202.

TEC61049

MATH CENTERS

Fraction Fun

Create task cards similar to the ones shown. Program the back of each card for self-checking; then laminate the cards for durability. Place the task cards, crayons, and a class supply of drawing paper at a center. A student divides a sheet of paper into six squares and numbers them from one to six. Next, she reads a task card and completes the activity in the corresponding square. She then flips the card to check her work. She repeats this process with the additional cards. Periodically add new task cards to keep student interest high. **Fractions**

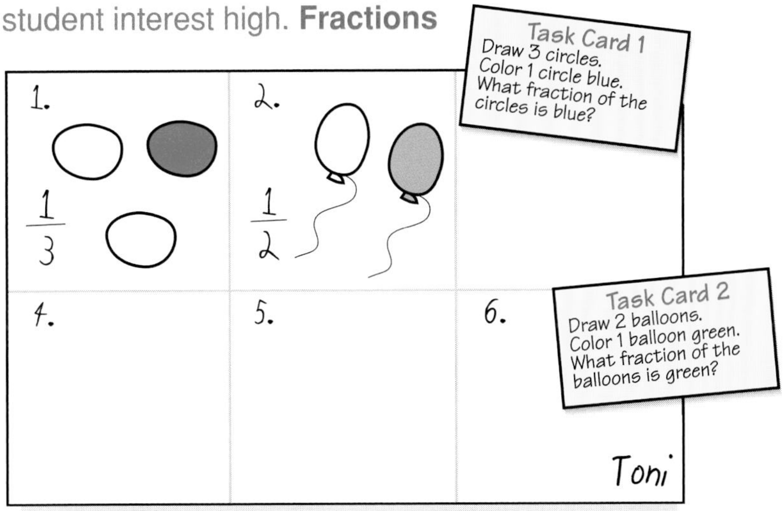
Task Card 1
Draw 3 circles.
Color 1 circle blue.
What fraction of the circles is blue?
1.
1/3
2.
1/2
Task Card 2
Draw 2 balloons.
Color 1 balloon green.
What fraction of the balloons is green?
4.
5.
6.
Toni

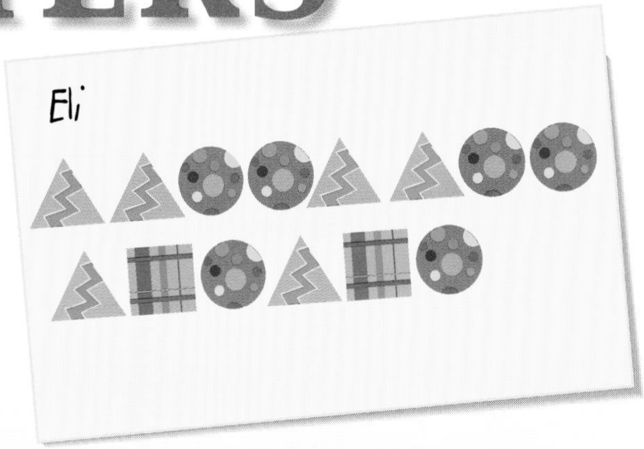
Eli

Perky Patterns

Cut a large supply of basic shapes—such as squares, circles, and triangles—from leftover gift wrap, wallpaper samples, or fabric. Place the shapes, glue, and a supply of paper at a center. A student uses the shapes to create a predetermined number of different patterns. He then glues the patterns onto a sheet of construction paper. Display the completed patterns on a bulletin board for an eye-catching display. **Geometric patterns**

Munchable Math

Students can review a variety of math skills at this tasty learning center. Place a box of colorful breakfast cereal and a supply of three-ounce paper cups at a center. A student visits the center and fills one cup with cereal. Then she uses the pieces to complete a variety of tasks, such as

- estimating how many pieces are in the cup and then counting to find the actual number
- determining whether the total is an odd or even number
- counting the pieces by twos
- counting the pieces by fives
- determining which color appears on the most (or fewest) pieces
- creating a color or shape pattern

After she completes the tasks, invite the student to munch her manipulatives as a reward for her hard work. Math

Guess: 62
Actual: 70
even
Red is the color I have the most pieces of.
Purple is the color I have the fewest pieces of.
My Pattern

Fishing for Facts

Cut a large fish shape from paper. Glue each top edge of several construction paper semicircles to the fish cutout to make scales as shown. Number the top corner of each scale; then program the scales with math problems. Lift each scale and write the answer to each problem underneath. Place the fish at a center along with paper and pencils. A student numbers a sheet of paper, answers the corresponding problems, and then lifts the scales to check her work. **Basic facts**

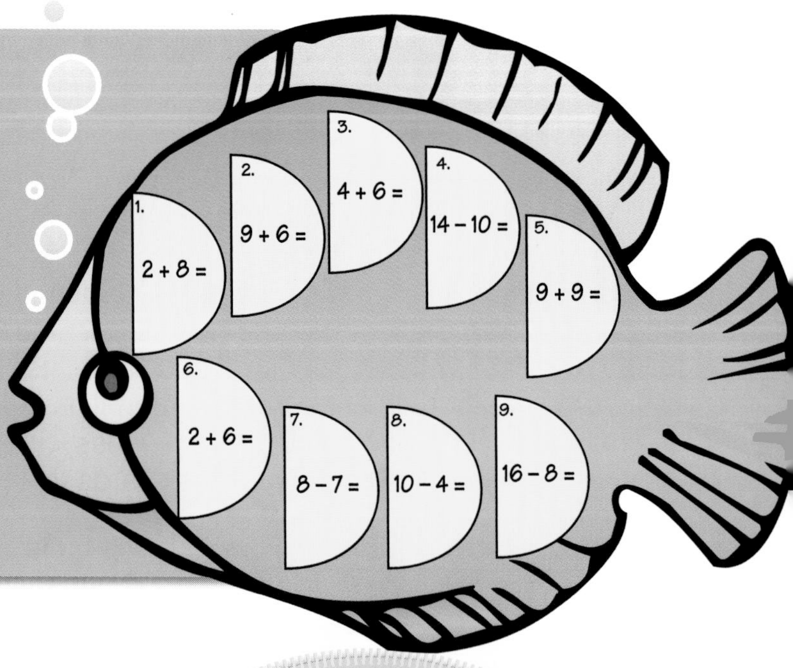
1. 2 + 8 =
2. 9 + 6 =
3. 4 + 6 =
4. 14 – 10 =
5. 9 + 9 =
6. 2 + 6 =
7. 8 – 7 =
8. 10 – 4 =
9. 16 – 8 =

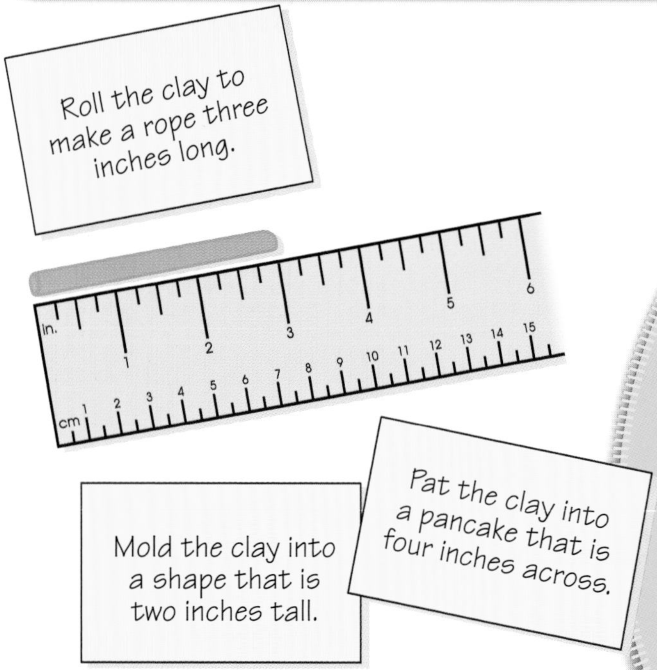
Roll the clay to make a rope three inches long.
Mold the clay into a shape that is two inches tall.
Pat the clay into a pancake that is four inches across.

Partner Measurement

To set up this partner center, create several task cards similar to the ones shown. Laminate the cards for durability; then place the cards, two rulers, and a supply of modeling clay at a center. A student selects a task card, uses a ruler to mold the clay to the desired length, and then asks his partner to check his work with the other ruler. Challenge your students to complete four task cards each time they visit the center, taking turns molding the clay. No doubt students' measurement skills will really take shape! **Linear measurement**

A Day in the Life

Review time-telling skills with this booklet activity. To make a booklet, staple five sheets of blank paper between two construction paper covers. Place a class supply of booklets, a clockface stamp, an ink pad, and crayons at a center. A student writes "A Day in the Life of [student's name]" on the front cover of a booklet and decorates it as desired. Then he stamps a clockface on the next five pages. He chooses five different times of the day and uses a crayon to sequentially program each clock with one of the times. Then, on the bottom of each page, he writes the time and illustrates what he might be doing at that time of the day. Have students share their completed booklets with their classmates. **Telling time**

7:00

Collecting Facts

To reinforce basic facts, make several copies of the bucket and shell patterns on page 208. Cut out the patterns and then program each bucket cutout with a number between 1 and 20. Next, label each of four shells with an addition or subtraction problem that equals the number on the bucket. Then repeat the process with another bucket and set of shells. Put the shells in a resealable plastic bag and place the bag at a center with the buckets, pencils, and paper. A child chooses a bucket and locates the shells with facts that equal the number named. He places the shells on the bucket, and when he has all four, he records the facts on his paper. Then he selects another bucket and repeats the process. If desired, have the student check his work with a calculator. **Basic facts**

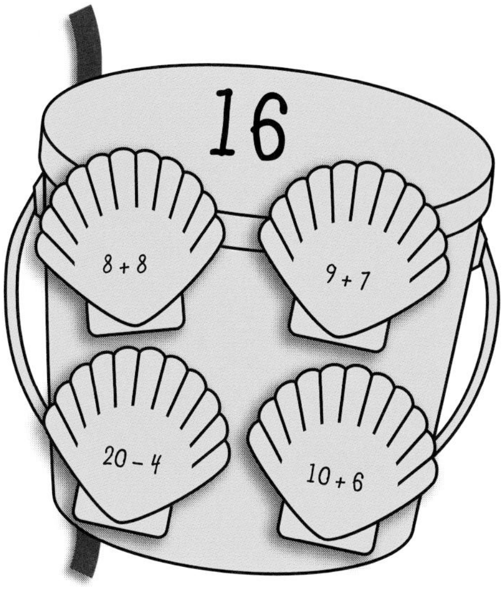
16
8 + 8
9 + 7
20 – 4
10 + 6

Multitasking Numbers

Make a class supply of the place-value model patterns on page 209. Next, cut a class supply of six-inch-long sentence strips in three different colors. A student stacks three different-colored strips and staples them together along the top at each end and in the middle. Next, he cuts the top two layers between the staples to make three equal sections. Then he writes a digit on each section of the top layer. He writes the word for each value on the middle layer. After that, he cuts out and glues the matching place-value models onto the bottom layer. Use the completed booklets at a later date to order or compare numbers. **Number sense**

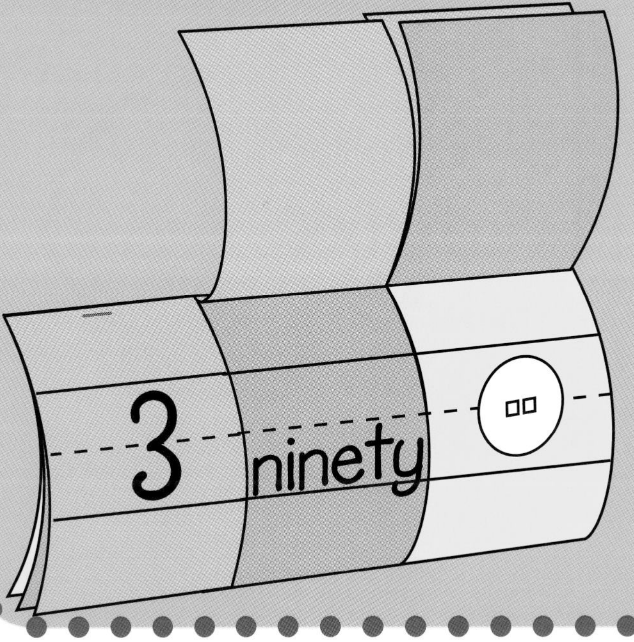
3
ninety

Money Bags

Enlarge the pocket pattern on page 208 and then make five copies. Write a price on and cut out each pocket. Next, glue paper or plastic coins that total these prices onto paper strips, preparing one set of coins for each pocket. Place each strip inside a snack-size plastic bag and use a permanent marker to label each bag with a letter. Then make an answer key by writing each letter and the value of the coins in its bag. Put the pockets, bags, and answer key at a center. A child chooses a pocket and finds the bag with the matching coin amount. She places the bag with the pocket. After all of the matches have been made, she uses the answer key to check her work. **Coin sets**

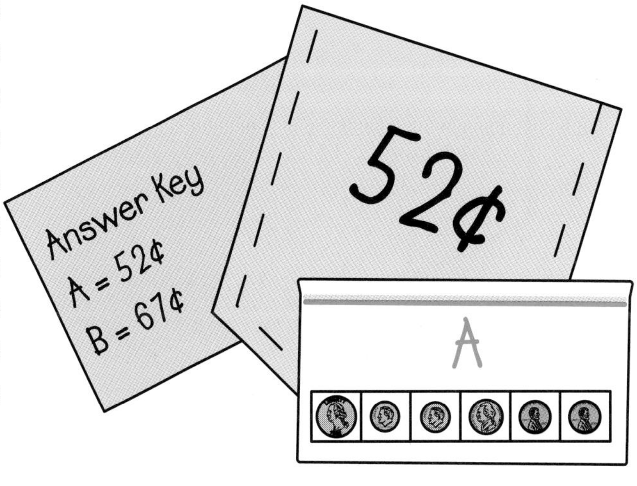
Answer Key
A = 52¢
B = 67¢
52¢
A

Bucket and Shell Patterns

Use with "Collecting Facts" on page 207.

TEC61049

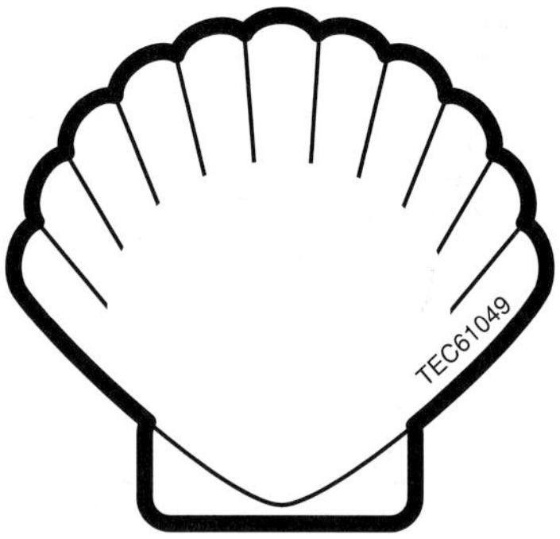
TEC61049

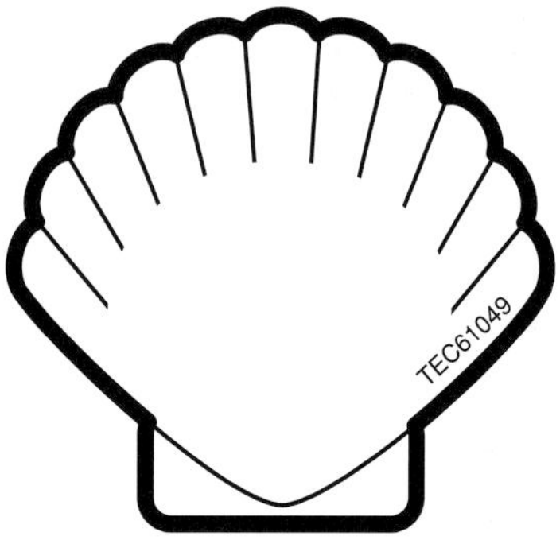
TEC61049

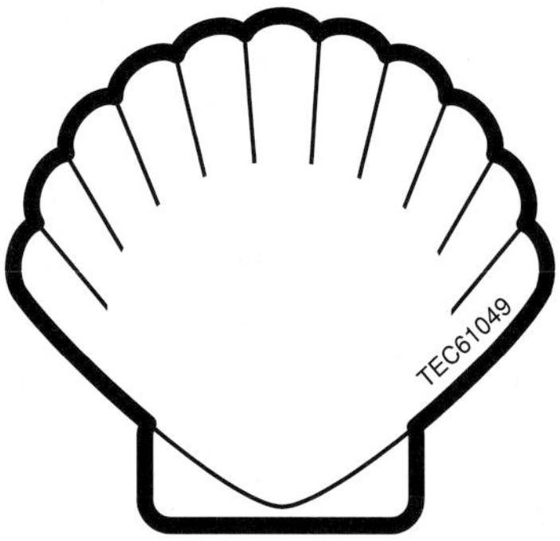
TEC61049

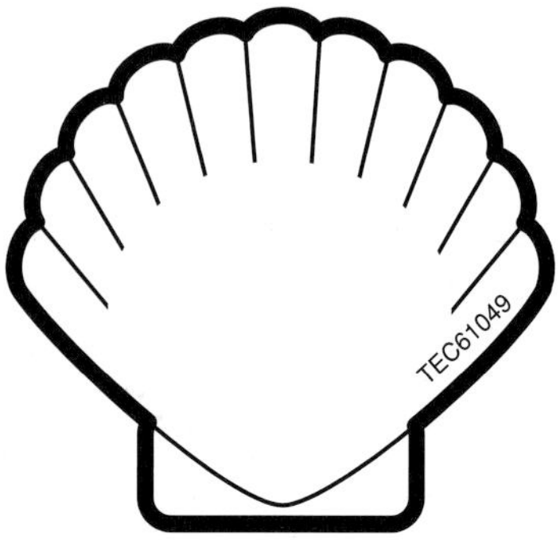
TEC61049

Pocket Pattern

Use with "Money Bags" on page 207.

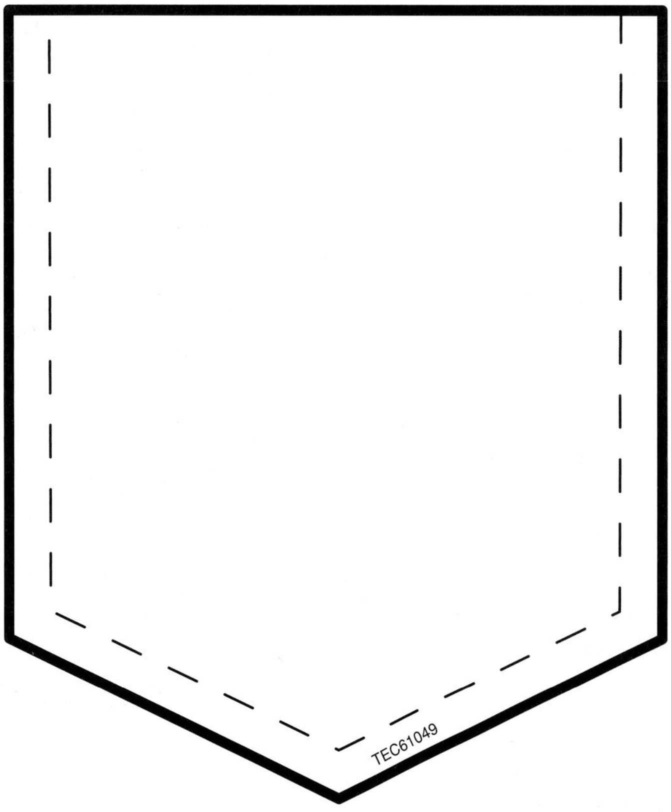
TEC61049

Use with “Multitasking Numbers” on page 207.

Hundreds

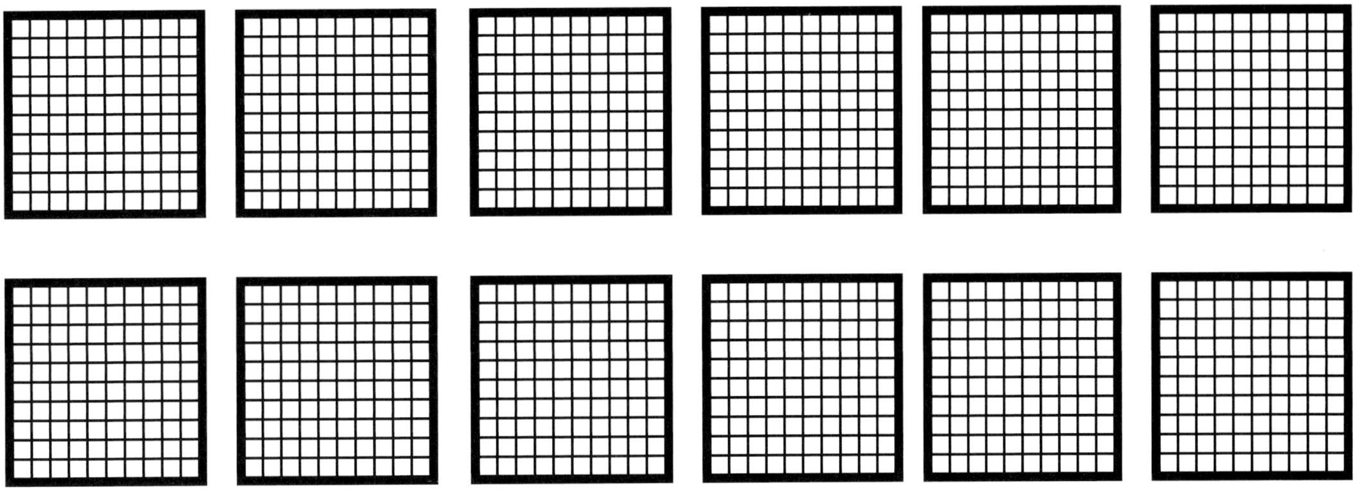

Tens

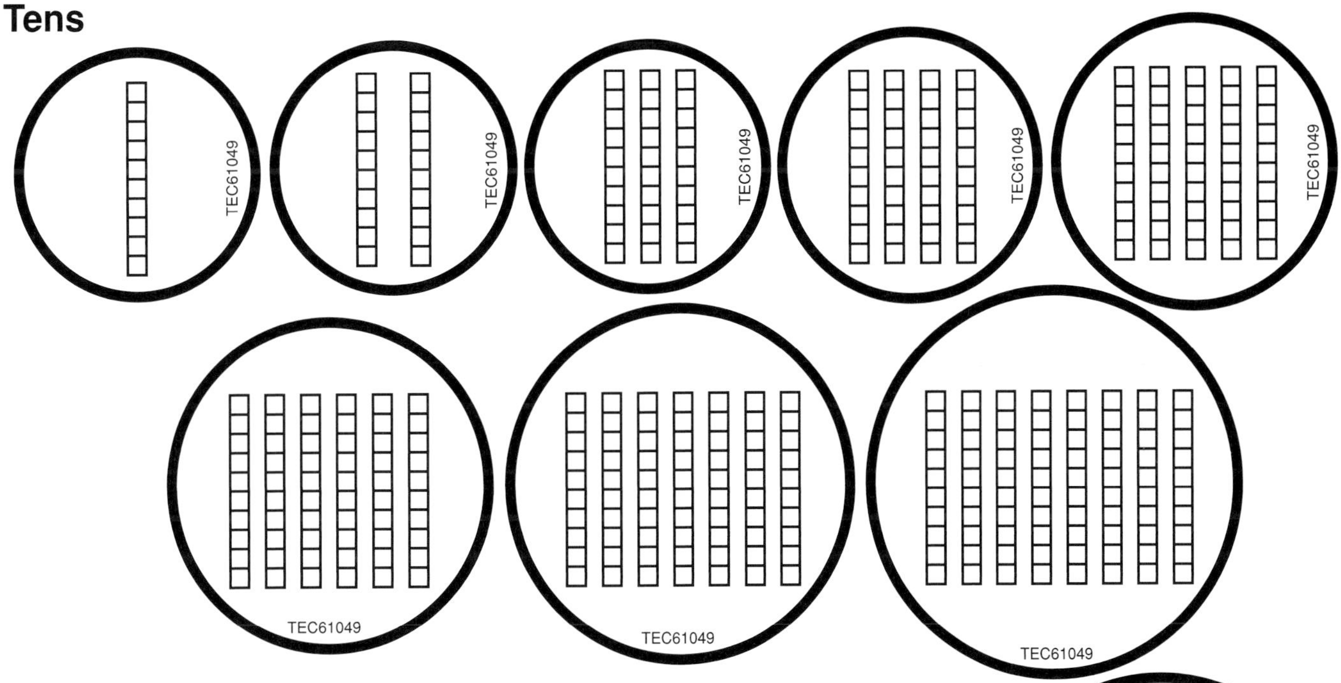
TEC61049
TEC61049
TEC61049
TEC61049
TEC61049
TEC61049
TEC61049
TEC61049

Ones

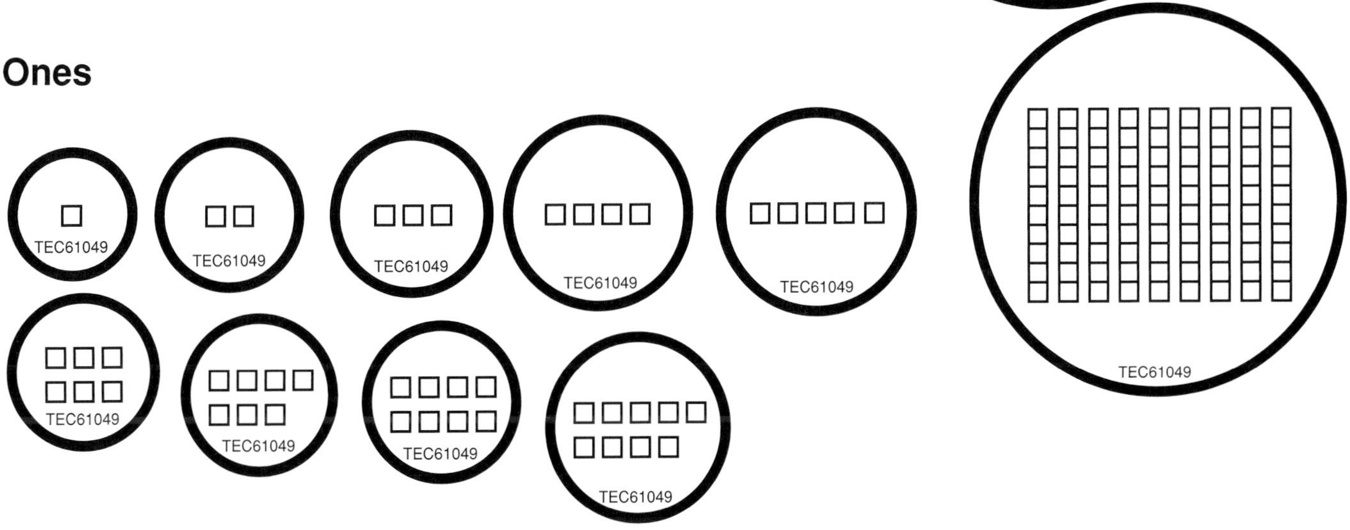
TEC61049
TEC61049
TEC61049
TEC61049
TEC61049
TEC61049
TEC61049
TEC61049
TEC61049
TEC61049

Games

Teaming Up

Team games are a lot of fun, but having student captains choose teammates can result in hurt feelings. Try this approach to placing students in teams. Gather a class supply of craft sticks and divide them into the number of teams you wish to create. Select a color to represent each group. Color the tips of each group's sticks with the designated color. Store the sticks—colored tips down—in a container. When it's time to form teams, have each student randomly select a stick. Have students with like colors form a team. Then save the sticks for the next team game or activity.

Shake, Rattle, and Spell

S K A T E

Prepare for this spelling game by collecting two empty, clean potato chip cans. Fill each can with a set of plastic alphabet letters or paper squares programmed with letters. Divide the class into two teams and line up each team single file behind a desk. Have the first player on each team sit at the desk; then hand each player a container of letters and announce a spelling word. Both players roll their cans on their desks to scramble the letters. Then each player shakes the letters out and finds the letters needed to spell the word. (If a letter appears in a word more than once, it will be necessary to provide extra letters during preparation.) The first player to arrange the letters to spell the word stands up. If he spelled the word correctly, he wins a point for his team. If he is incorrect, the other player may try to win the point by correctly spelling the word. At the end of the turn, each player returns to the end of his line, and another round begins. Continue play until all students have had a chance to participate. Spelling

Spelling Detectives

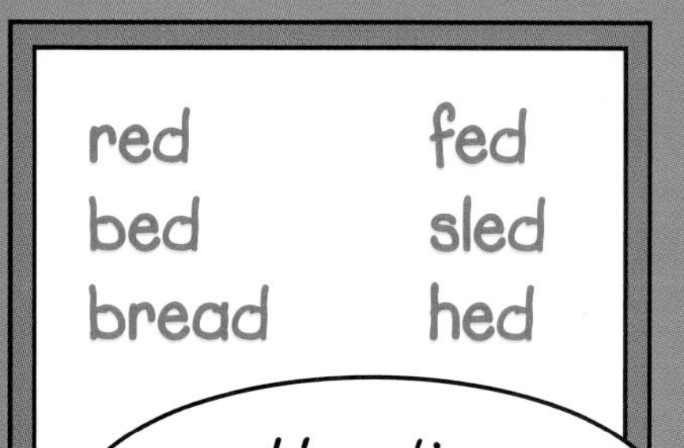
red
fed
bed
sled
bread
hed
Head is misspelled.

Sharpen your students' observation skills with this spelling review game. Write the weekly spelling words in random order on the board. Instruct the class to study the words for one minute; then have everyone turn away from the board. Erase one of the words; then rewrite it, spelling it incorrectly. Ask the class to turn around and study the words again, this time for 30 seconds. At the end of the time period, call on a volunteer to identify the misspelled word. If she answers correctly, award the class one point. Award the class an additional point if the student can give the correct spelling of the word. If she answers incorrectly, identify the word and give yourself the point. Challenge the class to earn more points than you do in ten rounds of play. Spelling

Drawing Digraphs

To prepare, cut out a copy of the digraph cards on page 214; then place them in a container. (Set aside any cards that have a digraph you do not want to include.) Invite a volunteer to remove a card and silently read the word. The volunteer writes the featured digraph on the board and then draws a representation of the word. As he works, the rest of the class tries to guess the word. The student who correctly identifies the word becomes the next drawer. If this student has already drawn, he chooses a classmate who has not. Play continues in this manner for each remaining card. **Initial digraphs**

ch
chin

Verb Village
Noun Town
to run
to leap
the dog
the park
Adjective Alley
pretty
soft

The Right Place

To prepare, label a class supply of blank cards with different nouns, verbs, and adjectives. Also label each of three different areas of your classroom with one of the following: "Noun Town," "Verb Village," "Adjective Alley." To play, gather students in a central classroom location and give each child a card. On your signal, each student reads her card and proceeds to the appropriate area. After all students are in place, have each child, in turn, read her card aloud to check for accuracy. Then have students return to the original location and redistribute the cards for another round of play. **Parts of speech**

On a Roll!

Cover a cube, such as an empty tissue box, with paper. Label each of three sides with different prefixes and each of the remaining sides with different suffixes. Divide your class into several small teams; then assign one member of each team to be the recorder. To play, invite a student to roll the cube and announce the affix that is faceup. On your signal, have each group compile a list of base words that can be combined with the prefix or suffix while each recorder writes the list on a sheet of paper. After a predetermined amount of time, ask students to stop writing. Then have a member from each group share the group's list. Award one point for each correct word. The group with the most points wins that round. Continue in the same manner for additional rounds. **Prefixes and suffixes**

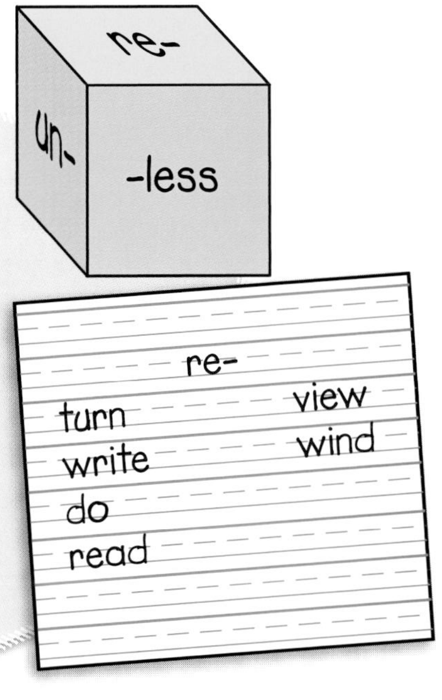
re-
un-
-less
re-
turn
write
do
read
view
wind

Busy Builders

Cut out two copies of the number cards on page 215; then place them in a container. Divide your class into two teams and label a pocket chart as shown. Invite one member from each team to take three cards and make the largest three-digit number possible. Have each child display her number in the pocket chart. Then award one point to the team with the greater number. After placing the cards back in the container, continue play in the same manner until each child receives a turn. Declare the team with more points the "Busiest Builders"! Place value

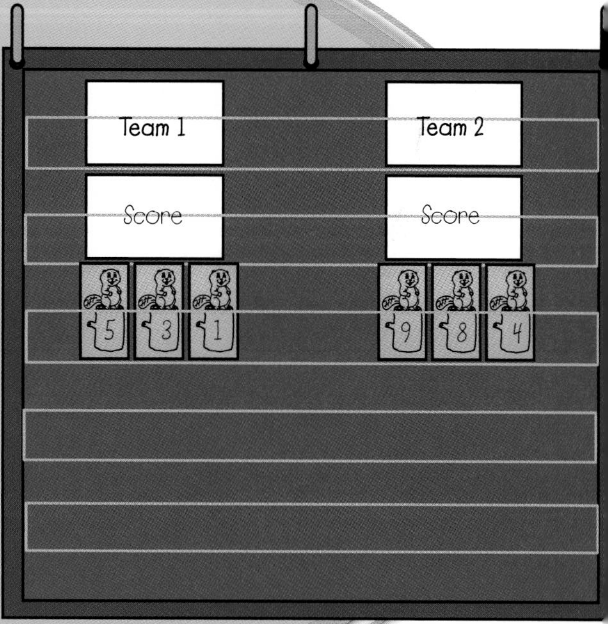
Team 1
Team 2
Score
Score
5
3
1
9
8
4

Pizza Delivery

Give each pair of students a copy of the gameboard on page 216, a copy of the game cards and answer key on page 217, two game markers, a paper clip, and a pencil. Show students how to use the spinner by standing the pencil in the paper clip and spinning the clip with your free hand. Then guide students through the directions below to play the game. Fractions

1. One player cuts the answer key from the game cards and places it facedown. Then he cuts apart the cards, shuffles them, and stacks them facedown.
2. Each player places his game marker on Start.
3. Player 1 draws a card, reads it aloud, and announces the answer.
4. Player 2 checks the key to confirm the answer. Once the answer is confirmed, Player 1 spins the spinner and moves his game marker as indicated. If the answer is not correct, his turn is over. He returns the card to the bottom of the stack.
5. Player 2 takes a turn in the same manner.
6. Players continue taking turns in this manner until one player reaches Finish.

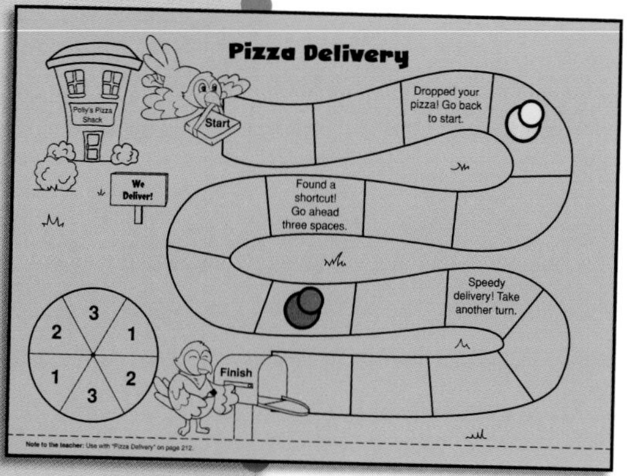
Pizza Delivery
Polly's Pizza Shack
Start
Dropped your pizza! Go back to start.
We Deliver!
Found a shortcut! Go ahead three spaces.
Speedy delivery! Take another turn.
Finish
3
1
2
3
1
2

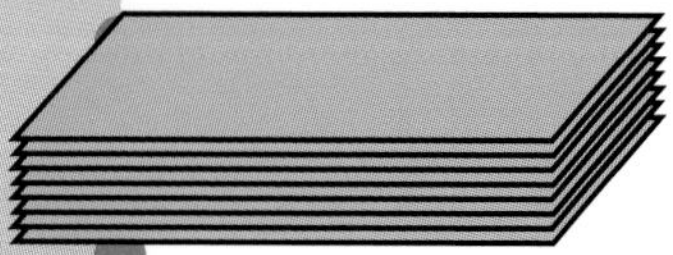

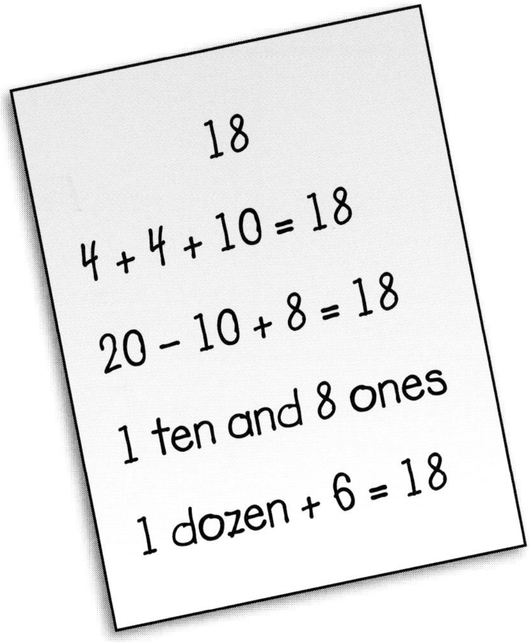
18
4 + 4 + 10 = 18
20 - 10 + 8 = 18
1 ten and 8 ones
1 dozen + 6 = 18

Make the Date

This game is a great time filler! Write the date on the board. Ask students to use mathematical concepts to form the corresponding number in different ways. For example, if the date is the 18th, students can form an addition, a subtraction, or a multiplication sentence that equals 18, write the number in place-value form, or combine operations to equal 18. Challenge students to write as many unique ways to form the number as they can in a predetermined amount of time. When the time is up, invite students to share some of their work. **Logical thinking**

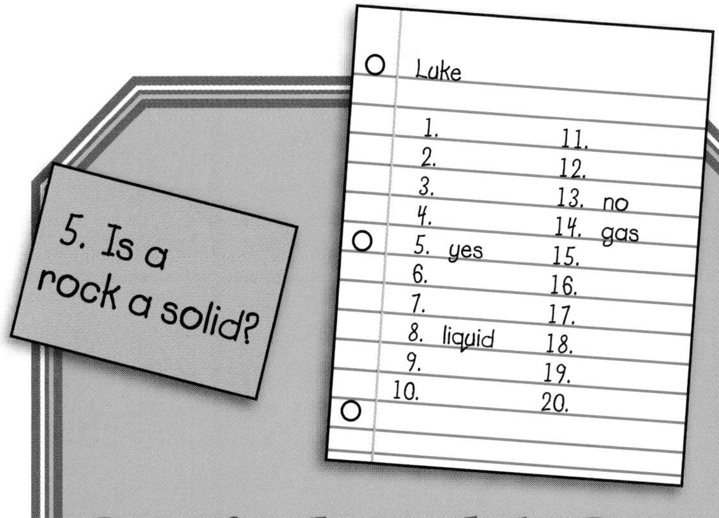
5. Is a rock a solid?
Luke
1.
2.
3.
4.
5. yes
6.
7.
8. liquid
9.
10.
11.
12.
13. no
14. gas
15.
16.
17.
18.
19.
20.

Practice Around the Room

Keep students moving along with this skill review game. For a desired skill or subject you would like students to practice, number a class supply of blank cards and then program each one with a different question or problem. Have each student number a sheet of paper to correspond with the number of cards. Then place one card facedown on each student's desk. On your signal, each child flips the card and writes his answer next to the corresponding number on his paper. After about a minute, direct students to rotate in a predetermined direction to the next desk. Continue in the same manner until each child is back at his desk. Then collect the cards and verify the answers with students. Skill review

Don't Wake the Bear!

Reinforce spelling, math, or curriculum-related skills with the help of a hibernating bear. Choose one child to sit on the floor and be the hibernating bear. Line up a row of five chairs on both sides of the bear. Divide the class into two teams, and have each team line up behind a row of chairs.

To play the game, ask the first member of one team to spell a word, solve a math problem, or answer a question. If he answers correctly, he walks to the end of the line. If he is incorrect, he sits in the chair farthest from the bear. Continue asking questions, alternating between the two teams. Each time an incorrect answer is given, that player takes the next available seat in his row. After all five chairs are filled, the next player on the team to give an incorrect response must "wake" the bear by gently tapping him on the head. The bear gives a roar and then trades places with any seated member on that team. After the two students switch, a new game begins. Skill review

Digraph Cards

Use with "Drawing Digraphs" on page 211.

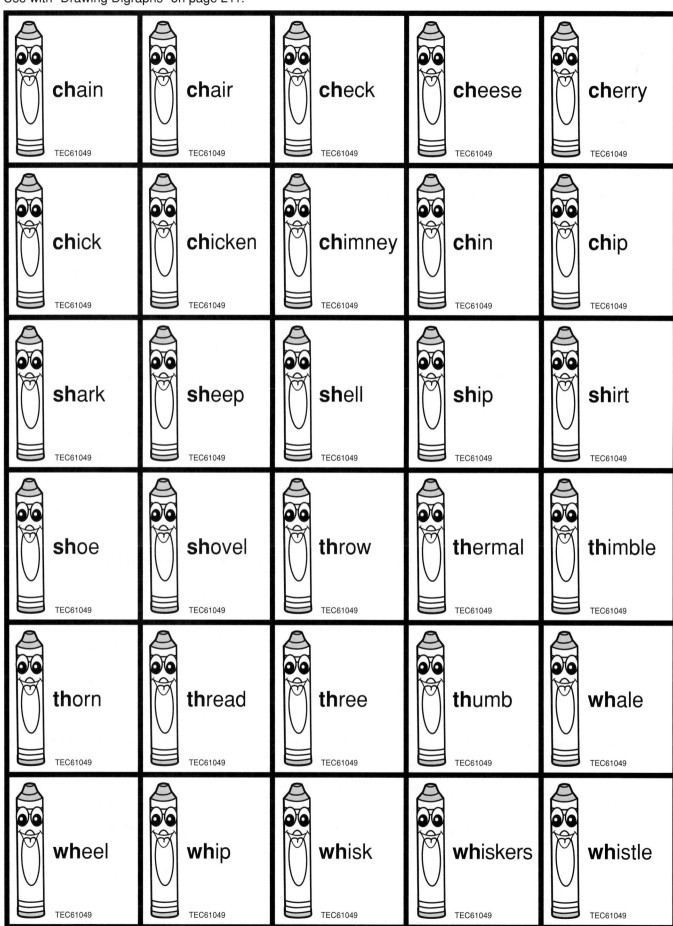

chain TEC61049	**ch**air TEC61049	**ch**eck TEC61049	**ch**eese TEC61049	**ch**erry TEC61049
chick TEC61049	**ch**icken TEC61049	**ch**imney TEC61049	**ch**in TEC61049	**ch**ip TEC61049
shark TEC61049	**sh**eep TEC61049	**sh**ell TEC61049	**sh**ip TEC61049	**sh**irt TEC61049
shoe TEC61049	**sh**ovel TEC61049	**th**row TEC61049	**th**ermal TEC61049	**th**imble TEC61049
thorn TEC61049	**th**read TEC61049	**th**ree TEC61049	**th**umb TEC61049	**wh**ale TEC61049
wheel TEC61049	**wh**ip TEC61049	**wh**isk TEC61049	**wh**iskers TEC61049	**wh**istle TEC61049

Number Cards

Use with "Busy Builders" on page 212.

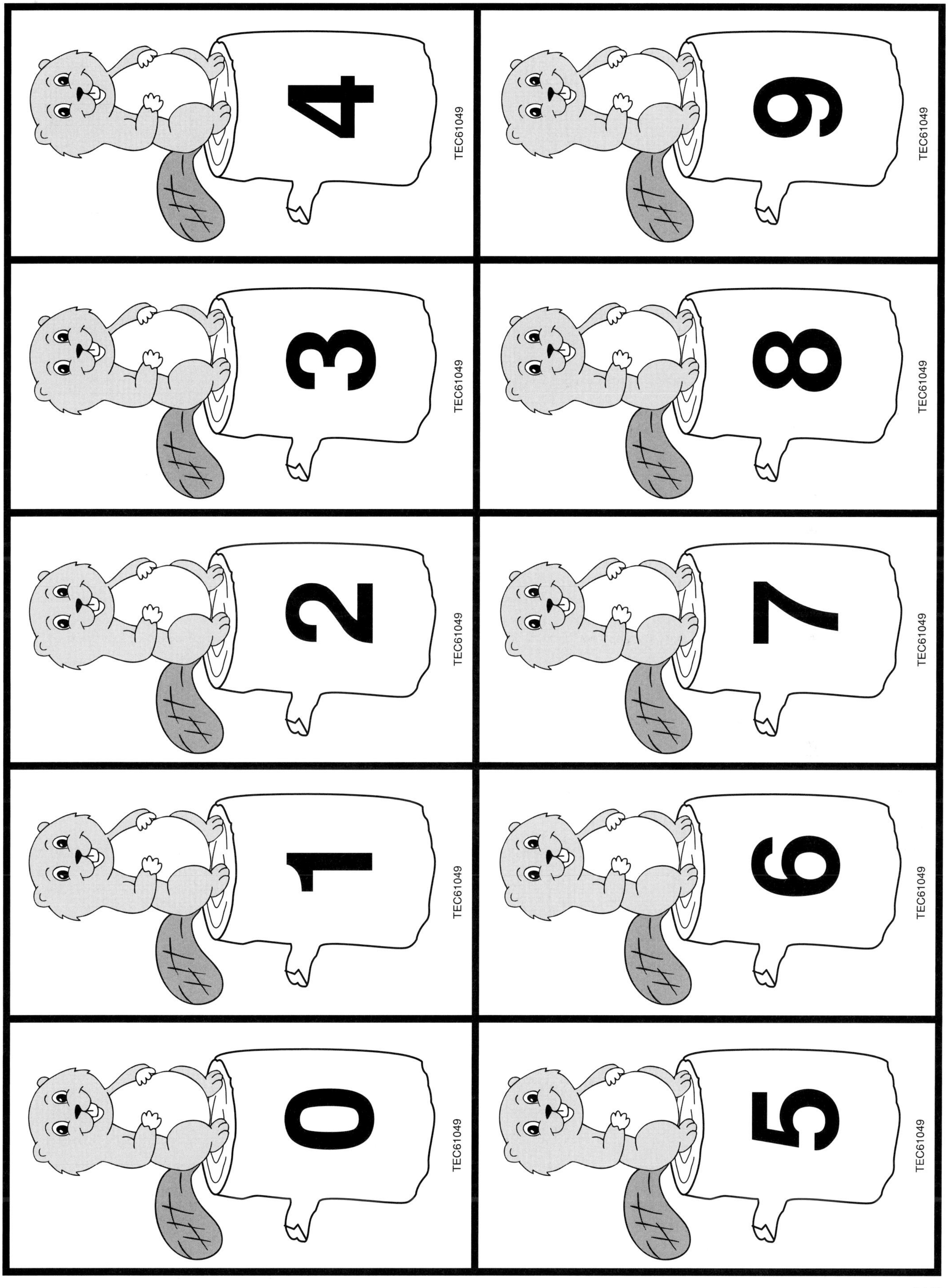
4
TEC61049
9
TEC61049
3
TEC61049
8
TEC61049
2
TEC61049
7
TEC61049
1
TEC61049
6
TEC61049
0
TEC61049
5
TEC61049

Pizza Delivery

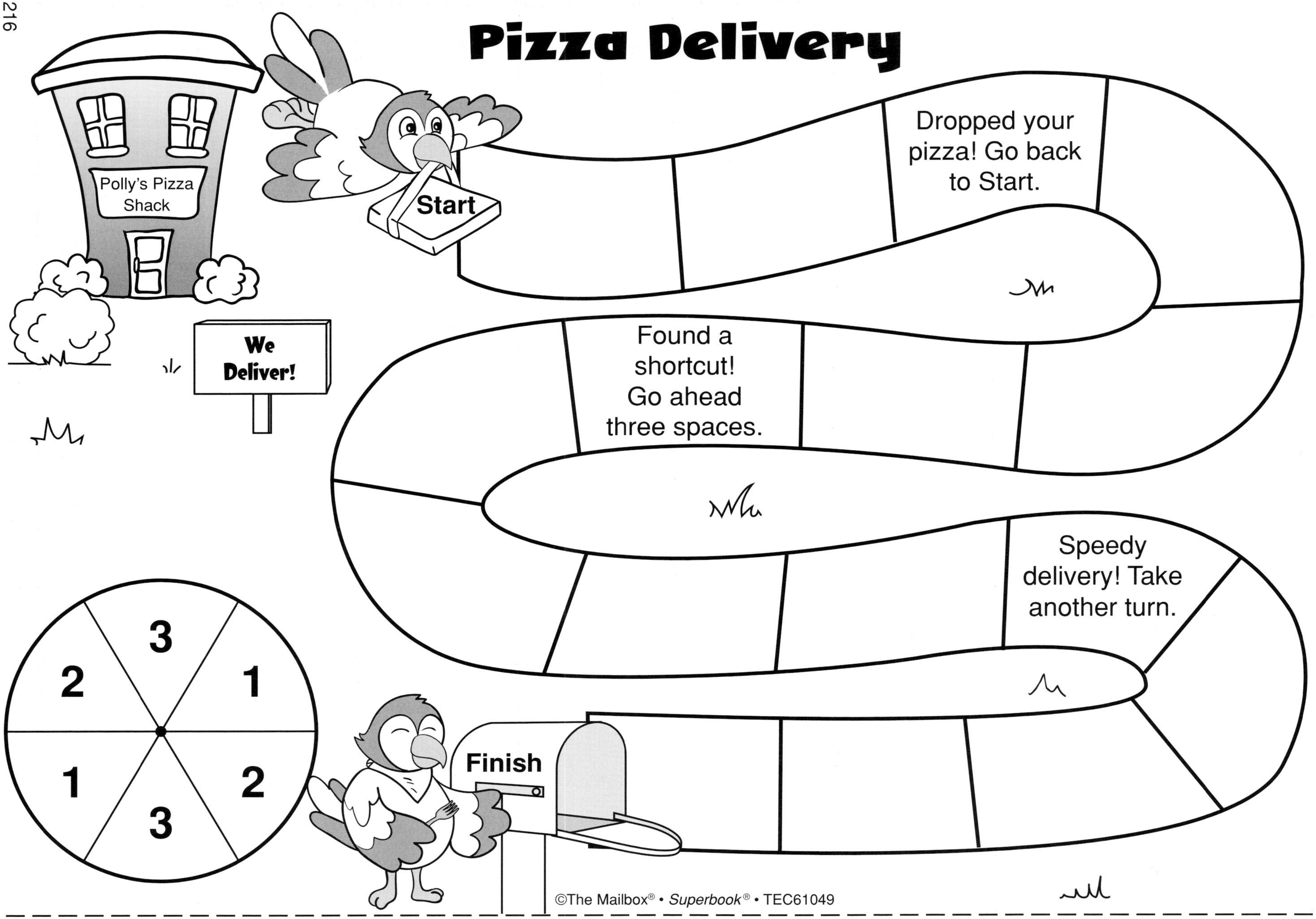
Polly's Pizza Shack
We Deliver!
Start
Dropped your pizza! Go back to Start.
Found a shortcut! Go ahead three spaces.
Speedy delivery! Take another turn.
Finish
3
1
2
3
1
2

Note to the teacher: Use with "Pizza Delivery" on page 212.

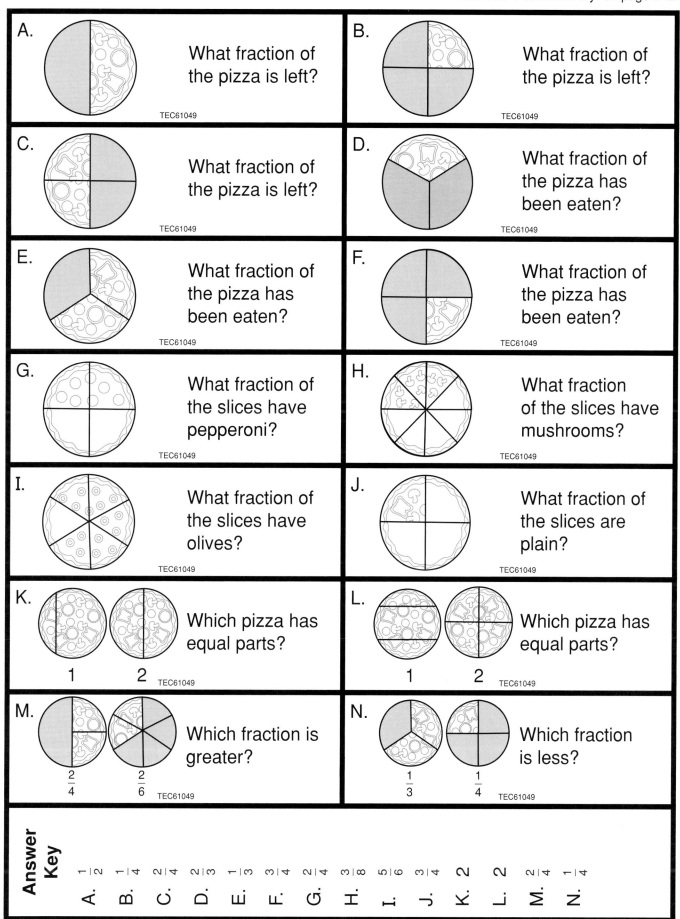

A.
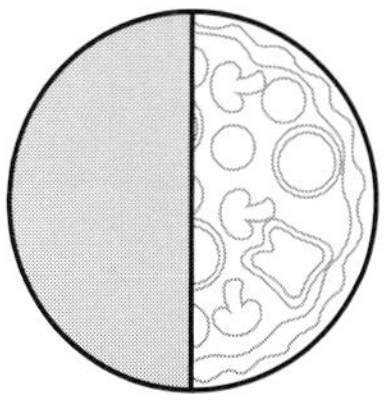
What fraction of the pizza is left?
TEC61049

B.
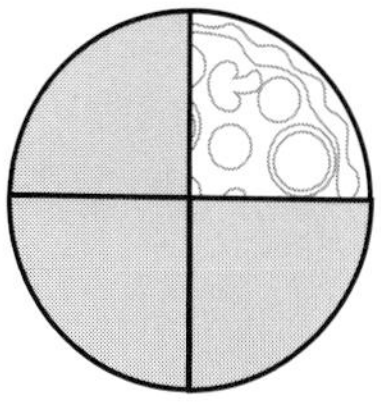
What fraction of the pizza is left?
TEC61049

C.
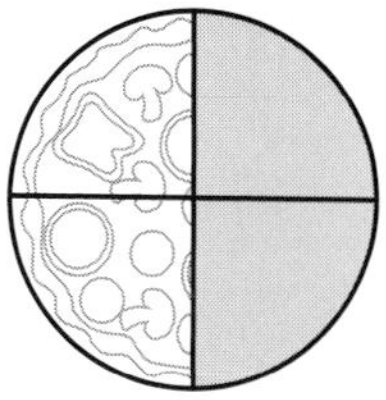
What fraction of the pizza is left?
TEC61049

D.
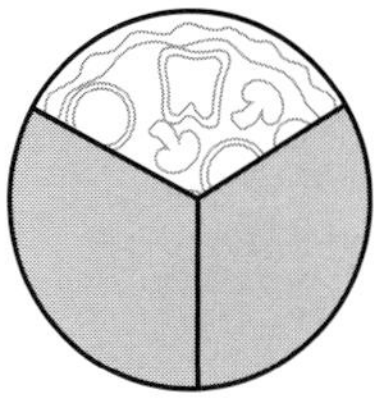
What fraction of the pizza has been eaten?
TEC61049

E.
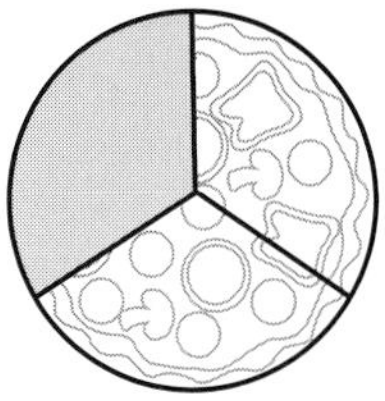
What fraction of the pizza has been eaten?
TEC61049

F.
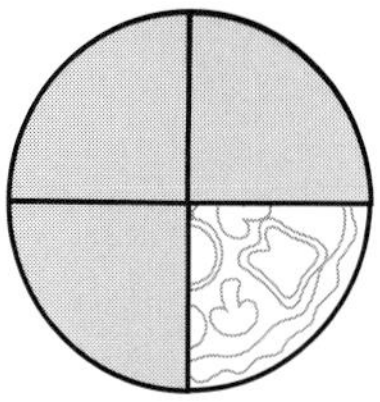
What fraction of the pizza has been eaten?
TEC61049

G.
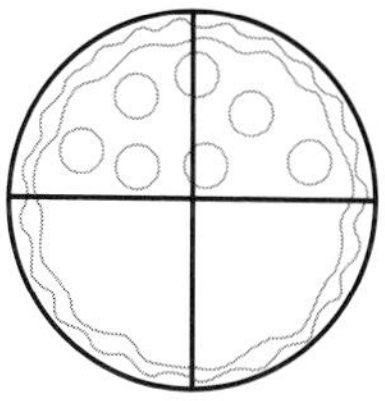
What fraction of the slices have pepperoni?
TEC61049

H.

What fraction of the slices have mushrooms?
TEC61049

I.
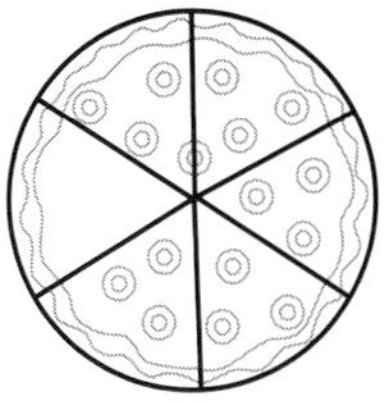
What fraction of the slices have olives?
TEC61049

J.
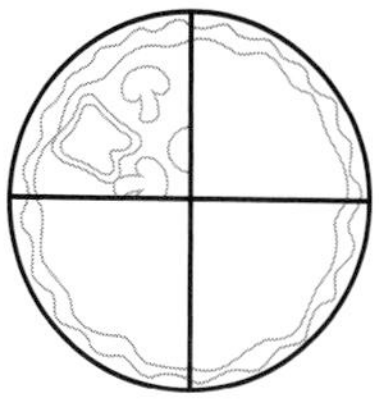
What fraction of the slices are plain?
TEC61049

K.
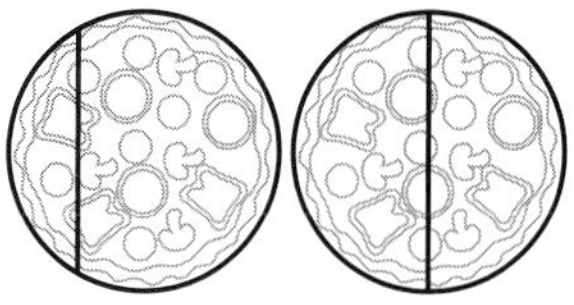
1 2
Which pizza has equal parts?
TEC61049

L.
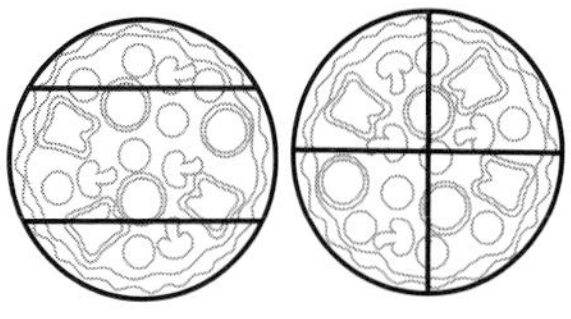
1 2
Which pizza has equal parts?
TEC61049

M.
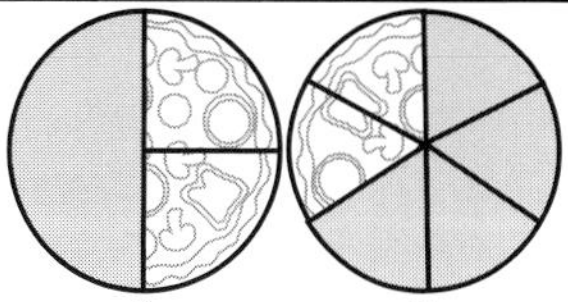
$\frac{2}{4}$ $\frac{2}{6}$
Which fraction is greater?
TEC61049

N.
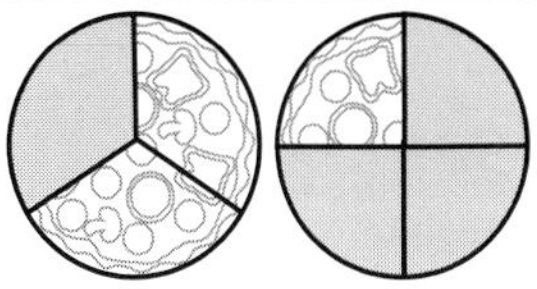
$\frac{1}{3}$ $\frac{1}{4}$
Which fraction is less?
TEC61049

Answer Key

A.	B.	C.	D.	E.	F.	G.	H.	I.	J.	K.	L.	M.	N.
$\frac{1}{2}$	$\frac{1}{4}$	$\frac{2}{4}$	$\frac{2}{3}$	$\frac{1}{3}$	$\frac{3}{4}$	$\frac{2}{4}$	$\frac{3}{8}$	$\frac{5}{6}$	$\frac{3}{4}$	2	2	$\frac{2}{4}$	$\frac{1}{4}$

Differentiation Tips

Leveled Centers

Here's a simple way to provide each student with just-right skill practice at center time! Write each student's name on a blank card and laminate the cards for reuse. To create a color-coding system, place a color dot sticker on each center activity to identify its level. Use a wipe-off marker to draw on each name card a color dot that corresponds with the center level you would like each student to complete. Have each youngster store her card in an accessible location. During center time, direct each youngster to choose an activity that matches her card. To adjust a student's level, simply wipe off the color dot and replace it with a different color.

Bridget
Writing Center

Math Groups

Keep children learning at their own pace by forming small instructional groups. Give a short pretest at the beginning of each new math unit. Assign each child to a group based on the results of the test. Then prepare packets of activities and skill sheets for each group. Each day distribute the packets. As children are working, meet with each group for a minilesson tailored to meet the group's needs. Periodically check each student's progress with his packet and answer any questions he may have. If a child masters a specific skill or if he needs more reinforcement, move him to a different group.

Ready Resources

To meet the varying needs of the students in your classroom, keep a variety of resource books on hand. Obtain skill books for the grade levels just above and just below the grade level you teach. Or plan to share materials with teachers in those grade levels. When a student needs reinforcement, extra practice, or enrichment, you'll always have a skill sheet to meet her needs.

The Mailbox
Leveled Skill Builders
Differentiated Practice for Language Arts and Math
Grade 1
Grade level page
Core skills covered in state standards
Provide practice for students working at different levels
Lower level page
Leveled Skill Builders
Grade 3

Group Guided Reading Group 3 Date March 3-7

Name	Skill: Recognizes and uses knowledge of spelling patterns when reading				
Joey	most of the time				
Sue	needs prompts				
Carlos	needs some assistance				
Savannah	reads text without errors				
Reilly	text was too hard				
Ari	almost always				

Group Records

This versatile chart helps you track the progress of the students in each of your small instructional groups. For each group, program a copy of the chart on page 220 with the group's name, the date, and its students' names. Then write a different skill or goal at the top of each column. When you're working with a small group, make notes on the corresponding chart as needed to monitor the progress of your students.

Handy Highlights

Encourage students to try the following bright ideas to help them with their classwork.

- Have youngsters highlight each word in the word bank on a skill sheet.
- Remind a student to write her name on her paper by having her highlight her name after she writes it.
- Ask children to highlight the key words in the directions on a skill sheet.
- Instruct students to highlight operational signs on math problems before they begin working.

Lesson Plan Labels

Looking for a way to keep track of student modifications? Try this simple solution! Use a computer to program large shipping labels with each student's initials and a list of his required modifications. Then print a sheet of the labels and affix one to each new week in your planbook. As you plan, refer to the label and write each student's initials and modifications next to each corresponding activity as needed.

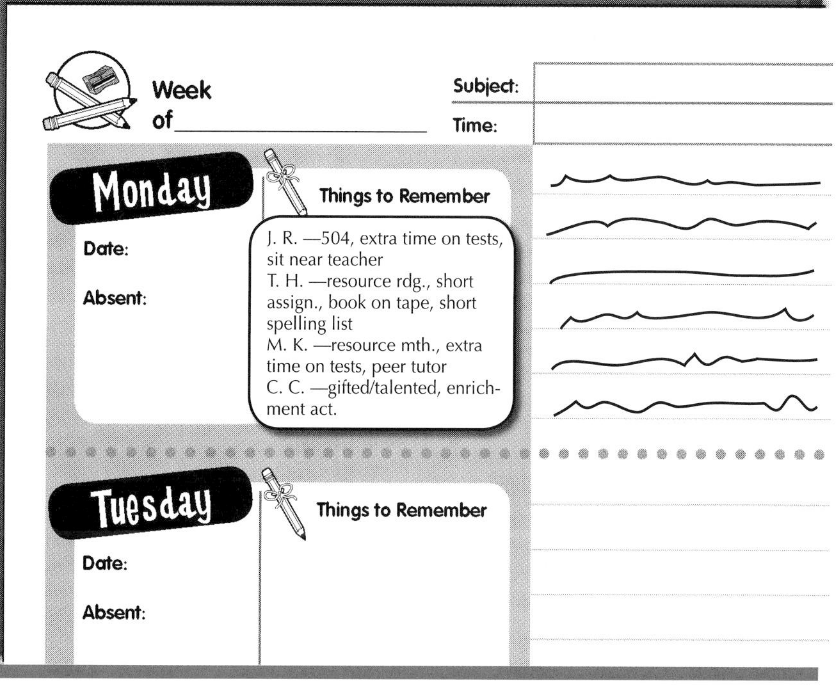
Week of
Subject:
Time:
Monday
Date:
Absent:
Things to Remember
J. R. —504, extra time on tests, sit near teacher
T. H. —resource rdg., short assign., book on tape, short spelling list
M. K. —resource mth., extra time on tests, peer tutor
C. C. —gifted/talented, enrichment act.
Tuesday
Date:
Absent:
Things to Remember

Group ____________________ Date ______________

Skill / Name					

Note to the teacher: Use with “Group Records” on page 219.

ASSESSMENT

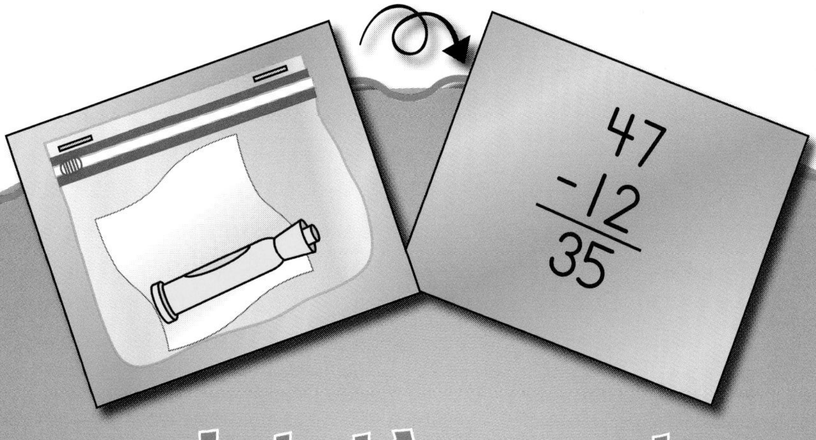

47
-12
35

Instant Assessment

Check each student's understanding of a skill or concept at a glance with this handy tool. For each student, staple a snack-size resealable plastic bag to the back of a 6" x 8" laminated poster board rectangle. Seal a dry-erase marker and a baby wipe inside each plastic bag. To assess how well students understand a skill, give each student a prepared board. Then ask each child to write a response to a question or to complete a task on his board. On your signal, have each student hold up his work for you to view. You can quickly and easily tell which youngsters have mastered the concept.

How Many Stamps?

This simple idea makes short work of grading student assessments. In advance, prepare a poster listing grading criteria similar to the one shown and post it in the classroom. Gather a small rubber stamp and an ink pad. When students are completing an assessment, circulate and talk with each student. Determine each student's level of understanding and then stamp his paper the corresponding number of times. To monitor student progress, collect the completed assessments and quickly scan to see the number of stamps on each paper.

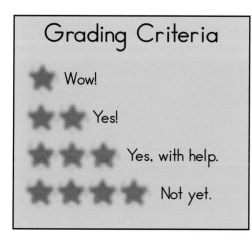

Grading Criteria

- ★ Wow!
- ★★ Yes!
- ★★★ Yes, with help.
- ★★★★ Not yet.

Ready to Read

Eliminate the pressure of oral reading assessments with this helpful idea. When you are ready to begin, announce that you will be the first reader's "coach." Then offer assistance when the child encounters unfamiliar words. When the first student is finished reading, invite him to be the coach for the next reader (offer assistance if necessary). Continue in this manner until you have assessed each child's oral reading skills.

The Gift of Knowledge

Wrap up a lesson or unit of study with this nifty idea. To prepare, list several assessment questions related to a chosen topic. Place a class supply of treats, such as stickers or small candies, inside a box and then wrap the box. Using a different patterned paper, wrap the box again. Continue to wrap the box in this manner until you've added one layer for each question on your list. At the end of the lesson or unit of study, present the box to the class and ask the first question. When a student volunteer correctly answers the question, invite her to unwrap one layer of the paper from the box. Once the box is completely unwrapped, give each child a treat from inside.

Writing Rubric

1	2	3	4
The story • leaves the reader with a lot of questions • has some complete sentences • has few details	The story • has a lot of complete sentences • creates a fuzzy picture • has several details that are not needed	The story • makes sense • has complete sentences • helps make a picture • has a few details that are not needed	The story • is easy to understand • has complete sentences • helps make a clear picture • "hooks" the reader

Writing Rubric

Give each student a copy of the rubric on page 223 and discuss the listed criteria. Then use the rubric as a class to assess anonymous pieces of writing or selected passages from children's books. After students are familiar with the rubric, instruct each youngster to keep her copy in an accessible location. Have her use the rubric to size up her completed stories and keep track of her writing growth.

In-Line Assessment

Take advantage of the time your students spend waiting in line with this quick assessment idea. Announce a spelling word, math problem, or other content-related question to the first youngster in your line. Continue asking questions down the line, and by the time you reach the end, the wait time will be over!

Use with "Writing Rubric" on page 222.

Writing Rubric

1	2	3	4
The story • leaves the reader with a lot of questions • has some complete sentences • has few details	**The story** • has a lot of complete sentences • creates a fuzzy picture • has several details that are not needed	**The story** • makes sense • has complete sentences • helps make a picture • has a few details that are not needed	**The story** • is easy to understand • has complete sentences • helps make a clear picture • "hooks" the reader

TEC61049

Writing Rubric

1	2	3	4
The story • leaves the reader with a lot of questions • has some complete sentences • has few details	**The story** • has a lot of complete sentences • creates a fuzzy picture • has several details that are not needed	**The story** • makes sense • has complete sentences • helps make a picture • has a few details that are not needed	**The story** • is easy to understand • has complete sentences • helps make a clear picture • "hooks" the reader

TEC61049

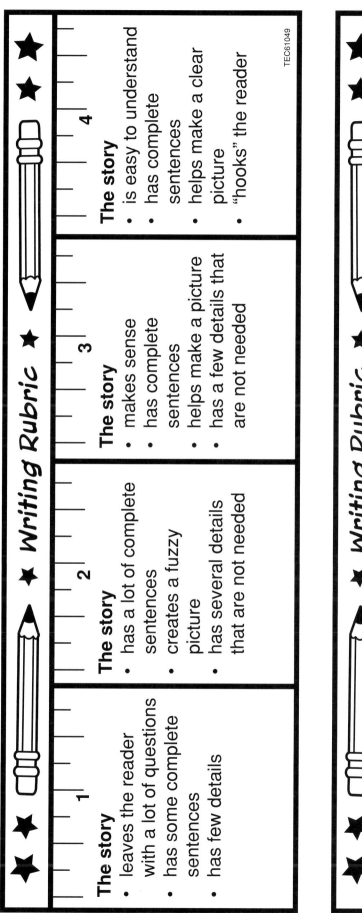

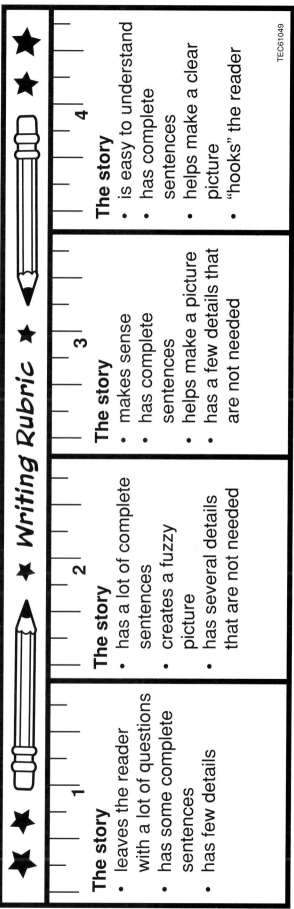

Test-Taking Strategies

Test Takers on Parade

Get students fired up the morning of a test with a little help from younger grades not testing that day. Several days before the test, have each student bring in an empty, clean plastic milk container. Have the student use construction paper and other craft materials to decorate the milk jug with art and words of encouragement. Next, have the students place a few beans in the container and then seal the cap shut with glue or tape. Give the noisemakers to the younger grades. On the morning of the test, have the youngsters line the halls, shake the noisemakers, and cheer as the test takers walk to class.

Go for it!
Work hard!
Try your best!

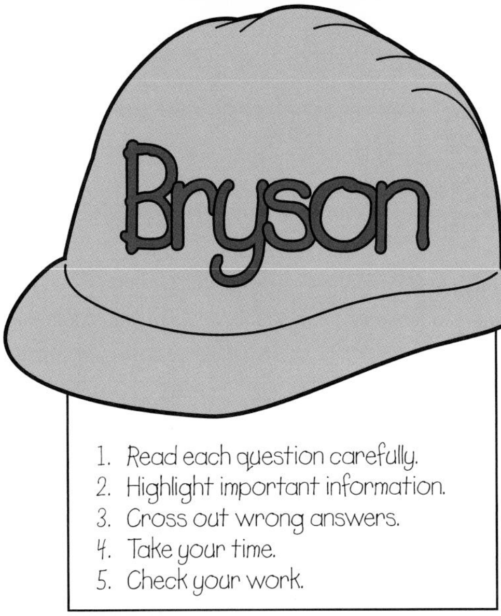
Bryson
1. Read each question carefully.
2. Highlight important information.
3. Cross out wrong answers.
4. Take your time.
5. Check your work.

Building Great Habits!

After reviewing various test-taking strategies, provide each student with a copy of the construction hat pattern on page 226. Each student labels the hat with his name and decorates it as desired. On another sheet of paper, he makes a list of test-taking strategies that he likes to use or that he feels will help others in the class. The student glues his decorated hat to the top of his paper. Display the hats on a board titled "Building Great Test-Taking Habits!" Encourage students to refer to the board as needed to practice test-taking skills.

Sticker Before the Test

Boost students' test-taking confidence with this quick tip. Occasionally surprise students by placing a sticker on each child's test before testing begins. Explain to students that you are rewarding them in advance because you know they will be trying to do their best. Be on the lookout for great test grades!

Three Cheers!

Cheer students to testing victory with this simple activity. Have small groups of students create a mnemonic device to help remember important information about taking a test. Then have the group present its mnemonic to the class using arms and legs to spell out each letter of the device.

Eat a good breakfast.
Focus on the questions being asked.
Follow the directions.
Organize your thoughts.
Recheck your answers.
Try your best.

Shhhh! We're Working!

Help children understand the need for quiet during testing by creating testing folders for each child. Give each child a colorful file folder and have her write her name and "Shhhh! I'm working!" on one side as shown. Collect the folders and then, on testing days, redistribute them. Direct each child to set up her folder on her desk, creating a wall that she can work behind. Explain to students that when the folders are up, no one may talk or get out of her seat. This serves as a great reminder to students that although each child works at her own pace, students should respect each others' right to work in a quiet, still environment.

Shhhh!
I'm
working!
Jessica

Test-Taking Checklist

Asking students to look over their tests before turning them in means different things to different children. Help them with this step by providing a checklist on the board or stapling one to each child's test. Students will appreciate knowing exactly what they are looking for, and they might even improve their test scores in the process!

Construction Hat Pattern

Use with "Building Great Habits!" on page 224.

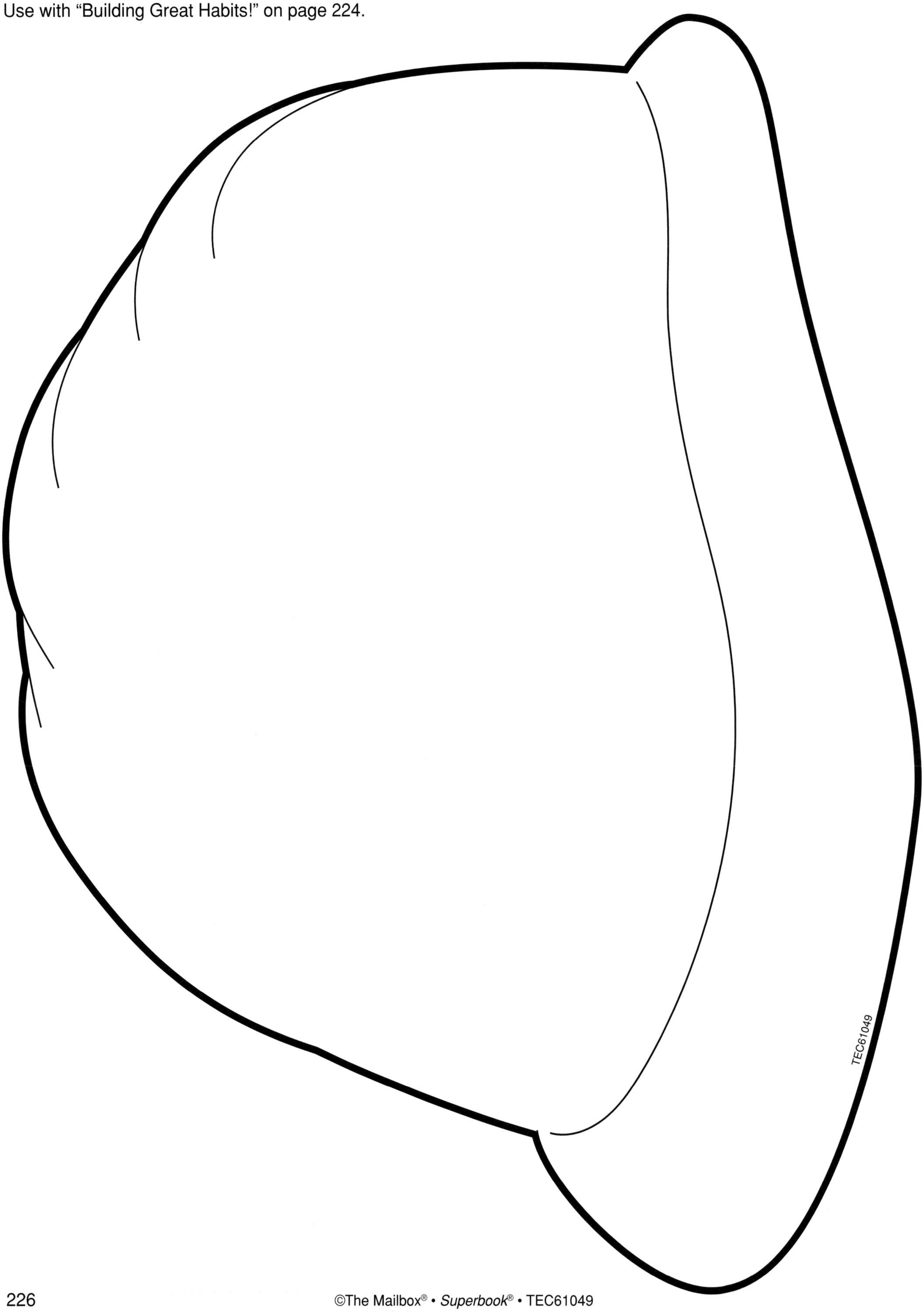
TEC61049

English Language Learners

Recording Reading

Help each English language learner share her school success with her family while boosting her reading skills. After a child is familiar with a book, guide her to record herself as she reads the book aloud. Then send the book and the tape home with the student in a resealable plastic bag. Invite her to play the tape for her family and then read along with it to build her reading skills.

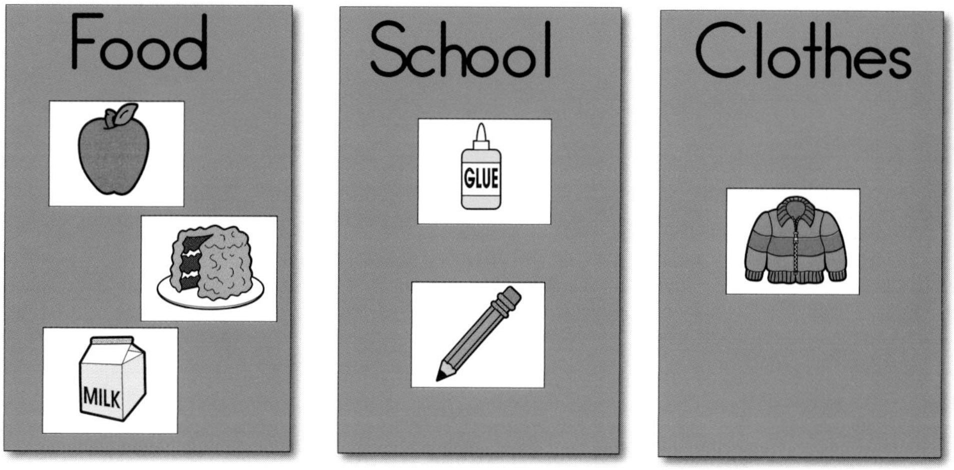
Food
School
Clothes
GLUE
MILK

School, Clothes, or Food?

Increase your English language learners' vocabulary with this sorting activity. Color and cut out a copy of the picture cards on page 229 and store them in a resealable plastic bag. Label each of three large sheets of construction paper with one of the following categories: "clothes," "food," "school." Place the prepared sheets within student reach. Invite a child to remove a card, name the pictured item, and match it to the corresponding category (provide assistance as necessary). After all of the cards are sorted, lead the youngster in reviewing each vocabulary word.

Daily Routine

Try this picture-perfect idea to help English language learners become familiar with your daily schedule. To prepare, take photos of students during routine activities and each special subject, such as music or art. Each morning, post the day's schedule as desired. Then display selected photos beside the corresponding times. Since students will know what to expect, they'll feel more comfortable in your classroom!

8:30 Morning Work
8:45 Reading
9:45 Writing
10:15 Music

A Welcoming Album

Help English language learners adjust to their new surroundings by preparing this visual tool. Obtain a small inexpensive photo album. Take photos of special people (such as the principal) and places (such as the playground) around the school. Label a separate sticky note for each photo and attach it to the corresponding photo. Then slip each labeled photo in the album. When a new English language learner arrives in your classroom, ask a student volunteer to assist him in looking through the album.

Principal
Dr. Adams

Please Repeat!

If your English language learners need extra time to process oral information, give this idea a try! When you assign students independent work, such as responding to a journal prompt, make a recording of yourself explaining the task. Arrange for each youngster who needs support to use headphones to listen to the recording. Encourage her to replay the recording as many times as she needs to gain understanding. She'll be able to work at her own pace, and you'll be free to monitor students.

Draw and Write

Drawings make the perfect bridge to help youngsters be successful writers. To respond to a prompt, have each English language learner draw a picture. Guide him to tell about his completed picture; then use sticky notes to add labels. Instruct each child to refer to his drawing as he completes the writing assignment. The labels will help boost his vocabulary as well as assist him with spelling.

sunshine
outside
me
dog
ball

Picture Cards

Use with “School, Clothes, or Food?” on page 227.

TEC61049

TEC61049

GLUE

TEC61049

MILK

TEC61049

TEC61049

TEC61049

CRAYONS

TEC61049

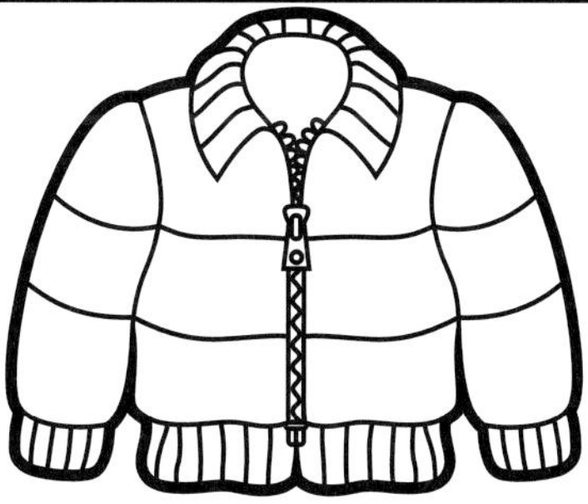

TEC61049

TEC61049

TEC61049

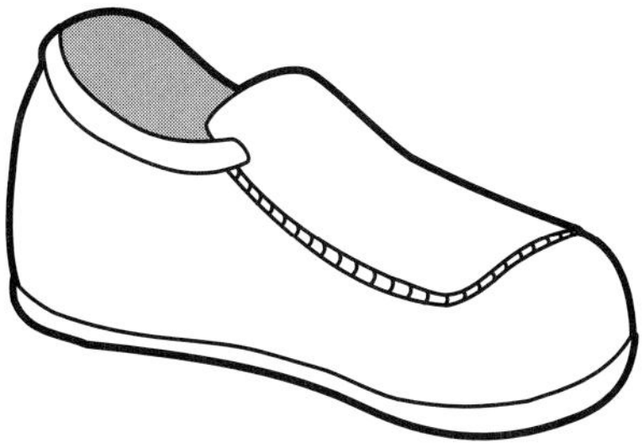

TEC61049

TEC61049

TEC61049

TEC61049

TEC61049

BULLETIN BOARDS

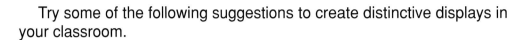

Try some of the following suggestions to create distinctive displays in your classroom.

Background Paper With Pizzazz

Let the theme of your bulletin board inspire your choice of background paper. Gift wrap comes in a variety of designs that can enhance a bulletin board display. Wrapping paper comes in many colors and patterns that are not available in standard background paper choices.

Create other interesting displays with the following background ideas:

newspaper
road maps
calendar pages
fabric
wallpaper
colored cellophane
plastic tablecloths
bedsheets

Distinctive Lettering

The title on a bulletin board can be a work of art in itself! Try cutting letters from the following materials:

wallpaper samples
sandpaper
greeting cards
foil
magazine pages
posters
paper bags

Keep It on File

Take a picture of each bulletin board before you take it down. Store the photos in an album or in an appropriate file. You'll have a wonderful collection of bulletin board ideas to choose from in the coming year, as well as a handy reference showing each completed display.

Borders That Beautify

If you're looking for just a touch of color to add to a bulletin board, use items from the list in "Background Paper with Pizzazz" to create borders for a board covered with a solid-color background. Make your own border by tracing several strips of precut border onto the new material. For added durability, laminate the strips before cutting them out.

Interesting borders can also be made using

doilies
cupcake liners
dried leaves
die-cut shapes
adding-machine tape that students have decorated

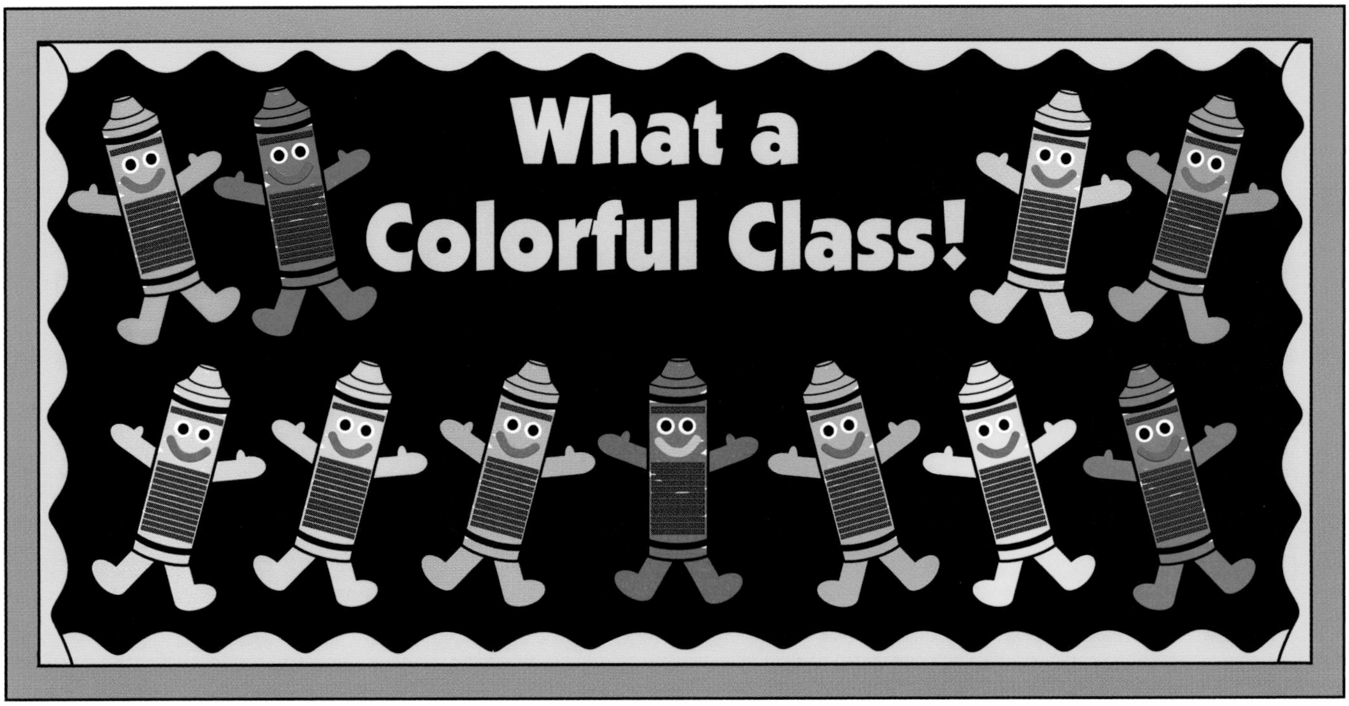
What a
Colorful Class!

Have each student write his name and complete the sentence about his favorite color on a copy of the crayon pattern on page 241. Next, have him color the crayon with his favorite color, cut it out, and add construction paper legs, arms, and facial features. Display the completed creations and the title shown on a bulletin board covered with black background paper.

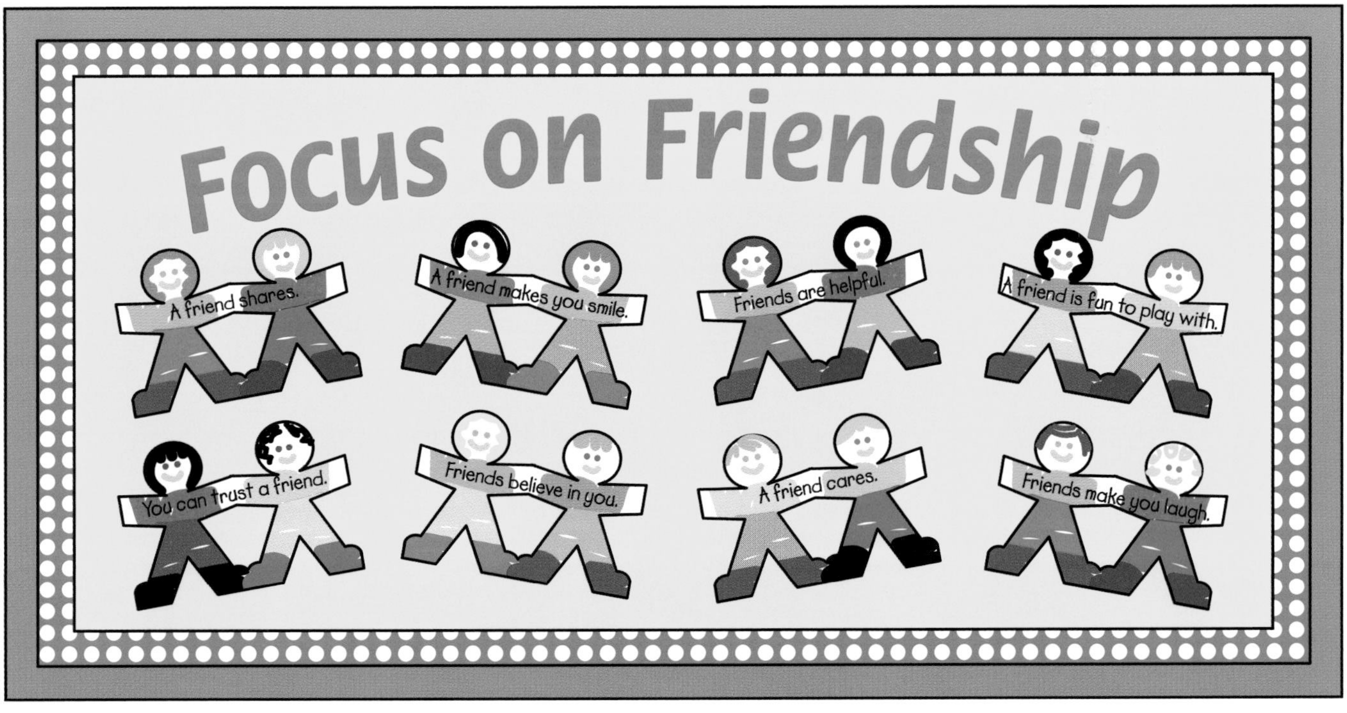
Focus on Friendship
A friend shares.
A friend makes you smile.
Friends are helpful.
A friend is fun to play with.
You can trust a friend.
Friends believe in you.
A friend cares.
Friends make you laugh.

Have each student cut out a buddy pattern (page 241), place it on a folded sheet of paper, and trace it. After cutting on the resulting outline, the child unfolds the paper and colors one of the buddies to resemble himself and the other to resemble a friend. He then writes a message of friendship across the cutout before displaying it on a colorful board.

Hats Off to Helpers!
Lunch Counter
Work Collector
Attendance Keeper
Line Leader
Plant Waterer
Annie
Joey
Sean
Alexa
Amy
Natalie
Juan
Rielly
Kurstin
Jenna
Gregg
Julia
Angela
Kaleb
Jan
Maria
Patrick
Kim
Lynne
Randy
Jon

Have each student cut out and personalize a construction paper copy of the buddy pattern on page 241 and then decorate it to resemble himself. For each classroom job, program an enlarged construction paper copy of a hat pattern (page 242) with a job description. Staple the hat cutouts to the board; then pin one student cutout below each job description. Pin the remaining cutouts around the border of the board. Each week assign new jobs using an established method of rotation.

WHAT A "HAND-SOME" SEASON!

Cover a bulletin board with white background paper. Paint a bare tree shape and add desired background details. Then have students trace their hands on sheets of red, orange, brown, and yellow construction paper and cut out the resulting shapes. Attach the handprints to the bulletin board as shown.

Have a "Purr-fectly" Safe Halloween!

Cover a bulletin board with black background paper. Add a construction paper moon and fence. After a discussion about Halloween safety, have each student write one safety rule on a copy of the cat pattern on page 243. Then have her color it and cut it out. Display the completed kitties along the fence to encourage a safe Halloween.

Give Thanks for Good Deeds!
Jenna
Ann
TJ
Jean
Tracey
Noah
Kelly
Alex
Danny
Rob

Encourage positive behavior with this terrific turkey. Color and cut out an enlarged copy of the turkey pattern on page 243 before mounting it on a bulletin board. Store a supply of colorful construction paper copies of the feather pattern on page 243 in a pocket attached to the board. When a student performs an act of kindness, write his name on a feather and staple it to the turkey.

Let It Snow!

Pop a supply of popcorn. Have each student cut and glue white construction paper circles to create a snowman. Then the child spreads a thin layer of glue on his snowman and attaches pieces of popcorn. If desired, tint a small amount of the popcorn with colored tempera paint for students to use to create eyes and buttons. Staple the completed creations and the title shown to a bulletin board covered with blue paper. Let it snow!

STAR-STUDDED WORK

Celebrate the Hanukkah season with this sparkling display of good work. Give each student two large triangles with the center sections cut out. Show the students how to glue the shapes together to form stars. Then have each student wrap yellow, white, and blue pieces of tissue paper around the eraser end of a pencil, dip them in glue, and apply them to his star. When dry, attach each star to a bulletin board along with a sample of each student's best work.

THE GIFT OF
GOOD WORK

Have each student decorate an eight-inch white construction paper square so it resembles holiday gift wrap. Then assist each student in attaching a length of curling ribbon to her package. Mount the packages on a bulletin board along with the title shown and a sample of each student's best work.

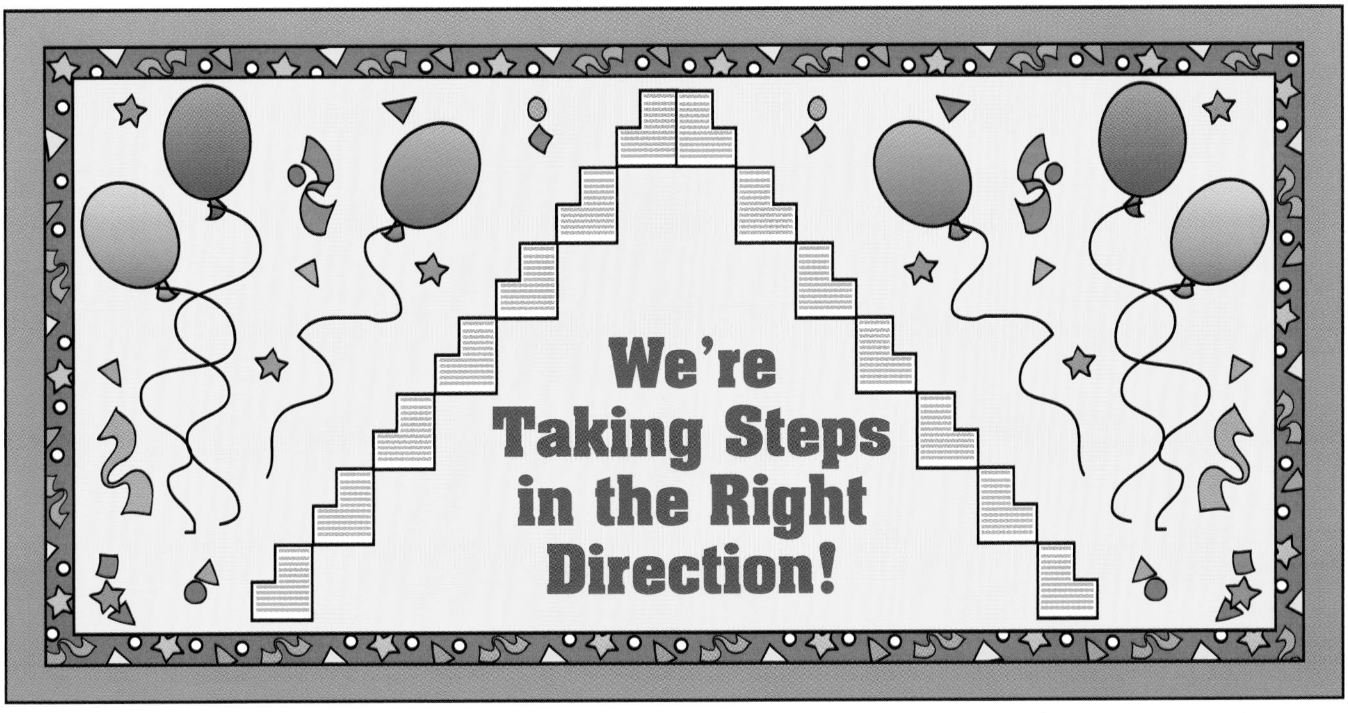
We're
Taking Steps
in the Right
Direction!

Ring in the new year with steps in the right direction! Cut a class supply of writing paper into step shapes. Have each student write his name and a self-improvement goal for the new year on a step. Staple the completed goals to a bulletin board as shown.

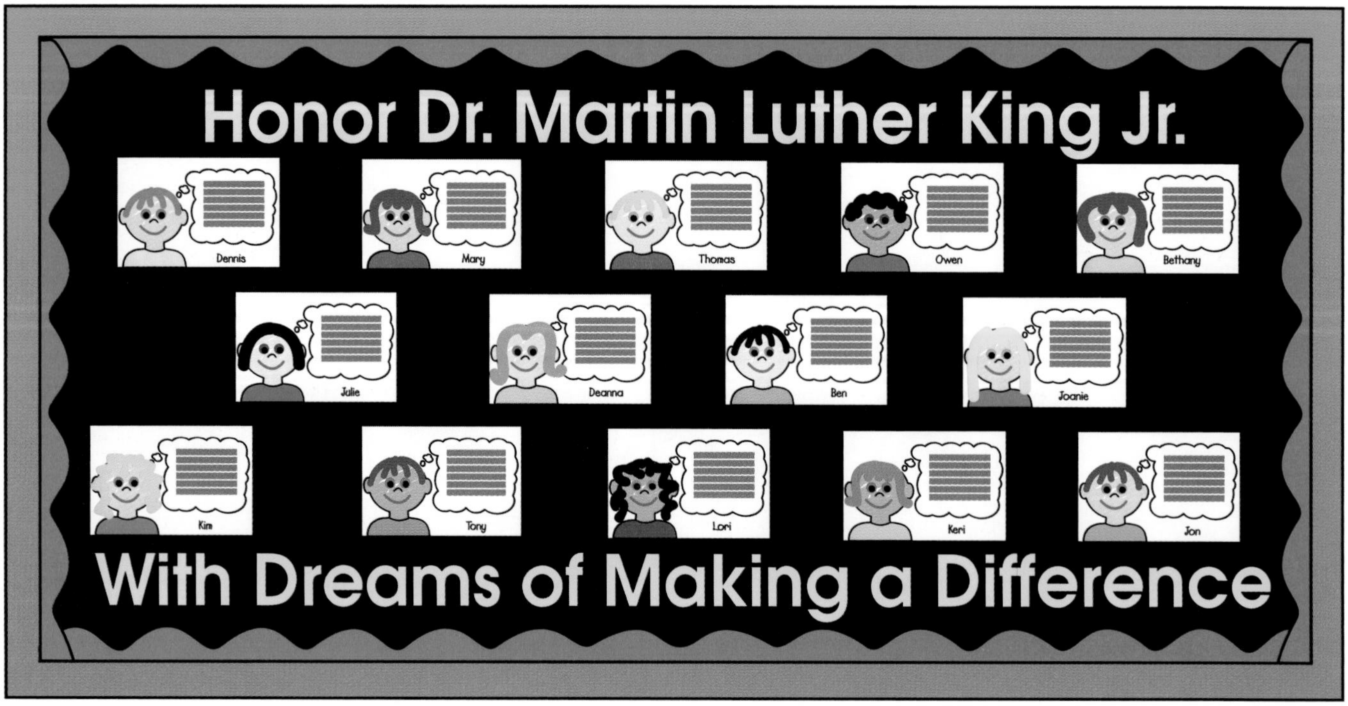
Honor Dr. Martin Luther King Jr.
Dennis
Mary
Thomas
Owen
Bethany
Julie
Deanna
Ben
Joanie
Kim
Tony
Lori
Keri
Jon
With Dreams of Making a Difference

Honor Dr. Martin Luther King Jr.'s dreams to make a difference. Have each student draw her likeness on a half sheet of paper and write her dream for making a difference in a thought bubble. Display the completed projects and the title shown on a bulletin board as a tribute to Dr. King.

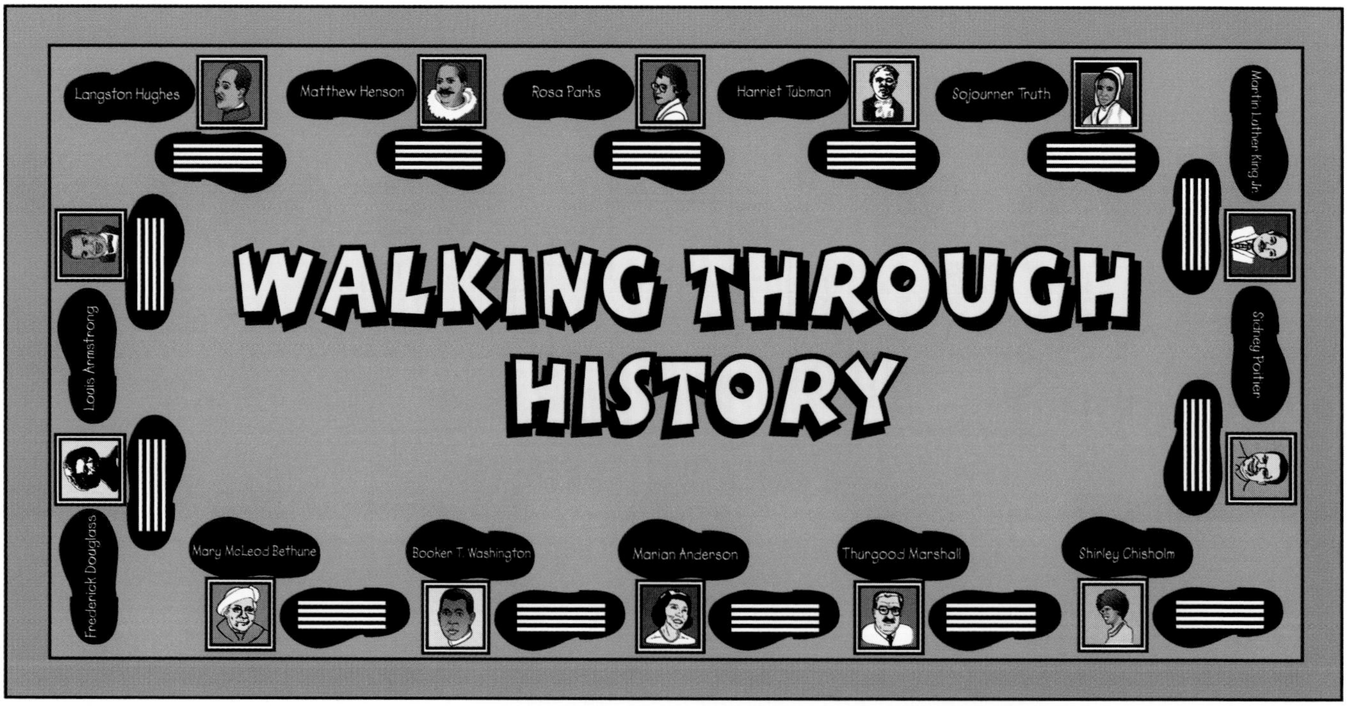
Langston Hughes
Matthew Henson
Rosa Parks
Harriet Tubman
Sojourner Truth
Martin Luther King Jr.
Sidney Poitier
Louis Armstrong
Frederick Douglass
WALKING THROUGH HISTORY
Mary McLeod Bethune
Booker T. Washington
Marian Anderson
Thurgood Marshall
Shirley Chisholm

Have each student trace his footprints on black construction paper and cut them out. Then have each student use a white crayon or paint pen to write the name of a famous Black American on one footprint. Next, have him write a sentence about that person on his other footprint cutout. Trail each footprint pair around the bulletin board along with a photo of each corresponding person. Add the title shown, and you're ready to celebrate Black History Month!

HOGS AND KISSES FOR VALENTINE'S DAY

To make a hog, a student traces two large and two small heart shapes onto construction paper and assembles the head and body of the hog as shown. Then she attaches facial features made from construction paper. She makes a kiss out of tagboard, cuts it out, and wraps a piece of slightly wrinkled foil around it. Staple the completed projects to a bulletin board for Valentine's Day fun!

Leapin' Leprechauns!

Have each student decorate a paper plate in her own likeness. Then give a copy of the form and leprechaun pattern on page 244 to each student. Instruct the student to color and cut out the leprechaun and then glue it to the top of the paper plate project. Then have her complete the form. Staple the projects on a bulletin board, add the title shown, and watch for smiles!

SOAR INTO SPRING
Kim
Ryan
Seth
Beth
Alice
Todd
Keith
Meg
Tina
Jon
Ben
Keri
Alex

Have each student write a message about spring on a copy of the balloon pattern on page 245. Next, have her personalize a copy of the basket pattern on page 245 and then color both copies. Hole-punch holes on the balloon and basket; then lace a 30-inch string through them in order, taping the ends in place. Staple the completed balloons to a blue bulletin board decorated with clouds; then add the title shown and soar into spring!

Reading Is
a Magical Experience!

Color and mount an enlarged copy of the carpet pattern on page 246 on a bulletin board. Have each student complete a copy of the lamp pattern on page 246 by writing the title of a favorite book and drawing a picture from the story. Staple the completed projects to the bulletin board. Add the title shown, and let the reading magic begin!

RED-HOT CHILI PAPERS
Kelly
Sam
Troy
Ryan
Elissa
Sara
Rob
Amy
Kim
Karen
Jonah
Adam

Show off students' good work with this sizzling display. Make a class supply of chili pepper cutouts on red construction paper. Program each cutout with a student's name. Then make a large pepper cutout and mount it in the center of the bulletin board. Staple to the board an example of each student's work topped with her personalized pepper.

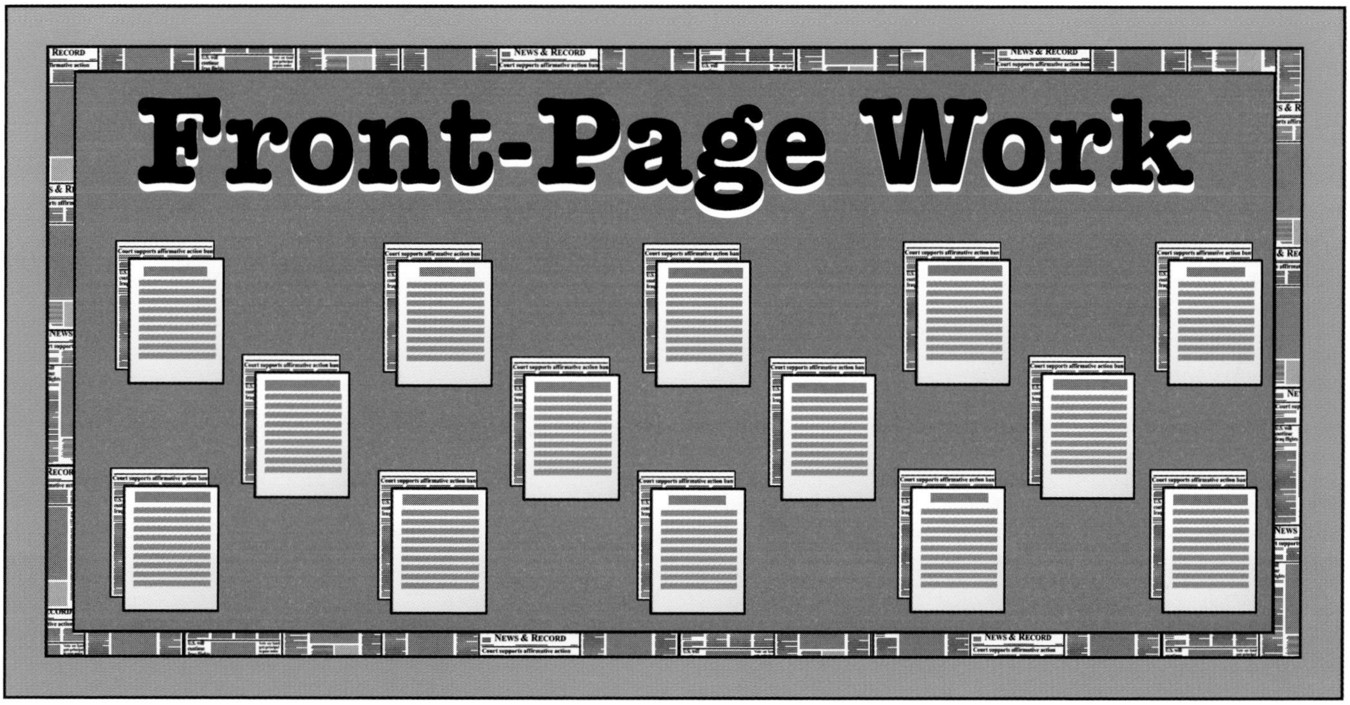
Front-Page Work

This easy display will spread the news about hardworking students. Cut a class supply of 8½" x 11" pages from newspaper. Staple them to the board to highlight student work as shown. Add a border cut from newspaper and a bright title.

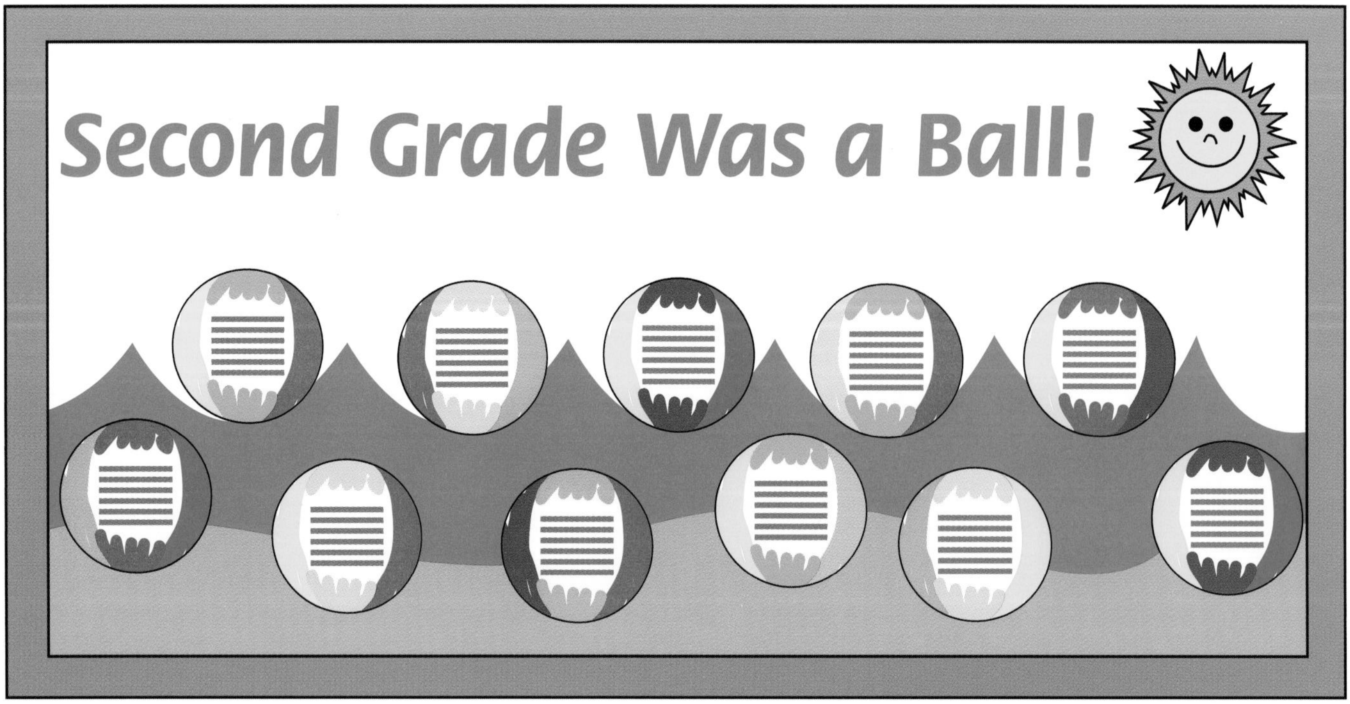
Second Grade Was a Ball!

Cover a bulletin board with white background paper. Add a strip of brown paper that resembles sand and a strip of blue paper cut to look like waves. Give each student a 12-inch white construction paper circle. In the center of the circle have each student write about his favorite experience in second grade; then instruct him to color the circle to look like a beach ball. Staple the colorful creations, the title shown, and a cheery sun character to the board for an end-of-the-year display.

GIVE A HIGH FIVE FOR SUMMER!

Have each student trace his hand on colored construction paper and cut it out. Each student writes his summer plans on the cutout. Staple the completed handprints to a bulletin board. Add the title shown and a border, and your display is complete.

Crayon Pattern

Use with "What a Colorful Class!" on page 231.

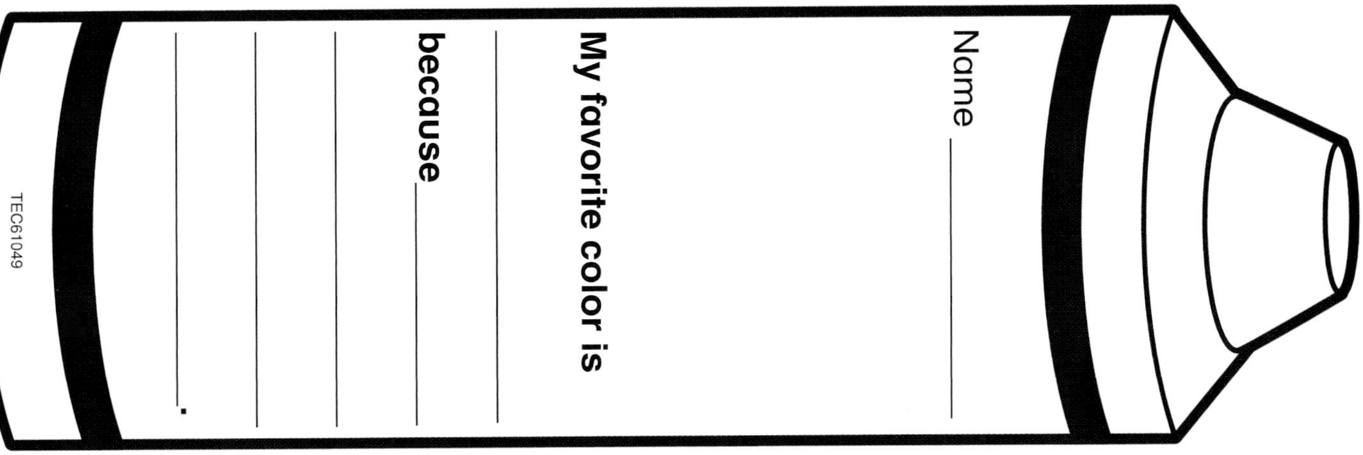
Name
My favorite color is
because
TEC61049

Buddy Pattern

Use with "Focus on Friendship" on page 231 and "Hats Off to Helpers!" on page 232.

TEC61049

Hat Patterns

Use with “Hats Off to Helpers!” on page 232.

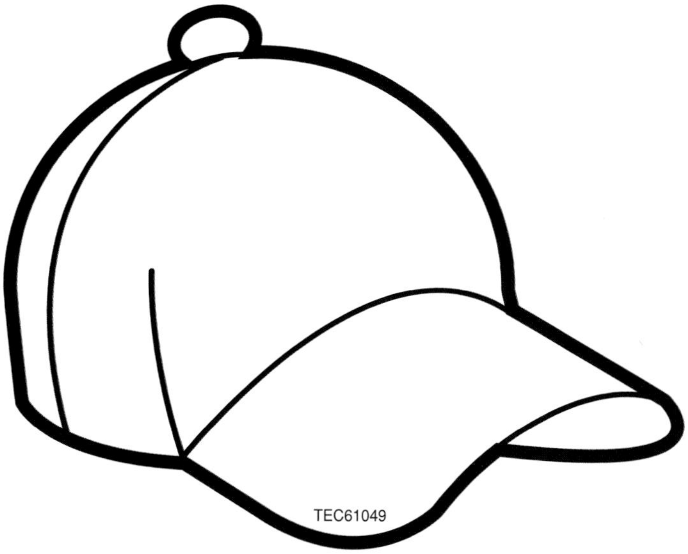
TEC61049

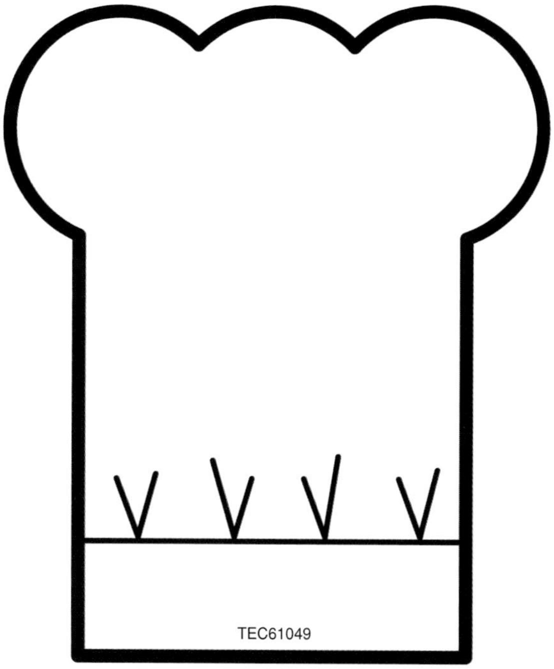
TEC61049

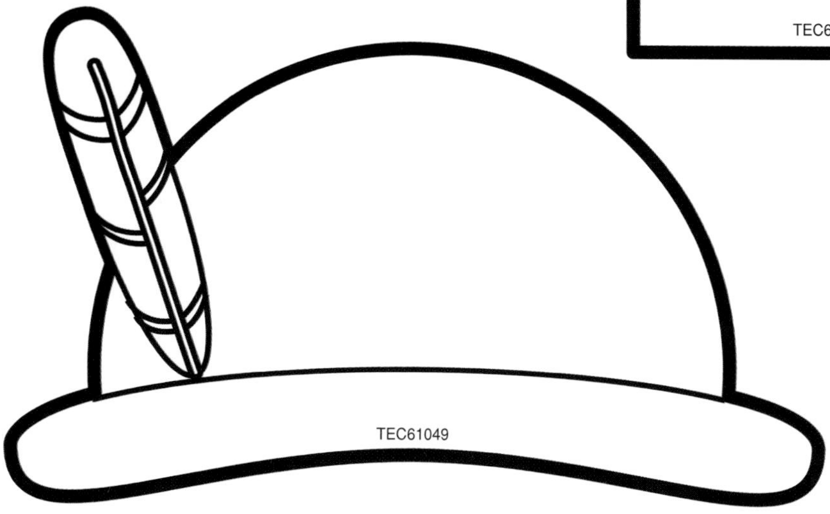
TEC61049

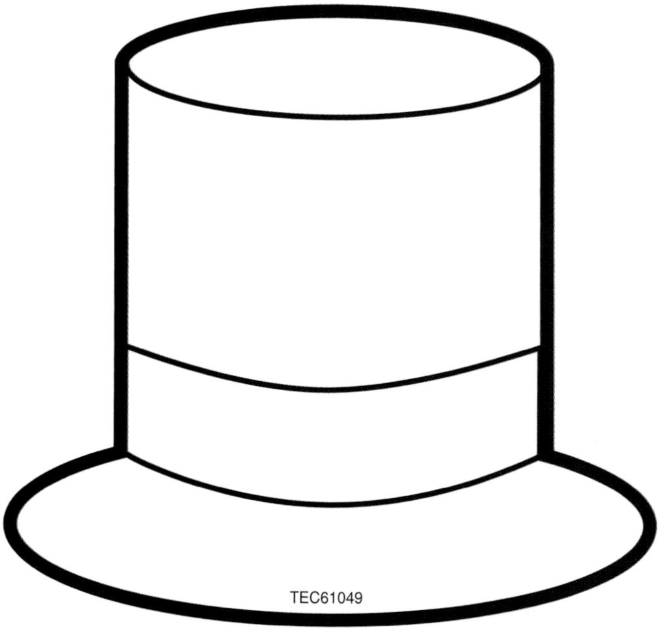
TEC61049

TEC61049

Cat Pattern

Use with "Have a 'Purr-fectly' Safe Halloween!" on page 233.

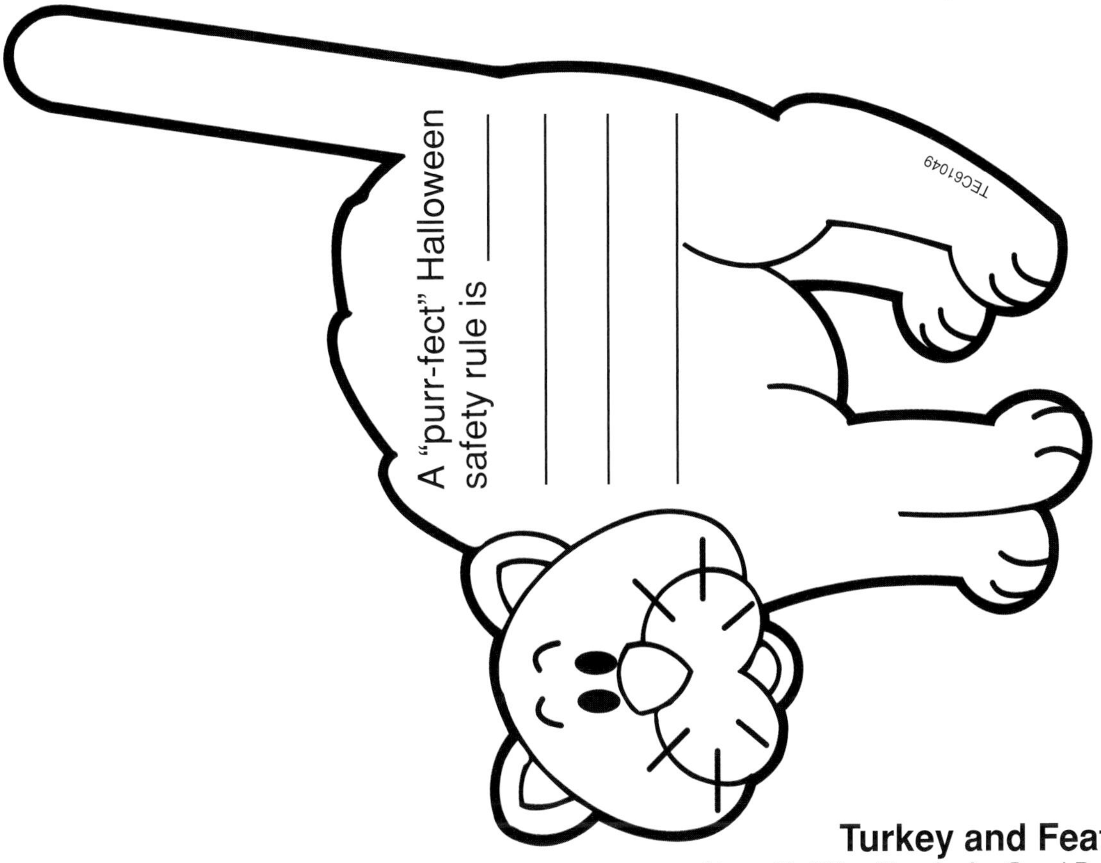
A "purr-fect" Halloween safety rule is
TEC61049

Turkey and Feather Patterns

Use with "Give Thanks for Good Deeds!" on page 233.

TEC61049

Leprechaun Pattern and Form

Use with "Leapin' Leprechauns!" on page 237.

I saw a little leprechaun;
He hopped upon my head.
He smiled and winked and tipped his hat,
And this is what he said:

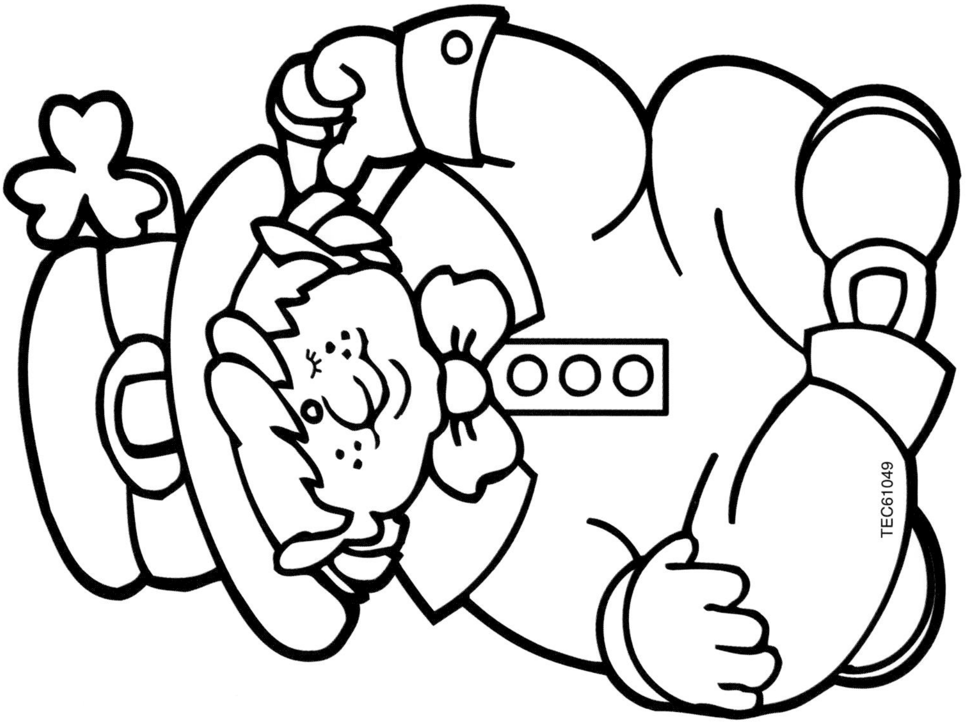
TEC61049

Balloon and Basket Patterns

Use with "Soar Into Spring" on page 238.

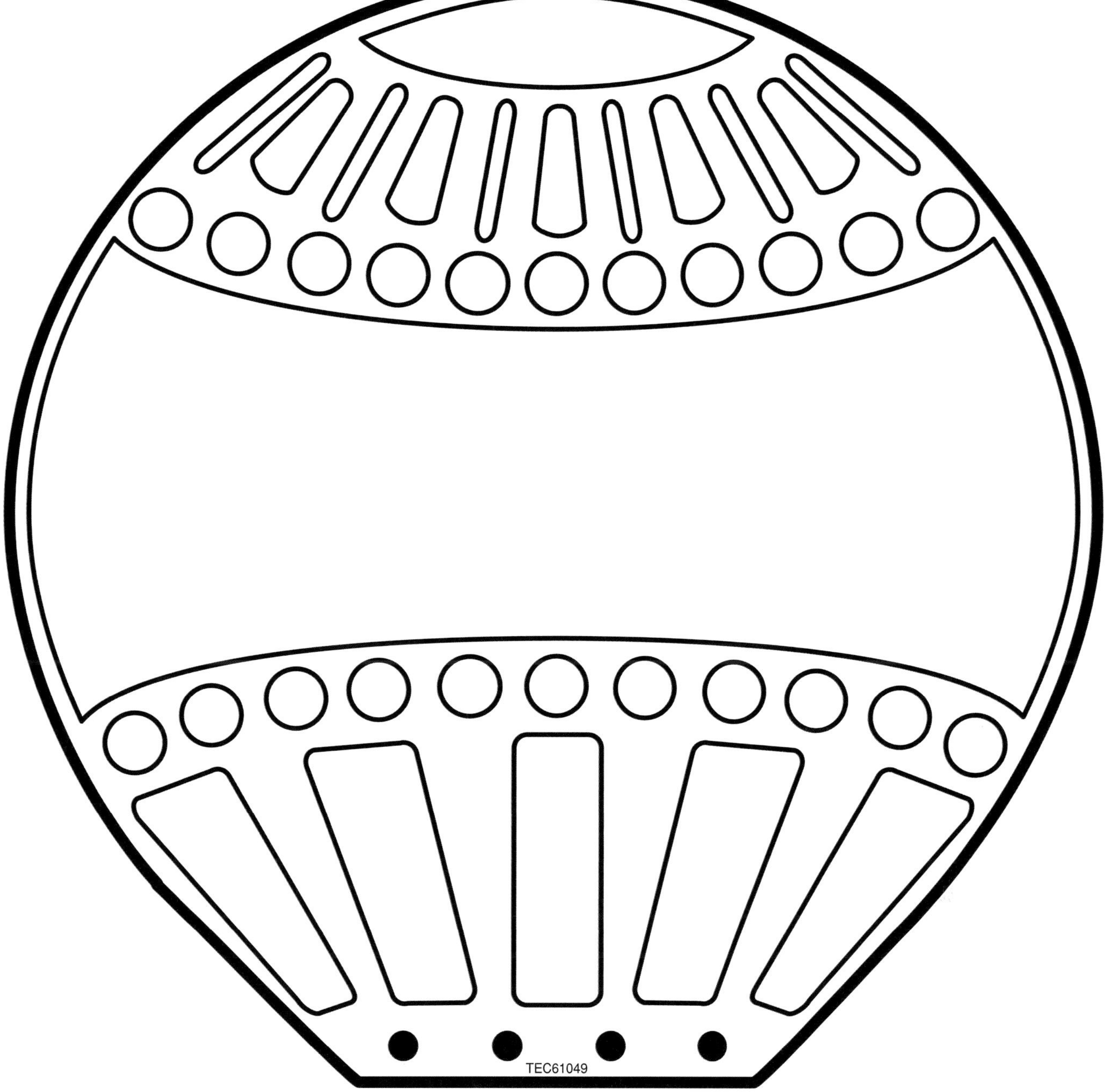
TEC61049

Carpet and Lamp Patterns

Use with "Reading Is a Magical Experience!" on page 238.

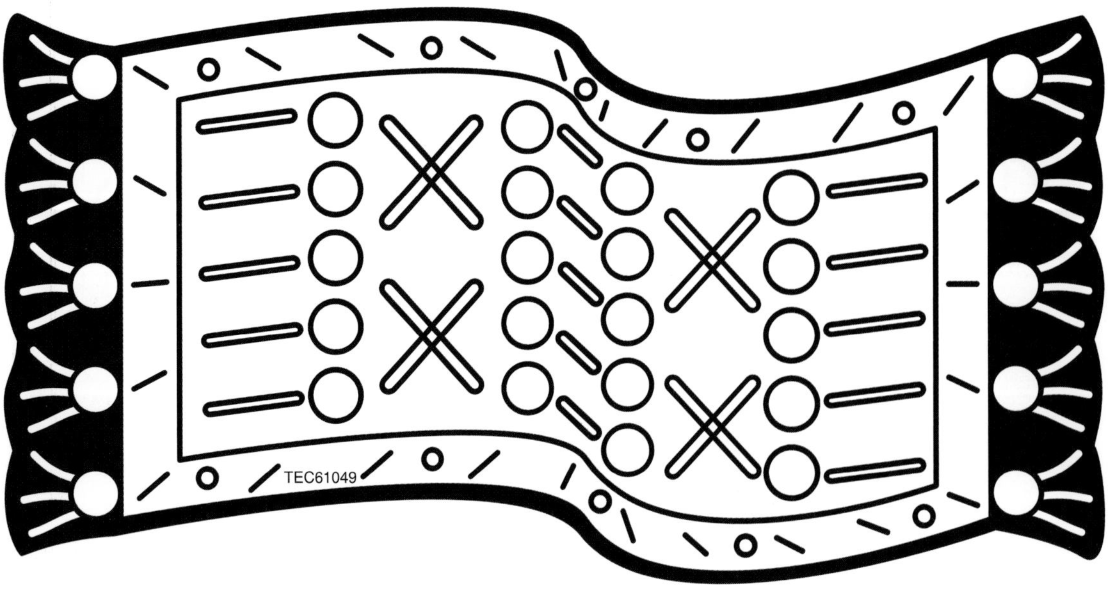
TEC61049

Title ______________________________
Name _______________________
TEC61049

Classroom Management

Follow the Dots

Colored, self-stick dots come in handy for placing students in small groups. Select a color for each small group you wish to create; then place a colored dot on the corner of each student's desk. Children with the same-colored dots will work together.

Use the dots for these purposes as well:

- Dots come in handy when you need a group of student helpers—just call out a color and your helpers are chosen!
- Use the dots to target a certain group for personal attention, praise, or extra help. Designate a color dot for each day of the week. Be sure that every student in that color group gets special treatment on his designated day.
- Color-code student journals and workbooks for easy collecting and distributing. Also keep up with writing journal responses by targeting a certain color to respond to each night.

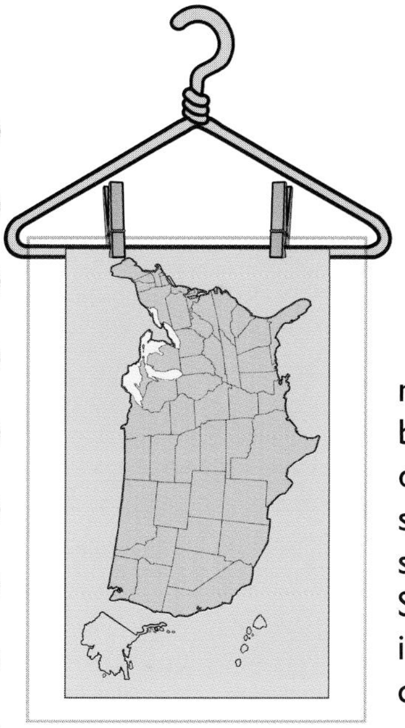

Storing Display Items

Store posters, maps, charts, and bulletin board displays with this simple and accessible method. Separate the items into the desired categories (by months, topics, or themes), and place each category in a see-through trash bag. Fold the top of each bag over a wire hanger and secure it with clothespins. Hang the bags in a closet or storeroom. When looking for a particular item, you'll be able to spot it hanging neatly in a bag.

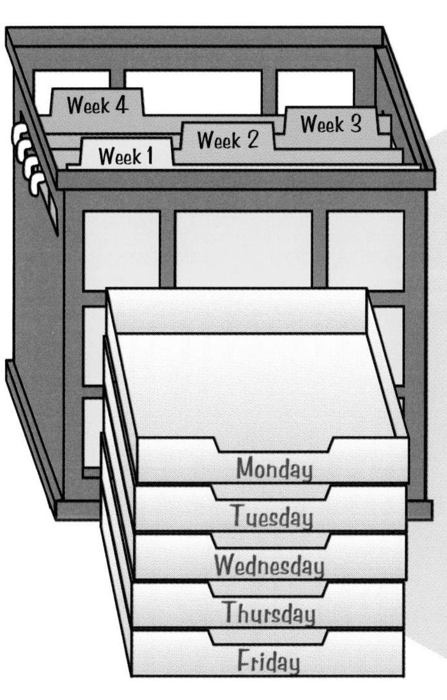
Week 4
Week 2
Week 3
Week 1
Monday
Tuesday
Wednesday
Thursday
Friday

Curriculum Organizer

Set up four hanging files and label each with a week of the upcoming month. At the beginning of the month, map out the activities and lessons you plan to teach during the next four weeks. File the plan sheet, along with all the books, worksheets, and resources needed, in the appropriate week's folder. Then organize for the upcoming week by removing the items from the folder and transferring them to a set of five stackable trays labeled "Monday" through "Friday." Place the appropriate materials in the tray labeled with the day that you will be using them. This plan will keep you prepared and organized for the week ahead!

To further organize and prepare for the next school year, keep a copy of the plan sheet filled out for each week. Clip copies of reproducibles, overhead transparencies, book lists, and other information pertinent to the lessons to each plan sheet. When the next school year rolls around, you will have copies of your previous lesson plans to refer to, as well as access to all the materials needed for each lesson.

Just Clip It!

Spring-type clothespins can be used in a variety of ways in the classroom. Keep a supply on hand for the following uses:

- Program a set of clips to be used as passes to the office, nurse, and restrooms.
- When a paper clip is too small for the job, use a clothespin!
- Display a chart or poster in a jiffy by using clothespins and a wire clothes hanger.
- Suspend several lengths of monofilament line from the ceiling. Attach a clothespin to the end of each length to hold student artwork or decorative displays.
- Program clothespins with the names of students. Use the programmed clips for emergency nametags, to label art projects and materials, and as manipulatives in graphing activities.
- Glue magnets to the backs of several clothespins and place them on filing cabinets as message holders, or attach them to magnetic chalkboards to hold posters, charts, and displays.
- Use clothespins for art projects that require pieces to be held in place while the glue dries.

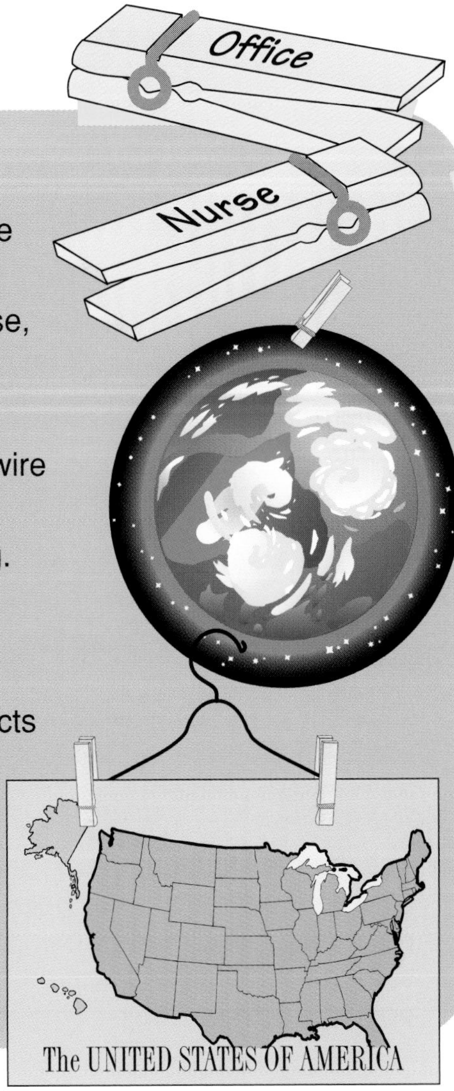
Office
Nurse
The UNITED STATES OF AMERICA

Pocket Organizers

Keep materials accessible at a glance with clear, plastic multipocket shoe bags.

- Hang a clear multipocket shoe bag by your desk to organize the basics you need every day. Place the following items in the pockets, and you'll have your necessary materials on hand in one central place:

Stickers
Glue
GLUE
Scissors
Dice
Spinner Cards
Index Cards
Bookmarks
Desktags
Incentive Punch Cards
Chalk
Passes
Hall Pass
Hall Pass
Hall Pass
Rubber Bands

lunch tickets
medical forms
office passes
overhead transparency markers
grading pens
a calculator
supplies
manipulatives

- Place a shoe bag in your art center, and stock it with supplies needed for the current project.
- Store laminated die-cut bulletin board letters in the pockets of the shoe bag.
- A see-through shoe bag can also serve as a classroom job chart. Use a permanent marker to label each pocket of the organizer with the title of a classroom job. Program a class set of index cards with students' names. To assign jobs, place a name card into a pocket.

HUNGRY AS A BEAR
Bring
Choice A
Choice B
Dave
Jane
Bobby
Sarah
Kevin
Sallie
Barbara
Tawnya
Seth
Jennifer
Rob
Cathy
Stacie
Cheryl
Joe
Annie
Lunch Clips
Daily Lunch Count

Lunch Count Made Easy

Duplicate and color the desired number of copies of the bear pattern on page 253. Label each pattern with an appropriate lunch choice. Staple the bears to a bulletin board and attach a construction paper necktie to each bear. Next, write each student's name on a spring-type clothespin, and clip it to a paper lunch sack stapled to the board. When each student arrives each morning, she attaches her clothespin to the appropriate tie. You'll be able to record the lunch count with a quick glance at the board, and reinforce graphing techniques and student responsibility too!

Right-Hand Man

Need a special helper? Then turn to your right-hand man! Fill a white cloth work glove with fabric stuffing or cotton balls. Glue wiggle eyes to both the ring and middle fingers as shown. Add a red felt mouth and a cloth bow tie; then fit a small tin can inside the opening of the glove to make it stand up. Place the character on a different student's desk each morning to signify that he is your right-hand man for the day.

Attendance Helpers

Each week give a class attendance list to a pair of students. As other students arrive, have them report to the two helpers. One helper is responsible for checking off attendance and will report to you any absences for the day. The other helper makes a tally of how many students are buying milk or a lunch, and provides that information for the lunch count. Keeping track of these daily tasks will be easier for you, and it will help develop students' organizational skills.

Super Signal

This bright idea will keep your classroom from sounding like a traffic jam! Make a tagboard copy of the traffic signal pattern on page 254. Use markers to color the lights the appropriate colors. Cut out a construction paper arrow, glue it to a spring-type clothespin, and clip it to the traffic signal. Tell students that when the arrow points to the red light, it is time to stop what they are doing. When the arrow points to the yellow light, they need to listen carefully to directions. The green light gives students the signal to begin their work. Simply move the arrow to indicate the desired classroom behavior!

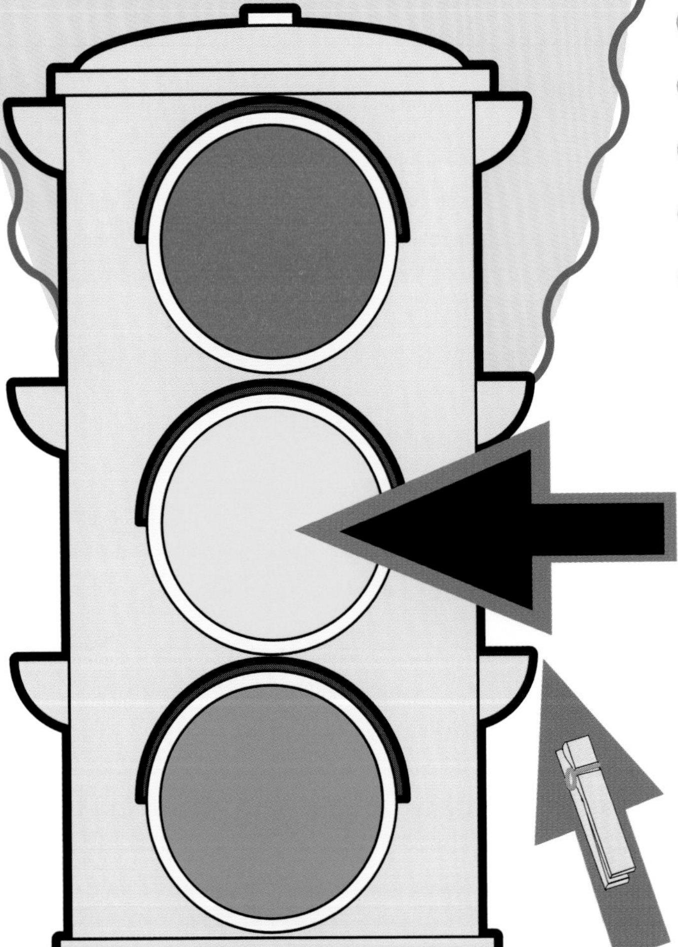

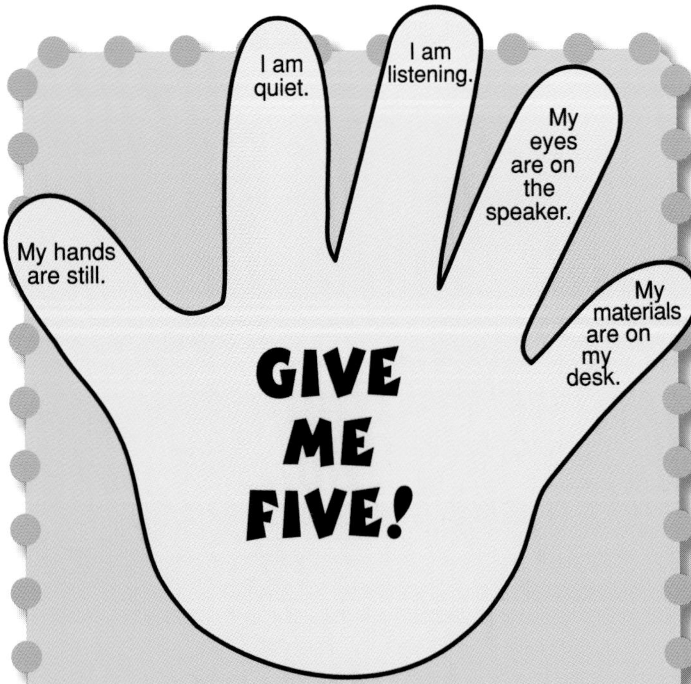
My hands are still.
I am quiet.
I am listening.
My eyes are on the speaker.
My materials are on my desk.
GIVE ME FIVE!

Give Me Five!

Enlarge a tagboard copy of the pattern on page 255 and display it in the classroom. Discuss with your students the five skills of a good listener as outlined on the pattern. When you desire students to display these skills, get their attention with the phrase, "Give me five!" Each student checks the chart to make sure he is demonstrating the five tasks, then raises his hand to show he is ready. What a "hand-y" way to encourage listening skills!

Transition Time

Tape an index card to each row of desks or table grouping. Each time a group of students prepares for the upcoming lesson in a timely and an appropriate manner, reward them by placing a sticker on their index card. When a group has accumulated a predetermined number of stickers, reward members with a special privilege, such as lining up first, sitting at a special table at lunchtime, or visiting a learning center of their choice. Students will quickly see that with cooperation and teamwork, their best efforts will be recognized.

Book-Order Box

Provide a handy box to collect student book orders. Request that each student bring her money and order form to school in an envelope labeled with her name. (Place a supply of blank envelopes by the box.) Have each student place her order inside the box instead of handing it to you. Then, when you have a chance during the day, check the contents of the box to make sure all forms are properly filled out and the correct money is enclosed. When it's time to send in the order, you'll have all forms and money ready to go!

Thinking Ahead

Keep notes about each unit in your plan book for the upcoming year. At the end of each day, jot down a few comments about each lesson. You may decide that it would be better to teach geometry in the spring, or that the units on time and money need additional reinforcement. Also write down the names of any books, videos, or manipulatives that enhanced the lesson. When the next year rolls around, you will have an easier time planning lessons, gathering materials, and making supply lists.

Review skip-counting before the lesson on cans.

Read *Inch by Inch* to introduce measurement.

Find applesauce recipe for Johnny Appleseed unit.

Challenge
Activities

Challenge Activities

Keep a supply of activities on hand for those students who are early finishers. Make a copy of several challenging reproducibles that you don't plan on using in your daily lessons. Mount each reproducible on construction paper, and attach a corresponding answer key to the back. Laminate the pages and place them in a decorated box labeled "Challenge Activities." Store several wipe-off markers in the box as well. When a student has extra time, encourage her to select a reproducible, complete and check her work, and then wipe away the programming before returning the activity to the box. Place new activities in the box periodically to provide new challenges.

Heading Helpers

If your students are having difficulty putting proper headings on their papers, try this cooperative suggestion. Make an oversized display of the paper heading and post it in a prominent place. Encourage students to check their papers against the heading each time they start a new assignment. For an added check, have each student ask a classmate to proofread her heading before she turns in her work. This will also be a big help to new students coming into your classroom.

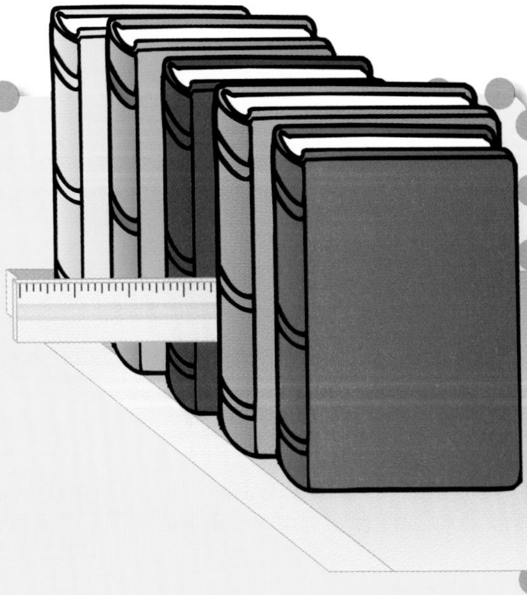

Library-Shelf Marker

Keep your classroom bookshelves in good order with a supply of wooden rulers (or paint-stirring sticks). Place the rulers (or sticks) in a decorated container on top of your bookshelf. When a student wishes to look at a book, she marks its place on the shelf by inserting the ruler in the book's place. If she decides to keep the book, she removes the ruler and places it back in the container. If she wants to put the book back, its proper place is marked.

No More Nameless Papers!

Here's a gentle reminder for students to write their names on their papers before turning the papers in. Place a pencil and a colored highlighting pen by the turn-in basket. If a child has written his name on his paper, he highlights it before placing his paper in the basket. If he has forgotten to write his name, he uses the pencil to do so, highlights it, and turns his paper in.

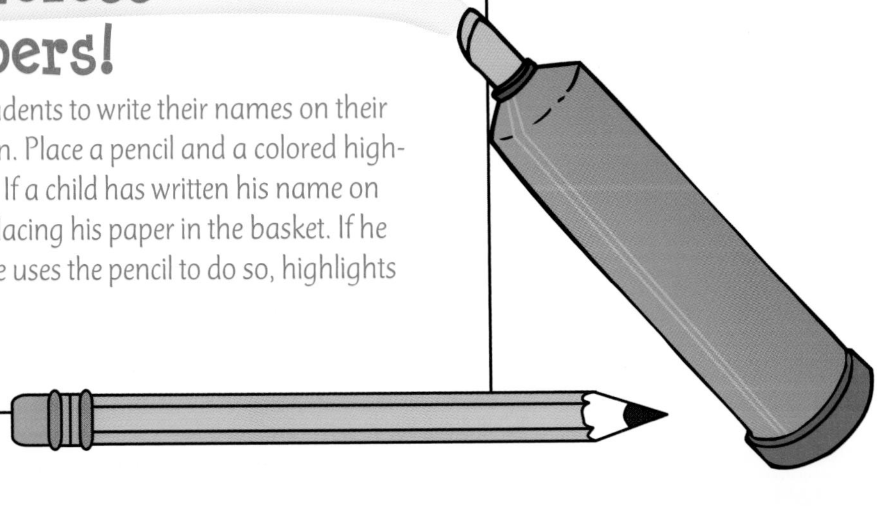

Bear Pattern

Use with "Lunch Count Made Easy"
on page 249.

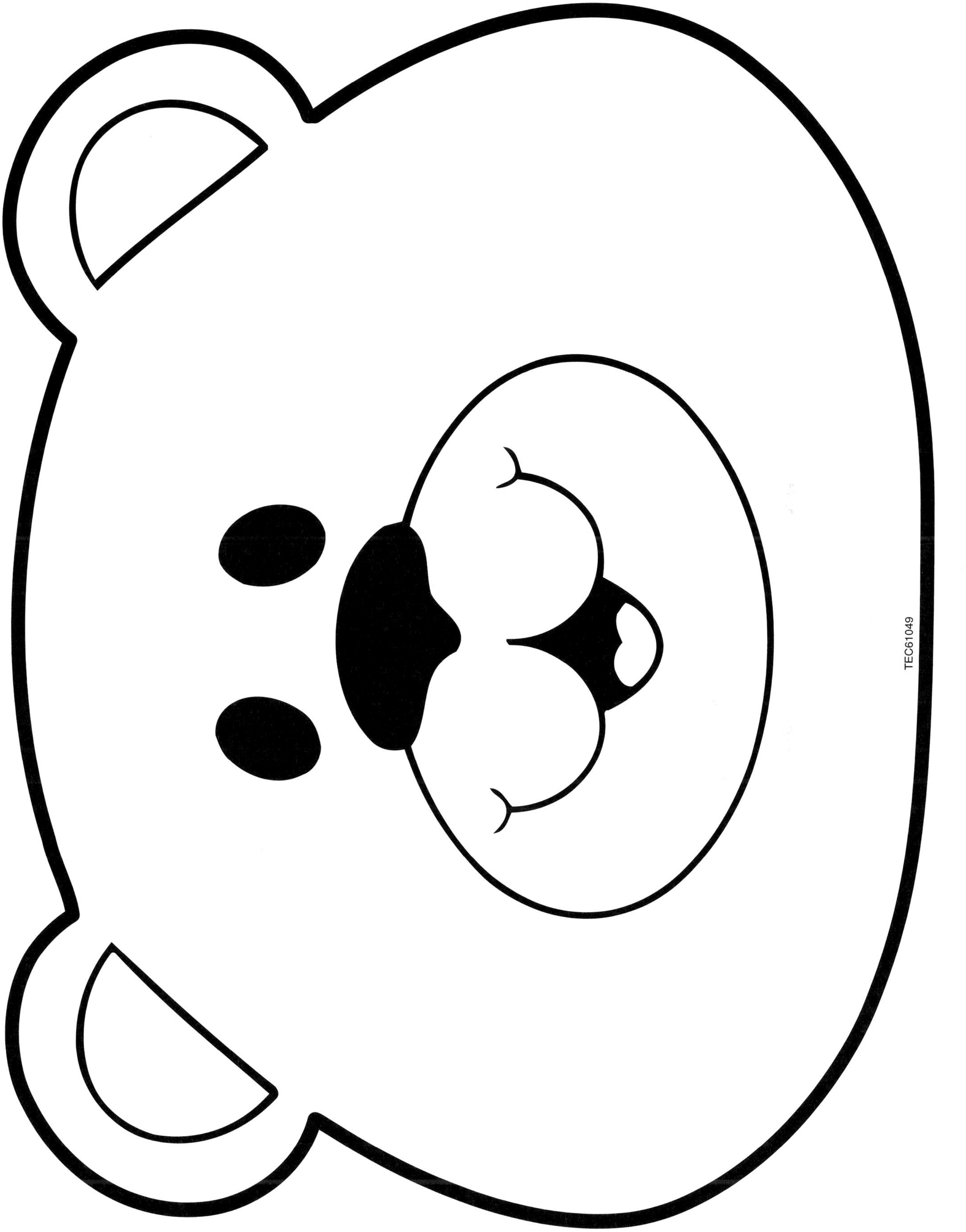
TEC61049

Traffic Signal Pattern

Use with "Super Signal" on page 250.

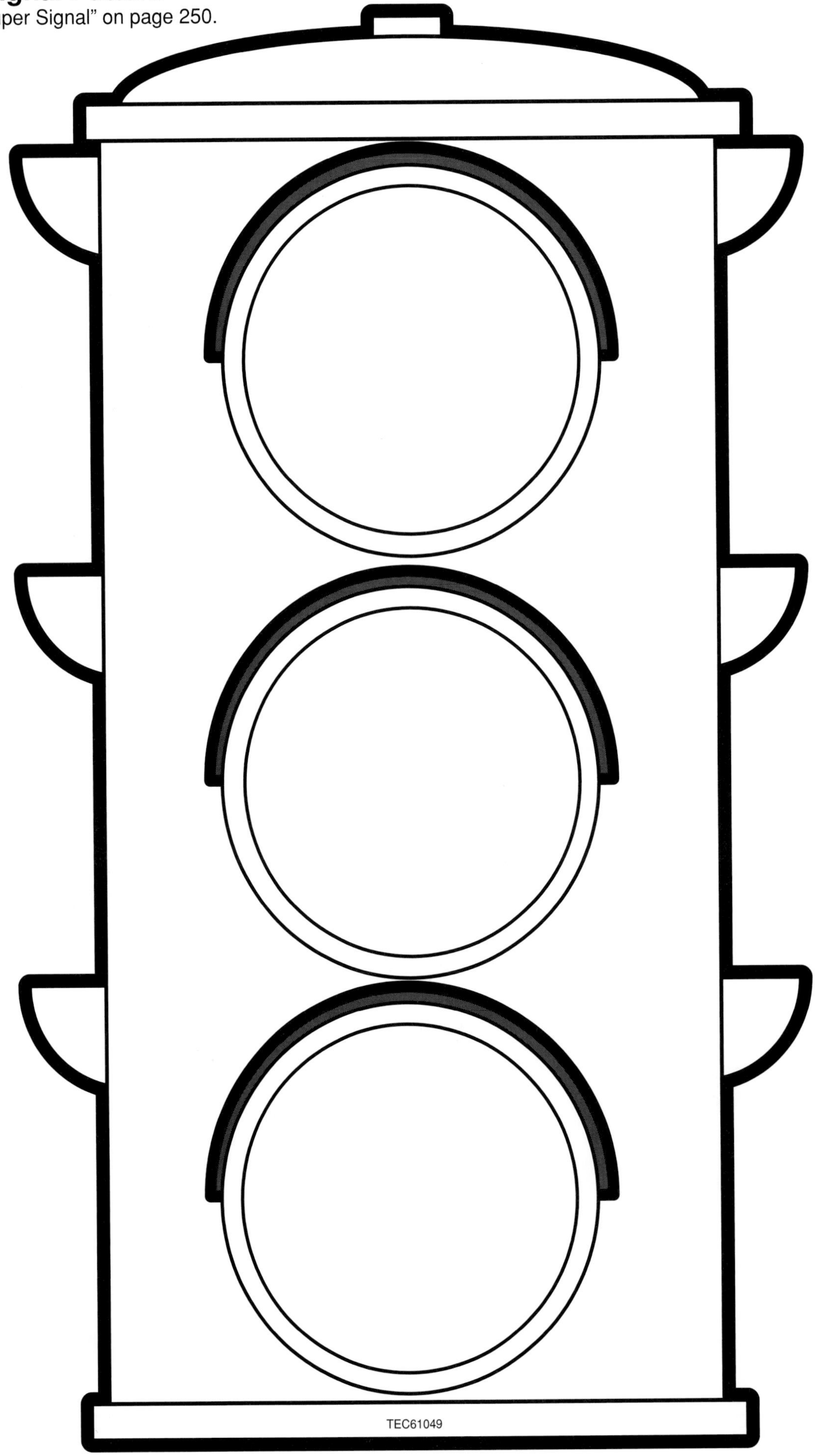
TEC61049

Hand Pattern

Use with "Give Me Five!" on page 250.

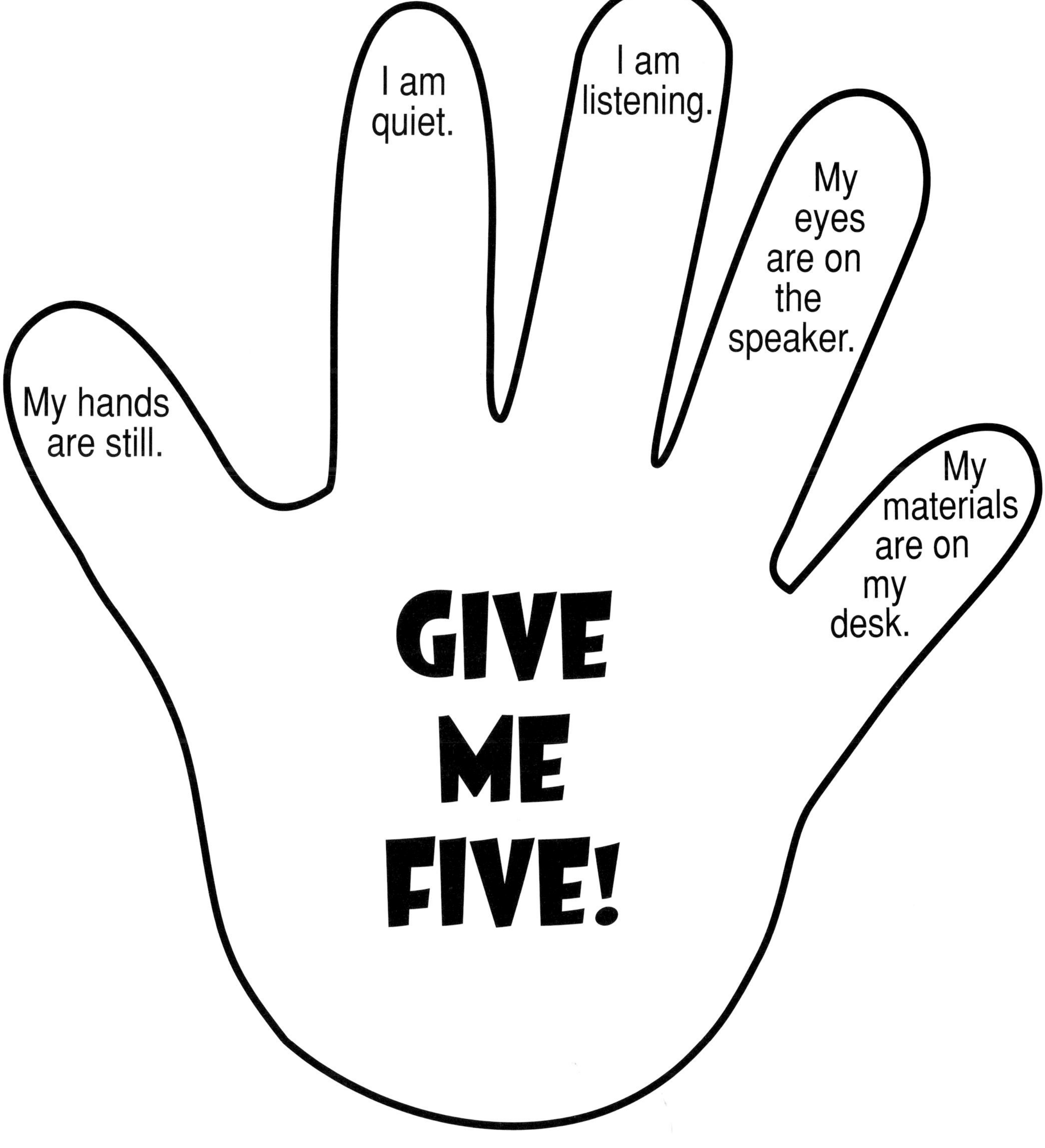
My hands are still.
I am quiet.
I am listening.
My eyes are on the speaker.
My materials are on my desk.
GIVE ME FIVE!

Behavior and Discipline Policies

Dear Parent,

Your child's success is very important. To create and maintain a positive learning environment for all students, I will follow the behavior and discipline policies below.

Please read them and discuss them with your child. Then sign the lower portion of the form and return it to school with your child. Be sure to keep this portion of the form for future reference.

Behavior Policy: ______________________________

____

____

____

Discipline Policy: ______________________________

____

____

____

Sincerely,

______________________ teacher signature ____________ date

I have read and do understand the behavior and discipline policies. I have also discussed these policies with my child.

______________________ parent signature ____________ date ______________________ student name

Homework Policy

Dear Parent,

Homework is an important part of your child's learning experience. Your child will benefit greatly from your support and encouragement of good work habits at home.

Please read the homework policy below and discuss it with your child. Then sign the lower portion of the form and return it to school with your child. Be sure to keep this portion of the form for future reference.

Homework Policy: ______________________________

____

____

____

____

Sincerely,

______________________ teacher signature ____________ date

I have read the homework policy. I have also discussed the policy with my child.

______________________ parent signature ____________ date ______________________ student name

It's a Celebration!

Dear Parent,

We are celebrating ______________________________

at ______________ on ____________, ______________.
time day date

You can help with the celebration by ____________________

____

____

____

Thank you for your help!

Sincerely, ____________________
teacher signature

Special Project Supplies

Dear Parent,
We are working on a special project related to ________________________.
subject

Your child needs to bring the following items by ________________________.
date

- ____
- ____
- ____
- ____

Thank you for helping!

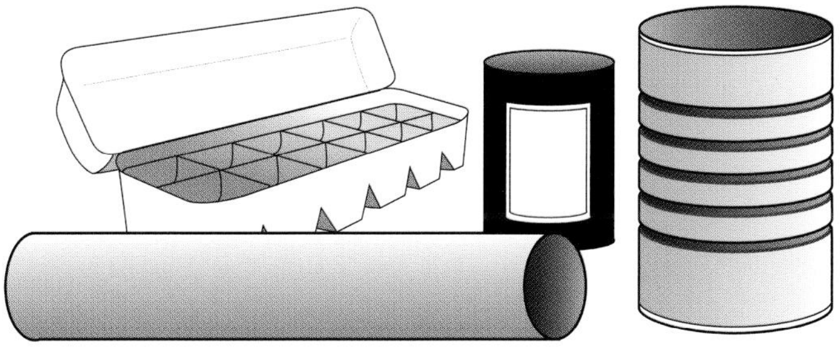

Sincerely,

____
teacher signature

date

Dear Parent,

Your child needs the following school supplies:

______ pencils
______ paper
______ crayons
______ glue
______ scissors
______ other: ______________

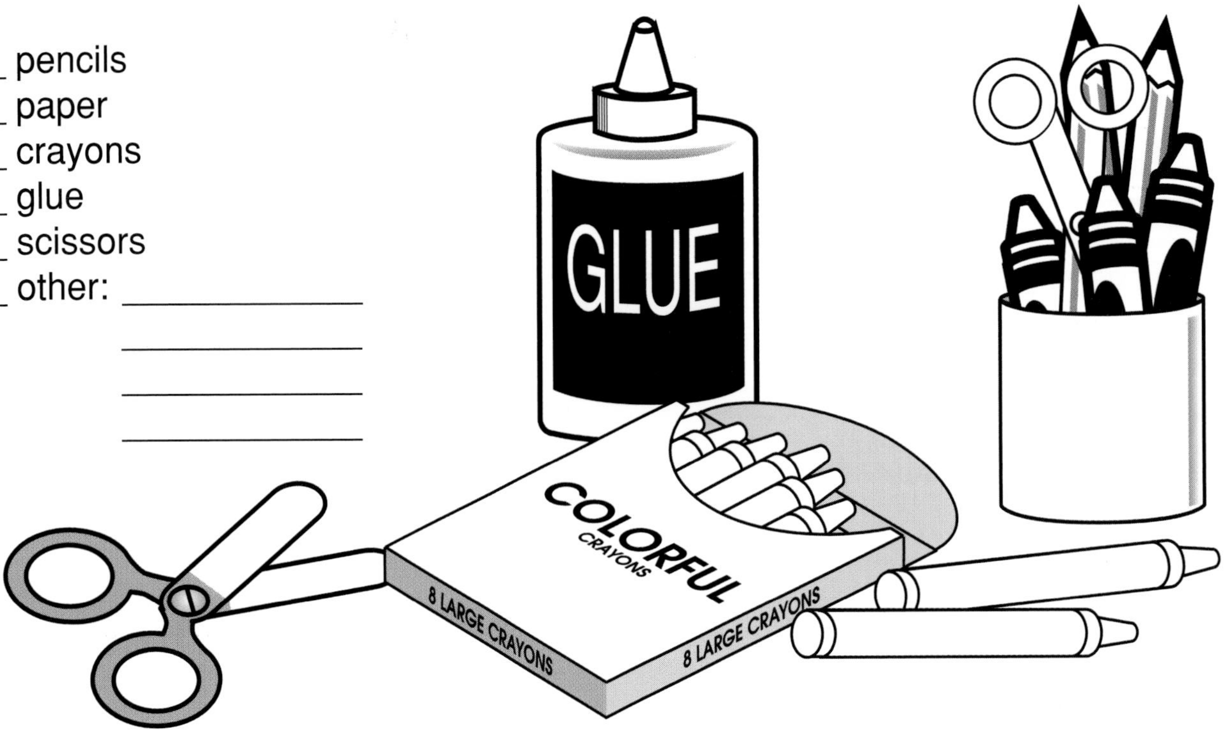
GLUE
COLORFUL
CRAYONS
8 LARGE CRAYONS
8 LARGE CRAYONS

---

date

Dear Parent,

Your child needs to complete the following assignments:

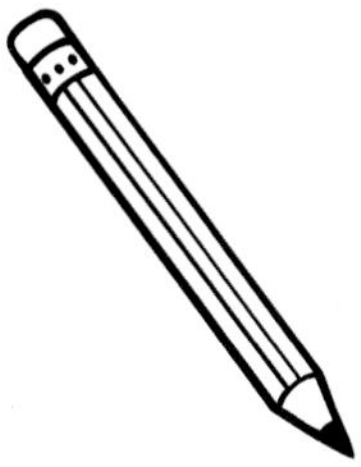

This work is due by ______________________________

Please sign and return this form.
Thank you for your help and support!

teacher signature

parent signature

Preconference Form

Student's Name ____

Parent's Name ____

Date ____

My child's attitude about school is ___________________________

____

I see growth in my child's abilities in these areas: ______________

____

I have concerns about my child's progress in these areas: _________

____

Topics I would like to discuss: ______________________________

____

Student Self-Evaluation

Name______________________________ Date__________________

- [ ] I do my best work.
- [ ] I use my manners.
- [ ] I follow the rules.
- [ ] I am kind to my classmates.

Most of the time

Sometimes

Not very often

I think I am good at ____.

I would like to do better in __________________________________.

My feelings about school are _________________________________

____.

©The Mailbox® • *Superbook®* • TEC61049

Motivation and Positive Discipline

Motivation by the Letter

Entice your students to use their best behavior with this teamwork approach. Begin by selecting a specific behavior that needs improvement. Then, as a class, decide on an incentive for reaching the goal. Use half-inch graph paper to spell out the reward in large block letters. Post the graph paper in a prominent location. Each time you notice a student displaying the target behavior, invite him to color a square on the graph lettering. When all the letters are colored, celebrate with the reward!

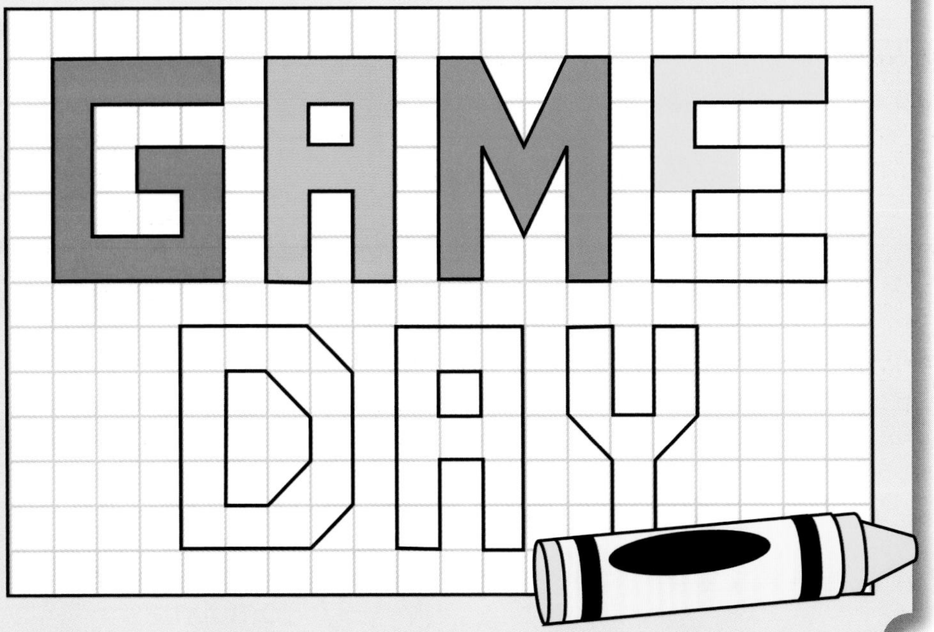
GAME
DAY

Instant Awards

Keep a supply of these little awards on hand to recognize individual achievements. Using colored paper, duplicate the awards on page 265. Each day, place several of the awards in your pocket or on the corner of your desk. When you spot a student demonstrating good behavior or trying his best at a task, present him with an award to show that you appreciate his efforts. What a nice way to say, "Keep up the good work!"

Funny Money

Cash in on good behavior with this motivational idea. At the beginning of each week, give a copy of one of the money patterns from page 264 to a different student. Give the student a black marker to design the funny money of the week. Copy the money to make a supply to use as rewards for good grades, appropriate behavior, completed assignments, or improved handwriting. At the end of the week, let students "spend" the funny money they have earned to purchase stickers, small treats, or special-privilege coupons.

Deanna Super Money
1
Funny Money
Deanna Super Money
1
Funny Money

Bloomin' Good Attendance

Motivate students to maintain good attendance with this bloomin' good idea. Draw a flowerpot in the bottom corner of your board. Each day that your class has perfect attendance, draw a flower in the pot. At the end of two weeks, reward the class with two minutes of free time for every flower in the pot. If desired, adapt the idea to reflect a different holiday or seasonal theme, using drawings such as feathers on a turkey, cherries on a tree, or eggs in a basket.

Quiet as a Mouse

Encourage students to work quietly with this soft and fuzzy incentive. Collect a supply of small stuffed animals or invite students to bring them from home. When it's time for students to work quietly at their desks, allow each child to place one of these silent, stuffed friends on his desktop. The stuffed animal may stay on the desk as long as the student remains quiet and on task. When the assignment is complete, the student returns the stuffed animal to the shelf until it's needed again.

Wall of Fame

Show students that you appreciate their best efforts with a classroom Wall of Fame. When a student makes significant progress in a certain subject, photograph her holding her good work. Mount the photo, along with a caption describing the achievement, on a bulletin board titled "Our Wall of Fame." At the end of every grading period, allow students to take their photos home to share with their parents.

Orderly Desk Incentive

Keeping desks neat and orderly is a task that is easily overlooked in the busy course of the school day. Keep students' desk clutter under control with a weekly desk inspection. Inform your students of the day you will check for neat desks, and remind them to have their desks neat and orderly by that day. Then choose a time when the students are out of the room and inspect each desk. If it is in good shape, tape a "Clean Desk" banner to the desk. When students come back into the room, they will be eager to see whether they have earned the special award.

CLEAN DESK

Pass the Paper

This quick and easy activity will make each student feel special. Have each child write her name at the top of a sheet of writing paper. When you say, "Pass the paper," each student hands her paper to the classmate on her right. The classmate writes a positive sentence about the student whose name appears at the top of the paper. Continue having students pass the papers until five or six statements have been written; then collect the papers and give them to their owners. Repeat the activity once a week, starting the papers at a different location each time to ensure that everyone has a chance to write about each classmate.

THE SWEET SMELL OF SUCCESS
Mary got a 100 on her spelling test.
Danny had a great day.
Jon wrote a poem.

The Sweet Smell of Success

Simmer a batch of self-esteem with this recipe for positive feedback. Obtain a cooking pot with a lid and place it on your desk. Each time you witness a student succeeding either academically or behaviorally, jot it down on a piece of paper and place it in the pot. (If desired, use vegetable- and noodle-shaped cutouts for this purpose.) At the end of the week, uncover the pot and read the notes aloud before giving them to the students to take home and share with their families.

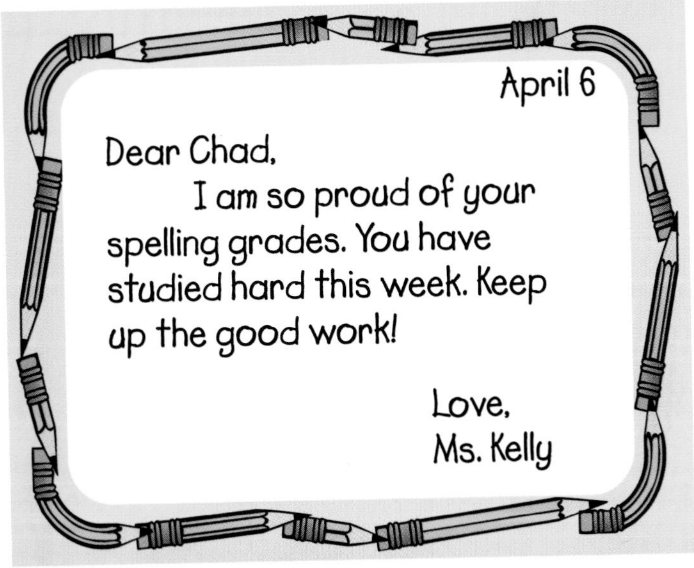
April 6
Dear Chad,
I am so proud of your spelling grades. You have studied hard this week. Keep up the good work!
Love,
Ms. Kelly

Special Delivery

Children love to receive mail. Capitalize on this by writing a letter to each student several times during the year. Take time during each grading period to write notes about good behavior and academic accomplishments to send to deserving students. (Indicate in your gradebook which students receive notes; make sure each student receives equal attention.) Even though it will take a little extra time, the payoff in student motivation and increased self-esteem is well worth the effort!

V. V. S. (Very Valuable Student)

Strengthen self-esteem by designating a V. V. S. (Very Valuable Student) in your classroom each week. During the week he is spotlighted as the V. V. S., the student is in charge of special events such as the following:

- selecting a book to read to the class
- choosing a topic for show-and-tell
- leading the line to lunch
- bringing a healthful snack to share with the class
- bringing pictures of his family to share with the class

To culminate the week, have each student draw a picture or write a message for the V. V. S. on a sheet of paper. (Be sure that you write a message too!) Bind the pages into a booklet and staple it between two construction paper covers. Then invite the V. V. S. to decorate the cover of his booklet. What a special tribute to a very valuable student!

Dear David,
I'm glad you were the V. V. S. this week! I loved the book you read to us.
Betsy

HAPPY BIRTHDAY, SUSAN!
Hooray! It's Your Birthday!
Have a great day! See you
HAPPY BIRTHDAY

Pal Pouch

This special-delivery idea is ideal for birthday students, but it can be used at other times during the year to boost a student's self-esteem. Make a student feel extra special by hanging a Pal Pouch from her chair. To make a pal pouch, attach a decorated manila envelope to the back of the selected student's chair. Encourage the other students to place positive notes in the pouch throughout the day. Provide a special place for the student to sit and read her mail before dismissal. What a treat and a self-esteem booster!

No More Monkey Business!

This class-effort progress chart will help eliminate monkey business in your classroom. Set a goal for your students, such as a week of having everyone seated before the tardy bell rings or having everyone's homework turned in on time. Color and cut out a copy of the monkey pattern on page 266. Cover a bulletin board with background paper and use markers to draw a palm tree as shown. Divide the tree into a desired number of sections for the steps required to reach the goal; then write the goal on a paper strip and post it by the palm tree. Pin the monkey to the bottom section of the tree. Each time the class makes progress toward the goal, move the monkey to the next level of the tree. When the monkey makes it to the top, celebrate with an afternoon of stories, an hour of math games, or free time at learning centers.

Turn in your homework on time.

Money Patterns

Use with "Funny Money" on page 260.

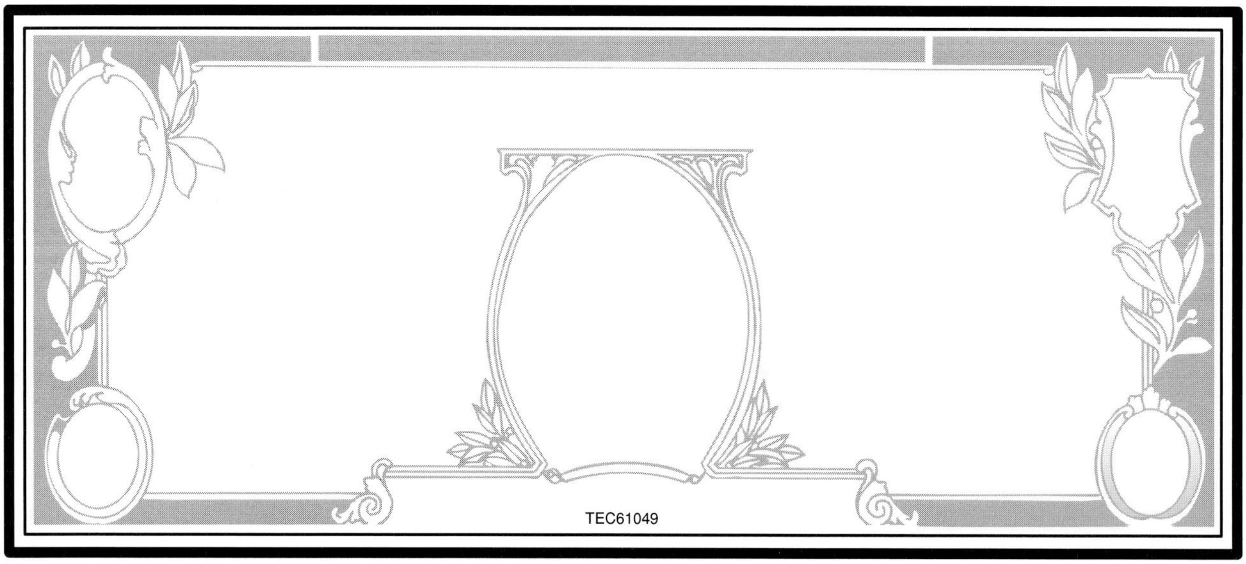
TEC61049

TEC61049

TEC61049

Use with "Instant Awards" on page 260.

CELEBRATE
GOOD
WORK!
TEC61049

You're
the Apple
of My Eye!
TEC61049

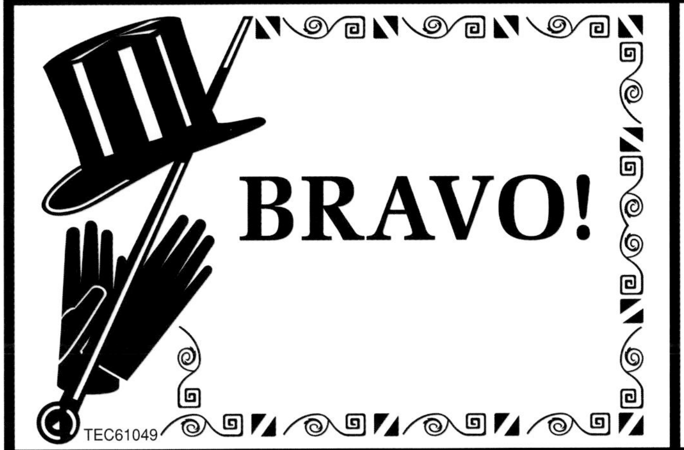
BRAVO!
TEC61049

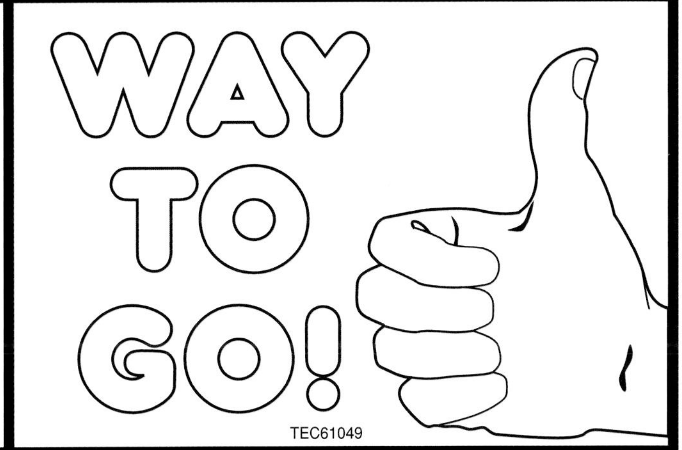
WAY
TO
GO!
TEC61049

Your
Work
Is Out of
This World!
TEC61049

1
AWARD-
WINNING
BEHAVIOR
TEC61049

ALL-STAR
STUDENT
TEC61049

You
Did a
Whale
of a
Job!
TEC61049

Monkey Pattern

Use with "No More Monkey Business!" on page 263.

TEC61049

Five-Minute Fillers

Rhyme Time

Write a word on the board and have students brainstorm rhyming words. Record their responses on the board. As the list progresses, point out the different spellings that create similar sounds. As an added challenge, have students use words from the list to compose simple couplets.

train

chain
pain
cane
plane
stain
rain/rein

Quick Fix

Write a list of scrambled spelling or vocabulary words on the board. Ask student volunteers to write the words correctly on the board. Then, if time permits, hold a bonus round for volunteers to define the words or name their parts of speech. In just a short time, you will have reinforced several important concepts!

Math Machine

Next time students are waiting in line, have the first student in line choose a number from one to ten. Announce an operation such as "Add three." The second student in line adds three to the first student's number. Continue down the line, having each student add three to the new total. For an added challenge, have students predict what the last number will be prior to their calculations. What a hardworking math machine!

Place-Value Scramble

This simple activity is perfect for a mini lesson on place value. Write three numerals on the board. Ask students to arrange the numerals to create the lowest possible number, the highest possible number, a number with the largest numeral in the tens place, and other similar arrangements. Complete the activity by asking students to assist you in arranging the resulting numbers in sequential order.

Graphing Games

Prepare for quick and easy graphing with this ready-to-go activity. Program a sheet of poster board with an open bar graph. Laminate the graph for durability. When you have a few extra minutes, display the graph and pose a question such as "How many buttons do you have on today?" Have each student write her answer on a sticky note while you label the graph with a wipe-off marker. Then have each student post her note in the appropriate place on the graph. Use the remaining time to have students interpret the information on the graph.

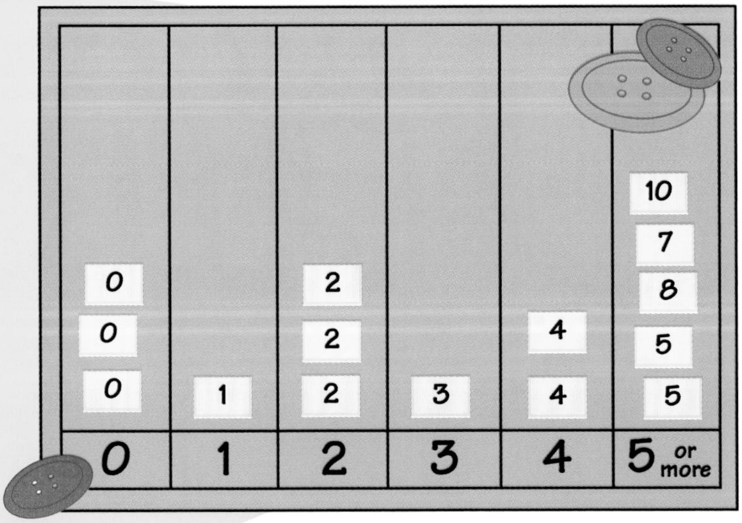
0
0
0
1
2
2
2
3
4
4
10
7
8
5
5
0
1
2
3
4
5 or more

Missing Vowels

Reinforce important decoding concepts with this easy time filler. Write several short-vowel words—with the vowels omitted—on the board. Ask the class to think of vowels that would make each word complete. Then have student volunteers come to the board to complete the words. Students will be amazed at the power vowels have to create different words!

Word Wizards

Divide students into four or five groups. Designate a recorder in each group and give her a blank sheet of paper. Write a letter combination such as *ad* on the board. Each group brainstorms as many words containing the letters as possible while the recorder lists them on the paper. Stop play after five minutes. In turn, call on each recorder to share a word from her list. If another group has that word listed, it is scratched from all lists. If no other group has the word, that team is awarded a point. Comparing continues until all answers have been exhausted. The group with the most points is dubbed Word Wizards for the day.

ad

had pad
bad sad
glad add
dad

Questions Only!

To fill a few minutes between activities, engage students in this questions-only game. Tell your students that you are thinking of an object related to a current topic of study. Give the students three clues about the object; then let the questioning begin. Each student may ask you one question that can be answered with *yes* or *no*. If a student guesses the object during his turn, he may lead a new round of questioning the next time the game is played.

???
I'm thinking of an animal that lives in the forest. It is covered with fur, and it walks on all four legs.
???

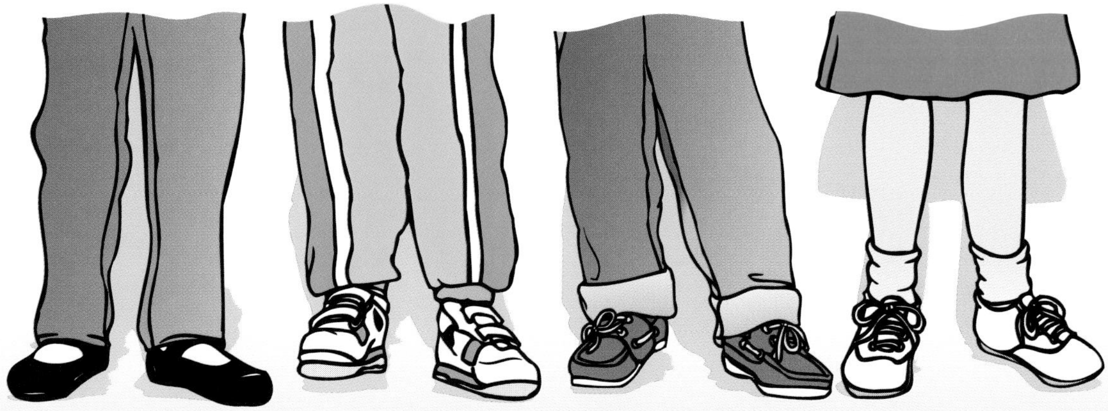

Pattern Power

With a few extra minutes, students can play this patterning game, which makes them the manipulatives. Ask four or five students to come to the front of the room and stand in line according to your directions. Have the rest of the class study the line to determine the pattern you used to organize the students. Try a few simple *ABAB* patterns (such as blue jeans, tennis shoes, blue jeans, tennis shoes) or *ABBA* patterns (such as boy, girl, girl, boy). Since appearances change every day, the possibilities are endless!

Line-Up Lesson

Students are lined up at the door, but there are still a few minutes before it's time to leave. Why not initiate a brainstorming session? Name a category with which students are familiar. Have students name an item in the category for each letter of the alphabet. By the time everyone has volunteered an answer, it will be time to go!

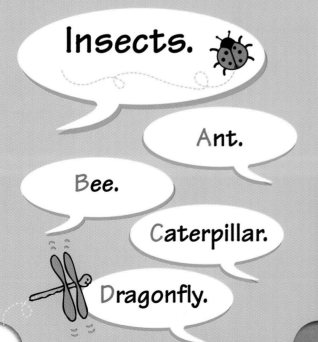

Insects.
Ant.
Bee.
Caterpillar.
Dragonfly.

Calendar Concepts

At the beginning of each month, provide each student with a copy of a blank calendar. Help your students fill in the appropriate dates, as well as information about holidays, student birthdays, and upcoming events. Have each student keep her calendar in her desk. When you have extra time throughout the day, instruct students to take out their calendars. Ask questions to practice calendar-related concepts or to remind students of special happenings. You'll stay on top of a busy school schedule while reinforcing important calendar skills.

Time Flies

Keep a large manipulative clock handy. When you have a few extra minutes, position the hands to show the current time. Ask a student volunteer to read the clock. Then ask a question such as "What time would it be if it were 15 minutes later?" Continue the activity as time allows.

ARTS and CRAFTS

Art projects are so much fun, but organizing the supplies can be a challenge. Arrange your materials in easy-to-use ways that make art time more enjoyable for you and your students.

- Keep balls of yarn and string tangle-free with a plastic funnel. Place the ball inside the funnel and pull the string out through the spout.
- Use baby-wipe containers to hold cotton balls, sponge shapes, paintbrushes, and craft sticks. The containers will stack neatly in your closet or cupboard.
- Store seasonal craft supplies in clear plastic boxes. Felt, pipe cleaners, and glitter in seasonal colors will be easier to find when grouped together.
- Stock up on project materials when you find them on sale. Some items to keep on hand are

clothespins
coffee filters
cotton balls
doilies
paper cups
paper lunch sacks
paper plates
pipe cleaners
wiggle eyes

Other materials can be obtained by asking parents to send specific items to school.

Tommy
POPCORN

Student Suitcases

Welcome the new school year with this get-to-know-me project. Have each student color and cut out an enlarged copy of the suitcase pattern on page 282. Then have him personalize the nametag on the suitcase. Next have the student cut pictures from old magazines of objects that are significant to him and glue them to the suitcase. Display the completed projects on a bulletin board titled "Look Who's Traveling Through Second Grade!"

Motivating Magnet

Encourage students to display schoolwork at home by having them create these unique take-home magnets early in the school year. To make a magnet, each child traces a half circle onto poster board and cuts it out. Next, he labels the half circle as shown. He then glues on two wiggle eyes and a one-inch pom-pom to create the facial features. If desired, have the student add yarn or paper hair to his creature before hot-gluing a magnet to the back. Students can proudly display their school papers at home using their self-made magnets.

LOOK WHAT I DID IN SCHOOL!

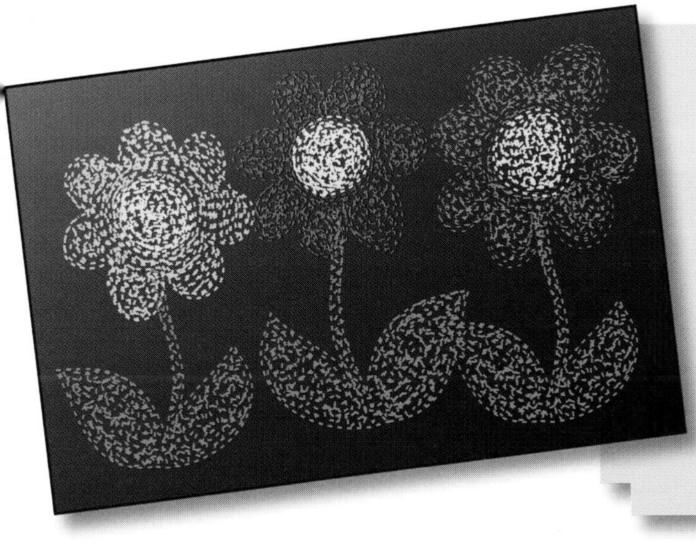

Pseudo Sand Painting

Students will get down to the nitty-gritty with this texturized project. Fill several resealable plastic bags with white cornmeal. Add a different color of food coloring to each bag. Seal each bag and gently knead the color into the cornmeal. Open the bags to allow the mixtures to dry. Have each student draw a design with glue on a sheet of black construction paper and then sprinkle the colored cornmeal onto the glue. After the glue dries, the student shakes off the excess cornmeal. Display these lovely creations on a bulletin board.

Spooky Spiders

Send shivers through your classroom with this display of creepy crawlers! To make a spider, have each student follow the directions below.

Materials needed for one spider:
4 black pipe cleaners
2 wiggle eyes
one $2\frac{1}{2}$" section of a cardboard tube
black tempera paint

Steps:

1. Paint the cardboard-tube section with black tempera paint. Allow it to dry.
2. Insert the four pipe cleaners through the tube so that equal lengths show on both sides.
3. Glue the pipe cleaners in place. After the glue dries, bend the spider legs in the desired positions.
4. Glue the wiggle eyes to the spider.

Display the completed spiders on a bulletin board covered with imitation spiderweb material.

Smiling Scarecrow Magnets

To make a magnet, each student traces a three-inch circle on a piece of tagboard and then cuts it out. Next she draws a face on the circle and glues several strands of raffia to the cutout to resemble hair. Next she cuts a hat from the remaining tagboard, colors it, and glues it atop the raffia. After the glue dries, she attaches a strip of magnetic tape to the back of her creation. Students can attach their magnets to metal objects in the classroom, or take them home for their families to enjoy.

Thanksgiving Gobblers

Brighten your classroom with a flock of turkey windsocks. To construct a windsock, each student rolls and staples a 9" x 12" sheet of brown construction paper to form a cylinder. Next she colors and cuts out a copy of the turkey head and feet (patterns on page 283) and glues them to the cylinder as shown. Then she uses a copy of the feather pattern (page 283) to trace and cut out several red and orange construction paper feathers, and glues them to the back of the cylinder. To complete the project, she staples a construction paper strip to the cylinder for the handle and glues tissue paper strips for the streamers.

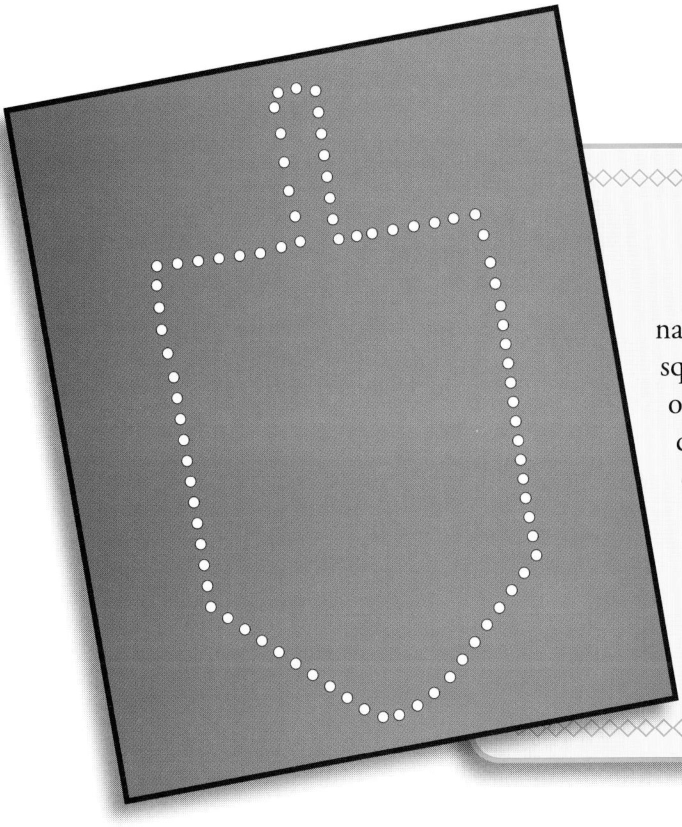

Hanukkah Lights

Honor the Festival of Lights with these illuminating projects. Have each student place an eight-inch square of construction paper atop an eight-inch square of cardboard. Then have him cut out a copy of the dreidel pattern (page 284) and trace it on the center of the paper. Next have him use a pushpin to punch holes along the traced lines. After all holes have been punched, have each student remove his cardboard. Then tape the construction paper squares to your classroom windows and watch as light streams through the tiny holes.

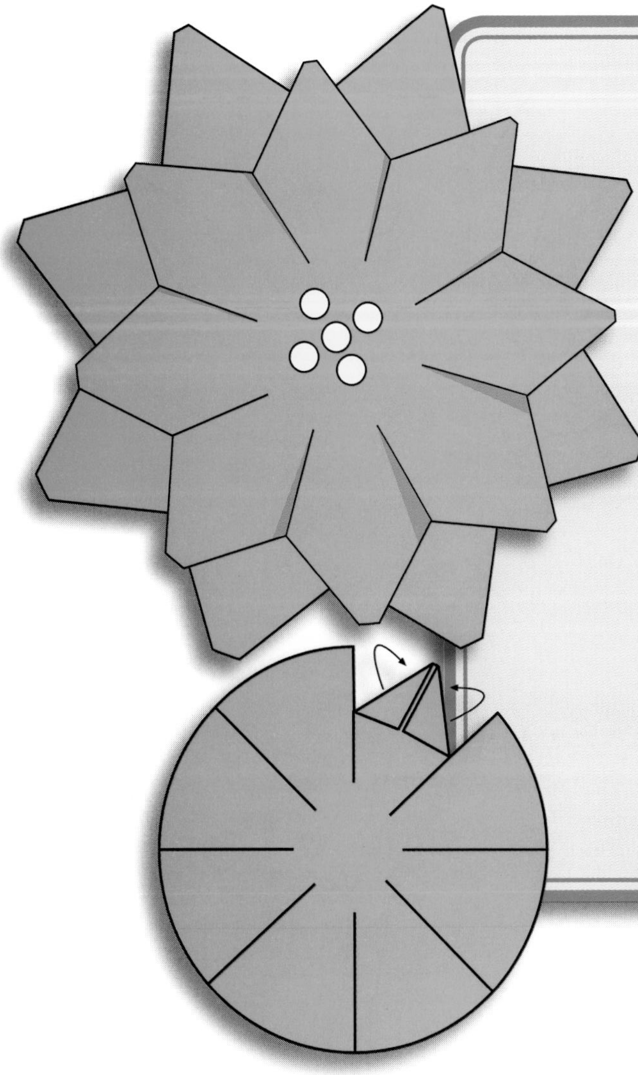

Pretty Poinsettias

These paper flowers add holiday flair to any classroom display. To make a poinsettia, a student folds both an eight-inch and a six-inch red construction paper circle in half, then in fourths, and finally in eighths. The student unfolds each circle and cuts each fold line three-fourths of the way down toward the center. For each circle, he folds back the corners of each section tab (to form a point) and secures the corners with glue. Then he glues the center of the smaller circle atop the larger circle. For a final touch, he hole-punches yellow construction paper and glues the dots in the center of the resulting poinsettia.

Christmas Countdown

To make a bell, a student copies the poem shown onto a large self-adhesive label. Next she gathers as many paper strips (half green and half red) as there are days until Christmas. She then uses the strips to create a paper chain. Next she inverts a red plastic cup and pokes a hole in what is now the top of the cup. Next have her thread the ends of a length of colorful ribbon through the hole—leaving a loop of ribbon at the top of the cup—and tie the two ribbon ends into a knot. Staple one end of the chain to the bottom of the cup, and then attach the poem as shown. Watch the excitement grow as students remove a link with each passing day.

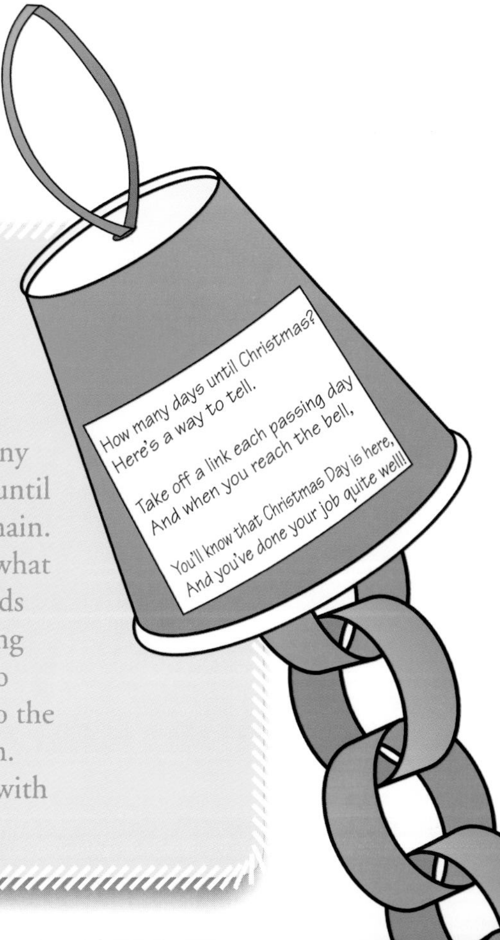
How many days until Christmas?
Here's a way to tell.
Take off a link each passing day
And when you reach the bell,
You'll know that Christmas Day is here,
And you've done your job quite well!

Abstract Art

Splash some color into the new year with these creative collages. To create a collage, a student glues crinkled tissue paper strips and confetti shapes onto an eight-inch white construction paper square as desired. Encourage each student to arrange the materials on his paper to create an abstract design. When the collage is dry, the student frames his creation by gluing it to a nine-inch, colored poster board square. Mount the colorful creations on a bulletin board for a dazzling New Year's display.

Sparkling Snowflakes

The forecast is for winter blizzards with these winter wonders. To make a snowflake, a student uses glue to draw a snowflake (with thick lines) onto a sheet of waxed paper. While the glue is still wet, she sprinkles glitter onto the shape. Allow the glue to dry for approximately two days; then help the student carefully peel her snowflake from the waxed paper. Use fishing line to suspend each youngster's snowflake.

On St. Patrick's Day,
All the things I had seen,
When viewed through my shamrock,
Were a nice shade of green.

Shamrock Viewers

Celebrate the glory of green with these snazzy shamrock viewers.

Materials needed for one viewer:

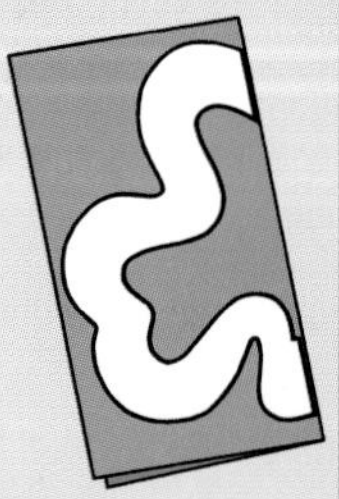

two $8\frac{1}{2}$" squares of green construction paper
one 8" square of green cellophane
1 craft stick
1 copy of the shamrock, leprechaun, and pot-of-gold patterns on page 285

Steps:

1. Fold both pieces of construction paper in half.
2. Cut out the shamrock pattern and trace it onto the sheets of folded construction paper (as shown) and cut out each shape.
3. Glue the cellophane between the two resulting cutouts, trimming away any excess cellophane.
4. Glue the craft stick to the bottom of the shamrock.
5. While the glue dries, color and cut out the leprechaun and pot-of-gold patterns.
6. Glue the patterns atop the shamrock as shown.

Have students recite the poem on the pot of gold before looking through their viewers to see a world of green.

Quilted Cards

These unique greetings are fun to make and a joy to receive! To make a card, a student traces a valentine-shaped template onto seasonal fabric and then uses fabric scissors to cut it out. Next she glues the bottom and sides of the shape to a sheet of poster board, leaving a two-inch opening at the top. When the glue dries, she stuffs the valentine with cotton balls and then glues the opening closed. To complete the card, she uses her best handwriting to pen a valentine greeting on the poster board.

To: Mom
Roses are red,
Violets are blue,
Thanks so much
For all you do!
Love,
Carol

"Eggs-traordinary" Easter Eggs

A student paints an inflated oval balloon with a diluted-glue mixture and covers it with colorful tissue-paper squares. Remind students to keep the tissue paper free of wrinkles as they cover the balloon with a double thickness. Then have students set the projects aside to dry.

When the paper is completely dry, have the student draw an egg-shaped opening on the balloon as shown. Then assist her in popping the balloon and cutting out her egg shape. Have students fill their "eggs-tra"-special eggs with cellophane grass, marshmallow bunnies, and jelly beans.

Fabulous Flower Prints

A bouquet full of celery prints? It makes a surprisingly lovely display! To prepare, cut several stalks of celery about two inches above the base. Pour two pastel colors of tempera paint into separate pie tins. To make the flower petals, a student dips a celery stalk into one color of paint and stamps its impression on a sheet of white construction paper. He continues in this same manner, alternating with the other color of paint. After the paint has dried, he uses crayons or markers to add stems, leaves, and a vase to his picture. Display the pretty prints for a lovely springtime scene.

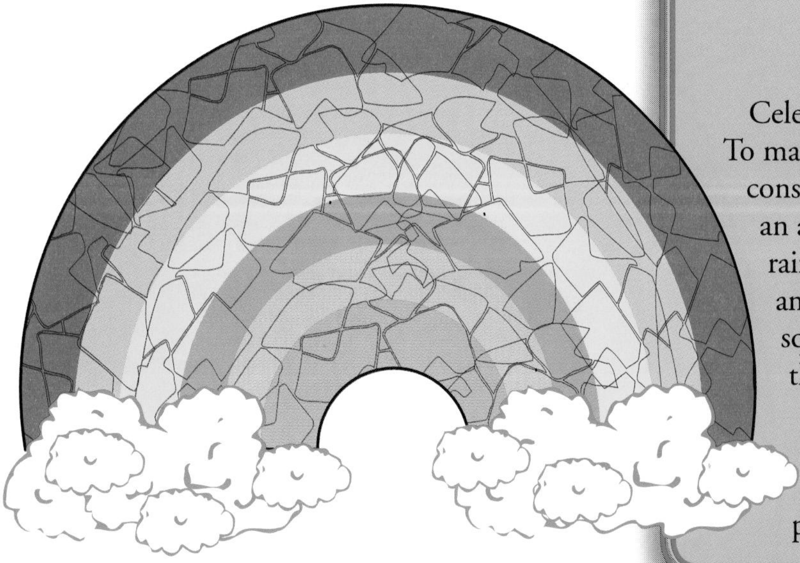

Remarkable Rainbows

Celebrate springtime with these colorful creations. To make a rainbow, a student cuts a ten-inch construction paper circle in half. Then he cuts an arc in the bottom of the half circle to make a rainbow shape. Next he lightly pencils in six arcs and glues appropriate-colored construction paper squares in the arcs of the rainbow. To complete the project, he glues cotton balls to both ends of the rainbow to resemble clouds. Decorate classroom windows, a bulletin board, or a doorway with these remarkable rainbow projects.

Mother's Day Planters

These unique planters make wonderful gifts for moms and any other special person. In advance, gather a laundry-detergent scoop and two milk-jug lids for each student. To make a planter, a student glues a milk-jug lid to each side of her scoop as shown. After the glue dries, she places potting soil and a small plant inside the scoop. Then she sprinkles the soil with a few drops of water. For a finishing touch, she ties a length of colorful ribbon to the handle of the scoop. The receiver of this pretty planter is sure to feel showered with love!

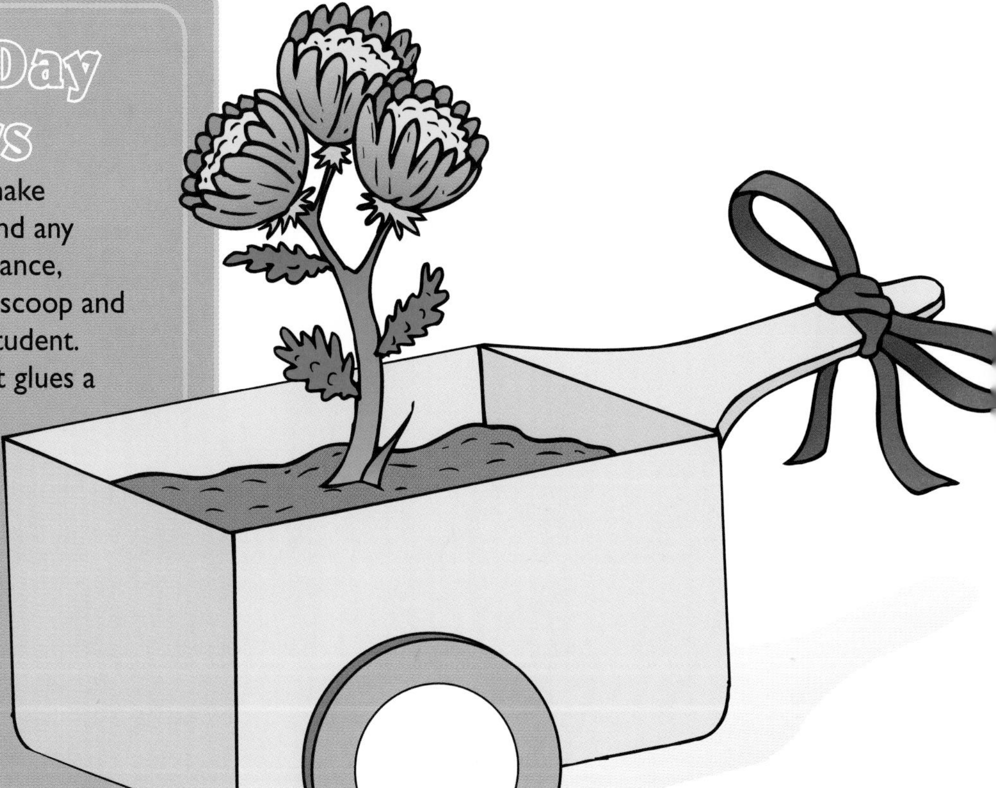

Lovely Ladybugs

Attract lots of attention with a display of these inviting insects. To make a ladybug, a student paints two-inch squares of red tissue paper onto a nine-inch paper plate using a diluted-glue mixture. When the glue is dry, the student cuts a four-inch black construction paper circle in half and glues one half to the plate (as shown) to create the ladybug's head. Next he glues two wiggle eyes to the head and several black construction paper circles to the body. He tapes three black pipe-cleaner halves to his plate, and bends them to create legs. To create the wings, he uses a black marker to draw a line down the center of the ladybug.

Dad,
You are
wonderful.
Thanks for
being my dad.
I ♥ you!
Love,
Jerome

Terrific Ties

Dad won't mind getting another tie for Father's Day when it's one of these treasures! Have each child trace a tie-shaped template onto colored construction paper and then cut it out. Next have him cut from old magazines pictures of his dad's favorite things and glue them on the tie. After the glue has dried, assist him in taping a safety pin to the back of the tie. Then have him write a personal message below the pin. Dads will delight in wearing these terrific ties for a funny Father's Day snapshot or keeping them as special mementos.

RECIPES

Sparkle Paint

light corn syrup
food coloring
glitter

In each of several small containers, mix corn syrup, a few drops of food coloring, and glitter. Have students use the mixture to paint on construction paper, paper plates, tagboard, or any other heavy paper. Allow several days' drying time.

Pastel Paint

evaporated milk
food coloring

Pour evaporated milk into several small containers. Add a few drops of food coloring to each container and mix. When painted on construction paper, the paint has a creamy, pastel appearance.

Wet-Look Paint

1 part white liquid glue
1 part tempera paint

Mix the paint and glue together, and apply to paper with a paintbrush. This paint retains a shiny, wet appearance when dry.

Colored Glue

white glue
food coloring

Pour glue into a small container and add the desired amount of food coloring. Stir until the color is blended. Have students apply the color with a paintbrush to a variety of materials.

Easy Dye

rubbing alcohol
food coloring

Use this simple method to color pasta, rice, seeds, or dried flowers. Put a small amount of rubbing alcohol into a container with a tight-fitting lid. Add the desired amount of food coloring. Place the objects to be dyed inside the container and secure the lid. Gently shake the container for one minute. Spread the objects on paper towels to dry.

Cooked Play Dough

1 cup flour
½ cup salt
2 teaspoons cream of tartar
1 cup water
1 teaspoon vegetable oil
food coloring

Mix the dry ingredients. Stir in the water, oil, and food coloring. Place the mixture in a heavy skillet and cook over medium heat for two or three minutes, stirring frequently. Knead the dough until it is soft and smooth. Store in an airtight container.

Simple Papier-Mâché

1 part liquid starch
1 part cold water
newspaper torn into strips

Mix together the starch and water. Have each student dip strips of newspaper into the mixture before applying to a balloon, chicken wire, or another form.

No-Cook Modeling Dough

2 cups flour
1 cup salt
water
tempera paint powder

Mix the ingredients, adding enough water to make the dough pliable. This dough will air-dry to harden, or can be baked at 300° for an hour, depending on the thickness of the object.

Suitcase Pattern

Use with "Student Suitcases" on page 271.

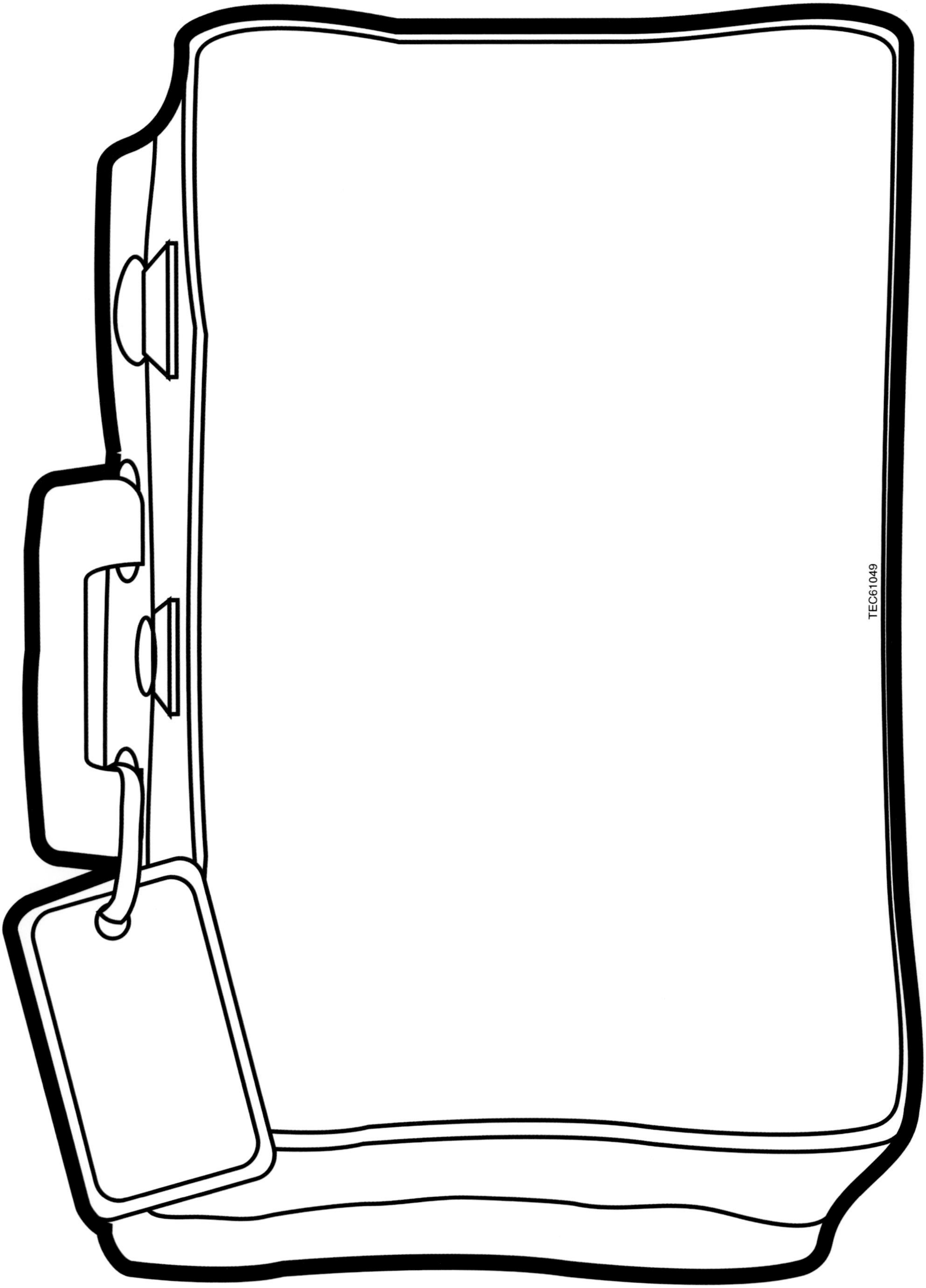
TEC61049

Turkey Patterns

Use with "Thanksgiving Gobblers" on page 273.

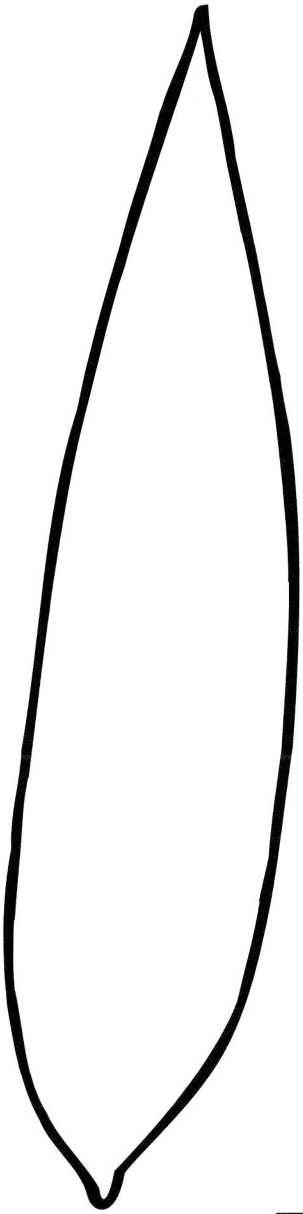

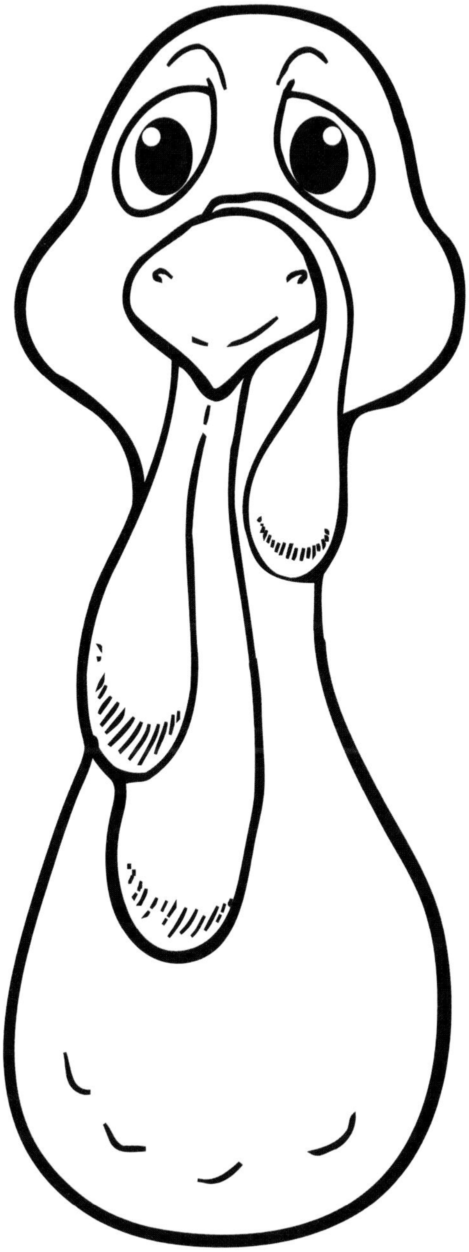

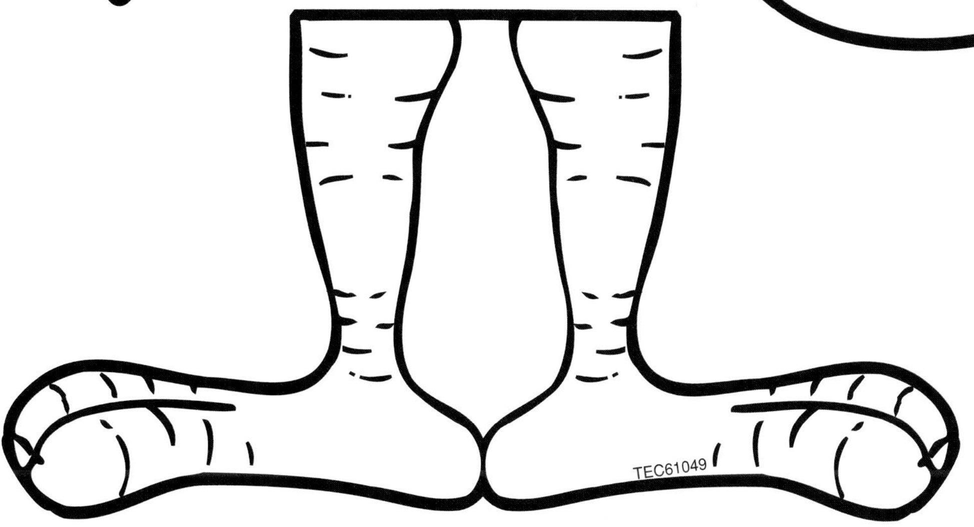
TEC61049

Dreidel Pattern

Use with "Hanukkah Lights" on page 273.

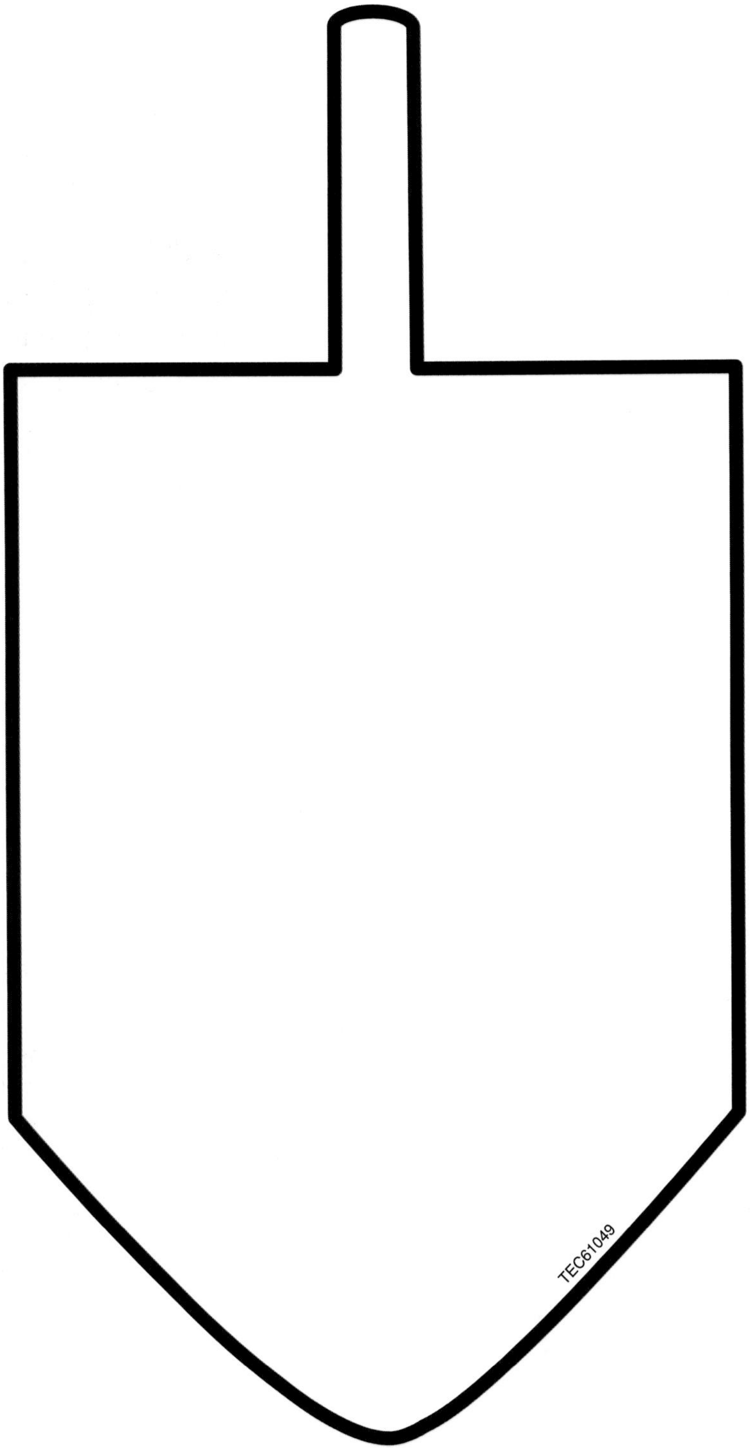
TEC61049

Shamrock, Leprechaun, and Pot-of-Gold Patterns

Use with "Shamrock Viewers" on page 276.

Place on fold.
Place on fold.

On St. Patrick's Day,
All the things I had seen,
When viewed through my shamrock,
Were a nice shade of green.
TEC61049

FALL

Getting-Acquainted Activity

Early in the school year, help students get over the hurdle of new introductions with this easy-to-implement idea. On an index card, have each student write one statement about herself that she would like everyone to know. Ask children not to sign their names. Place the cards in a container. When you have a few extra minutes, draw a card from the container and read it aloud. Have children guess who wrote the statement; then, if desired, ask the child to come forward and elaborate on her statement. This gives each student an opportunity to tell something about herself that others may not know.

I collect butterflies.
I went to China to visit my uncle.
I help my mom raise show dogs.

Grand Locations

Use this National Grandparents Day activity to incorporate map skills into your lessons. Post a U.S. map on a bulletin board in your classroom. Assist each student in inserting pushpins in the locations where his grandparents live. As an added activity, have each student write to his grandparents and request postcards from their homes. Surround the map with the postcards as they are received.

Nevada
WYOMING
CHICAGO
New York
UTAH!
New Mexico
WASHINGTON, D.C.

See Ya, Summer!
melting ice cream
sleeping late
flip-flops
days with Grandma
Hello, Autumn!
drinking apple cider
trick-or-treating
walking on crunchy leaves
watching football games with Dad

Seasonal Swing

Acknowledge the change of seasons while practicing categorization skills. Use bulletin board paper to create two door shapes. Add a title to each, as shown, and post them side by side. Next, brainstorm with students a list of favorite things from summer that they will give up in fall. Also have them name favorite things to which they look forward in fall. Then have each student draw and label pictures of her favorite idea from both seasons. After students share their pictures, post each one on its matching door.

Pumpkin-Patch Pleasers

When a student completes an assignment, encourage him to tiptoe to the pumpkin patch for some extra learning. To create the patch, cut several pumpkin shapes from orange tagboard. On each shape, write an activity for students to complete independently. (See the sample selection below.) Glue a craft stick to each pumpkin; then insert the stick into a large clay pot filled with potting soil. Place the pot on a table in a central location in your classroom. When a student visits the pumpkin patch, have him select a stick and complete the activity.

Suggested Pumpkin-Patch Activities

- Draw a pumpkin on a sheet of paper and design a jack-o'-lantern.
- Read a story with the word *pumpkin* in the title.
- Count and list all the orange things you see in the room.
- List words that begin with *p*.
- Write a story about eating orange foods.
- Write a recipe that has pumpkin as an ingredient.

Pumpkin Patch
Write an ending to this story: "One dark and stormy night..."

Halloween Writers

Let the ghosts and ghouls of Halloween inspire your students to become holiday writers. To begin, write a student-generated list of Halloween-related words on a large ghost cutout. Next, on a sheet of orange paper, have each child use the words from the list to write a Halloween story. If desired, provide students with story titles (similar to the ones shown) for inspiration. Invite students to decorate the borders of their completed stories with Halloween stickers. Then, for added fun, gather students in a circle, turn off the lights, and encourage your youngsters to read their "spook-tacular" stories!

candy
ghost
Halloween
scary
dark
The Ghost That Was Afraid
The Night I Met Gus the Ghost
Alone at the Pumpkin Patch

18
12
15

Facts of a Feather

Turkeys and math facts—perfect companions for creating a Thanksgiving bulletin board. Cover a display area with yellow bulletin board paper and a fall border. Make several turkey bodies from brown construction paper circles of two sizes as shown. Laminate the turkeys and staple them to the board so that feathers can later be placed behind the bodies. For each turkey, cut six feathers from a variety of colored construction paper and laminate them. Next, write a two-digit number on each turkey and a different math fact equaling that number on each of six feathers. Store all the feathers in a resealable bag at the corner of the board. A student solves the fact on each feather and places it behind its corresponding turkey. Change the answers and number sentences throughout the Thanksgiving season for additional math practice.

Check out the skill-building reproducibles on pages 288–291.

Name ______________________________

A Bushel of Addition

Add.

8 + 8
4 + 8
6 + 7
5 + 6
6 + 6
8 + 7
9 + 5
6 + 9
5 + 8
4 + 7
8 + 6
7 + 5
8 + 9
9 + 9

Interview a Grandparent

Ask a grandparent these questions.
Write the answer on the line.

1. When were you born? ____________ month ____________ day, ____________ year
2. What games did you play when you were my age?
   ____
3. What subject did you like best when you were in school?
   ____
4. What is your favorite food?
   ____
5. What job or jobs have you had as an adult?
   ____
6. What hobbies do you have now?
   ____

Draw a picture of your grandparent.
Draw something you learned from the interview.

Name ______________________________

Safety Is in the Bag

Cut apart the sentences at the bottom of the page. Glue only the trick-or-treating safety rules onto the bag.

Use the sidewalk.	Cross the street without looking.
Have your parents check the candy before you eat it.	Walk, don't run.
Wear dark clothing.	Only go to homes of people you know.
Wear makeup instead of a mask.	Walk with an adult.
Go to a strange house alone.	Carry a flashlight.

Winter Writing Wonderland

Here's a great way to get your students writing about a cool subject—snow! Read aloud a snowy story, such as *The Snowy Day* by Ezra Jack Keats. After discussing the book, ask students to brainstorm a list of snow-related words. (If you live in a warm climate, provide photographs of snowy conditions.) Record students' responses on a large sheet of bulletin board paper cut to the shape of a snow shovel. Then, on a sheet of writing paper, have each child write a snow story, using some words from the list as inspiration. Remind each student to include a beginning, a middle, and an ending in his story. After the student completes his story, have him illustrate a scene from his story on a sheet of light blue construction paper. To complete the illustration, have him repeatedly hole-punch a scrap piece of white paper and randomly glue the resulting snowflakes to his paper. Mount each story with its corresponding picture; then add the snow shovel and the title "Winter Writing Wonderland." The result—a blizzard of your students' best writing.

blizzard
chilly
freezing
ice
snow
flurry
blanket
storm
cold
winter
sleet
slippery

New Year's Goals

Welcome your students back to school after the New Year's holiday with this inspiring idea. Write a self-improvement goal for the new year and post it on a prominent bulletin board. Explain to students why you chose this goal and what you plan to do to accomplish it. Next have each student write a self-improvement goal on a blank sheet of paper cut into the shape of a party hat; then have her glue it atop a slightly larger sheet of festive gift wrap and trim the edges as shown. Post the resulting party hats on a bulletin board and add a title. To create an especially festive mood, attach New Year's party hats, horns, and inflated balloons to the border of the display. Students will love this three-dimensional display!

I am going to read at home every night.
Dee Dee

Recycled Calendars

Don't slip into the new year without reusing calendars from the previous year. These timeless treasures can serve many purposes in your classroom. After asking students to bring in their outdated calendars, try the following creative projects:

- Place the pictures or photographs in a writing center. Encourage students to select a picture as inspiration for creative writing assignments.
- Laminate the dated pages for use in a math center. Have students use wipe-off markers to write math equations equal to each number.
- Cut apart dated squares after laminating to use as number cards for various projects or games.
- Laminate each month and have students place them in chronological order.

African American Study

Use this unique report form to help students learn about accomplished African Americans. After studying several famous African Americans, have each child select one on which to do a report. Then give each student a 5½" x 9" sheet of colored construction paper to fold in half. On one side of the folded paper, have the student write the name of his chosen African American. On the other side of the paper, have him write an explanation as to why this person is considered famous. Glue students' folded papers to lengths of ribbon as shown. Then suspend the ribbons throughout your classroom and invite students to read about these famous African Americans during their spare time.

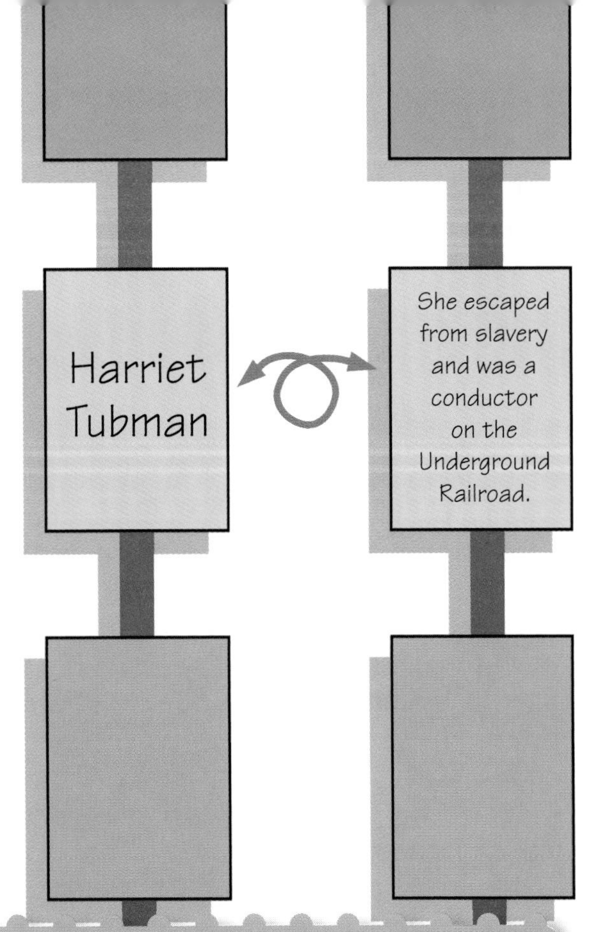
Harriet Tubman
She escaped from slavery and was a conductor on the Underground Railroad.

President Aikman
If I were president, I would make it a law that everyone must recycle.

If I Were President

Salute past and present presidents with these unique projects. Discuss with students the importance of the president's job and the major accomplishments of a few previous presidents. Then have each child imagine she is president, and have her write on a sheet of blank paper what she would like to accomplish. Have her glue her writing to a 9" x 12" sheet of construction paper. Next, have her trace a large oval template on a 9" x 12" sheet of drawing paper. Then have her draw a presidential portrait of herself inside the oval. (Remind students that you have to be at least 35 years old to be the president.) Instruct her to cut out the oval and mount it on the other side of the construction paper sheet. To complete the project, have her write her name on a yellow construction paper strip and glue it beneath her portrait. Hole-punch the top of each project, thread a length of yarn through the hole, and tie the yarn's ends. Suspend the projects throughout the classroom to celebrate Presidents' Day.

Groundhog Honors

Dig into these fun activities on February 2 to honor the weather-predicting groundhog—also known as a woodchuck.

- Begin with a tongue-twisting rendition of the time-honored tongue twister "How Much Wood Would a Woodchuck Chuck?"
- Have students brainstorm groundhog-related words, such as *burrow, hibernate,* and *shadow*. List students' responses on a word bank. Have students use the words for writing woodchuck poetry.
- Combine a math and science lesson by having students measure their shadows.
- Culminate the day with groundhog cupcakes. To make a cupcake, a student inserts two vanilla wafers into a frosted cupcake. Then she adds chocolate-covered candies for eyes and a nose, and two miniature marshmallows for teeth.

sun
shine

Mitten Match

Students will warm up to this compound-word game. Make several construction paper pairs of mittens. Program each left-hand mitten with the first half of a compound word. Write the second half of the word on the right-hand mitten. Create an answer key if desired. Laminate the mittens for durability; then store them in a resealable bag at a center. To play the game, two or more students turn the mittens facedown on a table. Each player takes a turn selecting two mittens and turning them faceup. If the mittens make a compound word, the player keeps them and takes another turn. If the mittens do not make a compound word, the player returns them to a facedown position and it becomes the next player's turn. Play continues in this manner until all mittens have been matched. The player with the most pairs wins.

To vary the game, program each mitten pair with a math problem and its answer, a vocabulary word and its definition, rhyming words, or a number word and the corresponding numeral.

Check out the skill-building reproducibles on pages 296–302.

Name ____ Problem solving

Which Hat?

Kate lost her hat. Use the clues to find her hat.

- My hat does not have circles.
- My hat does not have stripes.
- My hat has squares.
- My hat does not have a ball on top.

Color Kate's hat.

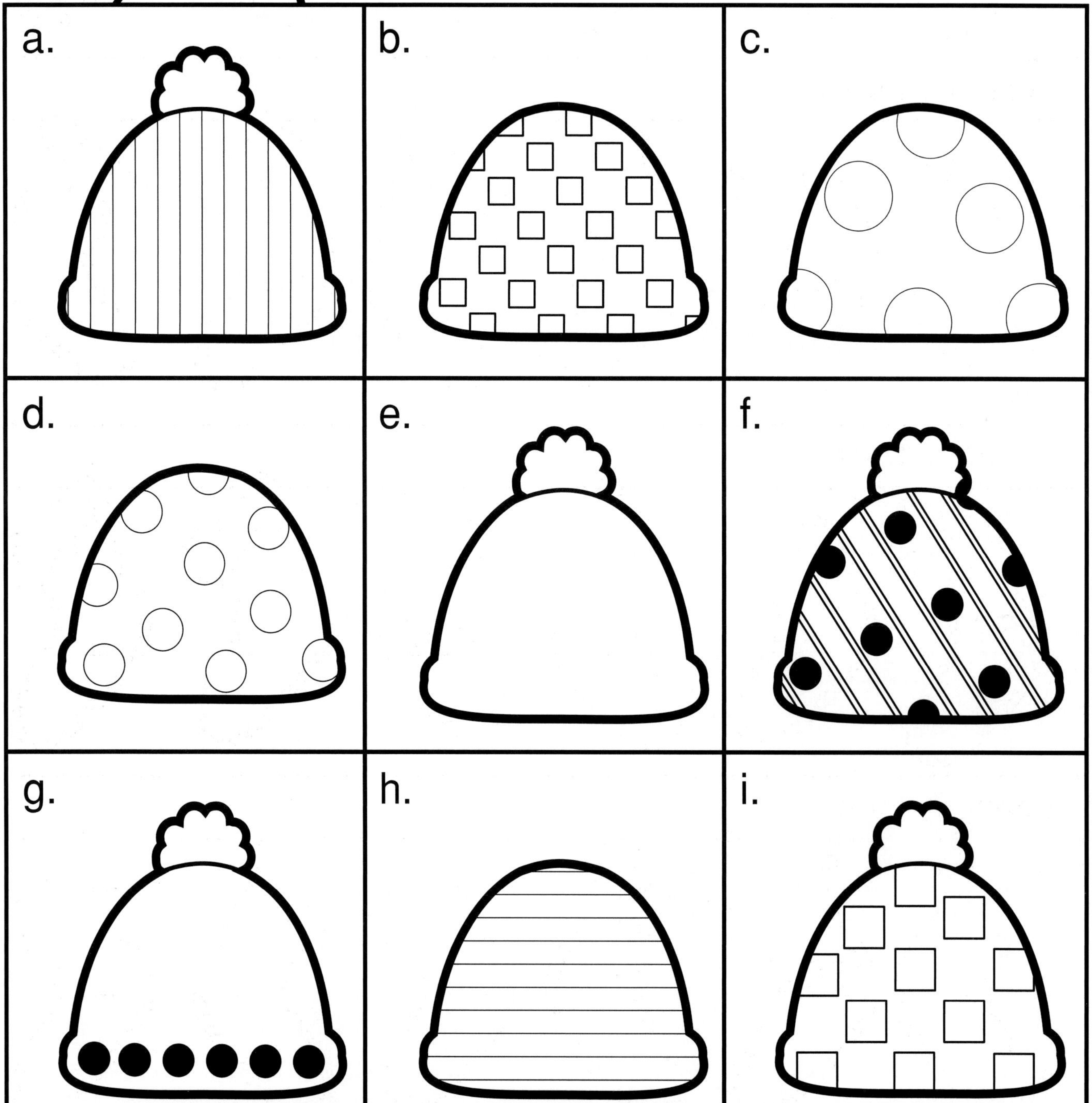
a.
b.
c.
d.
e.
f.
g.
h.
i.

Name ______________________________________ Skip-counting

Stocking Stuffers

Write each missing number.

count by fives

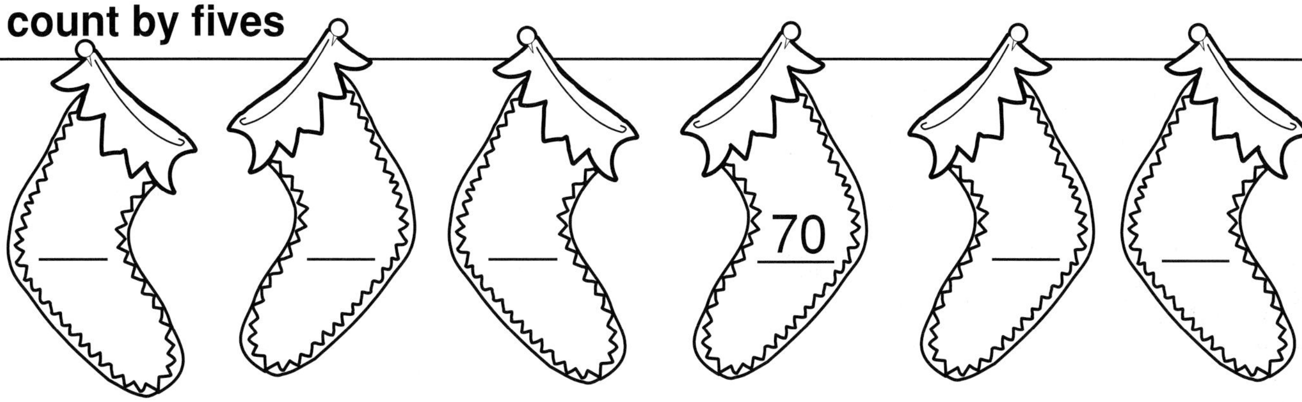
70

count by threes

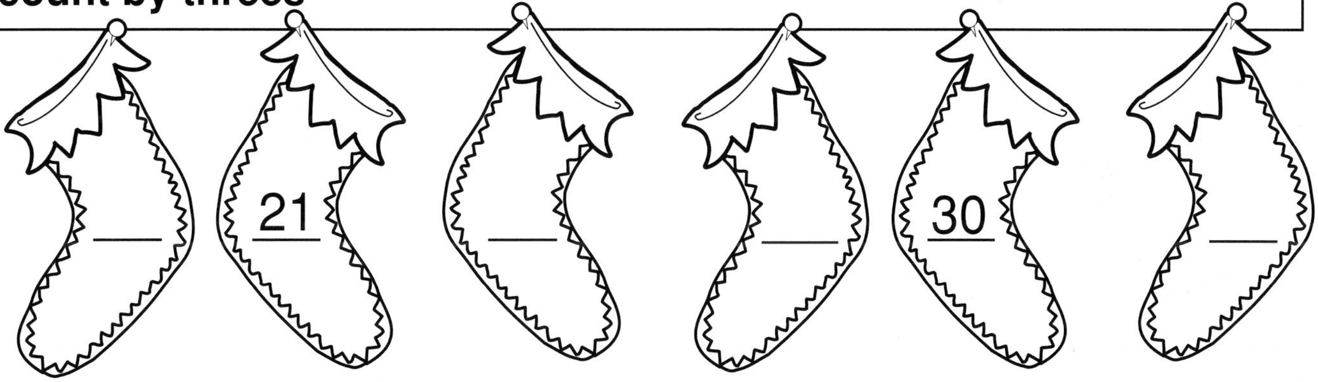
21
30

count by twos

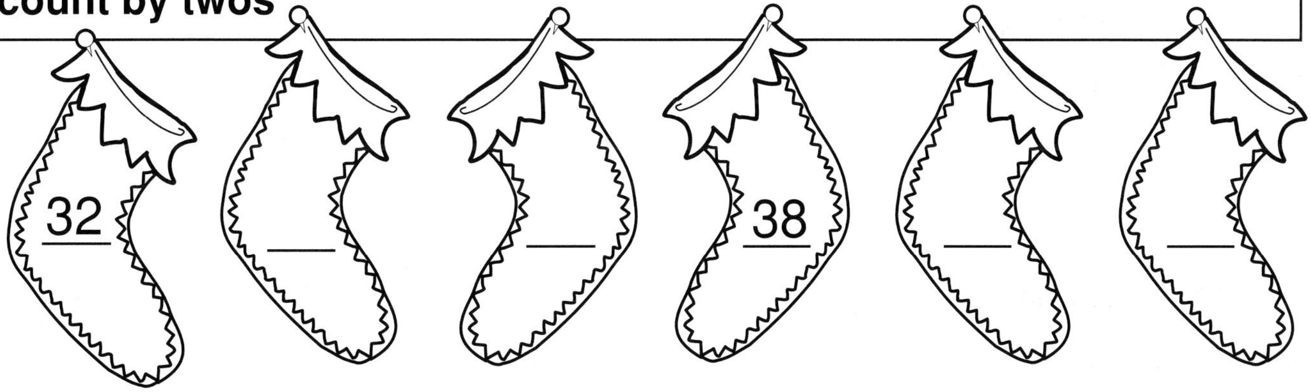
32
38

count by tens

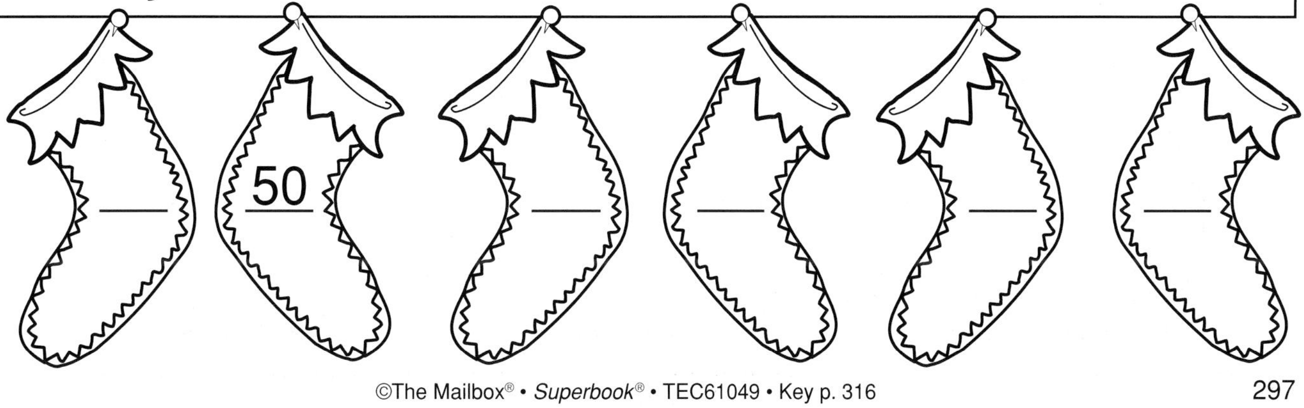
50

Name ____________________

Hanukkah Lights

Add. Cut the answers apart and glue each one in the right place.
There is one extra.

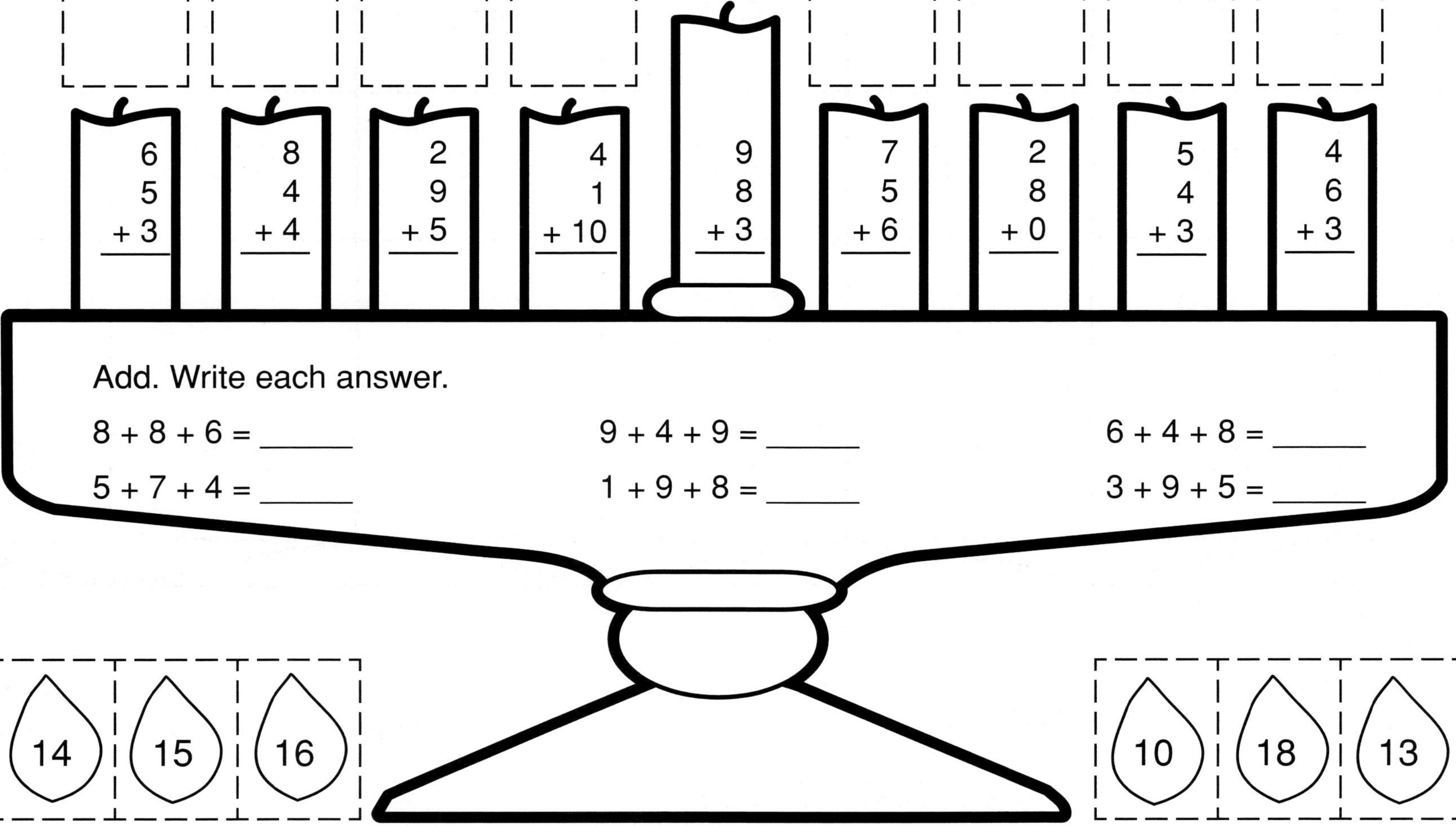

6	8	2	4	9	7	2	5	4
5	4	9	1	8	5	8	4	6
+ 3	+ 4	+ 5	+ 10	+ 3	+ 6	+ 0	+ 3	+ 3

Add. Write each answer.

8 + 8 + 6 = ______

5 + 7 + 4 = ______

9 + 4 + 9 = ______

1 + 9 + 8 = ______

6 + 4 + 8 = ______

3 + 9 + 5 = ______

16 | 20 | 14 | 15 | 16

12 | 10 | 18 | 13 | 19

Name ______________________________ Place value

A Mkeka for Kwanzaa

Look at the numeral 8 in each number.
Color by the code.

Color Code:
ones place = red
tens place = green
hundreds place = black

678	484	528	381	238	787	318
181	870	289	801	387	850	482
198	586	468	681	548	782	698
287	807	385	860	487	832	984
728	189	938	485	158	583	278

 • Key p. 316

Name ________________________________

A Page Turner

Stories of African American Leaders

Table of Contents

Section	Page
Community Leaders	
Martin Luther King Jr.	3
Rosa Parks	7
Colin Powell	9
Inventors	
George Washington Carver	10
Elijah McCoy	13
Sports Stars	
Hank Aaron	15
Wilma Rudolph	16
Tiger Woods	17
Writers	
Langston Hughes	20
Harriet Beecher Stowe	22

Use the table of contents.
Follow the directions.

1. Circle the title of the book.
2. Draw a box around the section title where you could find a story about Rosa Parks.
3. Put a star next to the name of each writer named in this book.

Answer the questions.

4. How many sections are in this book? ______
5. How many pages long is the story about Tiger Woods? ______
6. What do George Washington Carver and Elijah McCoy have in common?

____
____
____
____
____

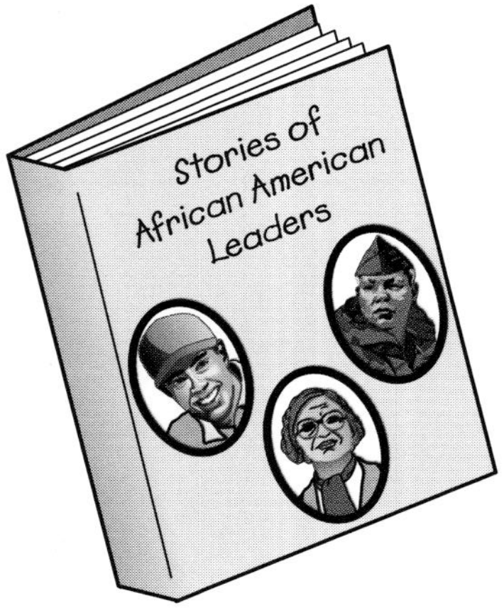
Stories of African American Leaders

Name ______________________________ Problem solving

Sweet Treat

CUTIE PIE
BE MINE

Solve.

Talos got 16 pieces of candy from his mother. He gave 6 pieces to his brother. How many pieces of candy did he have left? ______ C	Zach got 13 valentines. 6 valentines had gum. How many did not have gum? ______ L	Dan walked 6 blocks on one street and 8 blocks on another street to deliver valentines. How many blocks did he walk? ______ O
Kayla went to a Valentine's Day party. There were 14 boys and 8 girls at the party. How many more boys than girls were there? ______ C	Kate got 14 valentines. Meg got 15 valentines. How many valentines did the girls get in all? ______ H	Lisa got a necklace with 7 diamonds, 5 rubies, and 10 emeralds in it for Valentine's Day. How many jewels were in her necklace? ______ A
Rob ate 7 red, 4 yellow, and 6 pink candy hearts. How many candy hearts did Rob eat in all? ______ O	Sue got 12 heart stickers and 7 flower stickers to use on valentines. How many stickers did she have in all? ______ E	Cathy got 12 valentines, and Mac got 8 valentines. How many more valentines did Cathy get than Mac? ______ T

Write the letter that matches each answer to discover a yummy valentine gift.

6 29 14 10 17 7 22 4 19

Name____ Punctuation

Party Time!

Add the missing punctuation to each sentence.
Color the matching punctuation in the bowl.

1. Do you know what tonight is
2. Yippee, it is New Year's Eve
3. Owen and his family are having a party
4. Friends and neighbors are coming
5. They will have hats horns and noisemakers
6. Everyone will snack on chips pretzels and cookies
7. Owen plans to drink a lot of soda
8. He wants to stay up to see the fireworks
9. Do you think he can do it
10. Owen cannot wait to yell, "Happy New Year "

?
.
.
!
.
!
,
?
,
,
,
.
.
.

Spring

The Colors of Spring

Get spring off to a colorful start while teaching your students about plants. Fill three clear glasses with water and add ten drops of different-colored food coloring to each glass. Cut a few inches from the stems of three white carnations and place one carnation in each of the glasses. Ask students to predict what might happen to the flowers. The next day have students observe the colorful flowers and write comments about the changes. This quick science lesson is sure to brighten your students' day.

Green Graphing

Celebrate the color green with this graphing activity. On a large sheet of bulletin board paper, list several statements about green objects. Provide each child with several shamrock stickers. Read each statement and have each child, in turn, place a sticker next to each statement on the graph that applies to her. Have students use the completed graph to answer questions during a class discussion. Think green!

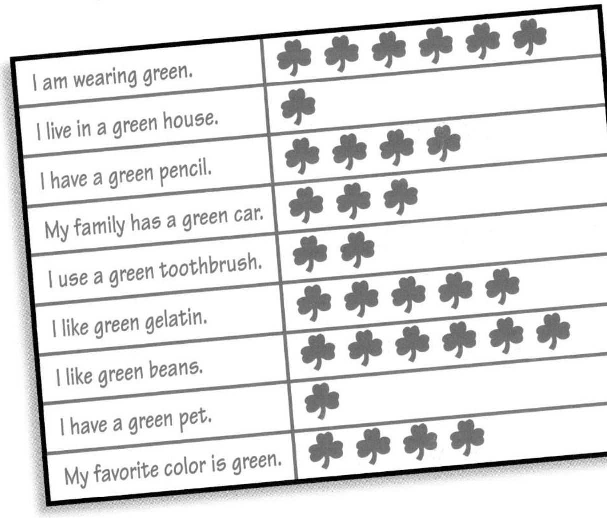
I am wearing green.
I live in a green house.
I have a green pencil.
My family has a green car.
I use a green toothbrush.
I like green gelatin.
I like green beans.
I have a green pet.
My favorite color is green.

Basket Bonus

Be ready to take advantage of a few free minutes by preparing a basketful of bonus-time activities. Write several short activities (similar to the ones shown) on separate slips of paper. Fold each slip and place it inside a separate plastic egg. Place the eggs in a basket filled with cellophane grass. When you have a few spare minutes, open an egg and read aloud the activity for students to complete.

Name animals that have fur.
Name animals that lay eggs.
Name things bunnies can do.
Name things you find in an Easter basket.
Name words that begin with *h*, like *hop*.

Name famous bunnies.

Paper Pals

Start a simple recycling effort right in your classroom in honor of Earth Day (April 22). Designate a box where students can put used paper. When they need a blank sheet, encourage them to use the back of a used piece from the box. Find a nearby recycling center that accepts paper and plan a field trip when your paper box is full. Interview the school custodian to see whether he notices less trash leaving your classroom. This class effort will help everyone see the value in recycling.

WE'RE PAPER PALS!
WE RECYCLE!

Cinco de Mayo Math

Teach your students the number words from one to ten in Spanish. (If you have Spanish-speaking students in your class, enlist their help in teaching the other students.) After a little practice, have your students use the Spanish number words to answer math problems. Announce or write a problem that equals an answer from one to ten; then ask a student volunteer to solve the problem using a newly learned Spanish number word. If desired, divide your class into two teams to create a competition. This fun activity is as easy as uno, dos, tres!

uno	**dos**	**tres**	**cuatro**	**cinco**
one	two	three	four	five
seis	**siete**	**ocho**	**nueve**	**diez**
six	seven	eight	nine	ten

Memorial Day Memories

Remind students that Memorial Day (the last Monday in May) is an American patriotic holiday that honors those who have died while serving our country in times of war. To extend students' knowledge of this holiday, create a bulletin board display featuring pictures of military personnel, medals, and monuments. Encourage students to contribute pictures of friends and family members who have served in the armed forces. For a follow-up, invite a veteran or an active-duty military person to speak to your students about his experiences. No doubt these activities will leave your students with a greater appreciation for the holiday!

Fantastic Mom

Your students will love making these Mother's Day fans as much as their moms will enjoy receiving them! In advance, obtain several discarded wallpaper sample books and cut an assortment of 8" x 14" sheets from the books. Also cut a class supply of 12-inch lengths of ribbon. To make a fan, a child accordion-folds a wallpaper sheet and staples one end. Next, she ties a bow with a length of ribbon. Hot-glue the bow to her fan. She then designs a card to accompany her gift that says "Mom, you're FANtastic!" Your students' mothers will be delighted with their fanciful Mother's Day presents!

Mom, you're FANtastic!

Mom's Homework

Challenge your students' moms to find their best qualities by completing this Mother's Day word search. Have your students brainstorm characteristics of their mothers. Write students' responses on the board. Next, give a copy of page 306 to each student. To make a word search, a student selects a word from the board and writes it at the bottom of his paper. Then he writes the word in the grid horizontally or vertically—one letter per box. He repeats the process until he has eight words in his puzzle. After checking his work, he fills in the remaining boxes with random capital letters. Have students take their puzzles home for their mothers to complete. No more searching for the perfect Mother's Day gift!

MOM

Mother's Day Munchies

Your students will enjoy making this special treat to show their moms how much they're loved. Purchase heart-shaped sugar cookies from a local bakery, or bake them in advance. (If desired, let your students assist with the cookie baking.) Purchase tubes of frosting in a variety of colors. Create a sample to show students basic decorating tips; then have each child decorate a cookie for her mother. Don't forget to have sandwich bags and ribbon on hand for wrapping your students' edible gifts.

Check out the skill-building reproducibles on pages 307–310.

Name______________________________ Puzzle

Homework for Mom

Word Bank

 Note to the teacher: Use with "Mom's Homework" on page 305.

Name ______________________________

Compound Coins

Write each compound word on the pot of gold.

rainbow
treasure
green
clover
luck
pot
horseshoe
smile
wishbone
coins
butterfly
gold
leprechaun
sunshine
dust
holiday
doghouse
cloudburst

Easter Fun

Find these words in the puzzle.
The words may be across or down.

Word List

basket	friends
bunny	fun
candy	grass
chick	holiday
chocolate	hunt
Easter	spring
eggs	

F	R	I	E	N	D	S	C	P
A	G	R	A	S	S	I	H	N
C	B	A	S	K	E	T	O	F
H	U	N	T	T	G	I	C	U
I	N	N	E	G	G	E	O	N
C	N	A	R	S	S	T	L	E
K	Y	H	O	L	I	D	A	Y
R	E	C	A	N	D	Y	T	G
S	P	R	I	N	G	G	E	S

Use a yellow crayon to color any letters in the puzzle that were not used.
Study the letters for something fun to do at Easter time. (**Hint:** Read the letters in order from left to right.)
Copy the message on the lines below.

_ _ _ _ _ _ _ _   _ _ _ _ _ _   _ _ _ _ _

Name ____________________

Spring Vowels

Write the missing vowels in each springtime word.
Cross off each vowel in the answer box.

Answer Box

e	a	i	a	i	i	e
e	e	e	i	e	e	a
e	u	o	a	u	i	i

1. fl__w__r

2. s__ __ds

3. g__rd__n

4. s__nsh__n__

5. __n__m__ls

6. r__ __n

7. k__t__s

8. __ns__cts

9. b__nn__ __s

Name ____

Thinkin' Like a Third Grader

Read. Write.

1. My favorite subject in second grade was ____________________.
   In third grade, I might like ____________________.
2. My favorite outdoor game in second grade was ____________________.
   In third grade, I might like to play ____________________.
3. My favorite stories in second grade were about ____________________.
   In third grade, I might like stories about ____________________.
4. My good friend in second grade was ____________________.
   In third grade, I might like ____________________.
5. My favorite food while I was in second grade was ____________________.
   In third grade, I might like to eat ____________________.
6. My favorite place to visit while I was in second grade was ____________________.
   In third grade, I might like to go ____________________.

Draw.

This is what I look like at the end of second grade.	This is what I might look like when I'm in third grade.

Answer Keys

Page 35

The Stone family started getting ready for a trip to the beach.
First, they packed their suitcases.
Next, they put some food and drinks into a cooler.
After that, they loaded up the car with their things.
Then the family climbed into the car.
The Stone family took off for the beach.
Oops! They forgot to bring the map.
After they went home for the map, the Stone family was on the road again.

Page 37

Answers may vary.

Cause	Effect
Ben tripped on his toys.	He got hurt.
Ben spilled orange juice.	He had to change his shirt.
Ben changed his shirt.	He missed the bus.
Ben forgot his lunch.	He had to eat spinach soup.

Page 56

	Yes	No
1. Fire T. Fly	**W**	E
2. will S. Wasp	W	**O**
3. Beth Ann Bee	**G**	L
4. Lady J. Bug	**T**	S
5. Andre v. Ant	G	**O**
6. B. k. beetle	T	**L**
7. Dragon Z. Fly	**S**	E
8. Butter P. fly	O	**P**
9. Rick r. Roach	S	**E**
10. Gina T. Gnat	**L**	P

"GLOW" TO SLEEP.

Page 57

Answers may vary.

1. Gus is going to plant a garden.
2. first, he drives to the garden store.
3. He chooses lots of plants and seeds.
4. He also buys soil and garden tools.
5. at home, Gus pours soil onto the ground.
6. He digs a hole for each plant.
7. he places a plant in each hole.
8. Next, he plants the seeds.
9. Gus carefully waters his garden.
10. next year, Gus will try to plant bananas!

First, he drives to the garden store.
At home, Gus pours soil onto the ground.
He places a plant in each hole.
Next year, Gus will try to plant bananas!

Page 58

1. Wow, this box is heavy!
2. Will you help me?
3. We can move it.
4. Is it time for lunch?
5. I am hungry too.
6. Let's order a pizza.

Page 59

Answers may vary, but each sentence should include a subject and a predicate. Possible answers include the following:

The coach is yelling.
One player threw the ball.
That hot dog tastes good.
The football is on the ground.
The crowd is cheering.

Page 60

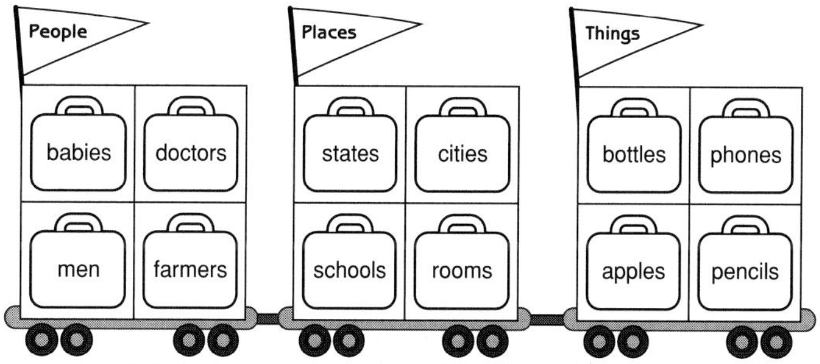

People
babies
doctors
men
farmers
Places
states
cities
schools
rooms
Things
bottles
phones
apples
pencils

Page 61

Order may vary.

-s	*-es*
rings	watches
soaps	rashes
spurs	wishes
dreams	boxes
sticks	matches
ducks	foxes

Page 62

1. Billy is building a new house.
   T P
2. He chews each tree down with his teeth.
   E B
3. Billy's friend Bert walks by.
   R M
4. Bert shows Billy what he is carrying.
   E S
5. Bert bought a new saw!
   R I
6. Billy laughs at Bert's saw.
   I R
7. Bert starts to cut down a tree.
   S E
8. Billy watches and begins to chew.
   ! E
9. Bert finishes and saws down another!
   B !
10. Billy stops chewing and borrows Bert's saw!
    T P

"SEP-TIMBER!"

Page 63

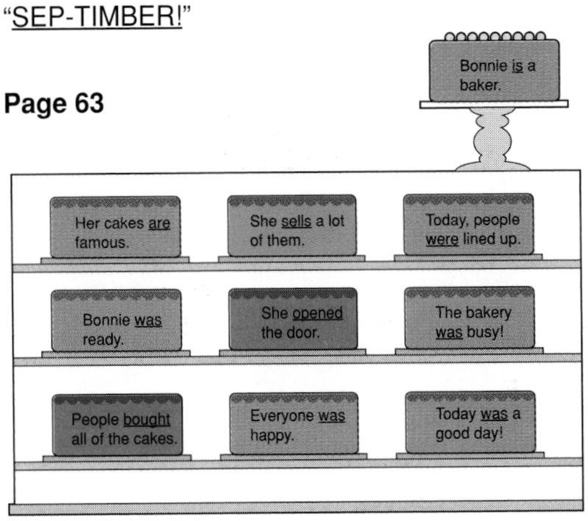
Bonnie is a baker.
Her cakes are famous.
She sells a lot of them.
Today, people were lined up.
Bonnie was ready.
She opened the door.
The bakery was busy!
People bought all of the cakes.
Everyone was happy.
Today was a good day!

Page 78

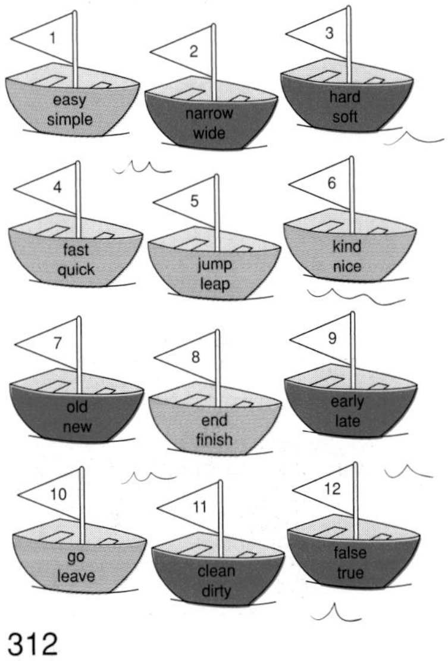
1
easy
simple
2
narrow
wide
3
hard
soft
4
fast
quick
5
jump
leap
6
kind
nice
7
old
new
8
end
finish
9
early
late
10
go
leave
11
clean
dirty
12
false
true

Page 79

1. would
2. no
3. buy
4. right
5. sale
6. cents
7. choose
8. piece
9. some
10. ate

Page 80

re-

refill	repay
retry	reread
replace	replay

un-

unfair	unclear
unknown	unequal
uneven	unhappy

Page 81

1. shyness
2. hopeless
3. homeless
4. sadness
5. softness
6. helpless
7. darkness
8. calmness
9. colorless
10. endless
11. calmness
12. homeless
13. hopeless
14. shyness
15. softness
16. colorless
17. sadness
18. helpless
19. endless
20. darkness

Because its horns don't work!

Page 106

A. 36 < 47	H. 70 > 69
B. 14 = 14	I. 63 > 43
C. 71 < 77	J. 29 < 31
D. 24 > 10	K. 62 = 62
E. 82 > 28	L. 94 > 46
F. 34 < 48	M. 3 < 13
G. 12 > 9	N. 45 < 54

Page 107

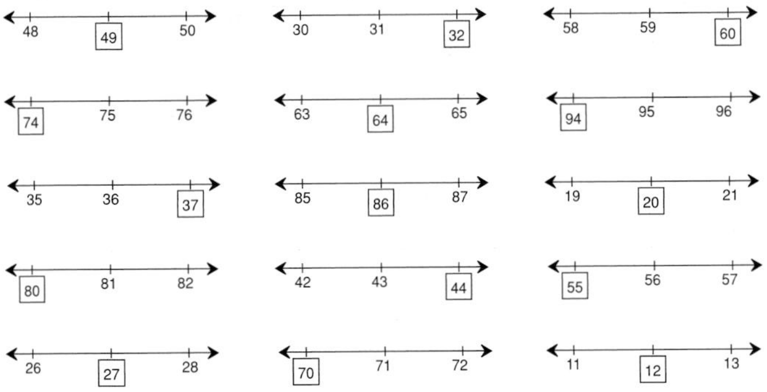
48 49 50
30 31 32
58 59 60
74 75 76
63 64 65
94 95 96
35 36 37
85 86 87
19 20 21
80 81 82
42 43 44
55 56 57
26 27 28
70 71 72
11 12 13

Page 108

A. 362 E. 715

B. 139 F. 647

C. 864 G. 291

D. 573 H. 456

Page 115

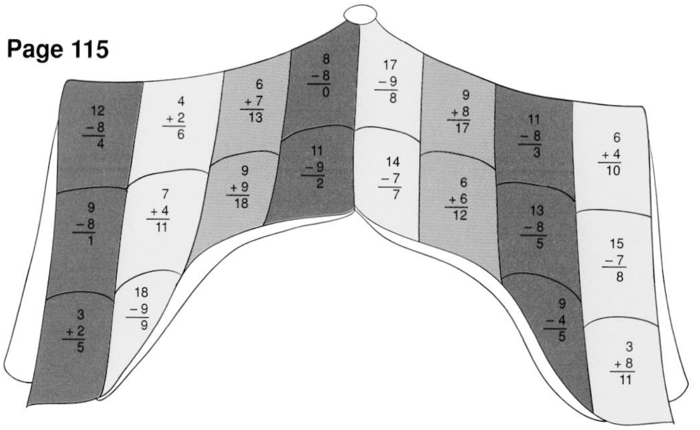
12 − 8 4
4 + 2 6
6 + 7 13
8 − 8 0
17 − 9 8
9 + 8 17
11 − 8 3
6 + 4 10
9 − 8 1
7 + 4 11
9 + 9 18
11 − 9 2
14 − 7 7
6 + 6 12
13 − 8 5
15 − 7 8
3 + 2 5
18 − 9 9
9 − 4 5
3 + 8 11

Page 116

15 + 34 49 A	50 + 19 69 Y	73 + 21 94 H	24 + 23 47 T	31 + 66 97 I
40 + 45 85 L	17 + 11 28 I	34 + 24 58 D	48 + 31 79 A	28 + 10 38 L
32 + 12 44 W	65 + 22 87 G	83 + 16 99 C	56 + 33 89 O	42 + 25 67 S

Because IT WAS A CHILLY DOG!

Page 117

A. 36 + 5 41 31 41	B. 62 + 8 70 70 60	C. 49 + 22 71 71 81	D. 56 + 38 94 85 94
E. 75 + 15 90 90 80	F. 23 + 58 81 75 81	G. 27 + 27 54 54 40	H. 19 + 38 57 47 57
I. 88 + 8 96 96 80	J. 37 + 14 51 43 51	K. 43 + 49 92 82 92	L. 55 + 28 83 83 73

Page 118

		33 − 16 17	74 − 16 58
31 − 27 4	73 − 26 47	56 − 28 28	91 − 12 79
60 − 55 5	93 − 15 78	70 − 14 56	85 − 28 57
67 − 38 29	82 − 45 37		

Page 122

Answers may vary.

1. 6 x 2 = 12
   4 x 3 = 12
2. 4 x 4 = 16
   8 x 2 = 16
3. 5 x 5 = 25
4. 6 x 4 = 24
   3 x 8 = 24
5. 6 x 6 = 36
   9 x 4 = 36
6. 10 x 3 = 30
   5 x 6 = 30

Page 126

A.
1/3 = shaded
2/3 = not shaded

B.
2/4 = shaded
2/4 = not shaded

C.
2/3 = shaded
1/3 = not shaded

D.
4/6 = shaded
2/6 = not shaded

E.
3/4 = shaded
1/4 = not shaded

F.
1/6 = shaded
5/6 = not shaded

G.
1/4 = shaded
3/4 = not shaded

H.
3/8 = shaded
5/8 = not shaded

I.
5/6 = shaded
1/6 = not shaded

Page 133

1. 3
2. 5
3. 1
4. 4
5. 2

Page 134

ounces

GLUE

pounds

Page 139
Order may vary.

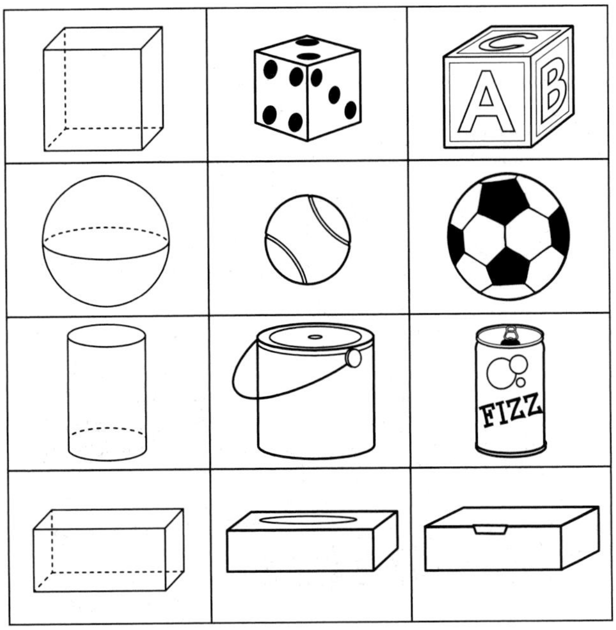
FIZZ

Page 140
1. cube
2. sphere
3. pyramid
4. cylinder
5. cone

Page 144
Predict.
1. orange
2. cherry

Think.
1. Answers will vary.
2. Answers will vary.

Page 145

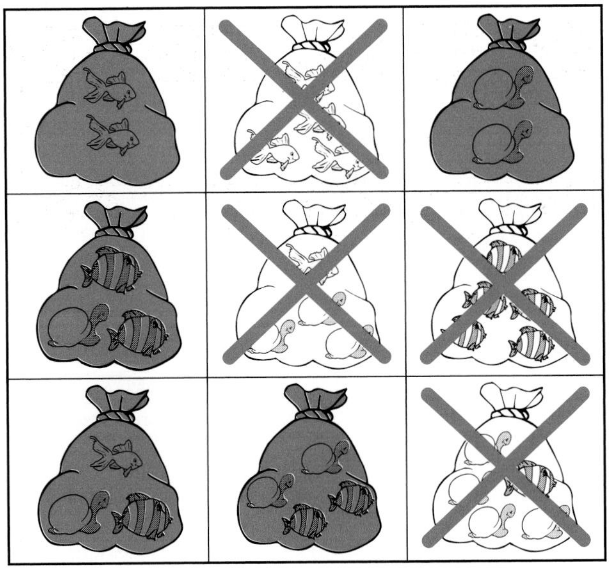

Page 152
Order may vary.

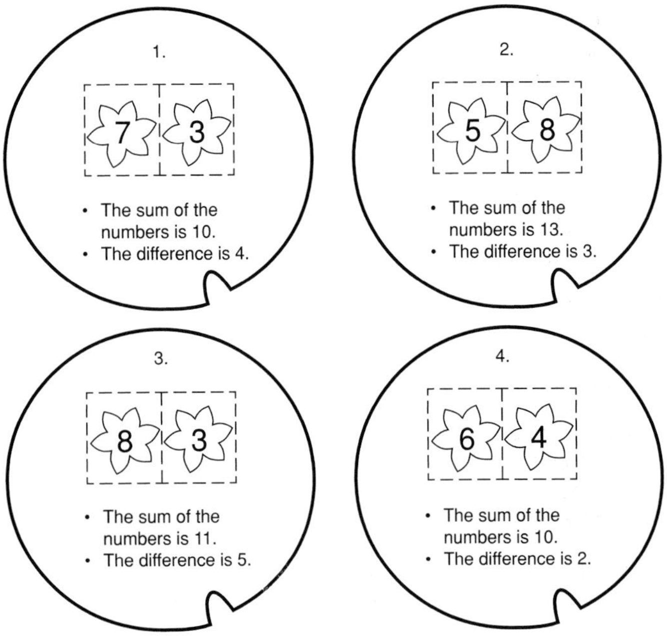
1.
7 3
• The sum of the numbers is 10.
• The difference is 4.
2.
5 8
• The sum of the numbers is 13.
• The difference is 3.
3.
8 3
• The sum of the numbers is 11.
• The difference is 5.
4.
6 4
• The sum of the numbers is 10.
• The difference is 2.

Page 153

	1st Place	2nd Place	3rd Place	4th Place	5th Place
Ray	X	X	X	X	✓
Rita	X	X	✓	X	X
Ron	X	X	X	✓	X
Ree	X	✓	X	X	X
Rob	✓	X	X	X	X

Page 154

Amount of Dog Food Needed for One Month									
Number of dogs	1	2	3	4	5	6	7	8	9
Pounds of dog food	10	20	30	40	50	60	70	80	90

1. 20 pounds
2. 5 dogs
3. 90 pounds
4. no

Page 168
1. thermometer
2. anemometer
3. weather vane
4. rain gauge
5. weather balloon

Page 181
Big cities have
lots of cars and buses
lots of tall buildings
lots of shops and big stores

Both have
schools
houses
children

Small towns have
fewer shops and stores
smaller buildings
fewer people

Page 185
1. They locked the doors and closed the windows.
2. They chose George Washington to do it.
3. They chose to have a vice president too.
4. They split the government into three parts.

Page 190

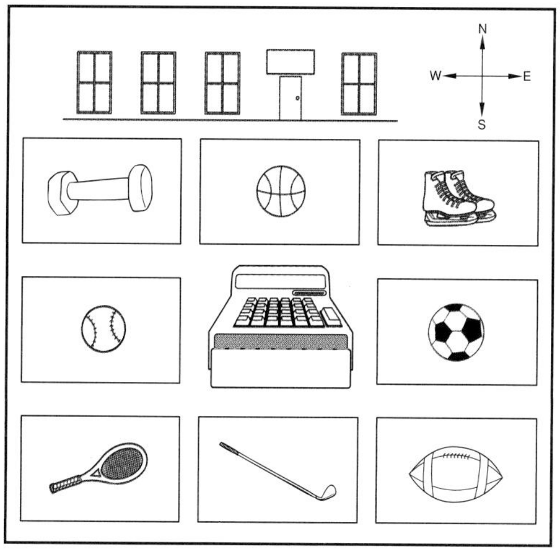

N
W
E
S

Page 191

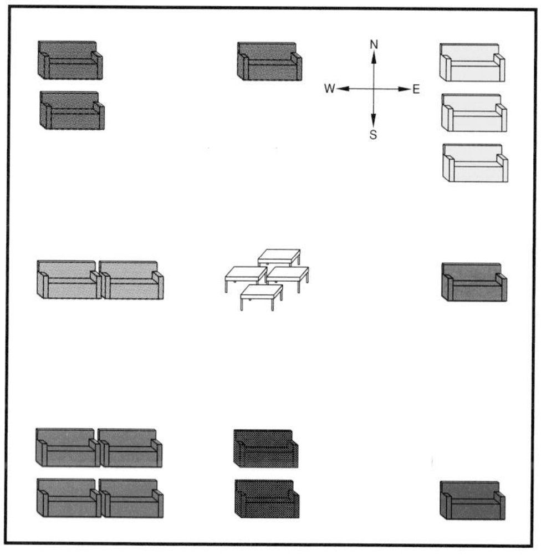

N
W
E
S

5 red
15 yellow
5 brown
10 black
20 blue
5 green
10 purple
10 orange

Page 288

8 + 8 = 16
4 + 8 = 12
6 + 7 = 13
5 + 6 = 11
6 + 6 = 12
8 + 7 = 15
9 + 5 = 14
6 + 9 = 15
5 + 8 = 13
4 + 7 = 11
8 + 6 = 14
7 + 5 = 12
8 + 9 = 17
9 + 9 = 18

Page 290
Walk with an adult.
Only go to homes of people you know.
Use the sidewalk.
Have your parents check the candy before you eat it.
Carry a flashlight.
Walk, don't run.
Wear makeup instead of a mask.

Page 291

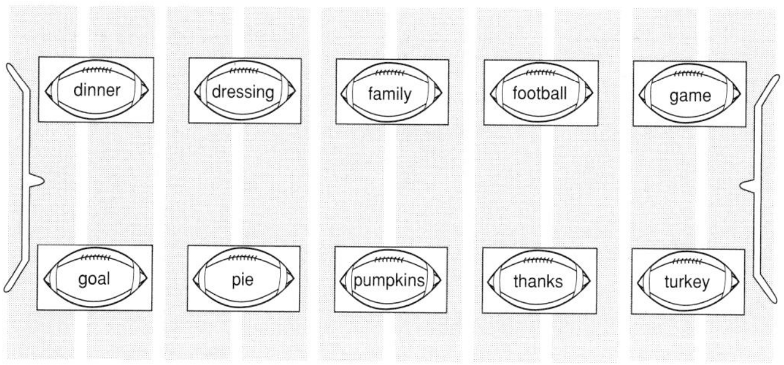

dinner
dressing
family
football
game
goal
pie
pumpkins
thanks
turkey

Page 296
b

Page 297

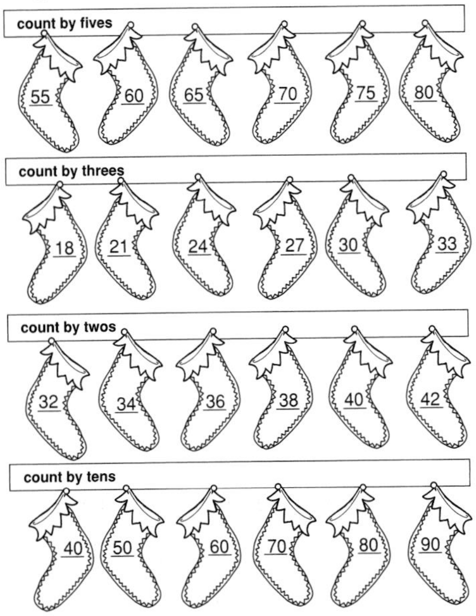

count by fives
55
60
65
70
75
80
count by threes
18
21
24
27
30
33
count by twos
32
34
36
38
40
42
count by tens
40
50
60
70
80
90

Page 298

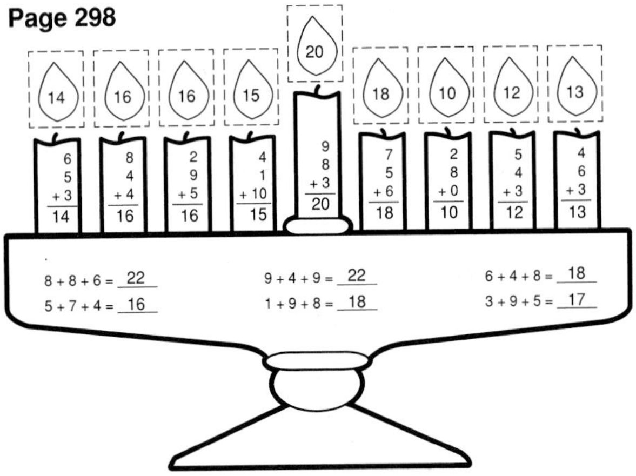

14
16
16
15
20
18
10
12
13
6 5 + 3 = 14
8 4 + 4 = 16
2 9 + 5 = 16
4 1 + 10 = 15
9 8 + 3 = 20
7 5 + 6 = 18
2 8 + 0 = 10
5 4 + 3 = 12
4 6 + 3 = 13
8 + 8 + 6 = 22
5 + 7 + 4 = 16
9 + 4 + 9 = 22
1 + 9 + 8 = 18
6 + 4 + 8 = 18
3 + 9 + 5 = 17

Page 299

678	484	528	381	238	787	318
181	870	289	801	387	850	482
198	586	468	681	548	782	698
287	807	385	860	487	832	984
728	189	938	485	158	583	278

Page 300

Stories of African American Leaders

Table of Contents

4. 4
5. 3
6. They are both inventors.

Page 301

10 C	7 L	14 O
6 C	29 H	22 A
17 O	19 E	4 T

C	H	O	C	O	L	A	T	E
6	29	14	10	17	7	22	4	19

Page 302

1. Do you know what tonight is**?**
2. Yippee, it is New Year's Eve**!**
3. Owen and his family are having a party**.**
4. Friends and neighbors are coming**.**
5. They will have hats**,** horns**,** and noisemakers**.**
6. Everyone will snack on chips**,** pretzels**,** and cookies**.**
7. Owen plans to drink a lot of soda**.**
8. He wants to stay up to see the fireworks**.**
9. Do you think he can do it**?**
10. Owen cannot wait to yell, "Happy New Year**!**"

Page 307

Order may vary.

rainbow
wishbone
horseshoe
sunshine
doghouse
cloudburst
butterfly

Page 308

F	R	I	E	N	D	S	C	P
A	G	R	A	S	S	I	H	N
C	B	A	S	K	E	T	O	F
H	U	N	T	T	G	I	C	U
I	N	N	E	G	G	E	O	N
C	N	A	R	S	S	T	L	E
K	Y	H	O	L	I	D	A	Y
R	E	C	A	N	D	Y	T	G
S	P	R	I	N	G	G	E	S

PAINTING EASTER EGGS

Page 309

1. flower
2. seeds
3. garden
4. sunshine
5. animals
6. rain
7. kites
8. insects
9. bunnies

Index